Chemistry
for the IB Diploma

Workbook

Jacqueline Paris

CAMBRIDGE
UNIVERSITY PRESS

CAMBRIDGE
UNIVERSITY PRESS

University Printing House, Cambridge CB2 8BS, United Kingdom

One Liberty Plaza, 20th Floor, New York, NY 10006, USA

477 Williamstown Road, Port Melbourne, VIC 3207, Australia

4843/24, 2nd Floor, Ansari Road, Daryaganj, Delhi – 110002, India

79 Anson Road, #06 –04/06, Singapore 079906

Cambridge University Press is part of the University of Cambridge.

It furthers the University's mission by disseminating knowledge in the pursuit of education, learning and research at the highest international levels of excellence.

www.cambridge.org
Information on this title: www.cambridge.org/9781316634950 (Paperback)

First published 2017

20 19 18 17 16 15 14 13 12 11 10 9 8 7 6 5 4 3 2 1

Printed in Spain by GraphyCems

A catalogue record for this publication is available from the British Library

ISBN 978-1-316-63495-0 Paperback

Cambridge University Press has no responsibility for the persistence or accuracy of URLs for external or third-party internet websites referred to in this publication, and does not guarantee that any content on such websites is, or will remain, accurate or appropriate. Information regarding prices, travel timetables, and other factual information given in this work is correct at the time of first printing but Cambridge University Press does not guarantee the accuracy of such information thereafter.

All exam-style questions and sample answers have been written by the authors.

....

Contents

How to use this book

Chapter outline

Each Chapter begins with a Chapter outline to briefly set out the learning aims and help with navigation through the topic.

> **Chapter outline**
> - Recall that the periodic table is arranged into groups, periods and into four blocks associated with the four sub–levels: s, p, d and f.
> - Recall that the period number is the outer energy level that is occupied by electrons.
> - Recall that the number of the principal energy level and the number of the valence electrons in an atom can be deduced from its position on the periodic table.
> - Explain the trends in atomic radius, ionic radius, ionisation energy, electron affinity and electronegativity across a period and down a group.
> - Recall that the oxides change from basic through amphoteric to acidic across a period.
> - Recall the equations for the reactions of Na_2O, MgO, P_4O_{10} and the oxides of nitrogen and sulfur with water, and the pH of the solutions formed.
> - Describe the reactions of the elements of group 1 and group 17.
> - Recall the definition of a transition element and their characteristic properties. **HL**
> - Explain the formation and shapes of complex ions. **HL**
> - Explain why transition metal complex ions are coloured. **HL**

Key terms and Key formulas

A list of Key terms and Key formulas at the start of each Chapter provide clear, straightforward definitions for the Key vocabulary. Key formulas can be referred to throughout the Chapter, to help with Exercises and Exam-style questions.

> **KEY TERMS**
>
> **Acid deposition:** A more general term than acid rain; it refers to any process in which acidic substances leave the atmosphere and are deposited on the Earth's surface.
>
> **Brønsted–Lowry acid:** A proton (H^+) donor.
>
> **Brønsted–Lowry base:** A proton (H^+) acceptor.
>
> **pH:** A measure of the concentration of hydrogen ions in an aqueous solution. $pH = -\log_{10}[H^+]$
>
> **Strong acid/base:** An acid/base that is completely dissociated into its ions in aqueous solution.
>
> **Weak acid/base:** An acid/base that is only partially dissociated into its ions in aqueous solution.

Exercises

Each Chapter contains a number of Exercises that relate to each chapter topic. Exercises can help to practice and consolidate learning.

HL Exercise 8.2 – Lewis acids and bases

The idea of Lewis acids was developed at the same time as the Brønsted–Lowry theory. It has a broader scope than Brønsted–Lowry as it is not restricted to species that contain a hydrogen ion.

It should be remembered that all Brønsted–Lowry acids are Lewis acids but not all Lewis acids are Brønsted–Lowry ones; similarly, with bases.

In organic chemistry Lewis acids are termed electrophiles and Lewis bases are referred to as nucleophiles. This is covered in Topic 10.

1 **a** Define the terms 'Lewis acid' and 'Lewis base'.
  b What type of bond is always formed in a Lewis acid–base reaction?

Tips

Tip boxes feature on many pages and offer helpful hints to aid understanding of the topic, provide exam tips or offer prompts to help with a specific Exercise.

This question is very similar to Question 4 but with a different unknown. Imagine the amount of ester reacting is x, then the amount remaining at equilibrium = $0.01 - x$. Then follow a similar sequence of steps.

Exam-style questions

Each chapter concludes with a list of Exam-style questions. These Exam-style questions provide an opportunity to practise what has been covered in each topic, and prepare for the types of question that will appear in the IB Chemistry Diploma exams.

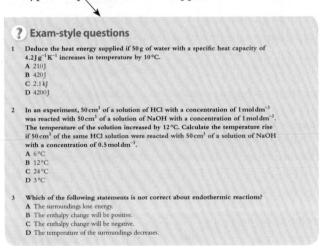

? Exam-style questions

1   Deduce the heat energy supplied if 50 g of water with a specific heat capacity of
    $4.2 \, J \, g^{-1} \, K^{-1}$ increases in temperature by 10 °C.
    A 210 J
    B 420 J
    C 2.1 kJ
    D 4200 J

2   In an experiment, 50 cm³ of a solution of HCl with a concentration of $1 \, mol \, dm^{-3}$
    was reacted with 50 cm³ of a solution of NaOH with a concentration of $1 \, mol \, dm^{-3}$.
    The temperature of the solution increased by 12 °C. Calculate the temperature rise
    if 50 cm³ of the same HCl solution were reacted with 50 cm³ of a solution of NaOH
    with a concentration of $0.5 \, mol \, dm^{-3}$.
    A 6 °C
    B 12 °C
    C 24 °C
    D 3 °C

3   Which of the following statements is not correct about endothermic reactions?
    A The surroundings lose energy.
    B The enthalpy change will be positive.
    C The enthalpy change will be negative.
    D The temperature of the surroundings decreases.

Introduction

This workbook has been written to support students studying the IB Diploma Chemistry syllabus for examination up to 2022 at both Standard Level (SL) and Higher Level (HL). The aim is to support learning by providing questions that check both knowledge and understanding whilst progressing through the course.

The content is arranged in chapters that follow the syllabus and the HL material is clearly marked both in the chapter outline and at question level. Definitions and key formulas are included at the beginning of each chapter. The chapters can be approached in any order; however, it is recommended that the chapter on stoichiometric relationships is met sooner rather than later as a knowledge of moles and equations is fundamental to many of the other areas of chemistry.

Each chapter aims to develop both knowledge and understanding by including questions ranging from those that require simple recall to those needing a detailed explanation of an idea or concept. The skills grid maps the questions according to some of the command terms given in the subject guide; these are arranged by assessment objective. Each chapter is broken into sections which gradually work through the content, each focusing on a particular idea or concept. Support is provided throughout by the use of guidance boxes. These offer suggestions about how to tackle a question, hints and tips, and general exam advice. This support is gradually reduced throughout each section as understanding develops. Each chapter then ends with exam-style questions which draw together the ideas met throughout the whole chapter.

All four option topics have been included although questions from only one of these are selected in paper 3 of the final examinations. As some of the content of the option topics may be less familiar than that in the compulsory part of the course, the questions in these sections include more background to each concept.

The nature of science is an overarching theme of the chemistry course. It examines the processes and concepts that are central to scientific endeavour, and how science serves and connects with the wider community. As this is an overarching theme, ideas about the nature of science have been integrated into the questions within each topic where applicable; the ability to analyse data without bias and an appreciation of random and systematic errors is an example of where an understanding of the objectivity of science is developed in many different areas of the course.

Answers to all the questions are provided with working where appropriate. Much can be learnt from the answers and it is recommended that these are used, not just to check numerical answers, but to look closely at the longer answer questions too. Key points are indicated as well as general advice. The answers to the exam-style questions are generally more detailed than those that might be met in an official mark scheme. The aim is to develop an appreciation of the level of detail needed in examinations rather than simply provide the bare minimum required to score a mark. This should lead to better quality answers which clearly demonstrate understanding and leave the examiner no room for doubt.

Skills grid

AO	Skill	1 Stoichiometric relationships	2 Atomic structure	3 Periodicity	4 Chemical bonding and structure	5 Energetics	6 Chemical kinetics	7 Equilibrium	8 Acids and bases	9 Redox processes	10 Organic chemistry	11 Measurement, data processing and analysis	12 Materials (Option A)	13 Biochemistry (Option B)	14 Energy (Option C)	15 Medicinal chemistry (Option D)
1	define	1.3 Q1, 1.4 Q1	2.2 Q1, 2.2 Q2, 2.4 Q1, 2.6 Q5, 2.7 Q1, 2.7 Q3	3.6 Q1, 14	4.2 Q1, 4.2 Q3, 4.3 Q1, 4.6 Q4	5.3 Q1, 5.4 Q1	6.1 Q1, 13		8.2 Q1, 8.4 Q1	9.8 Q1	10.1 Q1, 10.1 Q2, 10.2 Q3, 10.4 Q1, 10.5 Q1, 11		12.5 Q1	13.2 Q4, 13.3 Q3, 13.4 Q1, 13.5 Q1, 13.6 Q2, 13.8 Q3, 13.9 Q1, 3	14.1 Q1, 14.3 Q4, 1	15.1 Q1, 15.1 Q2, 15.3 Q1, 15.4 Q3, 15.5 Q1, 15.8 Q1, 15.8 Q2, 15.9 Q2
1	draw		2.6 Q4	3.6 Q4, 3.6 Q5, 15	4.1 Q2, 4.1 Q4, 4.2 Q2, 4.2 Q3, 4.2 Q4, 4.4 Q3, 4.6 Q1, 4.6 Q3, 4.6 Q4, 11, 12, 13	12, 14	13			9.8 Q3, 20	10.1 Q2, 10.1 Q3, 10.2 Q2, 10.3 Q2, 10.5 Q2, 11, 17	11.2 Q2, 11.2 Q3	12.5 Q2, 12.7 Q2, 12.8 Q2, 12.9 Q1, 6	13.3 Q2, 13.4 Q2, 1, 10		15.2 Q2
1	label	1.1 Q2				12, 13		7.1 Q2, 14		9.6 Q1				13.3 Q4, 13.4 Q1, 13.8 Q1, 13.9 Q1, 13.10 Q4, 7	14.3 Q1, 14.6 Q1	15.7 Q2
1	list		2.6 Q1		4.1 Q5		6.1 Q1						12.4 Q1	13.2 Q4	14.3 Q3	15.1 Q2
1	measure											11.1 Q2				
1	state	1.1 Q3, 1.2 Q2, 1.2 Q3, 14	2.1 Q1, 2.3 Q1, 2.4 Q1, 2.5 Q2, 2.6 Q1, 2.6 Q2, 2.6 Q5, 2.6 Q6, 2.7 Q1, 12	3.1 Q2, 3.5 Q1, 3.6 Q2, 3.7 Q1, 11, 16	4.1 Q2, 4.2 Q2, 4.3 Q1, 4.6 Q4, 4.6 Q6, 4.7 Q1, 12, 13	5.1 Q1, 5.5 Q4, 12	6.1 Q1, 6.1 Q1, 6.2 Q1, 6.2 Q2, 6.2 Q4, 6.3 Q1	7.2 Q2, 7.3 Q1, 7.4 Q1, 7.5 Q1	8.2 Q1, 8.3 Q1, 8.5 Q1, 8.7 Q1, 8.7 Q7, 13, 16, 17	9.6 Q1, 9.6 Q2, 9.8 Q1, 9.9 Q2, 19	10.1 Q1, 10.2 Q1, 10.2 Q2, 10.2 Q3, 10.2 Q4, 10.2 Q5, 10.3 Q1, 10.3 Q3, 10.3 Q4, 10.4 Q1, 10.5 Q3, 10.5 Q4, 11, 13	11.1 Q2, 11.3 Q2, 11.3 Q3, 11.3 Q4, 11.4 Q1, 11.4 Q3	12.1 Q1, 12.2 Q1, 12.2 Q2, 12.2 Q3, 12.2 Q5, 12.3 Q1, 12.4 Q1, 12.4 Q2, 12.5 Q1, 12.6 Q1, 12.6 Q2, 12.7 Q1, 12.7 Q2, 12.7 Q3, 12.7 Q4	13.1 Q1, 13.1 Q2, 13.2 Q1, 13.2 Q2, 13.3 Q1, 13.3 Q2, 13.3 Q3, 13.3 Q5, 13.3 Q6, 13.3 Q7, 13.4 Q1, 13.5 Q1, 13.6 Q1, 13.6 Q2, 13.7 Q2, 13.8 Q1, 13.9 Q1, 13.9 Q2, 13.10 Q1	14.1 Q2, 14.2 Q1, 14.2 Q2, 14.2 Q4, 14.2 Q5, 14.3 Q1, 14.3 Q2, 14.3 Q4, 14.4 Q1, 14.4 Q2, 14.5 Q1, 14.6 Q3, 14.6 Q4, 14.7 Q3, 14.7 Q4, 14.8 Q1, 14.8 Q2, 2, 3	15.1 Q1, 15.1 Q2, 15.2 Q1, 15.2 Q2, 15.3 Q1, 15.3 Q2, 15.4 Q1, 15.6 Q3, 15.7 Q1, 15.7 Q2, 15.8 Q1, 15.8 Q4, 15.9 Q2, 1, 4, 6, 7

AO	Skill	1 Stoichiometric relationships	2 Atomic structure	3 Periodicity	4 Chemical bonding and structure	5 Energetics	6 Chemical kinetics	7 Equilibrium	8 Acids and bases	9 Redox processes	10 Organic chemistry	11 Measurement, data processing and analysis	12 Materials (Option A)	13 Biochemistry (Option B)	14 Energy (Option C)	15 Medicinal chemistry (Option D)
1	state										15		12.8 Q2 12.8 Q3 12.10 Q2 3 5 7	13.10 Q4 1 4 5 8 10		
2	annotate								8.10 Q1							
2	calculate	1.3 Q1 1.3 Q2 1.4 Q3 1.4 Q4 1.4 Q5 1.5 Q1 1.5 Q2 1.5 Q3 1.6 Q1 1.6 Q2 1.6 Q3 1.7 Q1 1.7 Q2 1.7 Q3 1.7 Q4 2 3 4 5 6 10 11 12 13 15 16 17 18 19	2.1 Q1 2.1 Q2 2.2 Q2 2.3 Q1 2.7 Q2 8 11 13			5.1 Q2 5.1 Q3 5.2 Q1 5.2 Q2 5.3 Q1 5.3 Q2 5.4 Q2 5.4 Q3 5.5 Q3 5.5 Q5 1 2 10 11 12 13 14 15	6.3 Q1 12 14	7.6 Q1 7.6 Q2 7.6 Q3 7.6 Q4 7.7 Q1 7.7 Q2 7 8 9 10 11 12 13 14 15	8.4 Q2 8.4 Q3 8.4 Q4 8.7 Q3 8.7 Q4 8.7 Q5 8.7 Q6 8.9 Q1 2 13 14 15	9.5 Q1 9.5 Q2 9.5 Q3 9.7 Q3 9.7 Q5 9.9 Q5 9.9 Q6 9.9 Q7 8 11 12 14		11.1 Q2 11.1 Q3 2 3 11	12.2 Q2 12.5 Q3 12.8 Q3 12.10 Q5 2 7 8	13.3 Q3 13.6 Q5 13.7 Q3 13.7 Q4 3	14.1 Q1 14.2 Q5 14.3 Q4 14.6 Q3 14.6 Q5 14.7 Q1 14.7 Q2 1 3 4 5 6	15.4 Q3 15.6 Q3 15.8 Q2 15.9 Q2 1 3 6
2	describe	1.1 Q1 1.2 Q1 18	2.6 Q4 2.7 Q2	3.1 Q1 3.1 Q3 3.2 Q1 3.2 Q2 3.2 Q3 3.4 Q1 3.5 Q2 3.6 Q1 3.6 Q3 3.6 Q5 3.7 Q2 12 14 15 16	4.1 Q2 4.1 Q4 4.1 Q5 4.2 Q1 4.2 Q5 4.4 Q1 4.5 Q1 11 14	5.5 Q4 13 14		7.1 Q1 7.3 Q2 7.5 Q1 7.5 Q6 3	8.5 Q1 8.5 Q2 8.6 Q1 8.6 Q2 8.10 Q1 11 12	9.8 Q1 9.9 Q2 9.9 Q4 9.9 Q7 15 18 20	10.1 Q4 10.3 Q1 10.3 Q2 13 14 15 17	11.2 Q1 11.3 Q2	12.2 Q1 12.2 Q4 12.3 Q1 12.4 Q1 12.5 Q1 12.5 Q2 12.6 Q1 12.6 Q2 12.8 Q1 12.9 Q1 12.10 Q3 3 5	13.2 Q1 13.3 Q4 13.4 Q1 13.4 Q2 13.4 Q3 13.6 Q3 13.8 Q1 13.8 Q2 13.9 Q1 13.9 Q3 13.10 Q3 3 7	14.2 Q1 14.2 Q2 14.2 Q3 14.5 Q1 14.5 Q2 14.5 Q3 14.6 Q1 14.6 Q2 14.6 Q5 14.7 Q3 14.8 Q1 3 5	15.3 Q1 15.4 Q3 15.5 Q1 15.6 Q1 15.6 Q2 15.8 Q3 15.9 Q1 15.9 Q3 2 3 4 5
2	distinguish													13.2 Q5		

AO	Skill	1 Stoichiometric relationships	2 Atomic structure	3 Periodicity	4 Chemical bonding and structure	5 Energetics	6 Chemical kinetics	7 Equilibrium	8 Acids and bases	9 Redox processes	10 Organic chemistry	11 Measurement, data processing and analysis	12 Materials (Option A)	13 Biochemistry (Option B)	14 Energy (Option C)	15 Medicinal chemistry (Option D)
3	determine	1.2 Q2 7 8 18			4.1 Q3 4.2 Q4	5.5 Q5		7.5 Q3 11	8.4 Q1	9.2 Q4 9.3 Q3 9.3 Q4 9.5 Q3 9.6 Q3 9.7 Q1 9.9 Q3 3 13	10.5 Q3	11.2 Q1 11.3 Q1 14				
3	discuss													13.6 Q5	14.4 Q2 14.5 Q3	
3	evaluate											11.1 Q1				
3	explain	1.1 Q2 1.2 Q1	2.2 Q2 2.5 Q1 2.5 Q2 2.7 Q3 2.7 Q4 11 12 14	3.2 Q1 3.2 Q2 3.2 Q3 3.3 Q1 3.4 Q1 3.6 Q1 3.6 Q3 3.7 Q1 11 14 15	4.1 Q4 4.2 Q2 4.2 Q5 4.3 Q1 4.4 Q1 4.4 Q3 4.4 Q4 4.5 Q1 4.6 Q6 11 12 14	5.1 Q1 5.1 Q3 5.3 Q1 5.4 Q2 14	6.1 Q1 6.1 Q3 6.2 Q3 6.3 Q1 11 12 13 14	7.1 Q2 7.2 Q1 7.4 Q1 7.4 Q3 11 12 13	8.3 Q1 8.5 Q2 8.6 Q1 8.7 Q6 8.8 Q2 8.9 Q2 8.10 Q2 11 12 14 16 17	9.5 Q3	10.2 Q1 10.3 Q1 10.5 Q1 10.5 Q3 11 12 13 15	11.1 Q2 11	12.2 Q3 12.3 Q1 12.5 Q2 12.6 Q2 12.8 Q1 12.9 Q2 12.9 Q3 12.10 Q1 12.10 Q3 12.10 Q5 1 2 4	13.2 Q1 13.2 Q5 13.3 Q1 13.3 Q2 13.3 Q3 13.6 Q4 13.7 Q1 13.7 Q2 13.7 Q3 13.9 Q2 13.10 Q1 2 6 7	14.3 Q2 14.3 Q3 14.4 Q2 14.8 Q1 1 2 4 6	15.1 Q1 15.2 Q3 15.4 Q3 15.7 Q2 1 2 3 4 5
3	predict					5.5 Q2 13	12	7.5 Q4		9.4 Q1 9.7 Q4				13.5 Q1 13.9 Q2		
3	sketch		2.6 Q4 2.7Q4 13	15	4.6 Q3	5.1 Q1	6.1 Q2 6.1 Q3 6.2 Q3	13 14	8.8 Q1 14					13.7 Q2 6 9		
3	suggest		11	3.5 Q1 13 15	4.4 Q2 4.4 Q4 4.6 Q1 4.6 Q2 4.6 Q6 12	5.1 Q1 5.1 Q3 5.3 Q1 5.4 Q2 5.4 Q3 11 12	6.1 Q3 11 12 15		8.3 Q3 8.6 Q2 8.8 Q3 8.10 Q1 13		10.3 Q2 10.3 Q4 10.4 Q1	11.1 Q3 11.3 Q3 11.3 Q4 11.4 Q1 11.4. Q2 11 13 14	12.7 Q1 12.7 Q2 6	13.3 Q7 13.5 Q1 13.7 Q3	14.5 Q2	15.2 Q2 15.2 Q3 15.5 Q2 15.6 Q2 15.6 Q3 15.9 Q1 15.9 Q4 2 7

Stoichiometric relationships 1

Chapter outline

- Describe the three states of matter.
- Recall that atoms of different elements combine in fixed ratios to form compounds which have different properties from their component elements.
- Recall the difference between homogeneous and heterogeneous mixtures.
- Be able to construct and balance chemical equations.
- Recall the definitions for relative atomic mass, relative molecular/formula mass, empirical formula and molecular formula.
- Know how to solve calculations involving the composition of a compound, relative molecular/formula mass, empirical formula and molecular formula.
- Know that the mole is a fixed number of particles and refers to the amount of substance.
- Solve calculations involving the relationships between the number of particles, the amount of substance, the mass of a substance, the volume and concentration of a solution and the volume of a gas.
- Solve calculations using the ideal gas equation.
- Solve calculations involving theoretical and percentage yield including those involving a limiting reactant.

KEY TERMS AND FORMULAS

Avogadro's law: Equal volumes of ideal gases measured at the same temperature and pressure contain the same number of molecules.

Chemical properties: How a substance behaves in chemical reactions.

Empirical formula: The simplest whole-number ratio of the elements present in a compound.

Heterogeneous mixture: A mixture that does not have a uniform composition and consists of separate phases; it can be separated by mechanical means.

Homogeneous mixture: A mixture that has a uniform composition throughout the mixture and consists of only one phase.

Ideal gas: A theoretical model that approximates the behaviour of real gases.

Limiting reactant: The reactant that is used up first in a chemical reaction.

Mole: The amount of substance that contains the same number of particles (atoms, ions, molecules, and so on) as there are carbon atoms in 12 g of carbon-12 (6.02×10^{23}).

Molecular formula: The total number of atoms of each element present in a molecule of the compound; the molecular formula is a multiple of the empirical formula.

Physical properties: Properties such as melting point, solubility and electrical conductivity, relating to the physical state of a substance and the physical changes it can undergo.

Titration: An analytical technique used where one solution is reacted with the exact stoichiometric amount of another solution.

Water of crystallisation: Water that is present in definite proportions in the crystals of hydrated salts (e.g. $CuSO_4 \cdot 5H_2O$).

$$n = \frac{m}{M_r}$$

where n = amount of substance in mol, m = mass in g and M_r = molar mass in $g\,mol^{-1}$

Number of particles = $n \times L$
where n = amount of substance in mol, L = Avogadro's constant (6.02×10^{23}) in mol^{-1} – this value is given in the data book

% yield $= \dfrac{\text{actual yield}}{\text{theoretical yield}} \times \mathbf{100}$

$$n = \frac{\text{volume at a given temperature and pressure}}{\text{molar gas volume at the same temperature and pressure}}$$

where n = amount of substance in mol

$$\frac{P_1 V_1}{T_1} = \frac{P_2 V_2}{T_2}$$

P_1 = pressure under conditions 1 / any unit of pressure
V_1 = volume under conditions 1 / any unit of volume
T_1 = temperature under conditions 1 / K
P_2 = pressure under conditions 2 / any unit of pressure (same unit as for P_1)
V_2 = volume under conditions 2 / any unit of volume (same unit as for V_1)
T_2 = temperature under conditions 2 / K

$$c = \frac{n}{V}$$

c = concentration/$mol\,dm^{-3}$
n = amount of substance/mol
V = volume/dm^3

concentration in ppm $= \dfrac{\text{mass of solute} \times 10^6}{\text{mass of solution}}$

Exercise 1.1 – The particulate nature of matter

1 a Copy and complete Table 1.1, which describes the arrangement and movement of particles in solids, liquids and gases.

	Solids	Liquids	Gases
Diagram showing the arrangement of the particles			
Relative distance of the particles from one another			
Relative energy of the particles			
Relative speed of the particles			
Movement of the particles			
Relative force of attraction between the particles			

Table 1.1 Arrangement and movement of particles.

b Identify which of the descriptions of particles in Table 1.1 give rise to the fixed shape of solids and the lack of a fixed shape in liquids and gases.

c Which of the descriptions explain why, at a given temperature, the volume of a gas is not fixed but the volume of a liquid is?

2 Figure 1.1 shows the cooling curve for a substance.

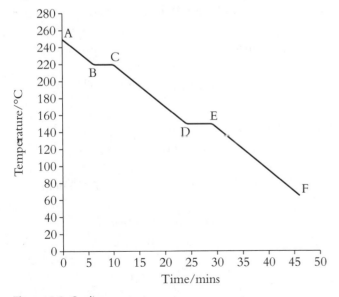

Figure 1.1 Cooling curve.

Remember this is a cooling curve so the change goes from gas to liquid to solid.
Melting points and boiling points are temperatures and should be read off the y-axis.

Label the diagram to show the following:
a the region where the substance is a solid
b the region where the substance is a liquid
c the region where the substance is a gas
d the region where the substance is freezing
e the region where the substance is condensing
f the melting point of the substance
g the boiling point of the substance.
h Explain, in terms of the movement and arrangement of the particles, why the temperature of the substance remains the same during a change of state.

3 Carbon dioxide and iodine are two examples of substances that undergo sublimation.
  a State what is meant by the term 'sublimation'.
  b State the term used to describe the reverse of sublimation.

Exercise 1.2 – Chemical change

1 **a** Identify whether the following substances are elements, mixtures or compounds:
  - air
  - water
  - sodium chloride solution
  - sodium chloride crystals
  - iron
  - chlorine gas
  - carbon dioxide gas

  b Describe what is meant by the terms 'homogeneous mixture' and 'heterogeneous mixture'.
  c Explain why a mixture of the solids sodium chloride and sand is not a homogeneous mixture.

2 A balanced equation shows the ratio of the number of each type of particle in a chemical reaction. This is normally expressed as the simplest whole-number ratio and fractions are not normally used. (The major exception to this is in the Energetics topic – see Chapter 5).
  Given the equation below for the combustion of butanol, answer the following questions

  $$C_4H_9OH(l) + 6O_2(g) \rightarrow 4CO_2(g) + 5H_2O(l)$$

  a Determine how many molecules of butanol would be required to produce 40 molecules of carbon dioxide.
  b What number of oxygen molecules would be needed to react with 100 butanol molecules?
  c State how the total number of molecules changes during this reaction.
  d State how the total mass of all the atoms changes during this reaction.

3 a Balance the following equations. Remember that only 'big' numbers can be used in front of a formula. 'Small' numbers are part of the formula of a substance and a formula must not be changed as this would change the identity of the substance.

  i $Na + Cl_2 \rightarrow NaCl$

  ii $N_2 + O_2 \rightarrow NO_2$

  iii $Li(s) + H_2O(l) \rightarrow LiOH(aq) + H_2(g)$

  iv $C_2H_6 + O_2 \rightarrow CO_2 + H_2O$

  v $Fe_2O_3 + CO \rightarrow Fe + CO_2$

  vi $Cu + HNO_3 \rightarrow Cu(NO_3)_2 + NO_2 + H_2O$

b Equation **iii** includes state symbols; what do the symbols (s), (l), (g) and (aq) indicate?

> If an element occurs in several different substances (e.g. oxygen in questions **iii** and **iv**) then it is often best to tackle this element last.

Exercise 1.3 – The mole concept

Although balanced equations tell us the number of units of each species reacting in an equation, they do not tell us the masses that react because not all atoms have the same mass. The mass of an atom is so small that relative atomic masses are usually used.

1 a In the terms 'relative atomic mass', 'relative formula mass' and 'relative molecular mass', to what does the word 'relative' apply?

b Define the terms 'relative atomic mass', 'relative formula mass' and 'relative molecular mass'.

c Calculate the relative formula mass or relative molecular mass of the following substances:

  i CO_2

  ii H_2O_2

  iii $NaNO_3$

  iv $(NH_4)_2SO_4$

  v C_2H_5OH

  vi $(CH_3CH_2COO)_2Mg$

  vi $H_3C_6H_5O_7$

> Always use the values from the data book and be consistent with decimal places.
> The data book gives relative atomic masses to 2 d.p. so answers should be given to 2 d.p.

2 Using the formulas $n = \dfrac{m}{M_r}$ and number of particles $= n \times L$, calculate the following:

    a the number of moles of sodium atoms in 10.0 g of sodium

    b the mass of 3 mol of $Cu(NO_3)_2$

    c the relative formula mass if 0.250 mol of the substance has a mass of 54.0 g

    d the number of water molecules in 2.50 mol of water

    e the number of oxygen molecules (O_2) in 64 g of oxygen

    f the number of oxygen atoms in 75.0 g of $CaCO_3$

    g the mass of one molecule of CO_2

    h the mass of hydrogen atoms in 0.040 mol of C_2H_6

Exercise 1.4 – Empirical and molecular formulas

1 Define the terms 'empirical formula' and 'molecular formula'.

2 Deduce the empirical formula from the following molecular formulas:

    a C_6H_6

    b H_2O_2

    c C_4H_{10}

    d $(COOH)_2$

    e NH_4NO_3

    f $CH_3CH_2CH_2COOH$

3 The formula of a substance can be used to find the percentage composition by mass of the substance using the formula

$$\% \text{ by mass of an element} = \frac{\text{number of atoms of the element} \times \text{atomic mass of the element}}{\text{relative formula mass}}$$

Calculate the % composition by mass of all the elements in $Mg_3(PO_4)_2$.

4 The composition of a compound can be found experimentally and can be used to determine the empirical formula of a compound. This is effectively the reverse of the calculation in Question 2 but it must be remembered that it always gives the empirical formula and not the molecular formula.

In an experiment, 0.36 g magnesium was reacted in an excess of oxygen and the oxide formed was found to have a mass of 0.60 g.

    a Calculate the mass of oxygen in the compound.

    b Deduce the empirical formula of the compound.

5 1.50 g of an organic compound containing only the elements carbon, hydrogen and oxygen with a relative molecular mass of 90.04 was combusted in excess oxygen. 1.47 g of CO_2 and 0.30 g of water were formed.

    a Calculate the empirical formula of the compound.

    b Deduce its molecular formula.

Exercise 1.5 – Calculations involving moles and mass

Calculations from equations can be broken down into three main stages:

1 Calculate the number of moles of the substance/substances for which you have some other information such as the mass.

2 Use the ratio in the balanced equation to find the number of moles of the substance that you are being asked about.

3 Convert this number of moles into the units that the question demands (e.g. mass or volume or concentration).

1 a Calculate the mass of carbon dioxide produced when 1.25 g of copper(II) oxide is reacted with methane, CH_4.

$$4CuO + CH_4 \rightarrow 4Cu + 2H_2O + CO_2$$

  b What mass of aluminium oxide is required to produce 1000 kg of aluminium?

$$2Al_2O_3 \rightarrow 4Al + 3O_2$$

  c What mass of magnesium can be burnt in 2.50 g of carbon dioxide?

$$2Mg + CO_2 \rightarrow 2MgO + C$$

2 Not all reactions produce the quantity of product that is theoretically possible. The amount produced is often quoted as a percentage of the theoretical maximum that could have been obtained.

  a Ethanol, C_2H_5OH, can be made from ethene, C_2H_4, using the following reaction:

$$C_2H_4(g) + H_2O(g) \rightarrow C_2H_5OH(g)$$

It was found that 10.0 g of ethene produced 14.6 g of ethanol. Calculate the percentage yield.

  b Calcium oxide is made by the thermal decomposition of calcium carbonate which is found in limestone.

$$CaCO_3 \rightarrow CaO + CO_2$$

Calculate the percentage yield if 3.0 g of calcium carbonate produced 1.5 g of calcium oxide.

3 Experiments are normally conducted using non-stoichiometric amounts. This means that the exact ratio of substances is not used; one or more of the reactants are in excess and so the amount of product that can be obtained is limited by the amount of the reactant that is not in excess. This is known as the limiting reactant.

  a 2.50 g of sulfur was heated with 2.50 g of iron to form iron(II) sulfide.

$$Fe(s) + S(s) \rightarrow FeS(s)$$

Identify which is the limiting reactant and calculate the theoretical maximum yield of iron(II) sulfide that could be formed.

  b Aluminium reacts with iodine according to the equation:

$$2Al(s) + 3I_2(s) \rightarrow 2AlI_3(s)$$

In an experiment 1.0 g of aluminium powder was mixed with 2.0 g of iodine. 2.0 g of aluminium iodide was produced. Identify the limiting reactant and calculate the percentage yield.

As with all calculations, use the same number of decimal places (for addition and subtraction) or significant figures (for multiplication and division) as are given in the original data and do not round any values until the last stage of the calculation.

If the number of moles of each reactant is divided by the coefficient in the balanced equation, the smallest number indicates the limiting reactant.

Exercise 1.6 – Calculations involving gas volumes

Watch out for the following when tackling questions involving gases:
- Units must be consistent. Remember $1000\,cm^3 = 1\,dm^3$ and $1000\,dm^3 = 1\,m^3$.
- When using $n = \dfrac{\text{volume at a given temperature and pressure}}{\text{molar gas volume at the same temperature and pressure}}$,
  any units can be used for the volume and for the molar gas volume as long as the same unit is used for both.
- When using $PV = nRT$, if the volume is in dm^3 then the pressure must be in kPa and vice versa.
- When using $PV = nRT$, if the pressure is in Pa then the volume must be in m^3 and vice versa.
- When using $PV = nRT$, the temperature must be in kelvin not °C.
- When using $\dfrac{P_1 V_1}{T_1} = \dfrac{P_2 V_2}{T_2}$, the temperature must be in kelvin not °C.
- When using $\dfrac{P_1 V_1}{T_1} = \dfrac{P_2 V_2}{T_2}$, any units for pressure and volume can be used as long as they are consistent on both sides of the equation.
- Think about the units!

For questions where the molar gas volume is known, for example at STP or where a value is given as in part **c**, then the expression
$$n = \frac{volume}{molar\ gas\ volume}$$
can be used as long as the conditions are not changing. Watch out for units.

1 The molar gas volume under standard conditions of temperature and pressure is $22.7\,dm^3\,mol^{-1}$. This is given in the data book.
   a Calculate the volume occupied by 0.75 mol of a gas at STP.
   b How many moles of gas occupy $500\,cm^3$ at STP?
   c At a given temperature and pressure, one mole of an ideal gas occupies $24.0\,dm^3$. Calculate the number of moles of gas that would occupy $150\,cm^3$ at the same temperature and pressure.
   d What volume would 2.50 g of carbon dioxide occupy at STP?

2 The expression $\dfrac{P_1 V_1}{T_1} = \dfrac{P_2 V_2}{T_2}$ can be used when any of the temperature, pressure or volume of a gas are changed.
   a $100\,cm^3$ of an ideal gas at a pressure of 100 kPa and a temperature of 330 K was cooled to a temperature of 250 K at the same pressure. What volume will the gas now occupy?
   b A fixed mass of gas was sealed in a flask with a volume of $1\,dm^3$ at a pressure of 200 kPa and a temperature of 25 °C. The flask was heated to a temperature of 100 °C. What pressure will the gas now exert?
   c At what temperature (in °C) would $200\,cm^3$ of an ideal gas at STP occupy $400\,cm^3$ at a pressure of 150 kPa?

3 The expression $PV = nRT$ can be used to find either the volume, pressure, temperature or the number of moles of gas when the conditions do not change.

  a Calculate the number of moles of gas that would occupy $400\,cm^3$ at a temperature of $298\,K$ and a pressure of $1.5 \times 10^5\,Pa$.

  b Calculate the pressure exerted by $2.40\,g$ of carbon dioxide with a volume of $1000\,cm^3$ at $25\,°C$.

  c If $73.07\,g$ of an ideal gas occupies $35.0\,dm^3$ at $50.0\,°C$ and a pressure of $200\,kPa$, calculate the molar mass of the gas.

  d A $0.25\,g$ sample of a metal that contained copper was reacted with concentrated nitric acid and the nitrogen dioxide gas produced was collected in a gas syringe.

$$Cu(s) + 4HNO_3(aq) \rightarrow Cu(NO_3)_2(aq) + 2H_2O(l) + 2NO_2(g)$$

The gas occupied $87\,cm^3$ at a pressure of $100\,kPa$. The temperature of the gas was measured to be $298\,K$. Assuming that only the copper in the metal mixture reacted, what is the percentage of copper in the sample?

Exercise 1.7 – Calculations involving solutions

Concentration is most commonly measured in $mol\,dm^{-3}$ but other units can also be used such as $g\,dm^{-3}$ or ppm (part per million).

1 a Calculate the concentrations of the following solutions in $mol\,dm^{-3}$.

    i $100\,cm^3$ of sodium chloride solution containing $0.75\,g$ of NaCl

    ii a solution of copper(II) sulfate ($CuSO_4$) with a concentration of $5.6\,g\,dm^{-3}$

    iii a solution of volume $250\,cm^3$ containing $4.50\,g$ of hydrated sodium carbonate ($Na_2CO_3 \cdot 10H_2O$)

  b The analysis of a contaminated water supply found that a $150\,g$ sample of the water contained 3.45 mg of Pb^{2+} ions. Calculate the concentration of lead ions in ppm.

  c What is the concentration of aluminium ions when $3.5\,g$ of aluminium sulfate ($Al_2(SO_4)_3$) is dissolved in water to give $200\,cm^3$ of solution?

2 a How many moles of solute are there in the following solutions?

    i $25.00\,cm^3$ of $0.100\,mol\,dm^{-3}$ $NaOH(aq)$

    ii $50.0\,cm^3$ of $0.025\,mol\,dm^{-3}$ $K_2Cr_2O_7(aq)$

  b What mass of potassium bromide, KBr, is required to make $250\,cm^3$ of solution with a concentration of $0.250\,mol\,dm^{-3}$?

  c What volume of calcium nitrate solution ($Ca(NO_3)_2$) with a concentration of $0.45\,mol\,dm^{-3}$ will contain $0.25\,mol$ of the solute?

> A formula with '·xH_2O' means that the solid is hydrated and contains water of crystallisation. The molar mass for the solid includes these water molecules.

3 A small piece of calcium was added to a beaker of water and the volume of hydrogen gas produced was measured. The solution formed was then made up to a volume of $200\,cm^3$.

$$Ca(s) + 2H_2O(l) \rightarrow Ca(OH)_2(aq) + H_2(g)$$

a What mass of calcium is required to produce $75\,cm^3$ of hydrogen gas at a temperature of $20\,°C$ and a pressure of $101\,kPa$?

b What is the concentration of the calcium hydroxide solution formed?

c What volume of hydrochloric acid of concentration $0.500\,mol\,dm^{-3}$ would be required to react with the calcium hydroxide formed in this reaction?

$$Ca(OH)_2(aq) + 2HCl(aq) \rightarrow CaCl_2(aq) + 2H_2O(l)$$

4 a A titration experiment was performed to find the concentration of a solution of sodium hydroxide. It was found that an average titre of $20.45\,cm^3$ of sulfuric acid with a concentration of $0.200\,mol\,dm^{-3}$ was required to neutralise $25.00\,cm^3$ of the sodium hydroxide solution.

    i Give the equation for the reaction.

    ii Calculate the number of moles of sulfuric acid used per titre.

    iii Use the balanced equation to find the number of moles of sodium hydroxide per titre.

    iv Calculate the concentration of the sodium hydroxide solution.

b $1.25\,g$ of hydrated oxalic acid crystals, $H_2C_2O_4 \cdot xH_2O$ were dissolved in water and made up to a volume of $250.0\,cm^3$. $25.00\,cm^3$ portions of this were then titrated against dilute sodium hydroxide of concentration $0.100\,mol\,dm^{-3}$. The average titre was found to be $19.85\,cm^3$.

    i Calculate the number of moles of sodium hydroxide used per titre.

    ii The balanced equation for the reaction is:

$$H_2C_2O_4(aq) + 2NaOH(aq) \rightarrow C_2O_4Na_2(aq) + 2H_2O(l)$$

    Deduce the number of moles of oxalic acid in $25.00\,cm^3$ of solution.

    iii Calculate the number of moles of oxalic acid in the original crystals.

    iv Calculate the mass of oxalic acid present in the crystals.

    v Calculate the mass of the water of crystallisation.

    vi Calculate the number of moles of water of crystallisation.

    vii Calculate the ratio of the number of moles of water to the number of moles of oxalic acid and hence determine the value for x in the formula of the hydrated oxalic acid.

c Succinic acid has a molar mass of $118.1\,g\,mol^{-1}$. In an experiment to find the number of hydrogen ions per succinic acid molecule, $1.01\,g$ of succinic acid crystals were dissolved in water to make a solution of volume $250\,cm^3$. This was then titrated against $25.00\,cm^3$ portions of $0.100\,mol\,dm^{-3}$ sodium hydroxide until concordant results were obtained. It was found that an average titre of $24.40\,cm^3$ was required. Determine the ratio for the reaction between succinic acid and sodium hydroxide.

> The mass (and hence the molar mass) of oxalic acid excludes the water of crystallisation as this water is released when the solid is dissolved.

> This question has not been structured so at first sight appears difficult. Start, as always, by calculating the number of moles of what you know. Set your work out clearly, showing the examiner each step.

? Exam-style questions

1   Which of the following statements is true of heterogeneous mixtures?
    A Their components cannot be separated by physical means.
    B They have the same composition throughout the mixture.
    C The components are in a fixed ratio.
    D The components are in separate phases.

2   Calculate the sum of the coefficients when the following equation is balanced with
    the smallest possible whole numbers.
    $H_2O_2 + KI + H_2SO_4 \rightarrow I_2 + K_2SO_4 + H_2O$
    A 6
    B 7
    C 8
    D 9

3   Calculate how many atoms there are in 4.4 g of carbon dioxide.
    A 3.01×10^{22}
    B 6.02×10^{22}
    C 9.03×10^{24}
    D 1.80×10^{23}

4   Molten iron can be produced by the reaction of iron(III) oxide with aluminium
    powder according to the equation:
    $Fe_2O_3 + 2Al \rightarrow 2Fe + Al_2O_3$
    Calculate how many moles of iron would be produced when 120 mol of
    iron(III) oxide is completely reacted with aluminium.
    A 60 mol
    B 120 mol
    C 180 mol
    D 240 mol

5   Calculate the volume of carbon dioxide produced when 65 cm³ of butane is burnt
    in 65 cm³ of oxygen.
    $2C_4H_{10}(g) + 13O_2(g) \rightarrow 8CO_2(g) + 10H_2O(l)$
    A 40 cm³
    B 65 cm³
    C 130 cm³
    D 260 cm³

6   Calculate the mass of solute needed to make 100 cm³ of 0.100 mol dm⁻³ of
    $MgSO_4 \cdot 7H_2O$.
    A 2.46 g
    B 1.5 g
    C 15.0 g
    D 24.6 g

7 A hydrocarbon was found to have a composition by mass of 2.4 g carbon and 0.2 g hydrogen. It has a molar mass of 78.66 g mol^{-1}. The molecular formula of the substance is:

A C_2H_6 B C_2H_2 C C_6H_{12} D C_6H_6

8 Which of the following would halve the volume of an ideal gas?

A Changing the temperature from 100 °C to 200 °C at constant pressure.

B Changing the pressure from 100 kPa to 200 kPa at constant temperature.

C Changing the number of moles of gas from 2 to 4 at constant pressure.

D Changing the pressure from 300 kPa to 150 kPa and the number of moles of gas from 4 to 2 at constant temperature.

9 The graphs in Figures 1.2–1.5 show the different relationships between pressure, volume and temperature of an ideal gas.

Identify each graph correctly from the options in Table 1.2.

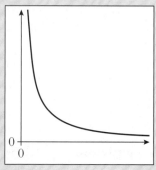

Figure 1.2

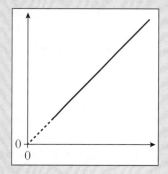

Figure 1.3

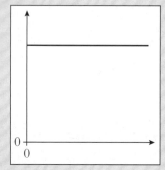

Figure 1.4

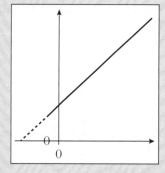

Figure 1.5

	Graph 1	Graph 2	Graph 3	Graph 4
A	x-axis: V/cm^3 y-axis: P/Pa	x-axis: $(1/V)$/cm^{-3} y-axis: P/Pa	x-axis: P/Pa y-axis: PV/cm^{3}Pa	x-axis: T/°C y-axis: V/cm^3
B	x-axis: T/°C y-axis: V/cm^3	x-axis: V/cm^3 y-axis: P/Pa	x-axis: $(1/V)$/cm^{-3} y-axis: P/Pa	x-axis: V/cm^3 y-axis: P/Pa
C	x-axis: V/cm^3 y-axis: P/Pa	x-axis: $(1/V)$/cm^{-3} y-axis: P/Pa	x-axis: P/Pa y-axis: PV/cm^{3}Pa	x-axis: T/K y-axis: V/cm^3
D	x-axis: $(1/V)$/cm^{-3} y-axis: P/Pa	x-axis: T/K y-axis: V/cm^3	x-axis: P/Pa y-axis: PV/cm^{3}Pa	x-axis: V/cm^3 y-axis: P/Pa

Table 1.2

10 In an experiment to produce iron(III) chloride, 5.6 g of iron wool was heated in a stream of chlorine gas. 8.13 g of iron(III) chloride, $FeCl_3$, was produced.

$2Fe(s) + 3Cl_2(g) \rightarrow 2FeCl_3(s)$ (A_r Fe = 55.85, M_r $FeCl_3$ = 162.20)

What is the percentage yield?

$$A = \frac{162.20 \times 55.85 \times 100}{5.6 \times 8.13}$$

$$B = \frac{5.6 \times 8.13 \times 100}{55.85 \times 2 \times 162.20}$$

$$C = \frac{8.13 \times 55.85 \times 100}{5.6 \times 162.20}$$

$$D = \frac{5.6 \times 100}{8.13}$$

11 In an experiment to find the identity of a group 2 element, M, 50.0 cm^3 of 0.100 mol dm^{-3} of sodium carbonate solution was mixed with 50.0 cm^3 of a solution of $M(NO_3)_2$ with a concentration of 0.200 mol dm^{-3}. The two solutions reacted together to form a precipitate according to the equation:

$Na_2CO_3(aq) + M(NO_3)_2(aq) \rightarrow MCO_3(s) + 2NaNO_3(aq)$

The precipitate was filtered, washed and dried carefully and was found to have a mass of 0.74 g.

   a Deduce which reagent was in excess. [1]
   b Calculate the number of moles of the group 2 carbonate precipitate formed. [1]
   c Determine the molar mass of the carbonate and hence suggest the identity of the group 2 element. [3]

[Total 5]

12 Silicon dioxide occurs as an impurity in the ores that are used to make iron. It is removed by reacting it with calcium oxide:

$CaO + SiO_2 \rightarrow CaSiO_3$

The calcium oxide is formed by the thermal decomposition of limestone:

$CaCO_3 \rightarrow CaO + CO_2$

   a Calculate the mass of calcium oxide required to remove each tonne (1 tonne = 1000 kg) of silicon dioxide. [2]
   b If limestone containing an average of 95% calcium carbonate was used, then what mass of limestone would be required per tonne of silicon dioxide? [2]
   c One of the main ores of iron is haematite (Fe_2O_3). This ore can be fed directly into an iron-making blast furnace along with the limestone.
      The ore is reduced according to the equation:

$Fe_2O_3 + 3CO \rightarrow 2Fe + 3CO_2$

   If the ore contains an average of 10% silicon dioxide, then what mass of limestone is required per tonne of iron produced? [4]

[Total 8]

13 Calomel is a mercury compound with a molar mass of $472.08\,g\,mol^{-1}$ and a composition of 84.98% mercury and 15.02% chlorine by mass.

    a Deduce the empirical and molecular formula of the compound. [3]

    b The compound decomposes on exposure to UV light to form mercury(II) chloride and elemental mercury.

       Give the balanced equation for this reaction. [1]

    c Calomel was a common ingredient in medicines but is toxic and is no longer used. It has an LD_{50} value of $210\,mg\,kg^{-1}$ in rats. This means that the lethal dose in 50% of cases is $210\,mg\,(kg\ body\ weight)^{-1}$. If an average adult has a mass of $70\,kg$ and the lethal dose in humans is the same as for rats, then what mass of calomel would need to be ingested to exceed the LD_{50} limit? [1]

    d Calomel has a solubility of $0.200\,mg\,/\,100\,cm^3$ at $25\,°C$. Calculate the concentration of a saturated solution in $mol\,dm^{-3}$ at this temperature. [1]

    e What volume of a saturated solution of calomel would be needed to exceed the LD_{50} limit? [1]

                                             [Total 7]

14 a State Avogadro's law. [1]

    b Gases deviate most from ideal behaviour at high pressure and low temperature. Give two assumptions about ideal gases which account for the deviation in the behaviour of real gases from that of an ideal gas. [2]

    c $50\,cm^3$ of an organic compound containing only carbon and hydrogen was burnt in $250\,cm^3$ of oxygen, an excess. At the end of the reaction the volume of the products and the unused oxygen was found to have contracted by $100\,cm^3$; some liquid water was also formed. The gaseous products were treated with sodium hydroxide which reacts with carbon dioxide and a further contraction of $100\,cm^3$ occurred. Assuming that all measurements were made at $298\,K$ and $1.0 \times 10^5\,Pa$, deduce the formula of the compound and give the balanced equation for its combustion. [6]

                                             [Total 9]

15 In an experiment to find the relative molecular mass of a volatile liquid, $0.500\,g$ of the liquid was injected into an empty gas syringe and the end of the syringe was sealed. The syringe was placed into an insulated oven and heated to a temperature of $120\,°C$. At this temperature all of the liquid vaporised and the gas formed was found to have a volume of $124\,cm^3$. The pressure was measured and was found to be $99.8\,kPa$.

    a Calculate the relative molecular mass of the substance. [2]

    b A second $0.500\,g$ sample of the same liquid was analysed by burning it in an excess of oxygen. $0.999\,g$ of carbon dioxide and $0.409\,g$ of water were formed. There were no other products.

       Deduce the empirical formula and the molecular formula of the substance. [6]

                                           [Total 8]

16 Potassium manganate(VII) decomposes on heating according to the following equation:

$$2KMnO_4(s) \rightarrow K_2MnO_4(s) + MnO_2(s) + O_2(g)$$

In an experiment, 1.00 g of $KMnO_4$ was heated and produced 100 cm³ of oxygen. The gas was allowed to cool to 20 °C and its volume was found to have reduced to 65 cm³.

a Calculate the temperature of the hot gas if the pressure of the gas at both temperatures is 100 kPa. [2]

b Calculate what percentage of the potassium manganate(VII) decomposed. [4]

[Total 6]

17 A 0.100 g sample of magnesium was thought to be impure and was analysed by reacting it with 100 cm³ of 0.200 mol dm⁻³ of dilute sulfuric acid (an excess) using the apparatus shown in Figure 1.6.

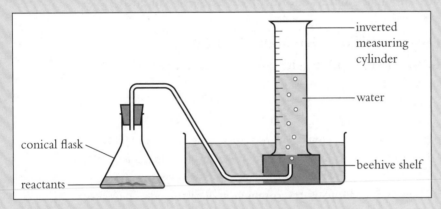

Figure 1.6 Apparatus for the reaction between magnesium and sulfuric acid.

a Give the equation for the reaction between magnesium and sulfuric acid, including state symbols. [2]

b Calculate the volume of gas that would be collected if the magnesium were 100% pure, the temperature of the gas was 24 °C and the pressure was 102 kPa. [2]

c If the volume actually collected was 86.0 cm³, calculate the percentage purity of the magnesium, assuming that none of the impurities reacted with the acid. [1]

d In case some of the gas had escaped before the bung was inserted, the contents of the conical flask were analysed by titration.

The contents of the flask were transferred into a volumetric flask, the conical flask was washed several times with distilled water and these washings were also transferred into the volumetric flask. The solution was made up to 250 cm³ with more distilled water and thoroughly mixed.

25.00 cm³ portions of this diluted solution were then titrated against 0.200 mol dm⁻³ NaOH using phenolphthalein indicator. An average titre of 16.05 cm³ of NaOH was required. Using the data from the titration experiment, calculate the percentage purity of the magnesium. [6]

[Total 11]

18 In an experiment to deduce the formula of $MgSO_4 \cdot xH_2O$, a sample of the solid
    was heated to constant mass in a crucible to remove the water of crystallisation.
    The following data were obtained.
    Mass of empty crucible/g = 18.27
    Mass of crucible and hydrated magnesium sulfate (before heating)/g = 21.19
    Mass of crucible and anhydrous magnesium sulfate (after heating)/g = 19.70
    a Describe what is mean by 'constant mass' and how these data could be obtained. [2]
    b Use the data to find the value of x in the formula. [4]
    c The balance used had an uncertainty of ± 0.01 g. Calculate the percentage uncertainties in
       the masses of both the hydrated and the anhydrous magnesium sulfate. [2]

                                                                                   [Total 8]

19 Ammonia is a very soluble gas. It is made industrially from nitrogen and hydrogen
    using the Haber process. In the laboratory, ammonia can be made by the reaction
    of an ammonium salt with an alkali such as sodium hydroxide or calcium
    hydroxide.

    e.g. $2NH_4Cl(s) + Ca(OH)_2(s) \rightarrow CaCl_2(s) + 2H_2O(g) + 2NH_3(g)$

    In such an experiment, 0.20 g of ammonium chloride was reacted with an excess
    of calcium hydroxide.
    a Give the minimum mass of calcium hydroxide that should be used. [2]
    b Calculate the volume of gas that would be collected at 400 K and 101 kPa. [3]
    c The hot products were passed through a drying agent to remove the water and allowed to
       cool. What volume will the dry gas now occupy if the temperature is reduced to 298 K at
       the same pressure? [3]
    d The dry ammonia gas was then bubbled into water in which it all dissolved. The water
       was made up to a volume of 250 cm^3. Calculate the concentration of the ammonia solution
       formed. [1]

                                                                                   [Total 9]

Atomic structure 2

Chapter outline

- Recall the structure of an atom in terms of protons, neutrons and electrons.
- Recall the definitions for mass number, atomic number and isotope.
- Calculate relative atomic mass and isotopic abundance from given data.
- Be able to write the electron configuration of an atom or ion using s, p, d notation and using orbital diagrams by applying the Aufbau principle, Hund's rule and the Pauli exclusion principle.
- Be able to describe the shapes of s and p orbitals.
- Be able to describe the emission spectrum of hydrogen and explain how it arises.
- Be able to solve equations involving $E = h\nu$. **HL**
- Be able to calculate the first ionisation energy from spectral data which gives the wavelength or frequency of the convergence limit. **HL**
- Be able to explain the trends in first ionisation energies across a period, including the discontinuities. **HL**
- Be able to deduce the group of an element from its successive ionisation energy data. **HL**

KEY TERMS AND FORMULAS

Atomic number, Z: The number of protons in the nucleus of an atom.

Aufbau principle: The idea that electrons always fill the sub-levels of the lowest energy first.

Degenerate: The term used to describe orbitals of equal energy.

Hund's rule: The idea that electrons fill degenerate orbitals so as to give the maximum number of electrons with the same spin. This leads to all the degenerate orbitals being half-filled rather than some being occupied by a pair of electrons and some empty.

Ion: An atom or group of atoms that have lost or gained one or more electrons and so is electrically charged. N.B. It is not correct to define an ion as a charged particle because protons and electrons are charged particles but they are not ions.

Ionisation energy: This can be thought of as the minimum amount of energy required to remove the outermost electron from a gaseous atom.

Isotope: Different atoms of an element; they have the same number of protons but different numbers of neutrons.

Mass number, A: The sum of the number of protons and neutrons in the nucleus of an atom.

Orbital: The region or **volume** (not area as orbitals are 3-dimensional) of space in which there is a high probability of finding a maximum of two electrons.

Pauli exclusion principle: The idea that two electrons within the same orbital must have opposite spins.

Principal quantum number: The number used to describe the main energy level or shell. The first shell has the principal quantum number 1, the second, 2 and so on. The symbol n is sometimes used. The maximum number of electrons in a given shell can be calculated using the formula $2n^2$.

Shielding: The idea that complete inner shells of electrons shield or screen outer electrons from the full attractive force of the nucleus.

Convergence limit: The lines in a line spectrum fall into several series or groups. Within each series the lines get closer together at higher frequency, eventually converging. The convergence limit is the frequency at which this convergence occurs.

Maximum number of electrons in a given energy level = $2n^2$
where n is the principal quantum number

Relative atomic mass $A_r = \dfrac{\text{sum of}\left(\text{mass} \times \text{abundance of each isotope}\right)}{\text{total abundance}}$

Exercise 2.1 – Atoms

Sub-atomic particle	Relative mass	Relative charge
proton		
neutron		
electron		

Table 2.1

1 An atom can be thought of as being composed of centrally located protons and neutrons, collectively referred to as the nucleus, surrounded by fast moving electrons arranged in shells.

   a Copy and complete Table 2.1 to show the mass and charge of each sub–atomic particle relative to each other.

   b The atomic number and mass number of an atom can be used to determine the number of protons and neutrons in an atom. Copy and complete Table 2.2.

Element	Atomic number	Mass number	Number of protons	Number of neutrons
phosphorus	15	31		
strontium	38	88		
		207	82	
bromine	35			44
	74			109

Table 2.2

2 Electrons can be relatively easily lost or gained by an atom to form ions. (Changes to the nucleus of an atom only occur during radioactive processes which are explored in Physics.) The formulas of an ion can therefore be deduced from the number of its sub-atomic particles. Copy and complete Table 2.3.

Formula	Atomic number	Mass number	Number of protons	Number of neutrons	Number of electrons
Na^+	11	23			
O^{2-}	8	16			
	29	65			28
Fe^{2+}			26	28	
			22	24	20

Table 2.3

Physical properties include melting points, solubility, electrical conductivity. Chemical properties refers to chemical reactions.

Exercise 2.2 – Isotopes

1 Most elements exist as isotopes.
What is meant by 'isotope' and what are the differences in the physical and chemical properties of isotopes?

Mass number is always an integer whereas the relative atomic mass is not.

2 a Define the term 'relative atomic mass' and explain the difference between this and mass number.
  b Calculate the relative atomic masses of the following elements from their relative abundances.
    i   Carbon: % abundance ^{12}C = 98.93 & ^{13}C = 1.07
    ii Argon: % abundance ^{36}Ar = 0.3365, ^{38}Ar = 0.0632 & ^{40}Ar = 99.6003
    iii Sulfur: % abundance ^{32}S = 94.93, ^{33}S = 0.76, ^{34}S = 4.29 & ^{36}S = 0.020

Exercise 2.3 – Mass spectrometry

1 Mass spectrometry can be used to find number and relative abundances of the different isotopes of an element.

   a What are the most common axes on a mass spectrum?

   b On the mass spectrum of copper in Figure 2.1 identify the species responsible for each peak and calculate the relative atomic mass of the element.

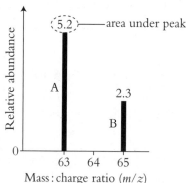

Figure 2.1 Mass spectrum of copper.

2 Given that the relative atomic mass of boron is 10.81 and that it has two isotopes, ^{10}B and ^{11}B, deduce the relative abundances of these isotopes.

This calculation is the reverse of those in Question 2 in Exercise 2.2. It is best approached using algebra. Imagine that the percentage abundance of one isotope is x and the other is $100 - x$.

Exercise 2.4 – Electron arrangement

The position of an electron is described in terms of its energy level rather than its distance from the nucleus because electrons are believed to be in constant motion. Electrons can only have discrete amounts of energy and these are known as energy levels. There is a limit to the number of electrons that can occupy a given energy level.

1 **a** What is the maximum number of electrons that can occupy each of the first five energy levels?

   b What is meant by the term 'principal quantum number'?

Look at the key formulas listed at the start of this chapter.

Exercise 2.5 – Hydrogen atom spectrum

1 All elements produce an emission spectrum but the hydrogen emission spectrum is particularly useful as hydrogen has only one electron so its spectrum is simpler to interpret.

   a Explain the difference between a continuous spectrum and a line spectrum.

   b Explain the origin of the lines in a hydrogen emission spectrum.

2 Figure 2.2 shows part of the hydrogen emission spectrum that appears in the visible part of the electromagnetic spectrum, which relates to transitions to the $n = 2$ energy level.

   a State what transitions give rise to the lines shown.

Spectrogram of visible lines in the Balmer series of hydrogen

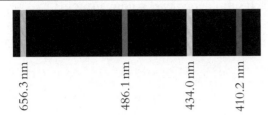

Figure 2.2 Balmer series for hydrogen.

b i Why do the lines in an emission spectrum series get closer together at shorter wavelengths?
  ii What name is given to the point at which they merge and what does this point represent?

Exercise 2.6 – Sub-energy levels

1 Each energy level in an atom can be subdivided into sub-energy levels: s, p, d and f.
  a Place the sub-energy levels that occur in the $n = 4$ energy level in order, starting with the sub-level of lowest energy.
  b What is the maximum number of electrons that each sub-energy level can hold?
  c Give the names of two elements in the first row of the d-block of the periodic table that do not obey the Aufbau principle.

> Another term for sub-energy level is sub-shell.

2 Give the full electron configuration of the following elements:
  a carbon
  b calcium
  c arsenic
  d manganese

3 Copy and complete Figure 2.3 to show the number of electrons and sub-energy levels in an atom of vanadium.

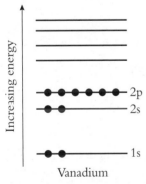

Figure 2.3 Arrangement of electrons in a vanadium atom.

4 a Describe what is meant by the term 'orbital'.

b How many orbitals make up each sub-energy level within an atom?

c In separate diagrams, sketch the shape of an s orbital and a p orbital.

d What is the only difference between the three p orbitals that make up a p sub-energy level?

5 The Pauli exclusion principle (paired electrons have opposite spins) and Hund's rule (degenerate orbitals are occupied singly by electrons with the same spin before electrons pair in the same orbital) can be applied to further refine the arrangement of electrons in an atom.

a What is meant by the term 'degenerate'?

b Copy and complete the orbital diagrams (electrons in boxes diagrams) in Figure 2.4 for phosphorus and copper.

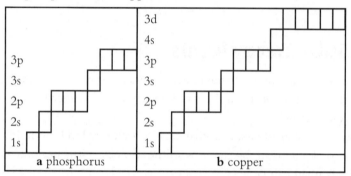

Figure 2.4 Electron configuration: a. phosphorus; b. copper.

6 When atoms lose electrons to become positive ions, the electrons lost are those that leave behind the most stable electron arrangement in the ion formed. This means that the electrons lost are most often those in the highest energy level.

a Which block of the periodic table does not obey this 'last in, first out' rule?

b Give the electron configurations of the following ions:

i Na^+

ii S^{2-}

iii Cr^{3+}

iv Cu^{2+}

HL Exercise 2.7 – Ionisation energies

1 a Define the term 'first ionisation energy'.

b Give an equation for the first ionisation energy of chlorine.

2 a How can the emission spectrum of an element be used to find the ionisation energy of its outermost electron?

b A line in the emission spectrum of sodium has a wavelength of 589 nm. Calculate the energy of the photon emitted.

c The convergence limit of helium is 50.4 nm; calculate the ionisation energy of helium.

3 The amount of energy required to remove the outermost electron depends on the force of attraction between the outer-shell electron and the nucleus. This depends on the nuclear charge and on the extent to which the outer-shell electrons are shielded from the nucleus by inner shells of electrons.

a Explain the trend in nuclear charge across a period.

b Explain the trend in nuclear charge down a group.

c Explain the trend in the amount of shielding across a period.

d Explain the trend in the amount of shielding down a group.

e Explain why there is a general increase in the first ionisation energy across a period of the periodic table.

f Explain why first ionisation energies decrease down a group.

g Define the second ionisation energy and explain why the second ionisation energy of an element is always higher than its first ionisation energy.

4 Table 2.4 shows the successive ionisation energies for magnesium.

Ionisation energy number	Energy / kJ mol^{-1}
1st	738
2nd	1451
3rd	7733
4th	10543
5th	13630
6th	18020
7th	21711

Table 2.4

a Explain why there is a large increase in the amount of energy required to remove the third electron compared to the second.

b Sketch a graph of the successive ionisation energies for silicon.

? Exam-style questions

1 **Which statement is not true about $^{138}_{56}\text{Ba}^{2+}$?**

   A It has 56 protons, 82 neutrons and 58 electrons.

   B The atomic number is 56 and the mass number is 138.

   C There are more neutrons than protons.

   D It has more protons than electrons.

2 **The relative atomic mass of chlorine is 35.45. Which of the following can be deduced from this information?**

   A Chlorine forms diatomic molecules, Cl_2.

   B Chlorine has two naturally occurring isotopes.

   C The relative molecular mass of Cl_2 is 70.90.

   D ^{35}Cl and ^{37}Cl exist in an approximate ratio of 3:1.

3 What is the correct electron configuration of Ni^{2+}?

A $1s^2\,2s^2\,2p^6\,3s^2\,3p^6\,4s^2\,4p^6\,3d^2$

B $1s^2\,2s^2\,2p^6\,3s^2\,3p^6\,4s^2\,3d^6$

C $1s^2\,2s^2\,2p^6\,3s^2\,3p^6\,3d^{10}$

D $1s^2\,2s^2\,2p^6\,3s^2\,3p^6\,3d^8$

4 What is the relative atomic mass of an element with the mass spectrum shown in Figure 2.5?

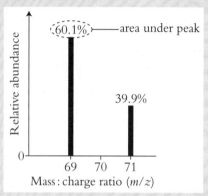

Figure 2.5 Relative abundances of the isotopes of an element.

A 70.0

B 70.2

C 69.5

D 69.8

5 Which statements about the hydrogen emission spectrum are true?

I The lines in the spectrum are due to electron excitation.

II The line of highest frequency represents the energy gap between the innermost and outermost energy levels.

III The series of lines in the ultraviolet region of the spectrum represents transitions involving the innermost energy level.

A I only

B II only

C I and II only

D II and III only

6 What is the total number of p electrons in an atom of arsenic?

A 3

B 7

C 15

D 33

7   **HL** The first 10 successive ionisation energies of an element are shown in Figure 2.6.

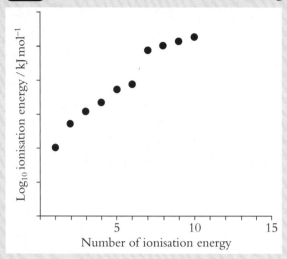

Figure 2.6 Successive ionisation energies of an element.

Which group of the periodic table could this element belong to?

A group 4
B group 6
C group 14
D group 16

8   **HL** Given that Planck's constant has a value of 6.63×10^{-34} Js, what is the energy of a photon of light with a frequency of 2.00×10^{14} Hz?

A 1.326×10^{-19} J
B 3.315×10^{-48} J
C 3.017×10^{47} J
D 1.326×10^{-20} J

9   **HL** Which of the following information can be deduced from the emission spectrum of an element?

A The first ionisation energy is deduced from the convergence limit of the series with the shortest wavelength.
B The convergence limits of each series can be used to determine the first, second, third ionisation energy and so on.
C The lines of the spectrum represent the movement of electrons between sub-energy levels.
D The number of lines on the spectrum indicates the number of electrons in an atom of the element.

10 **HL** Which elements are listed in order of increasing first ionisation energy?
A O < F < Ne
B Na < Mg < Al
C Si < P < S
D Cl < Ar < K

11 A metallic-looking sample was found at the back of a cupboard in a research facility with the label missing. It was thought that it was a mixture of two or more different metals. It was proposed that its elemental composition could be determined by mass spectrometry. It was analysed and the spectrum shown in Figure 2.7 was obtained.

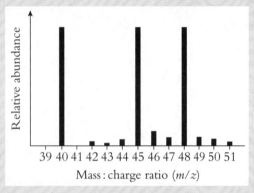

Figure 2.7 Mass spectrum of unknown substance.

a Given the data in Table 2.5, and assuming that all of the signals in the spectrum arise from 1+ charged ions, suggest the possible identities of the metals in the mixture and give reasons for your answer. [6]

Element	Natural abundance of each isotope
potassium	^{39}K, 93.26%; ^{40}K, 0.01%; ^{41}K, 6.73%
calcium	^{40}Ca, 96.94%; ^{42}Ca, 0.65%; ^{43}Ca, 0.14%; ^{44}Ca, 2.09%; ^{48}Ca, 0.18%
scandium	^{45}Sc, 100%
titanium	^{46}Ti, 8.25%; ^{47}Ti, 7.44%; ^{48}Ti, 73.72%; ^{49}Ti, 5.41%; ^{50}Ti, 5.18%

Table 2.5

b Using the data from Table 2.5, calculate the relative atomic mass of titanium. [2]
c Explain whether different isotopes of an element have similar or different chemical and physical properties. [2]

[Total 10]

12 a Give the full electron configuration of vanadium. [1]
b Explain why the part of the periodic table where chromium is found is called the d-block. [1]
c Represent the electron configuration of V^{2+} ions using 'electrons in boxes' notation. [1]

[Total 3]

13 a Sketch an energy-level diagram showing the transitions that lead to the lines in the series of the hydrogen emission spectrum with the shortest wavelength. **[3]**

b **HL** Indicate on your diagram the transition that corresponds to the convergence limit. **[1]**

c **HL** The line on the hydrogen emission spectrum representing the transition from $n = 6$ to $n = 2$ has a wavelength of 410 nm. Calculate the energy gap between these two energy levels. **[2]**

[Total 6]

14 **HL** **Figure 2.8 shows the first ionisation energies of the elements hydrogen to neon.**

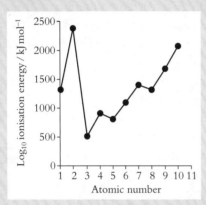

Figure 2.8 First ionisation energies of the elements hydrogen to neon.

Explain the following statements:

a Helium has the highest ionisation energy. **[2]**

b There is a large fall in the ionisation energy from helium to lithium. **[2]**

c There are slight falls in the first ionisation energies from beryllium to boron and from nitrogen to oxygen. **[2]**

d The first ionisation energy of neon is lower than that of helium. **[2]**

[Total 8]

15 **HL** **Figure 2.9 shows the $\log_{10}$ of the successive ionisation energies of an element. Identify the element and give a reason for your answer. [2]**

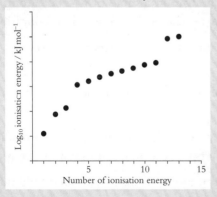

Figure 2.9 Successive ionisation energies of an element.

[Total 2]

3 Periodicity

Chapter outline

- Recall that the periodic table is arranged into groups, periods and into four blocks associated with the four sub–levels: s, p, d and f.
- Recall that the period number is the outer energy level that is occupied by electrons.
- Recall that the number of the principal energy level and the number of the valence electrons in an atom can be deduced from its position on the periodic table.
- Explain the trends in atomic radius, ionic radius, ionisation energy, electron affinity and electronegativity across a period and down a group.
- Recall that the oxides change from basic through amphoteric to acidic across a period.
- Recall the equations for the reactions of Na_2O, MgO, P_4O_{10} and the oxides of nitrogen and sulfur with water, and the pH of the solutions formed.
- Describe the reactions of the elements of group 1 and group 17.
- Recall the definition of a transition element and their characteristic properties. **HL**
- Explain the formation and shapes of complex ions. **HL**
- Explain why transition metal complex ions are coloured. **HL**

KEY TERMS

Amphoteric: A substance that can act as a base and as an acid.

Electron affinity: The energy change when one electron is added to each atom in a mole of gaseous atoms to form a mole of gaseous ions each with a 1− charge under standard conditions.

Electronegativity: A measure of the tendency of a covalently bonded atom to attract the shared pair of electrons towards itself.

First ionisation energy: The minimum amount of energy required to remove to infinity the outermost electron from each atom in a mole of gaseous atoms to form a mole of gaseous ions each with a 1+ charge under standard conditions.

Ionic radius: The distance between the nucleus and the electron in the outermost shell of an ion.

Transition element: An element that forms at least one stable ion with a partially filled d sub–shell.

Catalyst: A substance that increases the rate of a chemical reaction by providing an alternative pathway of lower activation energy and is not consumed by the reaction.

Complex: A species consisting of a central atom or ion surrounded by a number of ligands to which it is bonded by dative covalent bonds.

Diamagnetism: A weak magnetic force caused by the presence of paired electrons. Diamagnetic substances are repelled by a magnetic field.

Ligand: A species (neutral molecule or negative ion) which can donate a pair of electrons to form a dative covalent bond with an atom or ion to form a complex.

Oxidation number: The imagined charge on an atom if it were considered to be purely ionic. Oxidation numbers are covered in Topic 9 (redox processes).

Paramagnetism: A weak magnetic force caused by the presence of unpaired electrons. Paramagnetic substances are attracted to a magnetic field.

Exercise 3.1 – The arrangement of the elements

1 The elements of the periodic table can be broadly described as metals, non–metals and metalloids.
  a Identify the location of these different types of elements in the periodic table.
  b Describe the characteristic physical and chemical properties of metals and non–metals.

2 The location of an element can be described by its block, period and group number. Give the location of the following elements:
  a arsenic
  b caesium
  c tungsten
  d cadmium
  e rhenium

3 a Describe the relationship between an element's position in the periodic table and its electron configuration.
  b Deduce the identity of the element in the following positions of the periodic table:
    i   period 3, group 14
    ii   period 4, group 1
    iii period 5, group 9

Exercise 3.2 – Physical properties

Trends in first ionisation energies are introduced as part of the HL atomic structure topic but are also part of the SL periodicity topic.

1 This question explores the trends in the atomic radius around the periodic table.
  a Describe the trend in the atomic radius of the elements sodium to chlorine.
  b Explain the trend in the atomic radius of the elements sodium to chlorine.
  c Describe the trend in atomic radius down a group.
  d Explain the trend in atomic radius down a group.
  e Compare the radius of an atom to that of its 1+ and 1– charged ions.

2 This question focuses on ionisation energies.
  a Give an equation to represent the first ionisation energy of phosphorus.
  b Explain why there is a general increase in the first ionisation energy across a period of the periodic table.
  c Explain why first ionisation energies decrease down a group.

The trends in the physical properties of the elements across and down the periodic table are linked to the strength of the force of attraction between the nucleus of an atom and its outermost electrons. When considering these questions think about the nuclear charge, the amount of shielding by inner complete shells of electrons and the trend in the radii.

d Explain the slight discontinuities in the first ionisation energies between magnesium and aluminium and between phosphorus and sulfur as shown in the graph below.

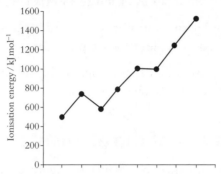

Figure 3.1 Variation in first ionisation energy across period 3.

3 Electron affinity is also dependent on nuclear charge, shielding and atomic radius.
   a Give an equation for the first electron affinity of chlorine.
   b Explain the trend in first electron affinity down group 17.
   c Describe the general trend in electron affinity across period 3.
   d Explain the trend in electronegativity across a period and down a group in the periodic table.

Exercise 3.3 – Group 1

1 Chemical and physical properties depend on the bonding and structure of a substance which is covered in more detail in Topic 4. In this topic you are asked to describe these trends and some of the typical reactions that can be used to illustrate them.
   a Explain the trend in the physical properties of group 1.
   b Explain the trend in the reactivity of the alkali metals.
   c Give equations for the reactions of potassium with oxygen, with chlorine and with water.

Exercise 3.4 – Group 17

1 **a** Describe the appearance of the halogens at room temperature.
   b Explain the variation in the melting points of the halogens.

2 Displacement reactions can be used to demonstrate the trend in the reactivity of the halogens. Design a simple experiment that could be performed in a school laboratory to show the trend for chlorine, bromine and iodine. Include observations and equations.

Exercise 3.5 – Oxides of periods 2 and 3

1 Give equations for the reactions of the following oxides with water. In each case suggest whether the solution formed is acidic or alkaline.
   a Na_2O
   b MgO
   c Al_2O_3
   d SiO_2

Although you are probably being taught this syllabus topic by topic, you should remember that the exams are all at the end of the course and the questions will not necessarily fall neatly into the chapter headings that you are used to.

Group 1 is known as the alkali metals. This should remind you about the acid/base nature of metal oxides.

Include state symbols in your answer.

e P_4O_{10}
f SO_2
g SO_3

The equations for these non-metal oxides at first appear difficult. In Topic 9 you will learn about oxidation numbers; these will help you to remember these equations as the non-metal does not change oxidation state. If you have only just started working towards the IB then this will probably not mean much at this stage. When you are nearer the end and are revising, it will help.

2 Nitrogen forms a number of different oxides including N_2O, NO and NO_2. Describe the acid–base nature of these oxides, giving equations as appropriate.

HL Exercise 3.6 – First–row d–block elements

Not all first–row d–block elements are transition elements. The term transition element can be defined in a number of ways; it is important for you to know the definition specified for this syllabus.

1 **a** Define the term 'transition element'.
  b Explain why zinc is not considered a transition element.
  c Describe the characteristic properties of transition elements.

2 Give the electron configurations of the following elements and ions:
  a Zn
  b Sc
  c Ti
  d Cr
  e Ni
  f Cu
  g Fe^{3+}
  h Mn^{2+}
  i V^{3+}
  j Co^{2+}

3 **a** Describe the variation in the first ionisation energies across the first–row d–block elements.
  b Explain why transition elements show variable oxidation states.

4 **a** Draw the orbital diagram for the atoms and ions in Question 2 and identify if each exhibits diamagnetism or paramagnetism.
  b Identify the atom or ion which will exhibit the strongest magnetic force.

The type of magnetism that most people are familiar with is ferromagnetism. In this topic only diamagnetism and paramagnetism are considered. These are much weaker effects. Virtually all substances contain some paired electrons and so exhibit diamagnetism. If they contain unpaired electrons, then they will also be paramagnetic which will dominate over any diamagnetism.

> Remember to use the periodic table and that the 4s sub–shell is both filled first in the elements and lost first when ions are formed.

> Parts **a** and **b** of Question 3 might at first seem unrelated but the answer to part **b** is linked to ionisation energies – not the first ionisation energies.

> An orbital diagram is also known as an 'arrows in boxes' diagram or 'electrons in boxes' diagram.

5 This question is about complex ions. Complex ions consist of a central atom or ion surrounded by ligands.
   a Describe the bonding in a typical complex such as $[CuCl_4]^{2-}$.
   b Draw the shape of the complex $[Fe(H_2O)_6]^{3+}$.
   c Determine the oxidation state of the transition element in the following complexes:
      i $[Ag(NH_3)_2]^+$
      ii $[Fe(H_2O)_5Cl]^{2+}$
      iii $[Pt(CO)_2(NH_3)Br]^+$
      iv $[Ni(CN)_4]^{2-}$

HL Exercise 3.7 – Colour in complexes

1 a Explain why transition metal complexes are often coloured.
   b A complex ion absorbs light of wavelengths between 650 and 700 nm. Deduce what colour the substance will appear. (The colour wheel can be found in the data book.)
   c State five factors that affect the colour of complexes.

2 The spectrochemical series (found in the data book) compares the size of the d–orbital splitting of different ligands. During a ligand substitution reaction water ligands were replaced by chloride ligands. Describe the effect that this will have on the d–orbital splitting and on the colour that the complex appears.

? Exam-style questions

1 Which of the following elements could be described as a metalloid?
   A S
   B Sb
   C Sc
   D Sn

2 Which is the correct electron configuration for chromium?
   A $1s^2\, 2s^2\, 2p^6\, 3s^2\, 3p^6\, 4s^2\, 3d^4$
   B $1s^2\, 2s^2\, 2p^6\, 3s^2\, 3p^6\, 3d^6$
   C $1s^2\, 2s^2\, 2p^6\, 3s^2\, 3p^6\, 4s^1\, 3d^5$
   D $1s^2\, 2s^2\, 2p^6\, 3s^2\, 3p^6\, 4s^2\, 4p^4$

3 Which of the following properties increases down group 17?
      i   melting point
      ii first ionisation energy
      iii electronegativity
   A I only
   B II only
   C I and II
   D II and III

4   The graph shows the variation in a property around the periodic table. Which property and for which elements?

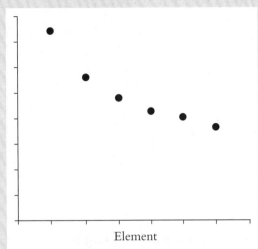

Figure 3.2 Periodic trends.

	Property	Elements
A	melting point	Na to S
B	electronegativity	He to Rn
C	first ionisation energy	Ra to Be
D	atomic radius	Li to O

Table 3.1

5   In a series of experiments between solutions of various halogen solutions with aqueous halides, the following results were obtained.

	Halide X⁻(aq)	Halide Y⁻(aq)	Halide Z⁻(aq)
Halogen X₂(aq)	no reaction	reaction	no reaction
Halogen Y₂(aq)	no reaction	no reaction	no reaction
Halogen Z₂(aq)	reaction	reaction	no reaction

Table 3.2

Which is the correct likely identity of X, Y and Z?
A X = fluorine, Y = chlorine, Z = iodine
B X = bromine, Y = iodine, Z = chlorine
C X = iodine, Y = bromine, Z = chlorine
D C = fluorine, Y = iodine, Z = bromine

6   Which of the following will form a solution in water with a pH of greater than 7?
A MgO
B Al_2O_3
C SiO_2
D P_4O_{10}

7   **HL** In which complex is the metal ion in oxidation state +2?
(If you haven't covered Topic 9 (redox processes) yet, then you may want to come back to this question.)

A $[Fe(CN)_6]^{3-}$

B $[Fe(H_2O)_5CO]^{3+}$

C $[Fe(NH_3)_4Cl_2]^+$

D $[Fe(H_2O)_3(CN)_6]^{4-}$

8   **HL** Which of the following compounds is likely to be coloured?

A CuI

B TiO_2

C $ScCl_3$

D V_2S_3

9   Table 3.3 gives the atomic radii, first electron affinities and first ionisation energies of the halogens.

Halogen	Atomic radius $/ \times 10^{-12}\,m$	First electron affinity / $kJ\,mol^{-1}$	First ionisation energy / $kJ\,mol^{-1}$
fluorine	60	-328	1681
chlorine	100	-349	1251
bromine	117	-325	1146
iodine	136	-295	1008

Table 3.3

   a Explain the trend in the first electron affinity and first ionisation energies of the elements. [5]

   b Give equations for the first electron affinity and first ionisation energy of chlorine. [2]

   c State how the radii of halide ions with a 1− charge will compare to the atomic radii for these elements. [1]

[Total 8]

10   **a** Describe the acid/base nature of the oxides of the elements sodium, magnesium, phosphorus and sulfur, giving equations of the reactions of the oxides with water as appropriate. [5]

   b Describe the acid/base nature of the oxides of nitrogen, NO, N_2O and NO_2. Use appropriate equations in your answer. [3]

[Total 8]

11   **Compare the following:**

   a The ionic radii of P^{3-} and S^{2-}. [4]

   b The atomic radii of potassium and sodium. [3]

   c The electronegativities of sulfur and oxygen. [3]

[Total 10]

12 **HL**

a Define the term 'transition element' and explain why not all d–block elements are described as transition elements. [2]

b One of the characteristic features of transition elements is that they have variable oxidation states.

 i Explain why the transition elements show this property. [2]

 ii Describe other properties which are characteristic of the transition elements. [4]

c Give the electron configurations of the Cu^+ and Cu^{2+} ions. Suggest the effect these different electron configurations have on some of the properties in your answer to **b ii**. [3]

[Total 11]

13 **HL** Transition metals commonly form complexes.

a Describe what is meant by a complex. [2]

b Complexes with a coordination number of 4 can adopt two possible shapes. Draw these and describe their different bond angles. [3]

c Cobalt forms a number of different complexes. One such complex was found to have a coordination number of six and to consist of a cobalt(III) ion with two water ligands and two ethanedioate ligands. The formula of the ethanedioate ion is shown in Figure 3.3.

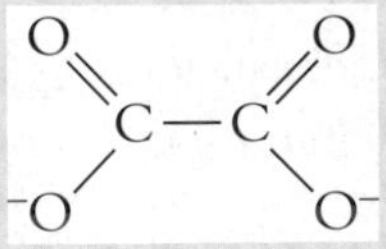

Figure 3.3 Ethanedioate ion.

 i Explain how the ethanedioate ion can act as a ligand. [1]

 ii Sketch a diagram of the complex, clearly indicating its overall charge. [3]

d Another cobalt(III) complex was found to have the composition 23.53% cobalt, 27.97% nitrogen, 6.04% hydrogen and 42.46% chlorine by mass.

 i Calculate the empirical formula of the complex. [3]

 ii The complex was further analysed by reacting 0.0100 mol of it with an excess of silver nitrate solution. Aqueous silver nitrate reacts with aqueous halide ions to form a precipitate of silver(I) chloride; 2.866 g of precipitate was formed. Suggest a possible formula for the complex. [3]

[Total 15]

14 **HL** Many transition metal compounds are coloured.

a Describe the origin of colour in simple transition metal compounds. [4]

b Describe the factors that affect the colour of a simple transition metal compound. [5]

c State what features of transition elements and their compounds enable them to often act as homogeneous or heterogeneous catalysts. [2]

d When a solution of 1, 2-ethanediamine (en) is added gradually to a solution of nickel(II) chloride solution, the colour of the solution changes from green to light blue to dark blue and finally to violet as the following complexes are formed. $[Ni(H_2O)]^{2+}$ (green) $[Ni(H_2O)_4(en)]^{2+}$ (light blue) $[Ni(H_2O)_2(en)_2]^{2+}$ (dark blue) $[Ni(en)_3]^{2+}$ (violet) With reference to the colour wheel in the data book, deduce the effect of the 1,2-ethanediamine ligand on the d–orbital splitting and explain your conclusion. [3]

[Total 14]

4 Chemical bonding and structure

Chapter outline

- Describe ionic, covalent, metallic and intermolecular bonding.
- Deduce the formula and name of an ionic compound from its component ions.
- Describe the structure of typical ionic, simple molecular, giant covalent and metallic compounds including alloys and explain the properties of a compound in terms of its structure.
- Draw Lewis diagrams for molecules and ions. (**HL** :calculate the formal charge of the atoms and use this to deduce the most likely Lewis structure.)
- Recall the relationship between covalent bond length and bond strength.
- Draw the shapes of molecules and predict bond angles for molecules with up to four electron domains (six at **HL**).
- Predict whether a molecule is polar or non-polar from electronegativity data and its shape.
- Describe σ and π bonds and explain resonance structures and delocalisation. **HL**
- Describe the mechanism of the catalysis of ozone depletion when catalysed by CFCs and NO_x. **HL**
- Explain the formation of sp, sp^2 and sp^3 hybridisation. **HL**

KEY TERMS AND FORMULAS

Delocalisation: The sharing of a pair of electrons between 3 or more atoms.

Dipole: The separation of charge due to its uneven distribution.

Electron domain: An area in which electrons are found around an atom or in a molecule. The number of electron domains refers to the number of lone pairs or bond locations; bond location is independent of whether the bond is a single, double or triple bond.

Hydrogen bonding: Intermolecular force between a lone pair of electrons on the nitrogen, oxygen or fluorine atom of one molecule and a hydrogen atom attached to a nitrogen, fluorine or oxygen atom of another molecule. These forces can also form intramolecularly.

Lewis structure: A diagram showing the arrangement of electrons in a molecule (or ion). Normally only the outer-shell electrons are shown.

London forces: Intermolecular forces arising from temporary dipole–induced dipole interactions.

Resonance structure: One of several Lewis structures for a substance. The actual structure of the substance is a hybrid of its resonance structures.

van de Waals' forces: The collective name for weak intermolecular forces. It includes London forces, dipole–induced dipole forces and permanent dipole–dipole forces but not hydrogen bonding or ion–dipole forces.

Formal charge: A concept used to identify the most likely Lewis structure for a molecule or ion. It is the charge that an atom would have if all the atoms had equal electronegativity.

Hybridisation: The mixing of atomic orbitals when a compound is formed to produce a new set of orbitals. The total energy and the total number of orbitals is conserved but their shape and orientation differ from the atomic orbitals from which they have been formed.

Pi bond: A bond formed from the sideways overlap of parallel p orbitals. The electron density lies in two regions above and below the inter-nuclear axis.

Sigma bond: A bond formed by the axial overlap of atomic orbitals. The electron density lies along the axis joining the two nuclei.

$$\text{Formal charge} = \text{Number of valence electrons on the un-combined atom} - \frac{1}{2} \times \text{number of bonding electrons} - \text{number of non-bonding electrons}$$

Exercise 4.1 – Ionic bonding and structure

Ionic bonding involves the transfer of one or more electrons whereas covalent bonding involves the sharing of electrons and so in simple terms can be thought of as opposites of one another. The reality is that it is not so simple; the distinction between ionic and covalent is a sliding scale on which ionic and covalent are at the two extremes.

1 a Copy and complete the paragraph below which describes the general distinction between ionic and covalent compounds.

_____ compounds are normally formed between metallic elements and non-metallic elements. _____ compounds are normally formed between non-metallic elements. There are exceptions to this: for example, ammonium chloride is _____. Generally, the _____ the difference in the electronegativity of the elements, then the more likely the compound is to be ionic. Elements with similar electronegativities tend to be positioned _____ in the periodic table. Group 1 elements combine with group 17 elements to form ionic compounds. The compound which can be thought of as being the most ionic is _____.

b Identify whether the following substances are ionic or covalent.

i K_2O
ii NO_2
iii CH_4
iv H_2O_2
v $NaClO$
vi HCl

Suggestions: ionic, covalent, larger, smaller, close together, far apart, CsF, $LiAt$, F_2, H_2. These words may be used once, more than once or not at all.

Only outer shell electrons are drawn on some occasions

2 a i In words, describe how a metal atom such as sodium forms an ion.

    ii Draw a diagram to represent this process.

    iii Write an equation to represent this process.

  b i In words, describe how a non-metal atom such as chlorine forms an ion.

    ii Draw a diagram to represent this process.

    iii Write an equation to represent this process.

  c Describe the relationship between the number of electrons in the outer shell of an atom and the charge on its ion.

3 This question is about the formulas of ionic compounds. The formula of a compound is fixed. When balancing equations, students often make up or change the formula of a compound to suit the balancing of the equation; this is wrong. A formula should never be changed; if it is changed, then it is a different substance.

  a Given the list of ions below, determine the formula of the following compounds.

    sodium, Na^+

    magnesium, Mg^{2+}

    aluminium, Al^{3+}

    fluoride, F^-

    oxide, O^{2-}

    nitride, N^{3-}

    i sodium fluoride

    ii sodium oxide

    iii sodium nitride

    iv magnesium fluoride

    v magnesium oxide

    vi magnesium nitride

    vii aluminium chloride

    viii aluminium oxide

    ix aluminium nitride

Compounds are neutral so the total number of positive and negative charges must be equal. Although the charges on the ions are used to deduce the formula and the ions in the compound are charged, the charges are not written as part of the formula. For example, sodium chloride is made up of Na^+ ions and Cl^- ions but the formula is written NaCl and not Na^+Cl^-.

b Given the list of ions below as well as using those listed in part **a**, determine the formula of the following compounds.

sulfate, SO_4^{2-}

nitrate, NO_3^-

hydroxide, OH^-

phosphate, PO_4^{3-}

carbonate, CO_3^{2-}

ammonium, NH_4^+

  i   sodium sulfate

  ii   magnesium carbonate

  iii magnesium hydroxide

  iv sodium phosphate

  v   aluminium nitrate

  vi aluminium sulfate

  vii aluminium phosphate

  viii ammonium carbonate

  ix ammonium nitrate

Consider these ions not as separate atoms but as a whole ion; for example, do not think of nitrate as one nitrogen atom and three oxygen atoms, consider it as a singly charged ion $(X)^-$ where $X = NO_3$. Never change the formula of an ion by changing the number of atoms in it. If more than one of these types of ions is needed, then brackets are used. For example, ammonium sulfate is made of NH_4^+ ions and SO_4^{2-} ions. To balance the charges, two NH_4^+ ions are need to combine with one SO_4^{2-} ion so the NH_4^+ ion is placed in brackets and the formula is $(NH_4)_2SO_4$.

4 a Explain what is meant by the term 'ionic bonding'.

  b i In words, describe the bonding in sodium chloride.

    ii Draw a diagram to show the bonding in sodium chloride.

  c i In words, describe the structure of sodium chloride.

    ii Draw a diagram to show the structure of sodium chloride.

  d What is the difference in the meaning of the terms 'bonding' and 'structure'?

5 a List the typical properties of ionic substances.

  b Link the following properties of ionic compounds to their correct explanations. The explanations can be used more than once.

Usually have high melting and boiling points.	Electrostatic forces of attraction are strong and exerted in all directions through the 3D lattice.
Usually have low volatility.	
Do not conduct electricity when solid.	When a force is applied, like charges become aligned and repel each other.
Conduct electricity when molten or dissolved.	Ions are held in a fixed lattice and cannot move.
Usually brittle.	Ions are free to move.

  c Describe why ionic substances are often soluble in polar solvents such as water but are not usually soluble in non-polar solvents.

Strictly speaking, there is no such thing as an ionic bond as this implies that one thing is joined by a bond to another. Electrostatic forces of attraction extend in all directions and so the oppositely charged ions in an ionic substance are **all** joined to each other. The correct term is ionic bond*ing*.

Include labels in your diagram.

Exercise 4.2 – Covalent bonding

Covalent bonding involves the sharing of electrons between atoms.

1 a Define the term 'covalent bond'.

  b The term 'valency' can be used to describe the 'combining power' of an atom; hydrogen has a valency of one as it only can only form one bond.

  Describe the relationship between the valency of an element and the number of electrons in its outer shell.

2 a Draw Lewis structures for the following compounds:

  i H_2O
  ii O_2
  iii NH_3
  iv CH_2Cl_2
  v CO_2
  vi N_2
  vii CO_3^{2-}
  viii BCl_3
  ix $BeCl_2$

  b State the relationship between the number of bonds (bond order) and bond strength and bond length.

  c Explain the relationship between the number of bonds and bond strength and bond length.

3 Coordinate covalent bonds (also known as dative covalent bonds) are a type of covalent bond in which both electrons come from the same atom. They are indistinguishable from ordinary covalent bonds in terms of their properties (bond length, bond strength and so on)

  a Draw Lewis structures for the following molecules and ions which all include coordinate bonds. Clearly indicate which bonds are coordinate bonds.

  i NH_4^+
  ii H_3O^+
  iii CO
  iv NH_3BF_3
  v NO_3^-

  b Electronegativity values can be used to determine whether or not a bond is polar.

  i Define electronegativity.

  ii Using the electronegativity values in the data book, rank the following bonds listed below in order of increasing polarity:

  N–H, O–H, C–H, C–l, H–S, F–F, O–Cl, P–Cl, C–Br, P–H

A Lewis structure or Lewis diagram is a 'dot–cross' diagram.
All of the outer-shell electrons must be shown for all of the atoms – don't forget the lone pairs!
Brackets and the charge are essential for ions.

Always take careful note of the command term in the question; 'state' and 'explain' do not have the same meaning.

Coordinate bonds can be shown by using dots and crosses rather than a line as this will show the origin of the electrons. Alternatively, an arrow can be used to represent a pair of electrons. The arrow points from the lone pair which is donated.

4 Some molecules or ions have more than one Lewis structure that are equally probable. The actual structure of the molecule or ion is likely to be neither of these but a mixture of the two known as a resonance hybrid.

    a Draw the resonance structures of the following species:
       i O_3
       ii HCO_3^-
       iii SO_3^{2-}

The molecule or ion does not flip between the different resonance structures but is a mixture of them. Part of the evidence for this is that the bond lengths in the actual structure are in-between the bond lengths that would be expected in the resonance structures; the bond lengths are not constantly changing which would be the case if the molecule was flipping between forms.

    b Determine the average bond order for the substances in parts **i** and **iii**.

5 **a** Describe the valence-shell electron-pair repulsion theory (VSEPR).
    b The VSEPR uses the idea of 'electron domains'. What is meant by this term?
    c Copy and complete Table 4.1 to show the relationship between the number of electron domains and the bond angles in a molecule or ion.

Number of electron domains	Bond angle
2	
3	
4	

Table 4.1

    d Copy and complete Table 4.2 to show the Lewis structure, shape and bond angles for the following species.

Species	Lewis structure	Sketch showing the shape	Bond angle	Name of the shape
H_2S				
PCl_3				
NO_2^-				
CCl_4				
CS_2				
NO_3^-				
NH_2^-				

Table 4.2

The term 'bond order' can be used to describe the number of covalent bonds between two atoms where a single bond has a bond order of 1, a double bond has a bond order of 2 and so on. For species that can be represented by resonance structures, the bond order is an average of these values.

To determine the shape of a molecule or ion, always begin by drawing the Lewis structure then count the number of electron domains to find the basic shape and bond angles. Finally, if there are lone pairs present on the central atom, adjust the name of the shape (lone pairs are invisible; the name of the shape depends on the atoms that can be seen) and bond angles (lone pairs are closer to the central atoms so repel other electron domains more than a bonding pair).

    e Both P–Cl and C–Cl bonds are polar; explain why PCl_3 is polar whereas CCl_4 is non-polar.

Exercise 4.3 – Covalent structures

Some covalent substances form giant structures rather than discrete molecules. Common examples include silicon dioxide and the allotropes of carbon.

1 a What is the meaning of the term 'allotrope'?
  b Figures 4.1–4.4 show four common allotropes of carbon; name these.

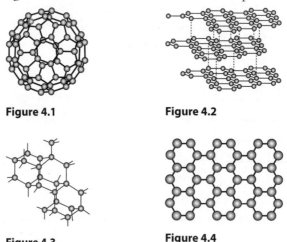

Figure 4.1   **Figure 4.2**

Figure 4.3   **Figure 4.4**

  c Explain the difference in the electrical conductivity of graphite and diamond.
  d Explain why graphite and diamond have high melting points whereas that of C_{60} fullerene is much lower.

Exercise 4.4 – Intermolecular forces

In this section, we are considering the nature of the forces which hold molecules together in the solid or liquid state and are overcome when a solid melts, a liquid evaporates or a solute dissolves in a solvent. These are known as intermolecular forces. The bonds that hold the atoms together in the molecule (intramolecular forces) are not broken during these processes; the molecules remain whole.

1 The intermolecular forces in non-polar molecules are known as London forces.
  a How do these forces arise?
  b Describe the relationship between the strength of these London forces and the boiling point of a substance.

c Figure 4.5 shows the trend in the melting points of the group 17 elements. Explain this trend.

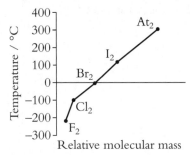

Figure 4.5 Trend in the melting points of the group 17 elements.

2 a Using the data in Table 4.3, choose two molecules that could be used to illustrate the relative strength of dipole–dipole interactions compared to London forces. Justify your choice.

Molecule	Lewis structure	Relative molecular mass	Boiling point/K
butane	H H H H $\|$ $\|$ $\|$ $\|$ H—C—C—C—C—H $\|$ $\|$ $\|$ $\|$ H H H H **Figure 4.6**	58	272
bromine	$\mid\overline{Br}\!-\!\overline{Br}\mid$ **Figure 4.7**	160	332
pentane	H H H H H $\|$ $\|$ $\|$ $\|$ $\|$ H—C—C—C—C—C—H $\|$ $\|$ $\|$ $\|$ $\|$ H H H H H **Figure 4.8**	72	309
butanone	H O H H $\|$ $\|\|$ $\|$ $\|$ H—C—C—C—C—H $\|$ $\|$ $\|$ H H H **Figure 4.9**	72	353
hydrogen bromide	H—$\overline{Br}\mid$ **Figure 4.10**	81	207

Table 4.3

> Dipole interactions depend not just on whether a molecule contains polar bonds but on the shape of the molecule. The dipoles on polar bonds may be cancelled by each other if the molecule is symmetrical in shape.

b Suggest whether the following molecules are polar:

i CO_2

ii H_2S

iii CCl_4

iv $CHCl_3$

In your answer to **3a**, include at least two molecules, at least one hydrogen bond, dipoles and lone pairs.

3 a Draw a diagram to show the hydrogen bonding in water.

  b Explain why some substances can form hydrogen bonds.

  c Does hydrogen bonding occur in each of the following substances?

  i H_2O_2

  ii

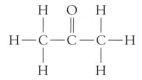

Figure 4.11

  iii

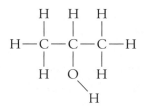

Figure 4.12

  iv

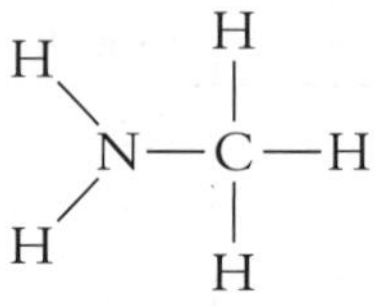

H, H
  N—C—H
H, H

Figure 4.13

  d What effect does the presence of hydrogen bonding have on the boiling point of a substance?

4 a Suggest whether or not the following substances are soluble in water:

  i C_4H_8

  ii CH_3OH

  iii CH_3COOH

  iv CCl_4

  b Explain your answers to part **a**; include a diagram in your answer to show the interaction between one of the soluble molecules and water.

Exercise 4.5 – Metallic bonding

1 a Describe the bonding and structure in metals.

  b Explain why the melting point of calcium is higher than that of sodium.

  c Explain which aspect of the structure and bonding in metals gives rise to the following properties:

  i high melting and boiling points

  ii good conductors of electricity

  iii malleable and ductile

2 Pure metals are very difficult to obtain but fortunately they are rarely required. Most metals are used in the form of alloys.

a What is meant by the term 'alloy'?

b Why are most alloys stronger than the metals from which they are made?

Diagrams can sometimes be useful in your answer.

🄷🄻 Exercise 4.6 – Covalent bonding, electron domains and molecular geometries

1 Exceptions to the octet rule include some species having incomplete octets and expanded octets.

a Suggest which groups of the periodic table include elements which are most likely to have incomplete octets.

b Suggest which periods of the periodic table include elements that are most likely to have expanded octets.

c Draw the Lewis structure of the following molecules which have expanded octets:

i PCl_5

ii SF_6

Examples of molecules with incomplete octets were met in Exercise 4.2.

2 Formal charge is a concept that can be used to deduce the most likely Lewis structure for a molecule or ion. It can be thought of as the charge that an atom would have if the electrons in a covalent bond were shared equally (i.e. all of the atoms have equal electronegativity). Atoms in a covalent bond have a formal charge if there are coordinate bonds or if the atom is part of an ion.

a Deduce the formal charge on each atom in the following species:

i

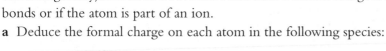

Figure 4.14 CO_2.

ii

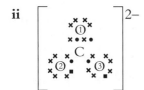

Figure 4.15 CO_3^{2-}.

iii

Figure 4.16 CO.

$$\begin{array}{llll}
\text{Formal} & = & \text{Number of valence} & - & \dfrac{1}{2} \times \text{number} & - & \text{number of} \\
\text{charge} & & \text{electrons on the un-} & & \text{of bonding} & & \text{non-bonding} \\
& & \text{combined atom} & & \text{electrons} & & \text{electrons}
\end{array}$$

For example, for a simple molecule like H–Cl, the formal charges can be worked out as follows:

Hydrogen: formal charge $= 1 - \left(\dfrac{1}{2} \times 2\right) - 0 = 0$ as hydrogen atoms have 1 outer-shell electron, there are 2 electrons bonding the H and Cl atoms together and there are no lone pairs.

Chlorine: formal charge $= 7 - \left(\dfrac{1}{2} \times 2\right) - 6 = 0$ as chlorine has 7 outer electrons, there are 2 electrons bonding the H and Cl atoms and there are 6 non-bonding electrons (3 lone pairs).

Note: The sum of the formal charges always equals the charge on the ion.

In general, the preferred Lewis structure is the one in which the formal charges are closest to zero (not add up to zero – they always add up to the charge on the species, so for neutral molecules they always add up to zero).

b The Lewis structures of the following molecules or ions can be drawn in a number of ways as shown in Figures 4.17 and 4.18. Deduce the formal charge on each atom.

i

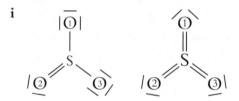

Figure 4.17a, b SO_3.

ii $:N\equiv N - \overset{..}{\underset{..}{O}}: \quad \overset{..}{\underset{..}{N}}=N=\overset{..}{\underset{..}{O}} \quad :\overset{..}{\underset{..}{N}} - N\equiv O:$

$\quad\quad\;\; 1 \quad\; 2$

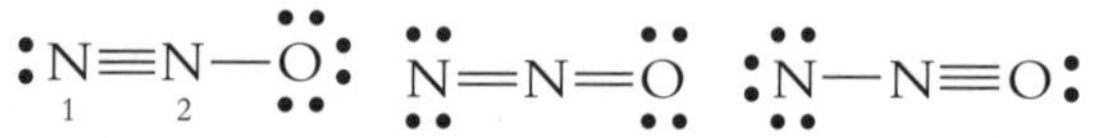

Figure 4.18a, b, c N_2O.

Make sure that your Lewis structures are different from each other and are not simply resonance structures of each other (see Question 5 below) The number of double and single bonds in the structures should be different.

c Using the concept of formal charge suggest which of the structures in part **b** is the most likely for each molecule.

d Deduce two possible Lewis structures for each of the following species and use the concept of formal charge to decide which structure is more likely.
  i ClO_3^-
  ii SCN^-

3 The shapes of molecules or ions with 5 or 6 electron domains around the central atom are based on a trigonal bipyramidal or octahedral shape.
  a Draw these shapes and give their bond angles.
  b Sketch the shape of the following species. In each one estimate the bond angles around the central atom.
    i IF_3
    ii $BrCl_5$
    iii SbF_5
    iv $PtCl_6^{2-}$
    v IBr_2^-

c Here are two possible structures for XeF_4. Suggest which structure is more likely and give a reason for your choice.

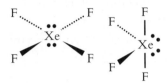

Figure 4.19a, b

d Draw a diagram to show the shape of $TeCl_4$ and estimate the bond angles in this ion.

4 Covalent bonding can also be described in terms of the overlap of atomic orbitals.
a Define the term 'atomic orbital'.
b Give the name for the type of bond formed by the overlap of the following atomic orbitals:
  i two s orbitals
  ii an s orbital and a p orbital
  iii two p orbitals overlapping end to end along an axis
  iv two p orbitals overlapping side by side along an axis
c Draw a diagram to represent the σ (sigma) and π (pi) bonds in O_2.
d Identify the number of s and p bonds in the substances shown in Table 4.4.

Substance	Number of σ bonds	Number of π bonds
H_2O		
CO_2		
N_2		
HCN		

Table 4.4

> A common mistake is to think that as π bonds involve p orbitals then σ bonds involve only s orbitals. This is not correct.

> Start by drawing the Lewis structure for each compound.

5 Delocalisation is a better model than the idea of resonance structures to explain equal bond lengths. It involves electrons that are shared by/between more than two atoms in a molecule or ion as opposed to being localised between a pair of atoms. It occurs when there are three or more p orbitals that overlap sideways with each other.
a Identify whether delocalisation occurs in the following molecules:
  i

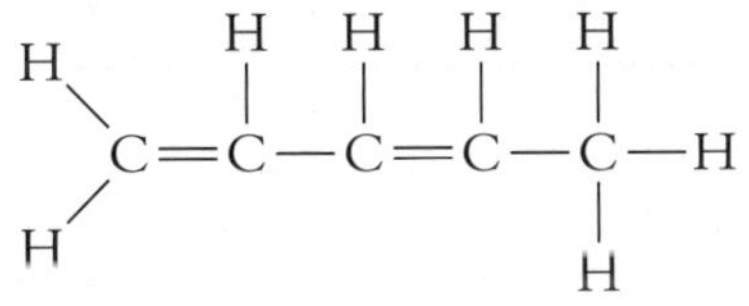

Figure 4.20 Penta-1,3-diene.

  ii NO_3^-
  iii CO_2
  iv

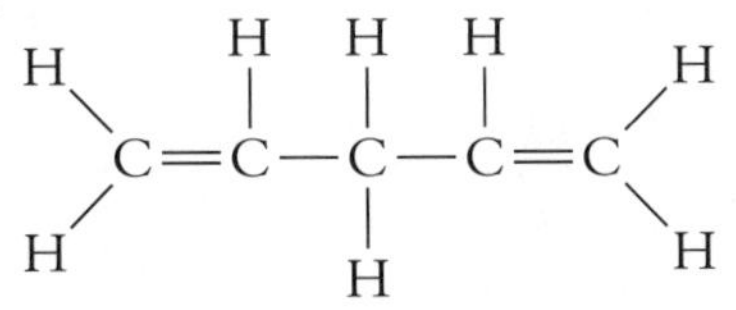

Figure 4.21 Penta-1,4-diene.

> Think about the shape of the molecules and whether the p orbitals are orientated such that they can overlap with each other.

6 Bond order and bond length are related to one another and bond energy is associated with reactivity.

    a UV radiation is divided into three different types according to the energy of the radiation, UV-A, UV-B and UV-C. UV-C has the highest energy and UV-A the lowest. Explain why O_2 molecules can only be dissociated into oxygen atoms by UV-C radiation whereas O_3 molecules are dissociated according to the equation $O_3 \rightarrow O_2 + O\cdot$ by lower energy UV-B radiation.

    b Chlorofluorocarbons are broken down by the absorption of UV radiation in the atmosphere.

      i Given the data below, suggest which carbon–halogen bonds are most likely to be affected by this process.
        C–F $492\,kJ\,mol^{-1}$
        C–Cl $324\,kJ\,mol^{-1}$
        C–H $414\,kJ\,mol^{-1}$

      ii Give equations to show how a halogen atom formed by the dissociation of a chlorofluorocarbon compound leads to the loss of ozone in the atmosphere.

      iii What name is given to the role of the halogen atom in this process?

> These equations need to be learnt.

HL Exercise 4.7 – Hybridisation

Hybridisation can be used to explain the shape of a molecule.

1 a State how the number of hybrid orbitals formed compares to the number of original atomic orbitals from which they were made.

    b Describe how the maximum number of electrons that can occupy a number of degenerate hybrid orbitals compares to the maximum number of electrons that could be held by the atomic orbitals from which the hybrid orbitals have been made.

    c Describe how the total energy of a number of degenerate orbitals compares to the total energy of the atomic orbitals from which they were made.

    d What is the meaning of the term 'degenerate' as used in part **c**?

    e Copy and complete Table 4.5.

> Using VSEPR is a useful way of determining the type of hybridisation. 2 electron domains = sp, 3 electron domains = sp^2 and 4 electron domains = sp^3.

Name of hybrid orbital	Number of degenerate hybrid orbitals formed	Type and number of original atomic orbitals	Bond angle of the hybrid orbitals
sp			
sp^2			
sp^3			

Table 4.5

> Always determine the Lewis structure first and use the shape/bond angles to identify the type of hybridisation.

    f Identify the type of hybridisation that occurs in the central atom of following species:
      i H_2S
      ii NI_3
      iii C_2H_4
      iv SCN^-
      v HCO^+

? Exam-style questions

1   Which is the correct formula for the compound formed between calcium and phosphorus?
    A   CaP
    B Ca_2P_3
    C Ca_3P_2
    D Ca_4P

2   Which property is not typical of ionic compounds?
    A   conduct electricity when molten
    B   often soluble in non-polar solvents
    C   have high melting points
    D   brittle

3   Which of the following molecules is polar?
    A H_2S
    B CH_4
    C CO_2
    D CCl_4

4   Which of the options in Table 4.6 shows the correct order of relative bond length and relative bond strength?

	Relative bond length	Relative bond strength
A	single > double > triple	single > double > triple
B	single < double < triple	triple < double < single
C	triple > double > single	single > double > triple
D	single > double > triple	triple > double > single

Table 4.6

5   Which of the following allotropes of carbon does not have a giant structure?
    A   graphene
    B   graphite
    C   diamond
    D C_{60} fullerence

6   What is the shape of the CO_2 molecule?
    A   linear
    B   bent
    C   trigonal planar
    D   trigonal pyramidal

7 Which of the following molecules does not form hydrogen bonds?
   A CH_2F_2
   B $CH_3CH_2NH_2$
   C CH_3OH
   D NH_2F

8 **HL** What is the approximate bond angle in KrF_4?
   A $90°$
   B $104.5°$
   C $109.5°$
   D $120°$

9 **HL** How many s and p bonds are there in an NO_2^- ion?

	Number of σ bonds	Number of π bonds
A	2	0
B	1	1
C	2	1
D	2	2

Table 4.7

10 **HL** The Lewis structure of SO_2 can be drawn as shown in Figure 4.22:

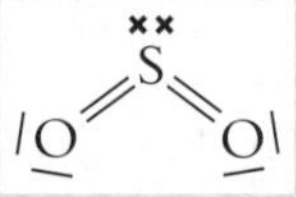

Figure 4.22

What is the type of hybridisation of the sulfur atoms and oxygen atoms in this molecule?

	Sulfur	Oxygen
A	sp^2	both sp^3
B	sp^2	both sp^2
C	sp^3	sp^2 and sp^3
D	sp	both sp^3

Table 4.8

11 a Draw a diagram to show the bonding and structure of magnesium. [2]
    b Explain why magnesium is malleable. [2]
    c Magnesium reacts with oxygen to form magnesium oxide.
      Describe the bonding in magnesium oxide. [2]
    d Compare the physical properties of magnesium and magnesium oxide and how these
      are related to the structures of these substances. [6]

                                                                    [Total 12]

12 **HL**
    a Nitrogen forms a number of different oxides including NO, N_2O, NO_2 and N_2O_4.
      NO and NO_2 both have an unpaired electron.
      i   Give the name of a molecule with an unpaired electron. [1]
      ii Draw the Lewis structures of NO_2 and N_2O_4. [2]
    b NO is formed in a number of ways in the high atmosphere including the reaction of N_2O and NO_2
      with oxygen atoms.
      These three play a key role in the depletion of ozone.
      i   Give equations for the formation of NO from NO_2 and from N_2O. [2]
      ii Give an equation to show the formation of oxygen atoms from ozone. [1]
      iii Give equations and explain how NO acts to reduce the amount of ozone in the atmosphere. [2]
    c Phosphorus also forms a number of oxides and, unlike nitrogen, can expand its octet. One oxide of
      phosphorus has the formula P_4O_{10} and is shown in Figure 4.23:

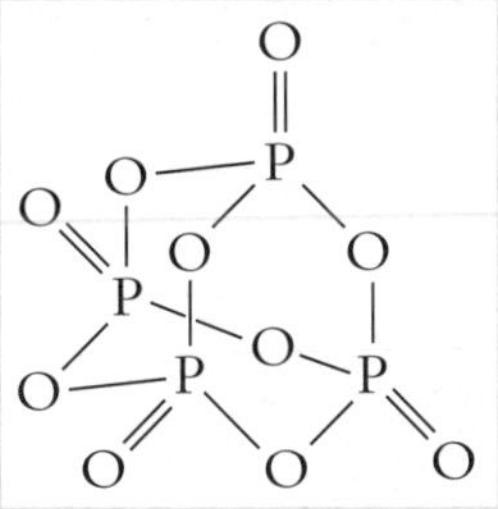

Figure 4.23 P_4O_{10}.

      i   State the hybridisation of the phosphorus atoms. [1]
      ii Estimate the P–O–P bond angle. [1]
    d Another compound of phosphorus is phosphorus oxytrichloride, $POCl_3$.
      The Lewis structure of this molecule can be drawn in a number of ways as shown in Figure 4.24.

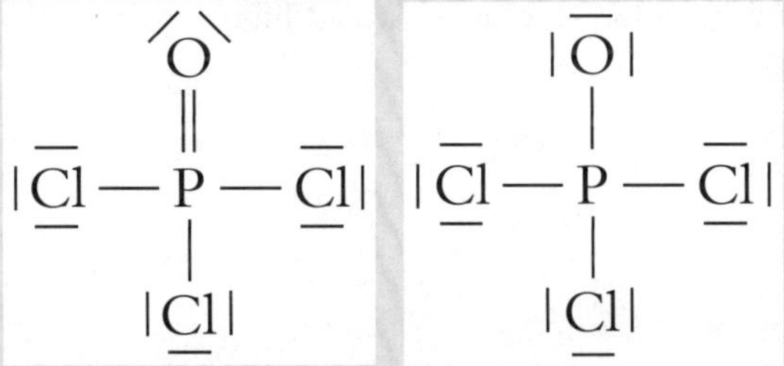

Figure 4.24a, b

      i   Give the name of the type of bond between the phosphorus and the oxygen atom in Figure 4.24b. [1]
      ii Using the idea of formal charge, deduce which structure is more likely and justify your choice. [3]

e Phosphorus also forms a number of compounds and ions with halogens.

Draw a diagram to show the shape of the following, clearly indicating the bond angles around the phosphorus atom in each case.

i PCl_3 [2]

ii PCl_5 [2]

iii PF_6^- [2]

iv PF_4^+ [2]

[Total 22]

13 **HL** (You may not be very familiar with these organic structures yet if you haven't studied Topic 10. Simply leave this question and come back to it later on in the course.)

a Describe the bonding in but-1,3-diene. [6]

Include the following ideas in your answer:

- Lewis structure
- delocalisation
- hybridisation
- shape
- bond angles
- σ and π bonding

b Figure 4.25 shows the structures of *cis*- and *trans*-but-2-ene-1,4-dioic acid.

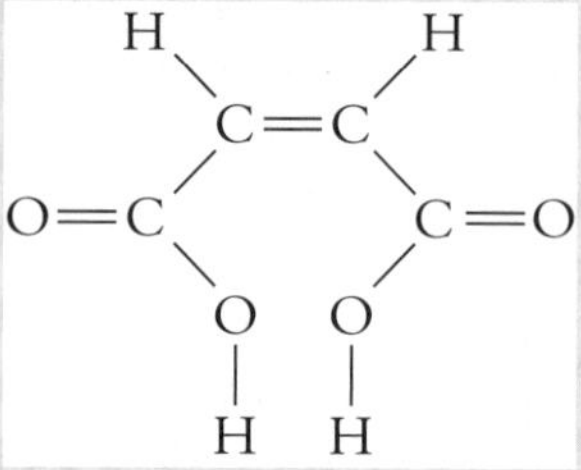

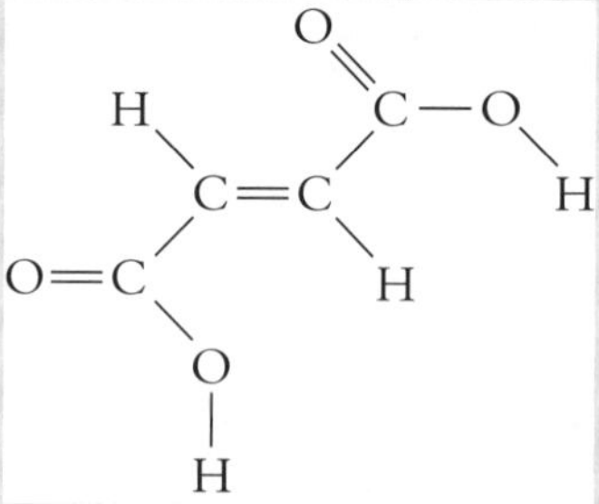

Figure 4.25a, b

i The melting point of the *cis* form is 130 °C whereas the melting point of the *trans* form is 287 °C. Explain this difference. [2]

ii Another difference between these two molecules is that, when heated, *cis*-but-2-ene-1,4-dioic acid forms the cyclic anhydride, *cis*-but-2-ene-1,4-dioic anhydride, as shown in Figure 4.26.

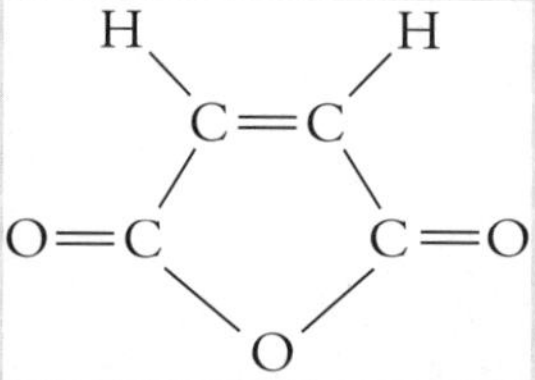

Figure 4.26

The *trans* form of the molecule does not form a cyclic anhydride.

With reference to the structure of the carbon-to-carbon double bond, explain this difference in behaviour. [1]

[Total 9]

Energetics 5

Chapter outline

- Know the difference between heat and temperature and draw enthalpy level diagrams for endothermic and exothermic reactions.
- Calculate the enthalpy change for a reaction from experimental data and solve calculations by applying Hess's Law.
- Recall the definitions for the enthalpy change of reaction, combustion, formation and average bond enthalpy.
- Relate the bond strength in ozone relative to that of oxygen to its importance in the atmosphere.
- Construct a Born–Haber cycle for a binary ionic compound and the enthalpy level diagram for the dissolving of an ionic substance in water. **HL**
- Recall the definitions for the energy changes associated with Born–Haber cycles and for the dissolving of an ionic substance in water. **HL**
- Explain the effect of the size and charge of an ion on lattice enthalpy and on the enthalpy of hydration.
- Explain what is meant by the term 'entropy' and predict the sign of the entropy change for a given reaction.
- Calculate the entropy change for a reaction from standard entropy values. **HL**
- Calculate the value of ΔG from data given and predict whether a reaction will be spontaneous at a given temperature. **HL**

KEY TERMS AND KEY FORMULAS

Average bond enthalpy: The average amount of energy required to break one mole of covalent bonds in a gaseous molecule under standard conditions. Average refers to the fact that the actual bond enthalpy will vary in different molecules. Bond enthalpies are always endothermic ($\Delta H^{\ominus}$ = +ve).

Standard enthalpy change of combustion, $\Delta H_c{}^{\ominus}$: The enthalpy change when one mole of a substance in completely burnt in oxygen under standard conditions of 298 K and 100 kPa.

Standard enthalpy change of formation, $\Delta H_f{}^{\ominus}$: The enthalpy change when one mole of a substance is formed from its elements in their standard states under standard conditions of 298 K and 100 kPa.

Standard enthalpy change of neutralisation, $\Delta H_n{}^{\ominus}$: The enthalpy change when one mole of water is formed by the reaction of an acid with an alkali under standard conditions of 298 K and 100 kPa.

Standard enthalpy change of reaction, $\Delta H_r{}^{\ominus}$: The enthalpy change when the molar amounts in a given a balanced equation react together under standard conditions of 298 K and 100 kPa.

Lattice enthalpy can also be defined as the energy when one mole of an ionic substance is **formed** from its gaseous ions; if defined this way then $\Delta H_{latt}^{\ominus} < 0$. The IB data book includes a table of lattice enthalpies which are all > 0 and so it can be assumed that lattice **dissociation** enthalpy is being used – watch for this difference if you use non-IB resources.

Entropy change, $\Delta S^{\ominus}$: The change in entropy under standard conditions. An increase in the entropy ($\Delta S^{\ominus} > 0$) represents an increase in the disorder; the energy is more spread out, for example, changing from liquid to gas.

Free energy change/Gibbs free energy, $\Delta G^{\ominus}$: This is related to the entropy of the universe. It can be used to predict whether a reaction will occur spontaneously at a given temperature; for spontaneous reactions $\Delta G < 0$ where $\Delta G = \Delta H - T\Delta S$

Standard enthalpy change of atomisation, $\Delta H_{at}^{\ominus}$: The enthalpy change to form one mole of gaseous atoms from an element under standard conditions of 298 K and 100 kPa.

Standard enthalpy change of hydration, $\Delta H_{hyd}^{\ominus}$: The enthalpy change when one mole of gaseous ions are surrounded by water to form an infinitely dilute solution under standard conditions of 298 K and 100 kPa.

Standard enthalpy change of solution, $\Delta H_{sol}^{\ominus}$: The enthalpy change when one mole of a substance is dissolved in excess solvent to form a solution of infinite dilution under standard conditions of 298 K and 100 kPa.

Standard lattice (dissociation) enthalpy, $\Delta H_{latt}^{\ominus}$: The enthalpy change when one mole of an ionic substance **dissociates** into its gaseous ions under standard conditions of 298 K and 100 kPa. $\Delta H_{latt}^{\ominus} > 0$.

$$\Delta H = -\frac{q}{n}$$

where
q = heat energy/J
ΔH = enthalpy change/J mol^{-1}
n = number of moles of limiting reactant

$$\Delta H_r^{\ominus} = \sum \Delta H_f^{\ominus}{}_{products} - \sum \Delta H_f^{\ominus}{}_{reactants}$$

where
$\Delta H_r^{\ominus}$ = enthalpy change of a reaction
$\sum \Delta H_f^{\ominus}{}_{products}$ = sum of the enthalpy change of formation of the products
$\sum \Delta H_f^{\ominus}{}_{reactants}$ = sum of the enthalpy change of formation of the reactants

$$\Delta H_{sol}^{\ominus} = \Delta H_{latt}^{\ominus} + \sum \Delta H_{hyd}^{\ominus}$$

where
$\Delta H_{sol}^{\ominus}$ = standard enthalpy change of solution/J mol^{-1} or kJ mol^{-1}
$\Delta H_{latt}^{\ominus}$ = standard lattice enthalpy/J mol^{-1} or kJ mol^{-1}
$\sum \Delta H_{hyd}^{\ominus}$ = sum of the standard enthalpy change of hydration/J mol^{-1} or kJ mol^{-1}

$$\Delta S^{\ominus} = \sum S_{products}{}^{\ominus} - \sum S_{reactants}{}^{\ominus}$$

where

$\Delta S^{\ominus}$ = the standard entropy change of the reaction/J K^{-1}mol^{-1}

$\sum S_{products}{}^{\ominus}$ = the sum of the standard entropy of the products (multiplied by their stoichiometric amounts)/J K^{-1}mol^{-1}

$\sum S_{reactants}{}^{\ominus}$ = the sum of the standard entropy of the reactants (multiplied by their stoichiometric amounts)/J K^{-1}mol^{-1}

Some reactions are easily recognised as being exothermic (combustion, respiration) or endothermic (thermal decomposition) and changes of state can be thought of as bond forming (exothermic) or bond breaking (endothermic). Most reactions involve both bond breaking and bond forming and so whether they are endo- or exothermic is not so easy to deduce.

Exercise 5.1 – Measuring energy changes

1 a Suggest whether the following reactions are exothermic or endothermic.

   i $C(s) + O_2(g) \rightarrow CO_2(g)$

   ii $6CO_2 + 6H_2O \rightarrow C_6H_{12}O_6 + 6O_2$

   iii $H_2O(l) \rightarrow H_2O(g)$

   iv $MgCO_3(s) \rightarrow MgO(s) + CO_2(g)$

  b Explain why the sign for the enthalpy change of an exothermic reaction is negative.

  c What is the difference between heat and temperature?

  d i   Sketch energy level diagrams for an endothermic and an exothermic reaction and clearly indicate ΔH on the diagrams.

     ii In which type of reaction are the products more stable than the reactants?

This question examines whether you understand what the enthalpy change is measuring.

2 a A block of copper of mass 20.0 g was heated using an electric heating element. 384 J were required to raise the temperature of the block by 50.0 °C. Calculate the specific heat capacity of copper.

  b The heated block was dropped into an insulated beaker containing 250 g of water at 25.0 °C and the temperature of the water and block were allowed to become equal. If the specific heat capacity of water is 4.18 J g^{-1} K^{-1} then calculate the final temperature of the water.

Another fundamental idea.

3 The apparatus in Figure 5.1 was used to determine the enthalpy change of combustion of a liquid fuel with the formula $C_5H_{11}OH$.

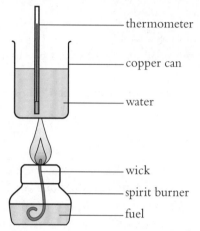

Figure 5.1 Apparatus to determine the enthalpy of combustion of a liquid fuel.

The following results were obtained.

Mass of empty copper can = 212.3 g
Mass of can and water before heating = 326.5 g
Temperature of water before heating = 21.5 °C
Mass of spirit burner before lighting = 104.0 g
Mass of spirit burner at the end of experiment = 99.3 g
Temperature of water after heating = 77.5 °C
Specific heat capacity of the water = 4.18 J g^{-1} K^{-1}

a Calculate the enthalpy of combustion of the fuel in kJ mol^{-1}.
b Explain why copper is a good choice of material for the can.
c Suggest two possible sources of experimental error in the experiment.
d Suggest ways to reduce the experimental errors suggested in part **c**.
e Other than experimental errors, suggest two reasons why the value for the enthalpy change of combustion of this fuel differs from the values quoted in data books.

Exercise 5.2 – Hess's law

The enthalpy changes for reactions that cannot be measured directly can be calculated using Hess's law.

1 In order to determine the enthalpy change for the reaction below, two separate experiments were performed. In each case, 2.0 g of the solid was added to an excess of dilute HCl with a mass of 50 g and the temperature changes recorded.

$2NaHCO_3(s) \rightarrow Na_2CO_3(s) + CO_2(g) + H_2O(l)$

In experiment 1 with 2.0 g of Na_2CO_3, the temperature rose by 11 °C.
In experiment 2 with 2.0 g of $NaHCO_3$, the temperature fell by 6.0 °C.
Assume that the specific heat capacity of the solutions is 4.18 J g^{-1} K^{-1} and the density is 1 g cm^{-3}.

  a i   Using $q = mc\Delta T$, calculate the heat energy gained by the liquid in experiment 1.
    ii   Calculate the number of moles of Na_2CO_3 used in experiment 1.
    iii   Using the values obtained in parts **i** and **ii**, calculate the enthalpy change, ΔH_1, for the reaction in kJ mol^{-1}.

b i Using $q = mc\Delta T$, calculate the heat energy gained by the water in experiment 2.

  ii Calculate the number of moles of Na_2CO_3 used in experiment 2.

  iii Using the values obtained in parts **i** and **ii**, calculate the enthalpy change, ΔH_2, for the reaction in $kJ\,mol^{-1}$.

c Complete the spaces in the Hess's cycle in Figure 5.2 and calculate ΔH_r.

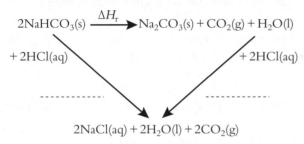

Figure 5.2 Hess's cycle for decomposition of $NaHCO_3$.

2 a Construct a Hess's cycle to connect the following three equations and calculate the value of ΔH_r.

$$PCl_5(g) \rightarrow PCl_3(g) + Cl_2(g) \qquad \Delta H_r = ?$$
$$P_4(s) + 6Cl_2(g) \rightarrow 4PCl_3(g) \qquad \Delta H = -2439\,kJ$$
$$4PCl_5(g) \rightarrow P_4(s) + 10Cl_2(g) \qquad \Delta H = 3438\,kJ$$

Think of a Hess's cycle as a triangle with a different equation on each side. The arrows on the cycle are the equation arrows; they can be written left to right, bottom to top or whatever, but they must travel from reactants to products. The values of the enthalpy changes must match their equations in the direction the equation is written so never change the sign of ΔH.

Start by picking one equation and writing that across the page. Then look for one substance that is common to the equation written and one of the other equations, these two equations must be on adjacent sides of the cycle. Make sure every equation balances.

b Construct a Hess's cycle to connect the following three equations and calculate the value of ΔH_r.

$$N_2H_4(l) + H_2(g) \rightarrow 2NH_3(g) \qquad\qquad \Delta H_r = ?$$
$$N_2H_4(l) + CH_4O(l) \rightarrow CH_2O(g) + N_2(g) + 3H_2(g) \qquad \Delta H = -37\,kJ$$
$$N_2(g) + 3H_2(g) \rightarrow 2NH_3(g) \qquad\qquad \Delta H = -46\,kJ$$
$$CH_4O(l) \rightarrow CH_2O(g) + H_2(g) \qquad\qquad \Delta H = -65\,kJ$$

See box on next page.

This cycle is more difficult as it includes four equations. This does not always mean that the cycle is a square, however. It could still be a triangle with two equations on one of the sides. Use the same principle as before: look for substances common to two equations. Here start with N_2H_4. CH_4O needs to be added on both sides so that the second equation can be used. Extra substances can always be added to the equations as long as they are added to both sides. It is a bit like adding x to both sides in maths. Remember these are not reactions that are actually going to happen — these cycles are just a way of calculating an enthalpy change. It's just algebra!

c Construct a Hess's cycle to find the enthalpy change for the following reaction using the data provided.

$C_2H_5OH(l) + CH_3COOH(l) \rightarrow CH_3COOCH_2CH_3(l) + H_2O(l)$

$\Delta H_c^{\ominus}(C_2H_5OH(l)) = -1367\,kJ\,mol^{-1}$

$\Delta H_c^{\ominus}(CH_3COOH(l)) = -874\,kJ\,mol^{-1}$

$\Delta H_c^{\ominus}(CH_3COOCH_2CH_3(l)) = -2238\,kJ\,mol^{-1}$

In this question the equations are not provided so you will need to construct them from your knowledge of the definitions of the various standard enthalpy changes; this is why learning definitions is so important.

The clue here is in the data provided. This is combustion data and so the substances that will form the missing corner of the Hess's cycle triangle will be the combustion products, CO_2 and H_2O.

d i Calculate the enthalpy of combustion of $C_6H_5COOH(s)$ using the data below.

$\Delta H_f^{\ominus}(C_6H_5COOH(s)) = -385\,kJ\,mol^{-1}$

$\Delta H_f^{\ominus}(CO_2(g)) = -394\,kJ\,mol^{-1}$

$\Delta H_f^{\ominus}(H_2O(l)) = -286\,kJ\,mol^{-1}$

This question can be approached using a Hess's cycle. Again the starting point is to write the equation of the enthalpy change that you need to calculate. Then consider the data that have been provided; as formation data have been provided, then the missing link is the elements in their standard states.

Alternatively, the formula $\Delta H_r^{\ominus} = \Sigma \Delta H_f^{\ominus}{}_{products} - \Sigma D H_f^{\ominus}{}_{reactants}$ can be used.

ii Construct an energy level diagram using these data.

Exercise 5.3 – Bond enthalpies

1 a Define the term 'average bond enthalpy'.

b i Using the average bond enthalpy values from Table 5.1, calculate the enthalpy change for the reaction shown in Figure 5.3.

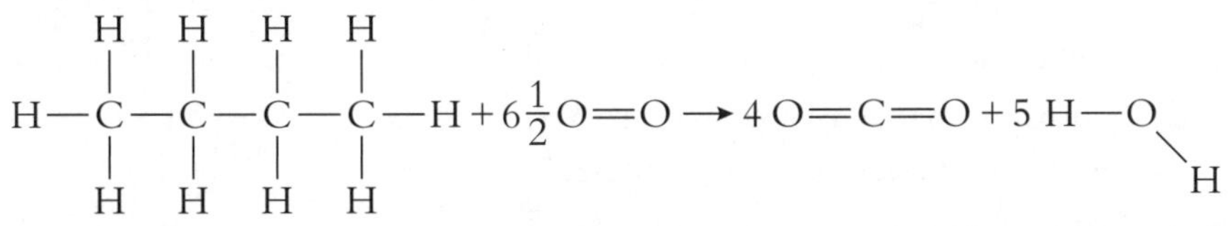

Figure 5.3 Combustion of butane.

Bond	Bond enthalpies at 298 K / kJ mol^{-1}
C–C	346
C–H	414
O–H	463
C=O	804
O=O	498

Table 5.1

ii The data book value for the standard enthalpy of combustion of butane is $-2878\,\text{kJ}\,\text{mol}^{-1}$. Suggest two reasons why this value is different from that calculated in part **b i**.

2 Ozone, O_3, in the upper atmosphere absorbs harmful UV-B radiation but does not absorb very much of the most harmful UV-C radiation. UV-C radiation is absorbed by diatomic oxygen, O_2. Neither diatomic oxygen nor ozone absorb UV-A radiation which passes through the atmosphere to reach the Earth's surface.

a Given that the average bond enthalpy in O_2 is $498\,\text{kJ}\,\text{mol}^{-1}$ and the enthalpy of formation of ozone is $143\,\text{kJ}\,\text{mol}^{-1}$, calculate the average bond enthalpy of an oxygen–oxygen bond in ozone.

b Oxygen and ozone both have an important protective effect in the upper atmosphere. With reference to the bond energies in oxygen and ozone, explain their role in absorbing UV-B and UV-C radiation and why UV-A radiation is not absorbed.

Always draw out the molecules showing all of the bonds as has been done for you in this question – the most common mistake is to miscount the bonds.

This question is not about a practical experiment so the difference is not due to experimental errors. Think about the definitions of 'average' bond energy and 'standard' enthalpy of combustion.

HL Exercise 5.4 – Energy cycles

Born–Haber cycles are energy level diagrams based on the enthalpy of formation of an ionic compound. Knowing the definitions for a variety of standard enthalpy changes is key to this section.

1 Define the following:
  a standard enthalpy change of atomisation, $\Delta H_{at}^{\ominus}$
  b standard enthalpy change of formation, $\Delta H_f^{\ominus}$
  c standard lattice (dissociation) enthalpy, $\Delta H_{latt}^{\ominus}$
  d first electron affinity
  e second electron affinity
  f first ionisation energy
  g second ionisation energy

> You may not have memorised these yet and so have either chosen to skip this question or simply copy the definitions from the start of the chapter. There are no shortcuts – these definitions have to be learnt. One way to do this is to write them out repeatedly.
>
> It is also worth noting that there is a pattern to these energy changes. Most of the definitions involve 'one mole' of something and 'standard conditions of 298 K and 100 kPa'.

2 Figure 5.4 shows the Born–Haber cycle for calcium oxide.

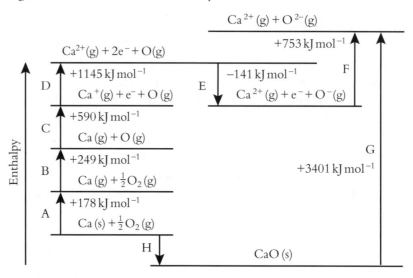

Figure 5.4 Born–Haber cycle for CaO.

  a Identify the enthalpy changes A–H.
  b Using the data given in Figure 5.4, calculate the enthalpy of formation of calcium oxide.

c The lattice enthalpy of MgO is 3791 kJ mol^{-1}. What does this suggest about the strength of the electrostatic force of attraction between the ions in MgO compared to those in CaO? Suggest a reason for this.

d The lattice enthalpy of CaF$_2$ is 2651 kJ mol^{-1}. The ionic radius of the O^{2-} ion is 140 nm and that of the F$^-$ ion is 133 nm. Explain the difference in the lattice enthalpies of CaO and CaF$_2$.

3 Figure 5.5 shows an energy profile diagram for the reaction when CaBr$_2$ dissolves in water.

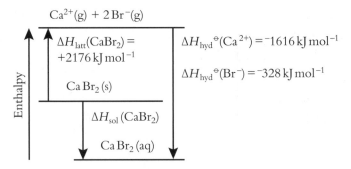

Figure 5.5 Dissolving of CaBr$_2$.

a Calculate the enthalpy of solution of CaBr$_2$.

b Suggest whether it is possible to deduce if the enthalpy of solution of calcium(II) chloride will be more or less exothermic than that of calcium(II) bromide given that the chloride ion has a smaller ionic radius than the bromide ion.

> Consider what factors affect the enthalpy of solution, lattice enthalpy and the enthalpies of hydration. What effect does ion size have on both of these?

HL Exercise 5.5 – Entropy and spontaneity

Entropy is most easily considered as a measure of the disorder of a system. Unlike enthalpy, where only enthalpy **changes** can be calculated, the actual value of the entropy of a substance can be known.

1 Identify which of the following substances in each pair has the higher entropy:
   a H$_2$O(l) or H$_2$O(g)?
   b NaCl(s) at 25 °C or at 100 °C?
   c nitrogen gas at a pressure of 200 kPa or at a pressure of 100 kPa?
   d 0.100 mol of NaCl(s) and 100 g of water separately or a solution made by dissolving 0.100 mol of NaCl in 100 g of water?

2 Predict the sign of the entropy change for the following reactions:
   a 2NaNO$_3$(s) → 2NaNO$_2$(s) + O$_2$(g)
   b C$_2$H$_4$(g) + H$_2$O(g) → C$_2$H$_5$OH(g)
   c 2CuSO$_4$(aq) + 4KI(aq) → 2CuI(s) + 2K$_2$SO$_4$(aq) + I$_2$(aq)

> ΔS is positive if the entropy increases (becomes more disordered) and ΔS is negative if there is a decrease in entropy (the system becomes less disordered).

3 Using the data from Table 5.2, calculate the entropy change for the following reactions at 298 K.

Substance	Entropy / $JK^{-1}mol^{-1}$
C(graphite)	5.7
C(diamond)	2.4
$CH_4(g)$	186
$O_2(g)$	205
$CO_2(g)$	214
$H_2O(l)$	70
$Al_2O_3(s)$	51
Fe(s)	27
Al(s)	28
$Fe_2O_3(s)$	87

Table 5.2

Remember to use the coefficients from the balanced equations in your calculation.

a $C(diamond) \rightarrow C(graphite)$
b $CH_4(g) + 2O_2(g) \rightarrow CO_2(g) + 2H_2O(l)$
c $2Al(s) + Fe_2O_3(s) \rightarrow Al_2O_3(s) + 2Fe(s)$

4 The free energy change of a reaction, $\Delta G^{\ominus}$, can be used to predict whether a reaction is spontaneous at a given temperature.
a Describe the meaning of the term 'spontaneous'.
b For what values of $\Delta G^{\ominus}$ is a reaction spontaneous?
c Give an equation that can be used to calculate $\Delta G^{\ominus}$.
d Copy and complete Table 5.3 to indicate the relationship between $\Delta H^{\ominus}, \Delta S^{\ominus}, \Delta G^{\ominus}$ and temperature.

$\Delta G^{\ominus}$ does not give an indication of the rate of a reaction. The relationship between rate and $\Delta G^{\ominus}$ is beyond this syllabus.

$\Delta H^{\ominus}$	$\Delta S^{\ominus}$	$\Delta G^{\ominus}$	Spontaneous?
positive			only at high temperatures
	negative	positive at all temperatures	
	positive	negative at all temperatures	always spontaneous
	negative	negative at low temperatures	

Table 5.3

5 Using the data provided, calculate the value of the free energy change for the following reactions at 298 K and state at what temperatures the reactions are spontaneous.
a $2H_2O_2(l) \rightarrow 2H_2O(l) + O_2(g)$
  $\Delta H^{\ominus} = -196\,kJ\,mol^{-1}$ and $\Delta S^{\ominus} = +125\,J\,K^{-1}\,mol^{-1}$
b $C_3H_8(g) + 5O_2(g) \rightarrow 3CO_2(g) + 4H_2O(l)$
  $\Delta H_c^{\ominus} = -2219\,kJ\,mol^{-1}$
  $S^{\ominus}(C_3H_8(g)) = 220\,J\,K^{-1}\,mol^{-1}$
  $S^{\ominus}(CO_2(g)) = 214\,J\,K^{-1}\,mol^{-1}$
  $S^{\ominus}(H_2O(l)) = 70\,J\,K^{-1}\,mol^{-1}$
  $S^{\ominus}(O_2(g)) = 206\,J\,K^{-1}\,mol^{-1}$
c $4KClO_3(s) \rightarrow 3KClO_4(s) + KCl(s)$

To determine whether a reaction is spontaneous, calculate the temperature when $\Delta G^{\ominus}$ is zero. If you are unsure whether the reaction is spontaneous above or below this temperature then calculate the value of $\Delta G^{\ominus}$ at a temperature 1 K higher than this. If $\Delta G^{\ominus}$ is now negative then the temperature must need to be higher than the one calculated. If $\Delta G^{\ominus}$ is positive using the higher temperature then the temperature needs to be below the one calculated.

Substance	$\Delta H_f^{\ominus}$ / kJ mol^{-1}	$S^{\ominus}$ / J mol^{-1}
KClO$_3$(s)	−398	143
KClO$_4$(s)	−433	151
KCl(s)	−437	83

Table 5.4

? Exam-style questions

1   Deduce the heat energy supplied if 50 g of water with a specific heat capacity of 4.2 J g^{-1} K^{-1} increases in temperature by 10 °C.
   A 210 J
   B 420 J
   C 2.1 kJ
   D 4200 J

2   In an experiment, 50 cm^3 of a solution of HCl with a concentration of 1 mol dm^{-3} was reacted with 50 cm^3 of a solution of NaOH with a concentration of 1 mol dm^{-3}. The temperature of the solution increased by 12 °C. Calculate the temperature rise if 50 cm^3 of the same HCl solution were reacted with 50 cm^3 of a solution of NaOH with a concentration of 0.5 mol dm^{-3}.
   A 6 °C
   B 12 °C
   C 24 °C
   D 3 °C

3   Which of the following statements is not correct about endothermic reactions?
   A The surroundings lose energy.
   B The enthalpy change will be positive.
   C The enthalpy change will be negative.
   D The temperature of the surroundings decreases.

4　Which equation represents the standard enthalpy change of formation of ammonia, NH_3?

A　$N(g) + 3H(g) \rightarrow NH_3(g)$

B　$N_2(s) + 3H_2(g) \rightarrow 2NH_3(g)$

C　$\frac{1}{2} N_2(g) + \frac{3}{2} H_2(g) \rightarrow NH_3(g)$

D　$NH_3(g) \rightarrow 3N\text{–}H(g)$

5　Which equation would give the correct value for the energy change, ΔH_r?

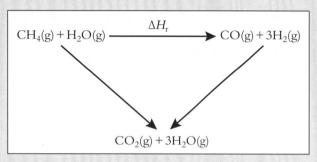

Figure 5.6 Calculation of ΔH_r.

A　$\Delta H_r = \Delta H_c(CH_4) - \Delta H_c(CO) - \Delta H_c(H_2)$

B　$\Delta H_r = \Delta H_c(CH_4) - \Delta H_c(CO) + (3 \times \Delta H_c(H_2))$

C　$\Delta H_r = \Delta H_c(CO) + \Delta H_c(H_2) - \Delta H_c(CH_4)$

D　$\Delta H_r = \Delta H_c(CH_4) - \Delta H_c(CO) - (3 \times \Delta H_c(H_2))$

6　Which equation represents the bond enthalpy of a C–H bond?

A　$CH_4(g) \rightarrow C(s) + 2H_2(g)$

B　$CH_4(g) \rightarrow C(g) + 4H(g)$

C　$\frac{1}{4} CH_4(g) \rightarrow \frac{1}{4} C(g) + H(g)$

D　$\frac{1}{4} CH_4(g) \rightarrow \frac{1}{4} C(s) + \frac{1}{2} H_2(g)$

7　**HL** Which of the following substances will have the most endothermic lattice enthalpy?

A　NaBr

B　CaO

C　KBr

D　$CaBr_2$

8　**HL** Which of the following reactions will have the largest increase in entropy?

A　$C_2H_5OH(l) \rightarrow C_2H_4(g) + H_2O(l)$

B　$C(s) \rightarrow C(g)$

C　$H_2O(l) \rightarrow H_2O(g)$

D　$C_2H_5OH(l) + 3O_2(g) \rightarrow 2CO_2(g) + 3H_2O(l)$

9 **HL** Which statement is true for the following endothermic reaction?
$CaCO_3(s) \rightarrow CaO(s) + CO_2(g)$

A The reaction is spontaneous at high temperatures.

B The reaction can never be spontaneous.

C The reaction is spontaneous at low temperatures.

D It is not possible to deduce whether the reaction is spontaneous or not from the information provided.

10 **HL** Calculate $\Delta G^{\ominus}$ for the following reaction at $400\,K$.

$C(g) + O_2(g) \rightarrow CO_2(g)$

$\Delta H^{\ominus} = -395\,kJ\,mol^{-1}$ and $\Delta S^{\ominus} = +5\,J\,k^{-1}\,mol^{-1}$

A $\Delta G^{\ominus} = -2395\,kJ\,mol^{-1}$

B $\Delta G^{\ominus} = -400\,kJ\,mol^{-1}$

C $\Delta G^{\ominus} = -393\,kJ\,mol^{-1}$

D $\Delta G^{\ominus} = -397\,kJ\,mol^{-1}$

11 In an experiment to determine the enthalpy change of a reaction, $50.0\,cm^3$ of a solution of copper(II) sulfate with a concentration of $0.100\,mol\,dm^{-3}$ was placed in a polystyrene cup and its temperature recorded every $30\,s$. After 3 minutes, $2.00\,g$ of magnesium powder was added to the cup and the temperature was measured every 30 seconds for a further 7 minutes.

The data shown in Figure 5.7 were obtained:

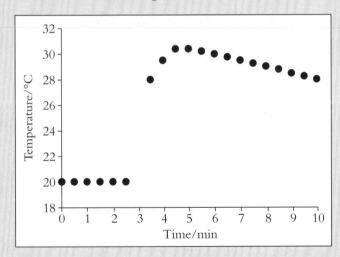

Figure 5.7 Temperature change for the reaction between $CuSO_4$ and Mg.

a Use the graph to find the temperature change for the reaction. [1]

b Calculate the heat energy produced by the reaction. [1]

Assume that the specific heat capacity of the mixture is the same as water: $4.18\,J\,g^{-1}\,K^{-1}$

c Calculate the number of moles of magnesium and the number of moles of copper(II) sulfate present and state which reactant was the limiting reactant. **[2]**

d Calculate the enthalpy change for the reaction **[2]**

$$Mg(s) + CuSO_4(aq) \rightarrow MgSO_4(aq) + Cu(s)$$

e What is the advantage of obtaining the temperature change for the reaction graphically rather than simply measuring the initial temperature and the maximum temperature? **[1]**

f Suggest two sources of error in this experiment. **[2]**

g Estimate the temperature change for the reaction if the reaction was repeated using $100\,cm^3$ of copper(II) sulfate of concentration $0.100\,mol$ and $2.0\,g$ of magnesium powder. **[1]**

[Total 10]

12 a State Hess's law. **[1]**

b i Label the Hess's cycle shown for the chlorination of benzene in Figure 5.8 to indicate the names of the enthalpy changes labelled A to C. **[3]**

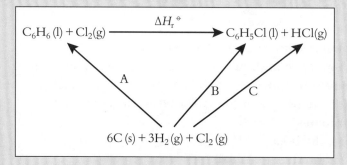

Figure 5.8 Chlorination of benzene.

ii Given the data below, calculate ΔH_r. **[2]**

$\Delta H_f(C_6H_6(l)) = +49.0\,kJ\,mol^{-1}$

$\Delta H_f(C_6H_5Cl(l)) = +11\,kJ\,mol^{-1}$

$\Delta H_f(HCl(g)) = -92.3\,kJ\,mol^{-1}$

c i Construct a labelled Hess's cycle to show how the enthalpy change for the following reaction can be calculated from the data below. **[3]**

$$3C(s) + 3H_2(g) \rightarrow C_3H_6(g)$$

$\Delta H_c(C(s)) = -394\,kJ\,mol^{-1}$

$\Delta H_c(H_2(g)) = -286\,kJ\,mol^{-1}$

$\Delta H_c(C_3H_6(g)) = -2058\,kJ\,mol^{-1}$

ii Give the name of this enthalpy change. **[1]**

iii Calculate the value for this enthalpy change. **[3]**

iv Draw and label and energy profile diagram for this reaction including the data given in part **i**. **[4]**

d The equation for the complete combustion of C_3H_6 can be written as shown in Figure 5.9:

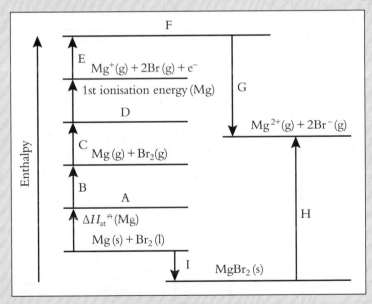

Figure 5.9 Combustion of C_3H_6.

i Given the bond enthalpy data below, calculate ΔH_c for C_3H_6. [3]
C–C 346 kJ mol^{-1}
C–H 414 kJ mol^{-1}
O=O 498 kJ mol^{-1}
O–H 463 kJ mol^{-1}
C=C 614 kJ mol-1
C=O 804 kJ mol-1

ii Suggest two reasons why the value calculated is not the same as the value quoted in the list of data given in part **c**. [2]

[Total 22]

13 HL

a Complete the Born–Haber cycle shown in Figure 5.10 for magnesium bromide by adding labels A–I. [4]

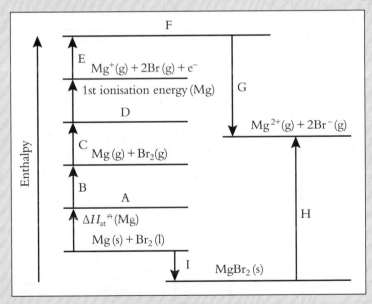

Figure 5.10 Born–Haber cycle for MgBr$_2$.

b Given the data below, calculate the lattice enthalpy of $MgBr_2$. [3]

$\Delta H_f^{\ominus}(MgBr_2) = -524\,kJ\,mol^{-1}$

Enthalpy of atomisation of magnesium = $129\,kJ\,mol^{-1}$

First ionisation energy of magnesium = $+738\,kJ\,mol^{-1}$

First electron affinity of bromine = $-325\,kJ\,mol^{-1}$

Enthalpy of vaporisation of bromine = $15\,kJ\,mol^{-1}$

Second ionisation energy of magnesium = $1450\,kJ\,mol^{-1}$

Bond enthalpy Br–Br = $+193\,kJ\,mol^{-1}$

c Describe the effect of the charge and size of the ions on the magnitude of the lattice enthalpy of a compound. [2]

d Predict whether the lattice enthalpy of calcium bromide will be more or less endothermic than that of magnesium bromide. Justify your answer. [3]

[Total 12]

14   **HL**   **The enthalpies of solution of the sodium halides are as follows**

$\Delta H_{sol}^{\ominus}(NaCl) = +3.88\,kJ\,mol^{-1}$

$\Delta H_{sol}^{\ominus}(NaBr) = -0.60\,kJ\,mol^{-1}$

$\Delta H_{sol}^{\ominus}(NaI) = -7.53\,kJ\,mol^{-1}$

a   **i**   Draw an energy level diagram to show how the lattice enthalpy of NaI can be calculated from its enthalpy of solution given that $\Delta H_{hyd}^{\ominus}(Na^+) = -424\,kJ\,mol^{-1}$ and $\Delta H_{hyd}^{\ominus}(I^-) = -287\,kJ\,mol^{-1}$. [3]

    ii   Calculate a value for this lattice enthalpy. [2]

    iii   Describe and explain the trend in the lattice enthalpies of NaCl, NaBr and NaI. [2]

    iv   Describe the trends in the enthalpies of hydration of the halide ions. [1]

    v   Explain why the enthalpies of solution of the sodium halides change from endothermic to exothermic from NaCl to NaI. [2]

b Explain why the dissolving of NaCl occurs spontaneously at room temperature despite this being an endothermic process. [2]

[Total 12]

15   **HL**

a Using the data in Table 5.5, determine $\Delta H^{\ominus}$, $\Delta S^{\ominus}$ and $\Delta G^{\ominus}$ for the following reaction at 298 K.

$Ba(OH)_2 \cdot 8H_2O(s) + 2NH_4Cl(s) \rightarrow 2NH_3(g) + 10H_2O(l) + BaCl_2(s)$ [3]

Substance	$\Delta H_f^{\ominus}$ / kJ mol^{-1}	$S^{\ominus}$ / J mol^{-1}
$Ba(OH)_2 \cdot 8H_2O(s)$	−3345	427
$NH_4Cl(s)$	−314	95
$NH_3(g)$	−46	192
$H_2O(l)$	−286	70
$BaCl_2(s)$	−859	124

Table 5.5

b Calculate at what temperatures the reaction is not feasible. [2]

[Total 5]

Chemical kinetics 6

Chapter outline

- Describe experimental methods for determining the rate of a chemical reaction, and analyse and interpret numerical and graphical data.
- Describe and explain the collision theory and the effects of concentration, temperature, the surface area of a solid, catalysts and pressure on the frequency and proportion of effective collisions.
- Draw the Maxwell–Boltzmann distribution and use it to explain the effect of temperature and of a catalyst on the rate of a chemical reaction.
- Draw enthalpy level diagrams which include activation energies and use these to explain the effect of a catalyst on the rate of a chemical reaction (**HL** : these can include multi-step reactions).
- Deduce the order of a reaction from experimental data and solve calculations involving the rate equation. **HL**
- Recall the meanings of the terms 'order', 'mechanism' and 'molecularity'. **HL**
- Sketch, identify and analyse graphical representations for zero-, first- and second-order reactions. **HL**
- Evaluate a proposed mechanism from a rate equation and vice versa. **HL**
- Recall that an increase in temperature causes an increase in the rate constant and that these are related to one another by the Arrhenius equation. **HL**
- Solve calculations using the Arrhenius equation and analyse graphical representations of it in linear form. **HL**

KEY TERMS AND FORMULAS

Activation energy: The minimum amount of energy that colliding species must have before a collision results in a chemical reaction.

Catalyst: A substance that increases the rate of a chemical reaction without itself being used up in the reaction; a catalyst acts by allowing the reaction to occur via an alternative pathway of lower activation energy.

Collision theory: A reaction can only occur when the particles collide in the correct orientation and with energy greater than or equal to the activation energy.

Rate of reaction: The change in the concentration of reactants or products per unit time.

Half-life: The time taken for the concentration of a reactant to fall to half of its original value.

Mechanism: A series of steps that make up a more complex reaction. Each step involves the collision of two particles.

Molecularity: The number of 'molecules' that react in a particular step (usually the rate-determining step) in a chemical reaction.

Order of reaction: The power to which the concentration of a substance is raised in the experimentally determined rate expression.

Overall order of reaction: The sum of the powers of the concentration terms in the experimentally determined rate equation.

Rate constant, k: The proportionality constant in the experimentally determined rate equation.

Rate-determining step: The slowest step in a reaction mechanism.

Rate equation/rate expression: An experimentally determined equation that relates the rate of a reaction to the concentrations of the substances in the reaction mixture.

Rate of reaction $= \dfrac{\text{change in concentration of reactant or product}}{\text{time}}$;

units are commonly mol $dm^{-3}\,s^{-1}$

Rate $= k[A]^n[B]^m$

where species A and B are substances in the reaction mixture

k = rate constant (units depend on the value of n and m)

n and m are the order of reaction with respect to A and B, respectively.

Rate equations can only be determined experimentally.

Exercise 6.1 – Collision theory and rate of reaction

1 The collision theory is used to explain the factors that affect the rate of a reaction.
   a State the collision theory.
   b Define the term 'rate of reaction'.
   c List the main factors that affect the rate of a chemical reaction.
   d In terms of the collisions between the particles, explain why the rate of a reaction decreases as a reaction proceeds.

2 The rate of a reaction depends on the frequency of collisions and on the proportion of collisions which are successful.
   a What name is given to the minimum amount of energy that the particles must have in order for a reaction to be successful?
   b Complete the boxes in Table 6.1 to indicate whether each factor affects the frequency of collisions, the proportion of successful collisions and/or the minimum energy required.

Factor	Frequency of collisions	Proportion of successful collisions	Minimum energy required for a successful collision
changing the concentration of a reactant			
changing the pressure of a gas			
changing the surface area of a solid			
using a catalyst			
changing the temperature			

Table 6.1

c Figure 6.1 shows the distribution of molecular energies at a particular temperature.

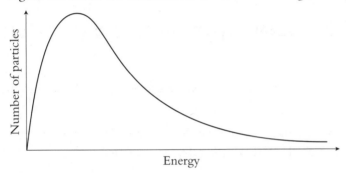

Figure 6.1 Distribution of molecular energy.

Add a line to represent the distribution at a higher temperature and use this to explain why the rate of a reaction increases at higher temperatures.

Details to consider include:
Should the curve start at (0,0)?
Should the curve touch the *x*-axis at high energies?
Should the maximum of the new curve be higher or lower than the first curve?
Where should the position of the maximum of the new curve be along the *x*-axis relative to the first curve?
Should the right-hand side of the new curve finish above, below or with the first curve?

d What does the total area under the curve represent?

Consider what happens to the concentration of the reactants as a reaction proceeds.

Any question about how a factor affects the rate of a reaction should be answered in terms of the effect on the *frequency* of collisions and on the *proportion of successful collisions*. An alternative to 'frequency' would be to describe the change in the number of collisions per unit time. The 'per unit time' is essential; more collisions on its own is incorrect.

Consider the
stoichiometry of
the equation. How
many moles of
iodine are used up
for each mole of
thiosulfate being
used?

3 The reaction between $25 \, cm^3$ of a solution of thiosulfate ions, $S_3O_3^{2-}$ of concentration $0.100 \, mol \, dm^{-3}$ and $25 \, cm^3$ of iodide ions with a concentration of $0.100 \, mol \, dm^{-3}$ proceeds according to the following equation:

$$2S_2O_3^{2-}(aq) + I_2(aq) \rightarrow S_4O_6^{2-}(aq) + 2I^-(aq)$$

The rate of the reaction can be followed colorimetrically.

a Explain what is meant by the term 'colorimetrically'.

b Sketch a graph to show the change in the concentration of iodine and of thiosulfate ions against time.

c On your graph, show how the initial rate of the reaction with respect to iodine could be calculated.

d Suggest how the rate of formation of iodide ions compares to the rate of formation of the $S_4O_6^{2-}$ ions.

HL Exercise 6.2 – Rate expression and reaction mechanism

The rate equation for a reaction can only de deduced experimentally and not from the chemical equation.

1 The rate equation describes the relationship between the rate of a reaction and the concentrations of substances in the reaction mixture, for example:

$$rate = k[A]^a[B]^b$$

a What name is given to k in the expression above and what does it represent?

b What name is given to terms such as a and b in the rate equation above?

c For the rate equation above, what name is given to the sum of a and b?

d What is the effect of temperature on the values of a, b and k in a rate equation such as that given above?

2 For each of the following examples, deduce the rate equation and calculate the value of k including its units.

a For the reaction $A + B \rightarrow C$ (using the data shown in Table 6.2):

Experiment	[A] / mol dm^{-3}	[B] / mol dm^{-3}	Rate / mol dm^{-3} s^{-1}
1	1	1	2
2	1	2	4
3	2	2	4

Table 6.2

Choose a pair of experiments in which one of the reactant concentrations does not change. This will enable you to determine the order with respect to the substance which does change.

Deduce the factor by which the concentration and the rate have both changed. If this change is the same, then the reaction is first order. If the change in the rate is the square of the change in the concentration, then the reaction is second order.

Remember the order of a reaction can be a fraction but you are not expected to do calculations which involve fractional orders.

b For the reaction A + 2B → C + D (using the data in Table 6.3):

Experiment	[A] / mol dm^{-3}	[B] / mol dm^{-3}	Rate / mol dm^{-3} s^{-1}
1	0.1	0.5	1.6
2	0.1	0.25	0.4
3	0.3	0.5	4.8

Table 6.3

Deduce the order with respect to F first and then use this information when deducing the order with respect to the other substances.

c For the reaction F + G → 2H (using the data in Table 6.4):

Experiment	[F] / mol dm^{-3}	[G] / mol dm^{-3}	[J] / mol dm^{-3}	Rate / × 10^{-2} mol dm^{-3} s^{-1}
1	0.2	0.5	0.10	3.0
2	0.1	0.5	0.10	1.5
3	0.6	0.5	0.20	18
4	0.3	0.25	0.40	4.5

Table 6.4

d In part **c**, substance J does not appear in the balanced equation. What name is given to a substance that appears in the rate equation but is not in the chemical equation?

3 The order of a reaction can be found graphically. For example, the half-life of a first order reaction is constant.
   a Explain what is meant by the term 'half-life'.
   b Sketch the shapes of the following graphs:
   i concentration of reactant against time for a zero-order reaction
   ii concentration of reactant against time for a first-order reaction
   iii concentration of reactant against time for a second-order reaction

Recognising the shapes of graphs is a useful skill. One way of developing this is to deduce their shapes. Try to answer the question by working out the shapes from the relationships rather than just memorising them.

   iv rate against concentration of reactant for a zero order reaction
   v rate against concentration of reactant for a first order reaction
   vi rate against concentration of reactant for a second-order reaction

4 Although a rate equation cannot be deduced from the balanced chemical equation, it can be deduced from the mechanism of the reaction. Strictly speaking, it is the mechanism that is deduced from the rate equation rather than the other way around.

a What is meant by the term 'mechanism'?

b The rate equation is related to the 'rate-determining step' of a mechanism. What is meant by this term?

c The mechanism for a reaction is given below:

Step 1: $NO_2 + Br_2 \rightarrow NOOBr + Br$

Step 2: $NO_2 + Br \rightarrow NOOBr$

The rate equation includes all the reactants in the rate-determining step, but rate equations can only include species which are found in the original reaction mixture. If any of these species are products of an earlier step and so are not found in the reaction mixture, then their concentration depends on the concentrations of the reactants in the equation by which they have been made.

For example, if the rate equation for the rate-determining step includes substance A and A is the product from an earlier step, then the concentration of A can be substituted by the concentrations of the reactants from which A was made.

  i   Deduce the overall equation for the reaction.

  ii Give the rate equation if step 1 is the rate-determining step.

  iii Give the rate equation is step 2 is the rate-determining step.

d The mechanism for a reaction is given below:

Step 1: $OCl^-(aq) + H_2O(l) \rightarrow HOCl(aq) + OH^-(aq)$

Step 2: $I^-(aq) + HOCl(aq) \rightarrow IOH(aq) + Cl^-(aq)$

Step 3: $IOH(aq) + OH^-(aq) \rightarrow IO^-(aq) + H_2O(l)$

  i   Give the overall equation for the reaction.

  ii Given that the rate equation for this reaction was found to be:
     rate = $k[I^-][OCl^-]$
     which is the rate-determining step in this mechanism?

  iii The 'molecularity' of this reaction is 2. What does this term mean?

  iv Which species in the mechanism act as intermediates?

  v   What is the role of water in this mechanism?

  vi Why does $[H_2O]$ not appear in the rate equation?

HL Exercise 6.3 – Activation energy

The relationship between the rate constant and temperature is described by the Arrhenius equation. This is given in the data book in three forms.

$$k = A\,e^{\frac{-E_a}{RT}}, \quad \ln k = \frac{-E_a}{RT} + \ln A \quad \text{and} \quad \ln\frac{k_1}{k_2} = \frac{E_a}{R}\left(\frac{1}{T_2} - \frac{1}{T_1}\right)$$

1 a What do the terms $\ln k$, A, T, E_a and R represent in these equations?

b Given that the activation energy of a reaction is $35\,\text{kJ}\,\text{mol}^{-1}$ and the exponential factor has a value of $12.5\,\text{dm}^3\,\text{mol}^{-1}\,\text{s}^{-1}$, calculate the rate constant at $25\,°\text{C}$.

In this question, you have one value of T, A and E_a so the expression $k = Ae^{\frac{-E_a}{RT}}$ should be used.

c The rate constant of a reaction was found to be $0.0245\,\text{dm}^3\,\text{mol}^{-1}\,\text{s}^{-1}$ at $50.0\,\text{C}$ and $0.0467\,\text{dm}^3\,\text{mol}^{-1}\,\text{s}^{-1}$ at $75.0\,\text{C}$. Calculate the value of the activation energy.

In part **c**, you have two values of T and k so the expression

$\ln\dfrac{k_1}{k_2} = \dfrac{E_a}{R}\left(\dfrac{1}{T_2} - \dfrac{1}{T_1}\right)$ should be used.

d Explain how can the expression $\ln k = \dfrac{-E_{a<}}{RT} + \ln A$ can be used graphically to find the activation energy of a reaction.

The form of this equation is similar to that of a straight line, $y = mx + c$

e Explain why is it appropriate to consider the Arrhenius equation as describing the relationship between *rate* and temperature even though *rate* does not appear in the equation?

What is the relationship between rate and k?

❓ **Exam-style questions**

1 Which of the following methods could not be used to follow the rate of the following reaction?

$CuCO_3(s) + 2HCl(aq) \rightarrow CuCl_2(aq) + H_2O(l) + CO_2(g)$

A measuring the mass of the reaction mixture with time
B measuring the volume of water produced with time
C measuring the pH of the reaction mixture with time
D measuring the volume of gas produced with time

2   **For the reaction: X + Y → 2W + Z**

Which graph (A, B, C or D) in Figure 6.2 shows the change in the concentration of the products with time when equal amounts of X and Y are mixed together?

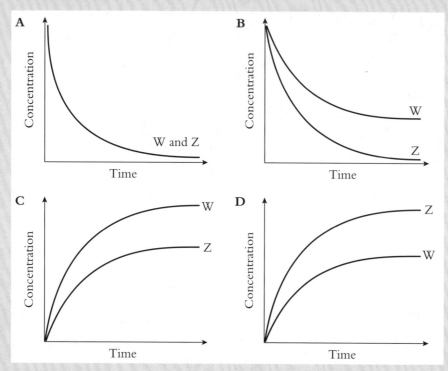

Figure 6.2

3   **Figure 6.3 shows the how the concentration of a product changes with time.**

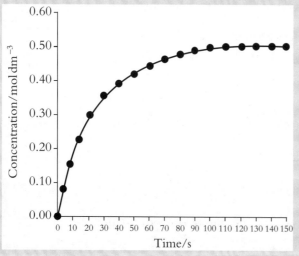

Figure 6.3 Concentration of a product against time.

Which row of Table 6.5 gives the correct values for the initial rate and the average rate of the reaction?

	Initial rate / mol dm^{-3} s^{-1}	Average rate / mol dm^{-3} s^{-1}
A	0.015	0.0050
B	0.30	0.00333
C	0	0.50
D	0.0050	0.0050

Table 6.5

4 Which statements best explain why increasing the temperature increases the rate of a reaction?

i The particles collide more frequently.

ii The proportion of collisions which are successful increases.

iii The activation energy is lower.

    A i and ii

    B i and iii

    C ii and iii

    D i, ii and iii

5 Which change is likely to have the greatest effect on the rate of reaction between a single lump of zinc of mass 1 g and 50 cm^3 of 0.200 mol cm^3 sulfuric acid at 25 °C?

A using 50 cm^3 of 0.200 mol dm^3 sulfuric acid at 25 °C with powdered zinc

B using 100 cm^3 of 0.200 mol dm^3 sulfuric acid at 25 °C with a single lump of zinc

C using 50 cm^3 of 0.200 mol dm^3 sulfuric acid at 10 °C with powdered zinc

D using 50 cm^3 of 0.250 mol dm^3 sulfuric acid at 40 °C with powdered zinc

6 **HL** The rate expression for the reaction $A + B \rightarrow C$ is rate $= k[A][B]^2$

What will the effect of doubling the concentrations of both A and B have on the overall rate?

A overall rate will increase by a factor of 2

B overall rate will increase by a factor of 4

C overall rate will increase by a factor of 6

D overall rate will increase by a factor of 8

7 **HL** Using the data from Table 6.6 deduce the rate expression for the reaction:

$Na_2S_2O_3(aq) + 2HCl(aq) \rightarrow 2NaCl(aq) + S(s) + SO_2(aq) + H_2O(l)$

$[Na_2S_2O_3(aq)]$ / mol dm^{-3}	$[HCl(aq)]$ / mol dm^{-3}	Rate / mol dm^{-3} s^{-1}
0.10	0.10	0.040
0.20	0.10	0.080
0.40	0.20	0.160

Table 6.6

A rate $= k[Na_2S_2O_3(aq)][HCl(aq)]$
B rate $= k[Na_2S_2O_3(aq)]$
C rate $= k[Na_2S_2O_3(aq)]^2$
D rate $= k[Na_2S_2O_3(aq)][HCl(aq)]^2$

8 **HL** The equation for the reaction of CH_3COCH_3 and I_2 is shown below

$CH_3COCH_3(aq) + I_2(aq) \rightarrow CH_3COCH_2I(aq) + H^+(aq) + I^-(aq)$

series of experiments were conducted and the rate equation was found to be
rate $= k[CH_3COCH_3][H^+]$
Which statement is not correct?
A The overall order of the reaction is second order.
B If the concentration of both reactants is doubled then the rate will also double.
C The hydrogen ions act as a catalyst.
D The reaction can be followed colorimetrically.

9 **HL** Which graph (A, B, C or D) in Figure 6.4 represents a first-order reaction?

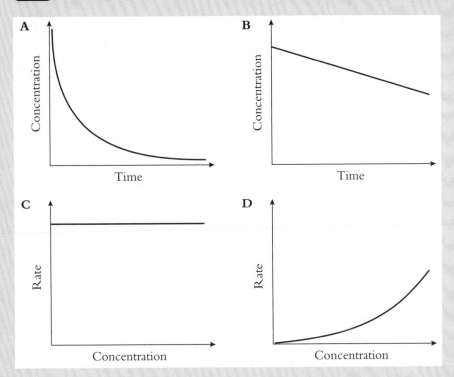

Figure 6.4

10 **HL** A series of experiments were conducted to measure the rate of a reaction at different temperatures.

Which of the following statements is correct?

A The gradient of a graph of rate vs temperature in Kelvin would equal the activation energy.

B The gradient of a graph of ln (rate) vs temperature in Kelvin would equal the activation energy.

C The gradient of a graph of ln (rate constant) vs $\dfrac{1}{\text{temperature (kelvin)}}$ would equal the activation energy.

D The gradient of a graph of ln (rate constant) vs $\dfrac{1}{\text{temperature (kelvin)}}$ would equal $\dfrac{-E_a}{R}$.

11 **a** Sketch a graph of the Maxwell–Boltzmann distribution including labels on both axes and explain what the graph shows. [3]

b Use your graph to explain the effect of a catalyst on the rate of a chemical reaction. [4]

c Add a second line to your graph to show the effect of decreasing the temperature on the shape of the curve. [2]

d Use your graph to explain the effect of decreasing the temperature on the rate of a chemical reaction. [2]

[Total 11]

12 Figure 6.5 shows the results of an experiment following the decomposition of 50 cm^3 hydrogen peroxide of concentration 1 mol dm^3 in the presence of 0.1 g of manganese(IV) oxide catalyst.

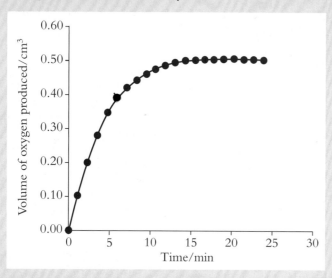

Figure 6.5 Decomposition of hydrogen peroxide.

The equation for the reaction is 2H$_2$O$_2$(aq) $\rightarrow$ 2H$_2$O(l) + O$_2$(g)

The reaction was followed by measuring the volume of oxygen produced.

a Calculate:

  i   the initial rate of reaction in cm^3 of O$_2$ per minute. [1]

  ii   the rate of reaction at 6 minutes in cm^3 of O$_2$ per minute. [1]

  iii the average rate of reaction in cm^3 of O$_2$ per minute. [1]

b Using the collision theory, explain your answers to parts **a i** and **ii**. [4]

c Predict how the graph produced would differ from that shown in Figure 6.5 if the following changes were made:

  i   the catalyst was ground to a finer powder but nothing else was changed from the original experiment. [2]

  ii   50 cm^3 of 0.050 mol dm^{-3} hydrogen peroxide was used but nothing else was changed from the original experiment. [2]

d It was decided to investigate the effect of the concentration of hydrogen peroxide on the rate of its decomposition by repeating the experiment at a number of different concentrations. It was noted that the decomposition of hydrogen peroxide is exothermic. Suggest what effect this would have on the accuracy of the data collected. [2]

[Total 13]

13 **The rate of a chemical reaction can be increased by the use of a suitable catalyst.**

a Define the term 'catalyst'. [1]

b In terms of the collision theory, explain how a catalyst increases the rate of a chemical reaction. [1]

c Draw a fully labelled sketch of the energy profile for an endothermic reaction with and without a catalyst. [3]

[Total 5]

14 **HL** Figure 6.6 shows the graph obtained during an experiment to determine the kinetics of the reaction between bromide ions and bromate ions which react according to the equation

$$5Br^- (aq) + BrO_3^- (aq) + 6H^+ (aq) \rightarrow 3Br_2 (aq) + 3H_2O (l)$$

The concentration of bromide ions was calculated by determining the concentration of bromine produced at timed intervals.

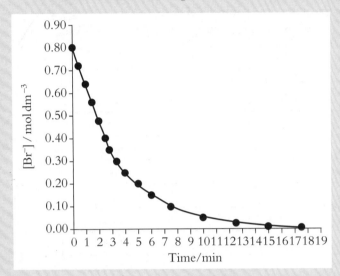

Figure 6.6 Kinetics of bromate/bromide reaction.

a Use the graph to determine the order of reaction with respect to bromide ions. [3]

b A series of further experiments were conducted and produced the results shown in Table 6.7:

Experiment	$[Br^-] / mol\,dm^{-3}$	$[BrO_3^-] / mol\,dm^{-3}$	$[H^+] / mol\,dm^{-3}$	Rate of reaction / $\times 10^{-5}\,mol\,dm^{-3}\,s^{-1}$
1	0.025	0.020	0.010	4.6
2	0.025	0.020	0.020	18.4
3	0.025	0.030	0.020	27.6
4	0.050	0.040	0.020	73.6
5	0.050	0.010	0.020	18.4

Table 6.7

  i   Deduce the order of reaction with respect to bromate and to hydrogen ions. [2]
 ii   Give the overall rate equation for the reaction and the overall order of the reaction. [1]
iii   Calculate the value of the rate constant for the reaction and its units. [2]

c Explain the effect of decreasing the temperature on the rate of the reaction and on the value of the rate constant. [3]

d Explain how the relationship between the rate constant and temperature can be used to determine the activation energy for this reaction. [2]

[Total 13]

15 **HL** The equation for the reaction between hydrogen and iodine monochloride is shown below

$$H_2(g) + 2ICl(g) \rightarrow I_2(g) + 2HCl(g) \quad \Delta H^\ominus = -155\,kmol^{-1}$$

The mechanism for the reaction to was found to have the following rate equation:
rate = $k[H_2][ICl]$

a Suggest a two-step mechanism for the reaction and identify the rate-determining step. [3]

b Sketch the energy profile diagram for your proposed mechanism. [4]

c The reaction was repeated at a range of temperatures and the data shown in Table 6.8 were produced:

Temperature/K	$\frac{1}{T}$ / K^{-1}	Rate constant / $\times$ 10^{-3} dm^3 mol^{-1} s^{-1}	ln k
270	0.00370	1.58	−6.45
280	0.00357	2.21	−6.11
290	0.00345	3.02	−5.80
300	0.00333	4.05	−5.51
310	0.00323	5.33	−5.23
320	0.00313	6.90	−4.98
330	0.00303	8.78	−4.74
340	0.00294	11.02	−4.51
350	0.00286	13.66	−4.29
360	0.00278	16.73	−4.09
370	0.00270	20.26	−3.90
380	0.00263	24.29	−3.72
390	0.00256	28.85	−3.55
400	0.00250	33.98	−3.38

Table 6.8

The relationship between temperature and the rate constant is described by the Arrhenius equation

$$\ln k = -\frac{E_a}{RT} + \ln A$$

i Plot a graph of ln k against $\frac{1}{T}$ and draw a line of best fit. [4]

ii Use your line of best fit to deduce the pre-exponential factor and the activation energy for the reaction. [4]

d Suggest what the magnitude of the value of A indicates about the likelihood that the particles collide with the correct orientation. [2]

[Total 17]

Equilibrium 7

Chapter outline

- Recall that in a closed system reversible reactions can reach a state of dynamic equilibrium and explain these terms.
- Recall what is meant by the term 'position of equilibrium'.
- Recall the equilibrium law and deduce an expression for the equilibrium expression for a given equation.
- Recall that the magnitude of the equilibrium constant indicates the extent of a reaction at equilibrium and is temperature dependent.
- Recall what is meant by the term 'reaction quotient'.
- Apply Le Chatelier's principle to predict the qualitative effect of a change in temperature, pressure, concentration or the addition of a catalyst to the position of equilibrium and the value of the equilibrium constant.
- Solve homogeneous equilibrium calculations using the expression for K_c. **HL**
- Explain Le Chatelier's principle using the equilibrium law. **HL**
- Solve calculations using $\Delta G = -RT\ln K$. **HL**

KEY TERMS

Closed system: A system where there is no exchange of matter with the surroundings.

Dynamic equilibrium: A system is said to be in a state of dynamic equilibrium when there appears to be no change in the macroscopic properties (e.g. all concentrations are constant); however, both forward and backward reactions are still continuing but at equal rates.

Equilibrium law: This states that the ratio of the products of the concentrations of the products (raised to the power of their coefficients in the balanced equation) to the product of the concentrations of the reactants (raised to the power of their coefficients in the balanced equation) is constant at a given temperature.

Le Chatelier's principle. This states that if a system in a state of dynamic equilibrium is subject to some change then the position of the equilibrium will shift in order to minimise the effect of that change.

Reaction quotient: The ratio of the products of the concentrations of the products (raised to the power of their coefficients in the balanced equation) to the product of the concentrations of the reactants (raised to the power of their coefficients in the balanced equation) at any given point in time (i.e. not just at equilibrium). At equilibrium the reaction quotient is equal to the equilibrium constant.

Reversible reaction: A reaction that can occur in either direction.

Exercise 7.1 – Reversible reactions and equilibrium

1 This question tests the basic ideas about equilibria.

   a Describe what is meant by the term 'dynamic equilibrium'.

   b Describe what is meant by the term 'closed system'.

   c The term equilibrium implies that something is 'equal' but what property is equal at equilibrium?

2 a Label the graph in Figure 7.1 to show the point at which equilibrium is reached.

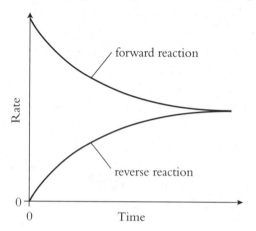

Figure 7.1 Rate of the forward and backward reactions for a reversible change.

This question probably addresses the most common misconception in this topic. Think carefully and check that you have the correct answer before moving on.

   b The rate of a reaction can be determined from the gradient of the graph at any given point. What is the gradient and therefore the rate of the forward and backward reactions at equilibrium for the reaction in Figure 7.1? Explain how this can be the case considering the definition of an equilibrium?

This is a very difficult question and is beyond the scope of the syllabus but it should make you think.

Exercise 7.2 – Physical equilibria

1 A state of equilibrium can also occur for processes that involve physical changes such as changing state or dissolving. The same conditions need to be met; constant temperature and a closed system.

Explain in terms of the movement of particles and the rates of the forward and backward processes how an equilibrium would be established when a volatile liquid is sealed in a container at constant temperature.

2 When adding increasing amounts of solid sodium chloride to a fixed volume of water, at what point would an equilibrium be established between the solid and dissolved sodium chloride?

Choosing the correct vocabulary is an important part of chemistry. If a question asks about the yield of a substance then the appropriate response would be to say that it increases, decreases or is unchanged. Position would be described by terms such as '**lying** to the left or right' or 'favouring the reactants or products'. A change in the conditions might lead to the forward or backward reaction being favoured or 'the equilibrium **moving** to the left or right'.

Exercise 7.3 – Position of equilibrium

1 The term 'position of equilibrium' is used to describe the relative amounts of products and reactants present at equilibrium.

    a A system at equilibrium contains relatively more reactants than products; how might the position of this equilibrium be described?

    b A system at equilibrium contains relatively more products than reactants; how might the position of this equilibrium be described?

2 Other descriptions of equilibria include ideas about the **yield** of a reaction or the forward or backward reaction being **favoured**.

    a A reversible reaction is said to have a high yield at a given temperature. What does this imply about the position of the equilibrium?

    b A change is made to a system in a state of dynamic equilibrium which favours the forward reaction. After a time, a new equilibrium position is established. Describe how the position of this new equilibrium will differ from the original position.

Exercise 7.4 – Le Chatelier's principle

It is important to differentiate between **describing** a change to the position of equilibrium and **explaining** it. Describing the change can be done in terms of stating whether it has shifted to the left or to the right whereas explaining it needs to include statements like: 'In order to minimise the effect of the change applied ...' These questions are often linked to questions about the rate of a reaction, especially with reference to industrial processes.

1 **a** State Le Chatelier's principle.

    b Explain the effect of increasing the temperature of a system in dynamic equilibrium if the forward reaction is exothermic.

    c Explain the effect of increasing the temperature of a system in dynamic equilibrium if the forward reaction is endothermic.

2 Explain the effect of increasing the pressure of the following systems in dynamic equilibrium

a $PCl_3(g) + Cl_2(g) \rightleftharpoons PCl_5(g)$

b $2NH_3(g) \rightleftharpoons N_2(g) + 3H_2(g)$

c $H_2(g) + I_2(g) \rightleftharpoons 2HI\ (g)$

d $CaCO_3(s) \rightleftharpoons CaO(s) + CO_2(g)$

e $H_2O(l) \rightleftharpoons H_2O(g)$

Equilibrium constants can be expressed in terms of the concentration of the species in the balanced chemical equation. The expression for the equilibrium constant can be deduced from the balanced equation. The equilibrium constant for a gas-phase reaction is normally described in terms of the partial pressure of the gases but this is beyond the scope of the syllabus and so concentration is used for these reactions in the same way as it is for reactions occurring in a liquid or aqueous phase.

3 Explain the effect of decreasing the concentration of the underlined species on the position of the following systems in dynamic equilibrium:

a $CH_3OH(l) + CH_3COOH(l) \rightleftharpoons \underline{CH_3COOCH_3}(l) + H_2O(l)$

b $Cu^{2+}(aq) + 4\underline{Cl^-}(aq) \rightleftharpoons CuCl_4^{2+}(aq)$

c $Fe^{3+}(aq) + \underline{SCN^-}(aq) \rightleftharpoons [FeSCN]^{2+}(aq)$

d What effect will adding alkali have on the position of the following equilibrium?

$Cr_2O_7^{2-}(aq) + H_2O(l) \rightleftharpoons 2CrO_4^{2-}(aq) + 2H^+(aq)$

Exercise 7.5 – Equilibrium constants

1 a State the equilibrium law.

b What is meant by the term 'reaction quotient'?

c Describe how the reaction quotient differs from an equilibrium constant.

2 Deduce the equilibrium expressions for the following reactions:

a $2H_2(g) + CO(g) \rightleftharpoons CH_3OH(g)$

b $CH_4(g) + H_2O(g) \rightleftharpoons CO(g) + 3H_2(g)$

c $H_2(g) + I_2(g) \rightleftharpoons 2HI(g)$

d $[Co(H_2O)_6]^{2+}(aq) + 4Cl^-(aq) \rightleftharpoons [CoCl_4]^{2-}(aq) + 6H_2O(l)$

3 Give equilibrium expressions for the following reactions and determine the relationships between their values:

Equation 1: $CO(g) + 2H_2(g) \rightleftharpoons CH_3OH(g)$

Equation 2: $\frac{1}{2}CO(g) + H_2(g) \rightleftharpoons \frac{1}{2}CH_3OH(g)$

Equation 3: $CH_3OH(g) \rightleftharpoons CO(g) + 2H_2(g)$

4 A reversible reaction has a reaction quotient of 0.258 at a given temperature. The mixture is allowed to reach equilibrium at the same temperature and it is found that the equilibrium constant is 0.123. Predict the difference in the composition of the mixture once the equilibrium has been established.

As well as being able to predict the effect of a change on the position of equilibrium, you also need to know the effect of a change on the value of the equilibrium constant. The remainder of the questions will check your understanding of this. It is best to approach these question through logic and to deduce the answers through reasoning rather than trying to memorise a large number of different scenarios.

5 The temperature of a reaction in a state of dynamic equilibrium is increased and the equilibrium is found to move to the right.

    a What can be deduced about the sign of the enthalpy change for the forward reaction?

    b What effect would this have on the value of the equilibrium constant?

6 Describe the effect of the following changes on the position of equilibrium and on the value of the equilibrium constant for the following reaction:

$$C_2H_4(g) + H_2O(g) \rightleftharpoons C_2H_5OH(g) \qquad \Delta H = -45\,kJ\,mol^{-1}$$

    a increasing the temperature

    b increasing the pressure of the system

    c removing ethanol from the mixture as it is formed

    d using a catalyst

HL Exercise 7.6 – Equilibrium calculations

It is important to always use equilibrium concentrations in equilibrium calculations and not equilibrium amounts. Concentration is measured in $mol\,dm^{-3}$. Although concentration is not the usual way of describing the amount of gas in a given volume, it can still be applied to gas-phase reactions.

1 An equilibrium mixture was found to have a concentration of $0.250\,mol\,dm^{-3}$ aqueous ammonia, $2.11 \times 10^{-3}\,mol\,dm^{-3}$ hydroxide ions and $2.11 \times 10^{-3}\,mol\,dm^{-3}$ ammonium ions.

    a Write an expression for the equilibrium constant for this reaction:

$$NH_3(aq) + H_2O(l) \rightleftharpoons NH_4^+(aq) + OH^-(aq)$$

    b Calculate the value of the equilibrium constant at this temperature for the reaction.

2 A sealed flask of volume $3\,dm^3$ and at temperature T at equilibrium was found to contain 1 mol of PCl_3, 2 mol of PCl_5 and 1.5 mol of Cl_2. The equation for the reaction is:
$$PCl_3(g) + Cl_2(g) \rightleftharpoons PCl_5(g)$$

    a Write an expression for the equilibrium constant for this reaction.

    b Calculate the concentrations of the three gases at equilibrium in $mol\,dm^{-3}$.

    c Calculate the equilibrium constant at this temperature.

3 1 mol of nitrogen was mixed with 4 mol of hydrogen in a sealed vessel of volume $2\,dm^3$ at a fixed temperature and allowed to reach equilibrium according to the equation:
$$N_2(g) + 3H_2(g) \rightleftharpoons 2NH_3(g)$$
Once established, it was found that the mixture contained only 2.2 mol of hydrogen.

    a Write an expression for the equilibrium constant for this reaction.

    b Deduce the amount of hydrogen that has been used in this reaction.

    c Deduce the amount of nitrogen used and hence the amount of nitrogen remaining at equilibrium.

    d Deduce the amount of ammonia formed.

    e Deduce the equilibrium concentrations of nitrogen, hydrogen and ammonia in $mol\,dm^{-3}$.

    f Use the answers for part **e** to calculate the value of the equilibrium constant.

This question is very similar to Question 3 but has not been structured. Follow a similar sequence of steps to determine the value of the equilibrium constant.

4 A solution containing $0.050\,mol$ of Fe^{3+} was added to an equal volume of a solution containing $0.050\,mol$ of SCN^- ions. On mixing, a blood-red solution of $[FeSCN]^{2+}$ was formed according to the equation:

$Fe^{3+}(aq) + SCN^-(aq) \rightleftharpoons [FeSCN]^{2+}(aq)$

The equilibrium concentration of the $[FeSCN]^{2+}$ ions was found to be $0.020\,mol\,dm^{-3}$. The total volume of the mixture was $0.50\,dm^3$. Calculate the equilibrium constant for the reaction.

This question is very similar to Question 4 but with a different unknown. Imagine the amount of ester reacting is x, then the amount remaining at equilibrium = $0.01 - x$. Then follow a similar sequence of steps.

5 A mixture of $0.01\,mol$ of ester and $0.01\,mol$ of water were allowed to reach equilibrium at room temperature according to the equation:

ester(l) + water(l) $\rightleftharpoons$ carboxylic acid(l) + alcohol(l)

Given that the equilibrium constant for this reaction is 0.25 at room temperature, deduce the composition of the equilibrium mixture.

HL Exercise 7.7 – K_c and ΔG

This is a particularly difficult section of the topic to understand but there are ways to simplify it.

1 Remember that the formula $\Delta G = -RT \ln K_c$ is given in the data book.

2 Understand that when ΔG is positive then K is small ($K < 1$) and the equilibrium lies to the left and when ΔG is negative then K is large ($K > 1$) and the equilibrium lies to the right. Type any random negative or positive value for ΔG into a calculator to demonstrate this.

3 The confusion is often linked to the statement that $\Delta G = 0$ at equilibrium; in this case, how can it also equal $RT \ln K_c$? The answer is complicated but, in simple terms, the expression $\Delta G = RT \ln K_c$ calculates ΔG for the reaction as if all the reactants turned into products, whereas at equilibrium this is not the case.

4 ΔG for $N_2 + 3H_2 \rightarrow 2NH_3$ is equal but opposite in sign to ΔG for $2NH_3 \rightarrow N_2 + 3H_2$. The amount of reactants turning into product for a reaction at equilibrium is such that $\Delta G = 0$.

Watch the units of T and of ΔG.

1 Calculate ΔG given the following values of K_c and comment on the position of equilibrium in each case.
   a $K_c = 4.56$ at a temperature of $298\,K$.
   b $K_c = 1.25 \times 10^{-4}$ at a temperature of $100\,°C$.

2 Calculate the equilibrium constant for the following values of ΔG and comment on the position of equilibrium in each case.

  a $\Delta G = 7.5\,\text{kJ}\,\text{mol}^{-1}$ at a temperature of $500\,\text{K}$.

  b $\Delta G = -20.0\,\text{kJ}\,\text{mol}^{-1}$ at a temperature of $25\,°\text{C}$.

? Exam-style questions

1 Which of the following statements about dynamic equilibria is true?

  A The forward and backward reactions have both stopped.

  B The rate of both the forward and backward reactions is zero.

  C The rate of both the forward and backward reactions is the same.

  D The concentrations of the reactants and of the products are the same.

2 Which of the following systems can reach a state of dynamic equilibrium?

  A an open container of water

  B a closed container of water

  C an open container of a saturated solution of sodium chloride

  D a closed container of sodium chloride crystals

3 Consider the endothermic reaction $2HI(g) \rightleftharpoons H_2(g) + I_2(g)$ Which option (A, B, C or D) in Table 7.1 describes the effect of increasing the temperature on the amount of hydrogen iodide, the position of equilibrium and on the value of the equilibrium constant?

	Amount of HI(g)	Position of equilibrium	Equilibrium constant
A	increases	shifts to the left	decreases
B	decreases	shifts to the right	stays the same
C	increases	stays the same	increases
D	decreases	shifts to the right	increases

Table 7.1

4 Which is the correct equilibrium expression for the reaction:
$4NH_3(g) + 5O_2(g) \rightleftharpoons 4NO(g) + 6H_2O(g)$

  A $K_c = \dfrac{[NO]^4 \times [H_2O]^6}{[NH_3]^4 \times [O_2]^5}$

  C $K_c = \dfrac{4[NO] \times 6[H_2O]}{4[NH_3] \times 5[O_2]}$

  B $K_c = \dfrac{[NO]^4 + [H_2O]^6}{[NH_3]^4 + [O_2]^5}$

  D $K_c = \dfrac{[NH_3]^4 \times [O_2]^5}{[NO]^4 \times [H_2O]^6}$

5 The value of the equilibrium constant for the reaction below is 4.00 at 100 °C.

2A(aq) + B(aq) ⇌ 2C(aq) + 2D(aq)

Deduce the value of the equilibrium constant for the following reaction at the same temperature.

C(aq) + D(aq) ⇌ A(aq) + $\frac{1}{2}$ B(aq)

    A 2.00   **C** 0.25

    B 16.00   **D** 0.50

6 Consider the reaction: $SO_3(g) + NO(g) ⇌ SO_2(g) + NO_2(g)$

Which of the following mixtures would not reach a state of dynamic equilibrium?

A a mixture of 1 mol of SO_3 with 1 mol of NO(g)

B a mixture of 1 mol of SO_3 with 1 mol of NO_2(g)

C a mixture of 1 mol of SO_3 with 2 mol of NO(g) and 1 mol of NO_2(g)

D a mixture of 1 mol of SO_2 with 1 mol of NO_2(g)

7 A mixture was found to contain $2.00\,mol\,dm^{-3}$ of substance A, $1.00\,mol\,dm^{-3}$ of substance B and $2.00\,mol\,dm^{-3}$ of substance C at a temperature of 50 °C. If the equation for the reaction is 2A + B ⇌ C, and its equilibrium constant = 2.0, then which statement is true?

A The reaction is at equilibrium.

B The reaction is not at equilibrium and will proceed to the left.

C The reaction is not at equilibrium and will proceed to the right.

D The reaction cannot reach equilibrium.

8 **HL** $100\,cm^3$ of a solution in a state of dynamic equilibrium mixture was found to contain 5 mol of A, 2 mol of B and 5 mol of C.

If the equation for the reaction is A(aq) + 2B(aq) ⇌ 3C(aq) then calculate the equilibrium constant for the reaction.

    A 6.25   **C** 12.5

    B 31.25   **D** 1.25

9 **HL** The equilibrium constant at a fixed temperature for the reaction below is 1.25.

$NO(g) + NO_2(g) ⇌ N_2O_3(g)$

Which statement correctly describes a mixture with a composition of $1\,mol\,dm^{-3}$ of NO, $1.5\,mol\,dm^3$ NO_2 and $2\,mol\,dm^{-3}$ of N_2O_3?

A $Q = 0.8$ and the system is not at equilibrium

B $Q = 1.33$ and the system is at equilibrium

C $Q = 0.75$ and the system is at equilibrium

D $Q = 1.33$ and the system is not at equilibrium

10 **HL** The reaction between carbon monoxide and hydrogen to produce methanol has a free energy change of $+8.82\,kJ\,mol^{-1}$ at 298 K.

The equation for the reaction is $CO(g) + 2H_2(g) ⇌ CH_3OH(g)$

What information can be deduced from this value?

A K_c must be negative as ΔG is positive.

B K_c must be positive because ΔG is positive.

C $K_c > 1$ and the position of equilibrium lies to the right.

D $K_c < 1$ and the position of equilibrium lies to the left.

11 Chlorine reacts with water to form a mixture of hydrochloric and chloric(I) acids according to the equation: $Cl_2(aq) + H_2O(l) \rightleftharpoons HCl(aq) + HClO(aq)$

  a Describe the features of a dynamic equilibrium. [5]
  b Deduce an expression for the equilibrium constant for this reaction. [1]
  c Determine the effect on both the position of the equilibrium and on the value of the equilibrium constant if additional chlorine gas was dissolved in the mixture. [2]
  d Explain the effect of adding alkali to the mixture. [4]

[Total 12]

12 A sealed flask containing a volatile liquid and its vapour are in state of dynamic equilibrium. The temperature of the flask is increased by a few degrees.
  Explain the changes that occur and describe the change to the composition of the flask at the new temperature. [6]

[Total 6]

13 The production of sulfur(VI) oxide is one stage in the industrial manufacture of sulfuric acid in the Contact process. $2SO_2(g) + O_2(g) \rightleftharpoons 2SO_3(g)$
  Figure 7.2 shows the energy profile for the reaction in the presence of vanadium(V) oxide which acts as a catalyst.

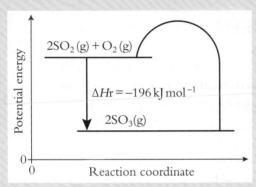

Figure 7.2 Energy profile diagram for the reaction $2\,SO_2(g) + O_2(g) \rightleftharpoons 2\,SO_3$ (g).

  a Sketch a diagram to show the energy profile of the un–catalysed reaction, clearly indicating its activation energy. [2]
  b Deduce an expression for the equilibrium constant, K_c, for this reaction. [1]
  c Describe the effect of the catalyst on the position of the equilibrium and on the value of K_c. [2]
  d Explain the effect of increasing the temperature and increasing the pressure on the position of this equilibrium and on the value of the equilibrium constant. [6]

[Total 11]

14 $4\,mol$ of NO_2 was placed in a sealed vessel of volume $1\,dm^3$ at a constant temperature. It gradually reacted according to the equation $2NO_2(g) \rightleftharpoons N_2O_4(g)$ Eventually the mixture reached a point of dynamic equilibrium. It was later found that the mixture contained $1\,mol$ of N_2O_4.

    a Deduce the number of moles of NO_2 used up in the formation of the N_2O_4. [1]

    b Sketch a graph of the concentration of N_2O_4 and of NO_2 against time. [2]

    c Label the point on your graph that clearly shows the time at which equilibrium is reached. [1]

    d The experiment was later repeated at a higher temperature. It was found that the amount of N_2O_4 in the mixture on this occasion was less than $1\,mol$. Deduce whether the dimerisation of NO_2 is endo- or exothermic and give your reasoning. [3]

                                                   [Total 7]

15 **HL** A mixture of $3\,mol$ of PCl_3 and $2\,mol$ of Cl_2 was allowed to react in a vessel of volume $2\,dm^3$. At equilibrium it was found that the mixture contained $1.5\,mol$ of PCl_5. The equation for the reaction is $PCl_3(g) + Cl_2(g) \rightleftharpoons PCl_5(g)$ Calculate the equilibrium constant for this reaction. [3]

16 **HL** In a laboratory experiment to investigate the hydrolysis of an ester, $4.00\,cm^3$ of the liquid ester of $M_r = 74.09\,g\,mol^{-1}$ and density $0.932\,g\,cm^{-3}$ was mixed with $2.00\,cm^3$ of hydrochloric acid of concentration $1.00\,mol\,dm^{-3}$. The water in the acid reacts with ester according to the following equation:

$CH_3COOCH_3(l) + H_2O(l) \rightleftharpoons CH_3COOH(l) + CH_3OH(l)$

ester   + water $\rightleftharpoons$ carboxylic acid + alcohol

The hydrochloric acid acts as a catalyst and remains at the end of the reaction. The mixture was allowed to stand for 24 hours at room temperature and then analysed by titration with sodium hydroxide solution to determine the amount of acid in the mixture. $28.50\,cm^3$ of $0.100\,mol\,dm^{-3}$ NaOH was required to neutralise all of the acid in the mixture.

    a Calculate the number of moles of ester in the initial mixture. [1]

    b Calculate the number of moles of water in the initial mixture. [1]

       (All of the hydrochloric acid solution can be assumed to be water with a density of $1.00\,g\,cm^{-3}$.)

    c Calculate the number of moles of acid in the initial mixture. [1]

    d Using the data from the titration, calculate the number of moles of acid in the mixture after it had been allowed to stand for 24 hours. [1]

    e Calculate the number of moles of acid produced by the hydrolysis of the ester. [1]

    f Using the equation above, calculate the number of moles of alcohol also produced and the number of moles of ester and water remaining at the end of the 24 hours. [3]

    g Calculate the concentrations of ester, water, carboxylic acid and alcohol at the end of the 24-hour period. [4]

    h Calculate the reaction quotient for the mixture. [1]

    i Given that the equilibrium constant for this hydrolysis is 0.235, comment on whether or not the mixture had reached equilibrium. [1]

                                                   [Total 14]

Acids and bases 8

Chapter outline

- Recall the definitions of Brønsted–Lowry acids and bases and deduce these in a chemical reaction, including the identification of conjugate acid–base pairs.
- Recall the terms 'amphoteric' and 'amphiprotic'.
- Describe the reactions of acids with metals, metal oxides, metal hydroxides, hydrogen carbonates and carbonates.
- Recall that pH is a measure of the concentration of aqueous hydrogen ions and solve problems involving pH and the concentration of hydrogen ions and hydroxide ions.
- Explain the difference between strong and weak acids and bases and describe experiments that could be used to distinguish these.
- Recall what is meant by acid deposition and explain some of the problems associated with acid deposition as well as pre- and post-combustion methods of reducing sulfur oxide emissions.
- Recall the definitions of Lewis acids and bases and recognise these in a chemical reaction. **HL**
- Deduce the dissociation constant for weak acids and bases. **HL**
- Sketch and explain the important features of titration curves including the composition and action of a buffer and use these curves to deduce the pK_a or pK_b value of a weak acid or base. **HL**
- Explain how an acid–base indicator works and select a suitable indicator for a titration. **HL**

KEY TERMS

Acid deposition: A more general term than acid rain; it refers to any process in which acidic substances leave the atmosphere and are deposited on the Earth's surface.

Brønsted–Lowry acid: A proton (H^+) donor.

Brønsted–Lowry base: A proton (H^+) acceptor.

pH: A measure of the concentration of hydrogen ions in an aqueous solution.
$pH = -\log_{10}[H^+]$

Strong acid/base: An acid/base that is completely dissociated into its ions in aqueous solution.

Weak acid/base: An acid/base that is only partially dissociated into its ions in aqueous solution.

Acid dissociation constant, K_a: The equilibrium constant for the dissociation of a weak acid. For an acid HA, then its dissociation can be represented by the equation

$$HA(aq) \rightleftharpoons H^+(aq) + A^-(aq) \text{ and } K_a = \frac{[H^+][A^-]}{[HA]}$$

Base ionisation (dissociation) constant, K_b: The equilibrium constant for the dissociation of a weak base. For a base B, then its dissociation can be represented by the equation

$$B(aq) + H_2O(l) \rightleftharpoons BH^+(aq) + OH^-(aq) \text{ and } K_b = \frac{[BH^+][OH^-]}{[B]}$$

Buffer solution: A solution that resists changes in pH when a small amount of acid or alkali is added to it.

Lewis acid: An electron (lone) pair acceptor.

Lewis base: An electron (lone) pair donor.

Salt hydrolysis: The reaction of the conjugate base of a weak acid or the conjugate acid of a weak base with water. This is why solutions of the salt of a weak acid or weak base are not neutral.

Exercise 8.1 – Brønsted–Lowry acids and bases

Man has long sought to make sense of the world by identifying patterns and classifying things into groups with similar properties, whether it be species or chemicals. Ideas about acids go back to the ancient Greeks who classified substances by taste; acids taste sour. The word 'acid' is believe to be derived from the Latin word for sour, *acere* and the common name for vinegar is acetic acid – an acid known for thousands of years.

The idea that the properties of acidic solutions is due to the presence of hydrogen is attributed to Svante Arrhenius in 1884. The Brønsted–Lowry theory (1923) about acid–base reactions involving the transfer of a hydrogen ion between species can be thought of as an extension of this idea.

Conjugate acid–base pairs are species that differ from each other by one proton (H^+). When an acid donates a proton it forms its conjugate base and vice versa. To find the conjugate base of an acid, remove H^+ from the formula. To find the conjugate acid of a base, add H^+ to its formula.

1 Deduce the conjugate acid–base pairs for the following species.

	Conjugate acid	Conjugate base
a	$HClO_4$	
b	H_2SO_4	
c	HCl	
d	HNO_3	
e		NO_2^-
f	H_2S	
g		SO_3^{2-}
h		HPO_4^{2-}
i	HCN	
j		NH_3
k	H_2CO_3	
l	HCO_3^-	
m		PO_4^{3-}
n		OH^-
o	NH_3	

Table 8.1

2 Identify the acid–base conjugate pairs in the following equations.
   a $H_2SO_4(aq) + HNO_3(aq) \rightarrow H_2NO_3^+(aq) + HSO_4^-(aq)$
   b $NH_3(aq) + H_2O(l) \rightarrow NH_4^+(aq) + OH^-(aq)$
   c $HSO_4^-(aq) + H_2O(l) \rightarrow H_3O^+(aq) + SO_4^{2-}(aq)$
   d $H_2PO_4^-(aq) + HCO_3^-(aq) \rightarrow HPO_4^{2-}(aq) + H_2CO_3(aq)$

There will be one acid and one base on both sides of the equation but the pairs will be across the arrow; the acid and its conjugate pair will be on different sides of the equation.

HL Exercise 8.2 – Lewis acids and bases

The idea of Lewis acids was developed at the same time as the Brønsted–Lowry theory. It has a broader scope than Brønsted–Lowry as it is not restricted to species that contain a hydrogen ion.
It should be remembered that all Brønsted–Lowry acids are Lewis acids but not all Lewis acids are Brønsted–Lowry ones; similarly, with bases.
In organic chemistry Lewis acids are termed electrophiles and Lewis bases are referred to as nucleophiles. This is covered in Topic 10.

1 a Define the terms 'Lewis acid' and 'Lewis base'.
  b What type of bond is always formed in a Lewis acid–base reaction?

Consider the
Lewis structure
(dot/cross
diagram) of each:
does it have a lone
pair of electrons
it can donate
(Lewis base)? or
a vacant orbital
into which it can
accept a lone pair
of electrons (Lewis
acid)?

c Indicate whether the following species can act as Lewis acids or Lewis bases:
   i NH_3
   ii $AlCl_3$
   iii Cu^{2+}
   iv Cl^-
   v CO

Exercise 8.3 – Properties of acids and bases

A salt can be described as a compound formed when the hydrogen ions in an acid are replaced by a metal ion or the ammonium ion. There are a number of reactions of acids in which salts are formed.

These word
equations are
essential learning.

1 a Give the general word equation for the reaction of an acid with the following:
   i   metal
   ii carbonate
   iii hydrogen carbonate
   iv metal oxide
   v metal hydroxide
   vi alkali
   vii base
  b Explain why all alkalis are bases but not all bases are alkalis.

2 Write balanced equations for the following reactions. State symbols are not required.

Knowing the
definition of
a base and of
an alkali are
important here.
Look at these
in the list of key
terms at the start
of this chapter.

> One of the most problematic aspects to these equations is the formulas of the salts. Learning the formulas and charges of a few common compounds and ions is recommended.
> A good starting point is: Cl^-, SO_4^{2-}, CO_3^{2-}, HCO_3^-, OH^-, NO_3^- CH_3COO^-, H^+, NH_4^+, HCl, H_2SO_4, HNO_3, CH_3COOH. Group 1 metals $= M^+$. Group 2 metals $= M^{2+}$.

  a zinc and hydrochloric acid
  b magnesium hydroxide and nitric acid
  c copper(II) carbonate and sulfuric acid
  d sodium hydrogencarbonate and phosphoric acid
  e calcium oxide and ethanoic acid
  f sulfuric acid and potassium hydroxide
  g hydrochloric acid and ammonia solution
  h ethanoic acid and barium hydroxide
  i ethanoic acid and magnesium
  j nitric acid and copper(II) carbonate
  k sulfuric acid and zinc oxide

3 Suggest suitable reagents that could be used to form solutions of the following salts:

Avoid the acid + metal reaction as this will only work for metals above hydrogen on the activity series (Topic 9).
Avoid acid + metal hydrogencarbonates, apart from group 1 and 2 and ammonium hydrogencarbonate, as most metals do not form these.

    a copper(II) sulfate
    b zinc nitrate
    c sodium ethanoate
    d ammonium chloride

Exercise 8.4 – The pH scale

The pH scale is used to indicate whether a solution is acidic, alkaline or neutral.
This section deals with what the numbers mean.

1 a Define the term 'pH'.
   b A solution of hydrochloric acid is diluted by a factor of 100.
      Determine the change in its pH.

pH is a log (base 10) scale. This means that 1 pH unit represents a 10-fold change in the hydrogen ion concentration.

Use the formula $pH = -\log_{10} [H^+]$. Practise this on your calculator.

2 a Calculate the pH of the following solutions:
    i 0.25 mol dm^{-3} HCl(aq)
    ii $0.025 \text{ mol dm}^{-3}$ H_2SO_4(aq) (assume that it is fully dissociated)

Note the $[H^+]$ in part **ii** is not the same as $[H_2SO_4]$ as sulfuric acid is diprotic (can donate two H^+ ions).

   b What is the hydrogen ion concentration of solutions with the following pH?

More calculator practice. You need to be able to get this conversion from pH to $[H^+]$ the correct way around. $[H^+] = 10^{-pH}$.

    i   pH = 3.0
    ii   pH = 4.5
    iii   pH = 7.0
    iv   pH = 10.2

In part **3b** you will need to firstly calculate the $[OH^-]$; this is not the same as $[Ba(OH)_2]$.

3 a How can the ionic product constant for water be used to find the pH of an alkaline solution?

b Calculate the pH of the following solutions:
  i 0.10 mol dm^{-3} NaOH
  ii 0.075 mol dm^{-3} Ba(OH)$_2$

Use the formula $K_w = [H^+(aq)][OH^-(aq)] = 1.0 \times 10^{-14}$ (at 25 °C)

c Calculate the hydroxide ion concentration of the following solutions:
  i HNO$_3$ of pH 2.50
  ii H$_2$SO$_4$ of pH 0.50

4 What is the concentration of the following solutions?
  a nitric acid with a pH of 3.70
  b sulfuric acid with a pH of 2.00, assuming it is fully dissociated

First calculate the $[H^+]$ from the pH, then consider the formula of the substance: how many H$^+$ ions are there in the formula of the acid?

  c potassium hydroxide with a pH of 11.2
  d barium hydroxide with a pH of 9.6

First calculate the $[H^+]$ from the pH, then calculate $[OH^-]$ using the value of K_w and finally consider the formula of the substance: how many OH$^-$ ions are there in the formula of the base?

Exercise 8.5 – Strong and weak acids and bases

The pH scale is not a measure of the strength of an acid, although it is hardly surprising that many people believe this to be the case as students are often introduced to the pH scale in this way early in their chemistry education. It is true to say that the pH of a weak acid will be higher than that of a strong acid of the same concentration; does the oversimplification of complex ideas aid understanding or hinder it?

Think about the arrow in the equation. How can you show that not all of the ethanoic acid has dissociated into its ions?

A weak base is a proton acceptor.

1 a Describe what is meant by the term 'the strength of an acid'?
  b Give an equation to show that nitric acid is a strong acid.
  c Give an equation to show that ethanoic acid is a weak acid.
  d Give an equation to show how ammonia acts as a weak base.
  e Describe the relationship between the strength of a base and the strength of its conjugate acid.

2 Describe and explain the differences in the observations for a strong and a weak acid of the same concentration in the following experiments:

   a A short length of magnesium ribbon is added to a small volume of each acid in a test tube.

   b The pH of each acid was measured using a pH probe.

   c The conductivity of a sample of each acid is determined using a conductivity meter.

The key word is 'observations': what would you see?

Exercise 8.6 – Acid deposition

Acid deposition refers to any process in which acidic substances are deposited on the surface of the earth. It is a broader term than acid rain because it also includes the deposition of gases and solids.

Dry deposition is caused by acidic gases rather than acidic solutions. Choose easy examples like sulfur and nitrogen oxides.

1 **a** Explain why rain water is naturally acidic. Use equations to explain your answer.

   b Give equations to show the formation of two substances that lead to dry acid deposition.

   c Describe the anthropogenic source of one of these substances.

   d Give three examples of the effect of acid deposition on the environment.

Anthropogenic means that they have been produced by human activity.

2 **a** Describe one pre-combustion and one post-combustion method of reducing sulfur oxide emissions.

   b Other than the methods described in the answer to part **a**, suggest how the amount of the substances that lead to acid deposition can be reduced in the following industries:

     i transport

     ii energy generation

   c Explain what is meant by the 'liming' of lakes and give equations to show how this can reverse the effect of acid deposition.

HL Exercise 8.7 – Acid and base calculations

The dissociation of a weak acid can be described by the equation:

$$HA(aq) + H_2O(l) \rightleftharpoons H_3O^+(aq) + A^-(aq)$$

The equilibrium expression for this equation can be written as:

$$K_c = \frac{[H_3O^+][A^-]}{[HA][H_2O]}.$$

As water is the solvent in this system, its concentration is constant and so its value is incorporated into the value of the equilibrium constant. This equilibrium constant is known as the acid dissociation constant, $K_a = \dfrac{[H^+][A^-]}{[HA]}$

K_b is the base dissociation constant and is the equivalent expression for a base.

$$B(aq) + H_2O(l) \rightleftharpoons BH^+(aq) + OH^-(aq)$$

$$K_b = \frac{\left[BH^+\right]\left[OH^-\right]}{[B]}$$

1 a Give the equation for the dissociation of ethanoic acid and write the expression for K_a.
  b Give the an equation to show how ammonia acts as a base in water and write the expression for K_b.

2 a Identify the strongest acid from the following pairs:
   i   chloroethanoic acid ($K_a = 1.35 \times 10^{-3}$) and dichloroethanoic acid ($K_a = 4.45 \times 10^{-2}$)
   ii   benzoic acid (p$K_a = 4.2$) and butanoic acid (p$K_a = 4.83$)
   iii phenol (p$K_a = 9.99$) and 3-nitrophenol ($K_a = 4.37 \times 10^{-9}$)
  b Identify the strongest base from the following pairs:
   i   methylamine ($K_b = 4.57 \times 10^{-4}$) and trimethylamine ($K_b = 6.3 \times 10^{-5}$)
   ii   sodium carbonate (p$K_b = 3.68$) and ammonia (p$K_b = 4.75$)
   iii phenylamine (p$K_b = 9.13$) and ethylamine ($K_b = 4.47 \times 10^{-4}$)

Look at the equations that represent acid or base dissociation and the equilibrium expressions. The larger the value of K then the more top-heavy the fraction (numerator is larger than the denominator) so the equilibrium must lie more to the right = more dissociated = stronger.
In paper 2 you will have your calculator so if you cannot remember the relationship between K and pK then enter any 2 random numbers for K. You will soon see that the larger the value entered then the lower the pK value is and vice versa.

3 a Calculate the acid dissociation constant for chloric(I) acid (HClO) at 25 °C if a 0.250 mol dm^{-3} solution dissociates to give a hydrogen ion concentration of 9.64×10^{-5} mol dm^{-3}. State any assumptions used in this calculation.

Start from the expression $K_a = \dfrac{\left[H^+\right]\left[A^-\right]}{[HA]}$

In a weak acid solution $[H^+] = [A^-]$ for monoprotic acids.

  b Calculate the base dissociation constant for dimethylamine at 25 °C if a 0.300 mol dm^{-3} solution dissociates to give a hydroxide ion concentration of 0.0127 mol dm^{-3}. State any assumptions used in this calculation.

4 a Calculate the pH of the following solutions.
   i   0.100 mol dm^{-3} pentanoic acid ($K_a = 1.48 \times 10^{-5}$)
   ii   0.500 mol dm^{-3} ethanoic acid (p$K_a = 4.76$)

Again use the expression $K_a = \dfrac{\left[H^+\right]\left[A^-\right]}{[HA]}$ but this time it is $[H^+]$ that is unknown.

b Calculate the pK_a of phenol if a $0.100 \text{ mol dm}^{-3}$ solution of it has a pH of 5.5. State any assumptions used in the calculation.

5 a Calculate the pOH of the following solutions. State any assumptions used in the calculation.

   i $0.250 \text{ mol dm}^{-3}$ ammonia ($K_b = 1.78 \times 10^{-5}$)

   ii $0.250 \text{ mol dm}^{-3}$ ethylamine ($pK_b = 3.35$)

$pOH = -\log_{10}[OH^-]$.

Use the expression $K_b = \dfrac{\left[BH^+\right]\left[OH^-\right]}{\left[B\right]}$

---

b Calculate the pH of the solutions in part **a**.

Use the expression for K_w.

---

6 K_a, K_b and K_w, like all dissociation constants, are dependent on temperature. As dissociation is an endothermic process, their values increase at higher temperatures.

  a What effect does temperature have on the values of pK_a, pK_b and pK_w?

  b The pH of pure water at $50\,^\circ C$ is 6.63. Is this water neutral? Explain your answer.

  c Calculate the pH of a $0.010 \text{ mol dm}^{-3}$ solution of potassium hydroxide at $10\,^\circ C$, given that pK_w at this temperature is 14.53.

> For part **a**, write expressions for K_a and K_b, then rearrange and substitute until only K_a, K_b and K_w remain. Part **b** is more difficult unless you are very confident in maths – best to just learn this one!

7 In solution an acid–base conjugate pair can be described by the following equations:

Equation 1: $HA(aq) \rightleftharpoons H^+(aq) + A^-(aq)$

Equation 2: $A^-(aq) + H_2O(l) \rightleftharpoons HA(aq) + OH^-(aq)$

K_a is the acid dissociation constant for acid HA in equation 1 and K_b is the base dissociation constant for base A^- in equation 2.

  a What is the relationship between K_a, K_b and K_w?

  b What is the relationship between pK_a, pK_b and pK_w?

8 a Identify the conjugate base of the following species and calculate its pK_b value.

   i CH_2FCOOH ($pK_a = 2.59$)

   ii CH_3OH ($pK_a = 15.5$)

   iii $CH_3CH_2NH_3^+$ ($K_a = 2.24 \times 10^{-11}$)

  b Identify the conjugate acid of the following species and calculate its pK_a value.

   i NH_3 ($pK_b = 4.75$)

   ii $C_6H_5NH_2$ ($pK_b = 9.13$)

   iii HCO_3^- ($K_b = 2.51 \times 10^{-8}$)

> Use the expressions deduced in Question 7.

HL Exercise 8.8 – Acid–base titrations

The shape of pH titration curves often comes as a surprise when these are first encountered, as most students expect pH to change proportionally as one solution is added to the other. With a little more thought, of course, titration would not work as a technique if there were not a large change in the pH at the equivalence point of a neutralisation reaction.

When sketching titration curves the following points should be considered:

- the initial pH (this can be calculated)
- the volume at equivalence (this can be calculated)
- the pH at the inflexion point (< 7, $= 7$, > 7)
- the shape of the curve
- the final pH (this can be estimated as tending towards a calculated value)

1 a Sketch the pH curve that would be produced during the following experiments:

  i A total of $50\,cm^3$ of $0.100\,mol\,dm^{-3}$ NaOH is added in small portions to $25\,cm^3$ of $0.100\,mol\,dm^{-3}$ HCl.

  ii A total of $100\,cm^3$ of $0.250\,mol\,dm^{-3}$ $NH_3(aq)$ is added in small portions to $50\,cm^3$ of $0.200\,mol\,dm^{-3}$ HCl.

  iii A total of $50\,cm^3$ of $0.100\,mol\,dm^{-3}$ CH_3COOH is added in small portions to $10\,cm^3$ of $0.200\,mol\,dm^{-3}$ NaOH.

  iv A total of $75\,cm^3$ of $0.100\,mol\,dm^{-3}$ CH_3COOH is added in small portions to $25\,cm^3$ of $0.200\,mol\,dm^{-3}$ $NH_3(aq)$.

2 a Explain why the point of inflexion of a pH titration curve is better described as the equivalence point rather than the neutralisation point.

  b Describe how the pK_a of a weak acid and the pK_b of a weak base can be deduced from a titration curve.

> Using the expression $K_a = \dfrac{[H^+][A^-]}{[HA]}$ then pH = pK_a when $[A^-] = [HA]$. This occurs when half of the HA has reacted to form A^- ions. This is known as the half-neutralisation point. Where will this be on a titration curve? What about for a base?

3 Indicators are often weak acids or weak bases where the conjugate acid–base pair have very different colours. Indicators that are weak acids are often represented by HIn and those that are weak bases as BOH.

  a An indicator with a formula represented by HIn is red in acid solutions and yellow in alkaline solutions. Give an equation to show the dissociation of the indicator and clearly indicate which species is red and which is yellow.

  b An indicator with a formula represented by BOH is green in acid solutions and purple in alkaline solutions. Give an equation to show the dissociation of the indicator and clearly indicate which species is green and which is purple.

  c Thymol blue is an acid–base indicator with a pH range of 8.0–9.6. It is yellow in acid solutions and blue in alkaline solutions. Suggest its pK_a value and explain whether or not it is suitable to use for a titration between HCl and NH_3.

Think about the shape of the titration curve for HCl and NH_3. Will the inflexion point be at, below or above pH 7?

HL Exercise 8.9 – Salt hydrolysis

The pH of the equivalence point of acid–base titrations involving weak acid or bases is not equal to 7 at 25 °C; this can be explained by salt hydrolysis.

1 In this question consider sodium ethanoate (CH_3COONa) and ammonium chloride (NH_4Cl) as examples of the salt of a weak acid and the salt of a weak base, respectively.

   a Give equations to represent the dissociation of sodium ethanoate and ammonium chloride in water.

Salts can be considered to be fully dissociated into their ions.

   b Give equations to show the reaction of the ethanoate ion and of the ammonium ion with water.

   c Calculate the pH of each solution if the concentration of each salt is $0.100\ mol\ dm^{-3}$. ($pK_b(CH_3COO^-) = 9.24$ and $pK_a(NH_4^+) = 9.25$)

Using the ethanoate as an example: the ethanoate ion can accept a proton, it acts as a base so the expressions to use are $K_b = \dfrac{\left[BH^+\right]\left[OH^-\right]}{[B]}$ and $[BH^+] = [OH^-]$.

You also need to use the expression that relates the dissociation constants of an acid (ethanoic acid) and its conjugate base (ethanoate ions):

$$pK_a + pK_b = pK_w$$

   d Given the pK_a and pK_b values in part c, estimate the approximate pH of a solution of ammonium ethanoate.

2 Salts of cations which have a high charge but small ionic radius are often acidic. This is because positive ions in solution are hydrated to form aqueous ions with formulas such as $[M(H_2O)_6]^{n+}$.
   Give an equation to show the dissociation of $[Fe(H_2O)_6]^{3+}$ in solution and use this to explain the pH of the solution.

HL Exercise 8.10 – Buffer solutions

A buffer solution resists a change in the pH of a solution when a small amount of acid or alkali is added. Buffers are used in foods, cosmetics and occur naturally in many biological systems.

1 a Describe the composition of an acidic buffer solution.
   b Describe the composition of a basic buffer solution.
   c Suggest two alternative types of substance that could be added to a solution containing $0.100\ mol$ of ethanoic acid in order to form a buffer solution. Approximately what quantity of each substance would be required?
   d Annotate the graphs in Figures 8.1 and 8.2 to show the 'buffer regions', justifying your choice.

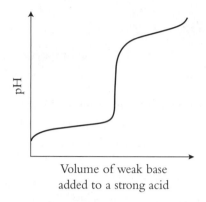

Figure 8.1 Buffer region for a strong acid/weak base titration.

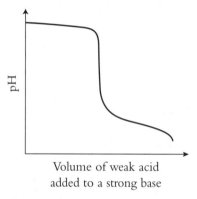

Figure 8.2 Buffer region of a weak acid/strong base titration.

> This question is a classic.

2 Explain how an acidic buffer works.

(?) Exam-style questions

1 Identify the correct acid–base conjugate pairs in the following reaction:
$HCO_3^-(aq) + OH^-(aq) \rightleftharpoons CO_3^{2-}(aq) + H_2O(l)$

	Acid & its conjugate base	Base & its conjugate acid
A	CO_3^{2-} / OH^-	H_2O / HCO_3^-
B	HCO_3^-/CO_3^{2-}	OH^- / H_2O
C	H_2O / HCO_3^-	CO_3^{2-} / OH^-
D	OH^- / H_2O	HCO_3^- / CO_3^{2-}

Table 8.2

2 Sufficient water was added to 25 cm³ of a solution of hydrochloric acid with a pH of 1 to make a solution with a total volume of 2.50 dm³. The solution was thoroughly mixed. What is the pH of the diluted solution?

A 1.0

B 2.0

C 3.0

D 4.0

3   The strengths of four bases are:
ammonia $K_b = 1.78 \times 10^{-5}$, aniline $pK_b = 9.37$, pyridine $pK_b = 8.71$,
diethylamine $K_b = 6.9 \times 10^{-4}$ Deduce the order of increasing base strength.
A aniline < pyridine < diethylamine < ammonia
B pyridine < ammonia < dethylamine < aniline
C diethylamine < aniline < ammonia < pyridine
D aniline < pyridine < ammonia < diethylamine

4   Which of the following can be used to distinguish between a monoprotic strong
and a monoprotic weak acid?
I Measuring the conductivity of solutions of equal concentration.
II Measuring the pH of solutions with equal concentration
III Measuring the volume of alkali required to neutralise equal amounts of acid
A I only
B I and II only
C II and III only
D all of them

5   Which substance is not responsible for acid deposition?
A CO_2
B NO_2
C SO_2
D SO_3

6   Which of the following reactions is used as a post-combustion method that might
be found in a power station to reduce acid deposition?
A $CaO(s) + H_2SO_4(aq) \rightarrow CaSO_4(aq) + H_2O(l)$
B $CaCO_3(s) + SO_2(g) \rightarrow CaSO_3(s) + CO_2(g)$
C $CaCO_3(s) + H_2SO_4(aq) \rightarrow CaSO_4(aq) + H_2O(l) + CO_2(g)$
D $Ca(OH)_2(s) + H_2SO_4(aq) \rightarrow CaSO_4(aq) + 2H_2O(l)$

7   **HL** Which statement is true about HCO_3^-?
A It can act as both a Brønsted–Lowry acid and a Brønsted–Lowry base.
B It can act as a both a Lewis acid and a Lewis base.
C It is both a Brønsted–Lowry acid and a Lewis acid.
D It is both a Brønsted–Lowry base and a Lewis acid.

8   **HL** Which of the following mixtures would act as a buffer solution?
A $25\,cm^3$ of $0.100\,mol\,dm^{-3}$ NaOH and $25\,cm^3$ of $0.200\,mol\,dm^{-3}$ propanoic acid
B $25\,cm^3$ of $0.100\,mol\,dm^{-3}$ ammonia solution and $25\,cm^3$ of $0.200\,mol\,dm^{-3}$ propanoic acid
C $100\,cm^3$ of $0.200\,mol\,dm^{-3}$ sodium ethanoate with $50\,cm^3$ of $0.200\,mol\,dm^{-3}$ sodium
hydroxide
D $50\,cm^3$ of $1.00\,mol\,dm^{-3}$ ammonia and $50\,cm^3$ of $1.00\,mol\,dm^{-3}$ hydrochloric acid

9   **HL** Figure 8.3 shows a typical titration curve. Which of the following procedures could have produced this curve?

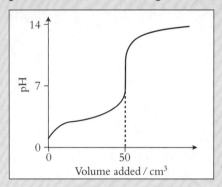

Figure 8.3 Typical titration curve.

A $100 \, cm^3$ of $0.100 \, mol \, dm^{-3}$ NaOH is added to $25 \, cm^3$ $0.100 \, mol \, dm^{-3}$ HCl.

B $50 \, cm^3$ of $0.100 \, mol \, dm^{-3}$ HCl is added to $25 \, cm^3$ $0.100 \, mol \, dm^{-3}$ NH_3 solution.

C $100 \, cm^3$ of $0.100 \, mol \, dm^{-3}$ NaOH is added to $25 \, cm^3$ $0.200 \, mol \, dm^{-3}$ CH_3COOH.

D $50 \, cm^3$ of $0.100 \, mol \, dm^{-3}$ HNO_3 is added to $25 \, cm^3$ $0.200 \, mol \, dm^{-3}$ CH_3CH_2COOH.

10   **HL** Which of the following salts will dissolve in water to form a solution with a pH of more than 7?

A KCl

B NH_4NO_3

C CH_3COONa

D $FeCl_3$

11   When chlorine 'dissolves' in water it actually forms a mixture of hydrochloric and chloric(I) acid. The formula for chloric(I) acid is HClO.

a Construct an equation for this reaction. [1]

b Hydrochloric acid is a strong acid whereas chloric(I) acid is a weak acid.

  i   Explain what is meant by the terms 'strong acid' and 'weak acid'. [1]

  ii Describe three simple laboratory experiments that could be used to distinguish between solutions of equal concentration of a strong and a weak acid. Include the expected observations in your answer. [6]

c Give equations to represent the dissociation of hydrochloric acid and chloric(I) acid into their ions and identify the conjugate base of both acids. [3]

d pH is a measure of the concentration of hydrogen ions in an aqueous solution. Explain why it would be incorrect to define it as describing the strength of an acid. State what term is used to describe the strength of an acid. [2]

[Total 13]

12   a Explain what is meant by the term 'acid deposition'. [1]

b Acid deposition can be classed as wet acid deposition or dry acid deposition. Give one example for each. [2]

c One source of acid deposition is sulfur which is found in fossil fuels. Describe how the burning of fossil fuels gives rise to the formation of both H_2SO_3 and H_2SO_4 in acid rain. Include any relevant equations in your answer. [7]

d Oxides of nitrogen such as NO and NO_2 also contribute to acid deposition. Outline the source of these pollutants and give equations for their formation. [3]

e Outline measures that can be taken to either reduce the production, or minimise the impact of acidic pollutants in the environment. [4]

[Total 17]

13 **a** Sulfuric(VI) acid is a strong diprotic acid with the formula H_2SO_4.

    i Explain what is meant by the term 'diprotic'. [1]

    ii Give equations to show the stepwise dissociation of sulfuric acid into its ions. [2]

    iii Calculate the pH of a solution of sulfuric acid with a concentration of $0.100 \ mol \ dm^{-3}$, assuming that it is fully dissociated. [2]

    iv The pH and conductivity of the solution were tested. The solution was then diluted by taking $25 \ cm^3$ of it and making it up to a total volume of $250 \ cm^3$ in a volumetric flask. Suggest a value for the pH of the diluted solution and the effect on its conductivity. [2]

b Potassium hydroxide is a strong base with the formula KOH.

    i Given that $K_w = 1.00 \times 10^{-14} \ mol^2 \ dm^{-6}$, calculate the pH of a $0.500 \ mol \ dm^{-3}$ solution of potassium hydroxide. [2]

    ii Barium hydroxide is a strong base with the formula $Ba(OH)_2$. Comment on how the pH of a $0.500 \ mol \ dm^{-3}$ solution of barium hydroxide would compare to that of a solution of $0.500 \ mol \ dm^{-3}$ potassium hydroxide. [2]

    iii Ammonia is a weak base. With reference to your answer to parts **b i** and **b ii**, comment on the pH of a $0.500 \ mol \ dm^{-3}$ solution of ammonia. [2]

[Total 12]

14   **HL**   **2-methylpropanoic acid ($CH_3CH(CH_3)COOH$) is a weak acid with a pK_a value of 4.84.**

a Calculate the pH of a $0.200 \ mol \ dm^{-3}$ solution of 2-methylpropanoic acid. [3]

b $25.0 \ cm^3$ of the $0.200 \ mol \ dm^{-3}$ 2-methylpropanoic acid solution is titrated with $0.150 \ mol \ dm^{-3}$ of sodium hydroxide solution.

Sketch a graph to show the pH changes as a total volume of $50 \ cm^3$ of the alkali is added to the 2-methylpropanoic acid solution. [4]

c Identify a suitable indicator for the titration from the table of acid–base indicators in the data book and justify your choice. [2]

d Explain why the pH of the mixture at the equivalence point of the graph is not equal to 7. Give an equation in support of your answer. [4]

[Total 12]

15   **HL**   **The strength of two acids with formulas represented as HX and HY were compared by measuring the pH of solutions of concentration of $0.100 \ mol \ dm^{-3}$. Acid HX was found to have a pH of 4.51 and acid HY had a pH of 3.78.**

a Calculate the value of K_a for the two acids. [3]

b Write an equation for the dissociation of the stronger of the two acids and identify its conjugate base. [2]

c Deduce the relative strength of the conjugates bases of both HX and HY. [1]

d The sodium salt of acid HY has the formula NaY.

    i Give an equation for the reaction of Y^- ions with water and explain why Y^- ions are acting as a base. [2]

    ii Using the information given about HY above, calculate the pK_b for the Y^- ion. [2]

    iii Calculate the pOH and pH of a $0.500\,mol\,dm^{-3}$ solution of NaY. [3]

                                                                            [Total 13]

16   **HL** **Ethylamine is a weak base with the formula $C_2H_5NH_2$.**
It dissociates in water according to the equation:

$$C_2H_5NH_2 + H_2O \rightleftharpoons C_2H_5NH_3^+ + OH^- \qquad\qquad pK_b = 3.35$$

When mixed with its salt, for example with ethylammonium chloride, a buffer solution is formed.

a State what is meant by a buffer solution. [2]

b Explain, with reference to the equation above, how this buffer solution works. [7]

                                                                             [Total 9]

17   **HL** **Figure 8.4 shows how the ionic product of water, K_w, varies with temperature.**

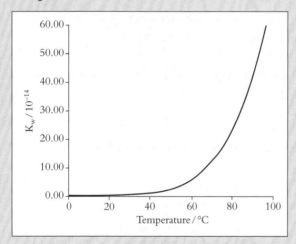

Figure 8.4 Values of the ionisation constant for water.

a Write an equation for the ionisation of water. [1]

b Write an expression for K_w and use the graph to explain whether the ionisation of water is endothermic or exothermic. [2]

c Use the graph to find the pH of water at 87 °C. [1]

d The pH of water at 25 °C is 7. Explain whether water is only neutral at this temperature. [2]

e The equation $2H_2O \rightarrow H_3O^+ + OH^-$ can be used to show that water is amphiprotic. Explain what is meant by the term 'amphiprotic'. [1]

f Water is also amphoteric.

    i Explain what is meant by the term 'amphoteric'. [1]

    ii Aluminium oxide, Al_2O_3, is also amphoteric but is not amphiprotic.
Use equations to illustrate the amphoteric nature of aluminium oxide and explain why it is not amphiprotic. [3]

                                                                             [Total 11]

Redox processes 9

Chapter outline

- Deduce the oxidation state of an atom in an ion or compound.
- Define the terms 'oxidation' and 'reduction' in terms of the loss/gain of oxygen, of hydrogen, or of electrons and in terms of a change in oxidation state.
- Deduce redox equations using half-equations in acidic or neutral solutions and identify the species oxidised, species reduced, the oxidising agent and the reducing agent.
- Deduce the feasibility of a redox reaction from the activity series or from reaction data.
- Recall that the Winkler method can be used to measure biochemical oxygen demand and is used as a measure of the degree of pollution in a water sample.
- Use a cell diagram convention to represent a voltaic cell and understand how it is used to produce electricity including relevant equations.
- Describe the features of an electrochemical cell and predict the products of electrolysis of a molten salt including the relevant half-equations.
- Describe the features of an electrochemical cell and predict the products of electrolysis of an aqueous salt including the relevant half-equations, and calculate the relative amounts of products formed during the electrolytic process including the process of electroplating. **HL**
- Describe the standard hydrogen electrode and explain the terms 'standard electrode potential' and 'standard cell potential'. **HL**
- Calculate the cell potential for a given cell, predict the feasibility of a redox reaction and use standard cell potentials to calculate $\Delta G^{\ominus}$ for a reaction. **HL**

KEY TERMS AND FORMULAS

Anode: The electrode at which oxidation occurs.

Cathode: The electrode at which reduction occurs.

Electrolysis: The breaking down of a substance (in molten state or in solution) by the passage of electricity through it.

Oxidation: The addition of oxygen or removal of hydrogen, loss of electrons or an increase in oxidation number.

Oxidising agent: The species in a reaction that oxidises another substance.

Redox reaction: A reaction that involves both oxidation and reduction.

Reducing agent: The species in a reaction that reduces another species.

Reduction: The removal of oxygen or addition of hydrogen, gain of electrons or decrease in oxidation number.

Standard cell potential: The voltage produced when two half-cells are combined under standard conditions.

Standard conditions: A common set of agreed conditions used to compare data. Most commonly a temperature of 298 K, a pressure of 100 kPa and with all solutions of concentration $1\,\text{mol}\,\text{dm}^{-3}$.

Standard electrode potential: The voltage of a half-cell connected to a standard hydrogen electrode measured under standard conditions. It shows the tendency of a species to be reduced compared to that of hydrogen ions.

Standard hydrogen electrode: The standard half-cell relative to which standard electrode potentials are measured. It is defined as having a value of 0.00 V.

The standard cell potential can be calculated using any one of the following formulas:

$$E_{\text{cell}}{}^{\ominus} = E_{\text{red}}{}^{\ominus} - E_{\text{ox}}{}^{\ominus}$$

where

$E_{\text{cell}}{}^{\ominus}$ is the standard electrode potential of the cell in volts, V

$E_{\text{red}}{}^{\ominus}$ is the standard electrode potential of the reduction half-equation in volts, V

$E_{\text{ox}}{}^{\ominus}$ is the standard electrode potential of the oxidation half-equation in volts, V

Relationship between standard free energy change and the standard cell potential

$$Q = It$$

where

Q is the charge in coulombs, C

I is the current in amps, A

t is the time in seconds, s

Exercise 9.1 – Oxidation and reduction

Knowing the definitions of oxidation and reduction correctly will enable you to identify each process more easily. Which definition is used depends on which fits more obviously for that reaction. These definitions never contradict each other; a reaction that can be described as oxidation will never be described as reduction using a different definition.

1 Identify whether the following definitions describe oxidation or reduction.

a gain of oxygen

b loss of oxygen

c gain of hydrogen

d loss of hydrogen

e gain of electrons

f loss of electrons

g increase in oxidation number

h decrease in oxidation number

2 **a** Identify whether the substance underlined in each equation has been oxidised or reduced.

   i $4\underline{Cu}O + CH_4 \rightarrow 4Cu + CO_2 + 2H_2O$

   ii $\underline{CH_3CHO} + [O] \rightarrow CH_3COOH$

   iii $2Ag^+(aq) + \underline{Zn}(s) \rightarrow 2Ag(s) + Zn^{2+}(aq)$

   iv $\underline{C_2H_4}(g) + H_2(g) \rightarrow C_2H_6(g)$

   b Identify the oxidising and reducing agents for the reactions in part **a**.

See Exercise 9.2 for practice deducing oxidation numbers.

Exercise 9.2 – Oxidation numbers

Oxidation numbers serve as a way of making oxidation and reduction processes easier to identify. They are a purely formal concept based on the idea that all compounds can be imagined to be ionic. The oxidation number is the imaginary charge on each atom in the compound. The concept of oxidation number is not particularly useful in organic chemistry but nonetheless it can be used.

Oxidation is brought about using an oxidising agent; the oxidising agent will be reduced in the process. Reduction is brought about using a reducing agent which will itself be oxidised.

1 Deduce the oxidation number of following atoms:

   a potassium in KBr

   b phosphorus in PCl_3

   c iron in Fe_2O_3

   d nitrogen in $NaNO_2$

   e chromium in $KCrO_4$

   f hydrogen in $LiAlH_4$

   g oxygen in Na_2O_2

   h carbon in C_2H_4

   i carbon in C_2H_6

   j cobalt in $K_3[Co(CN)_6]$

2 Deduce the formula of each of the following compounds:

   a iron(II) oxide

   b sodium chlorate(I)

   c potassium bromate(V)

   d iron(II) sulfate(VI)

   e sulfuric(IV) acid

   f potassium manganate(VII)

   g chromium(III) nitrate(V)

   h nitrogen(I) oxide

Oxidation numbers are written as a sign followed by a number e.g. +2 rather than 2+. The terms oxidation number and oxidation state can be used interchangeably.

Oxidation numbers can be used in the naming of compounds.

In transition metal compounds, Roman numerals are used to indicate the oxidation state of the metal.

In salts containing oxygen such as sulfate, nitrate, chlorate and so on (these are known as oxyanions), the Roman numeral indicates the oxidation state of the element combined with the oxygen.

In covalent compounds, the Roman numeral follows the name of the element to which it refers.

Roman numerals are only used in names and not when stating the oxidation number, e.g. the oxidation state of copper in copper(II) chloride is +2 not + II.

Number	Roman numeral
1	I
2	II
3	III
4	IV
5	V
6	VI
7	VII

Table 9.1

3 Deduce the names of the following compounds:
  a CuI
  b V_2O_5
  c Ru_2O_3
  d NH_4VO_3
  e K_2CrO_4

4 Determine the oxidation numbers of the substances in the following equations and use these to identify which substance has been oxidised and which has been reduced.
  a $Zn(s) + 2H^+(aq) \rightarrow Zn^{2+}(aq) + H_2(g)$
  b $Mg(s) + 2Fe^{3+}(aq) \rightarrow Mg^{2+}(aq) + 2Fe^{2+}(aq)$
  c $Mg(s) + H_2O(g) \rightarrow MgO(s) + H_2(g)$
  d $MnO_4^-(aq) + 8H^+(aq) + 5Fe^{2+}(aq) \rightarrow Mn^{2+}(aq) + 5Fe^{3+}(aq) + 4 H_2O(l)$
  e $CH_3CHO + [O] \rightarrow CH_3COOH$

Note this is the same equation as that in Exercise 9.1, Question 2 part **a ii**.

The oxidation state of [O] is zero.

The oxidation state of carbon can be calculated as an average value so in CH_3CHO, taking O as −2 and each H as +1 then the sum of the oxidation states of the two carbon atoms = −2 which is an average of −1.

This equation goes to show that, although oxidation states can be used in organic chemistry, they are not particularly helpful and ideas about the addition or removal of oxygen or hydrogen are more straightforward.

Exercise 9.3 – Constructing and combining half-equations

Half-equations are used to show either just the oxidation process or just the reduction process. Like all equations they must be balanced in terms of the number of each species and the overall charge. For species in solution, the IB syllabus only includes neutral or acidic conditions. Using oxidation numbers is an important first step in this process as the change in the oxidation number is equal to the number of electrons lost or gained.

1 Construct the following half-equations and identify whether each represents oxidation or reduction:
  a $H_2 \rightarrow H^+$
  b $Ce^{4+} \rightarrow Ce^{2+}$

In parts **a** and **b**, the number of each type of atom needs to be balanced and then the charges made to balance by adding electrons to the appropriate side of the equations; to the left if the equation represents reduction and to the right if it represents oxidation. Deducing the oxidation number is the easiest way of finding out if it is an oxidation or reduction reaction.

Question 2 is the same as Question 1 but is less straightforward. Part **a** is broken down into smaller steps to make the process easier. Follow the same sequence for part **b**.

2 a Construct the half-equation for $NO_3^- \rightarrow NO_2$ by following the steps below.
   i Deduce the oxidation numbers of the elements and identify which element is oxidised or reduced.
   ii Add the number of electrons to the equation that equals the change in oxidation state. For reduction, place these on the left; for oxidation, place these on the right-hand side of the equation. (Remember *OIL RIG.*)
   iii Calculate the total charge of all the substances on each side of the equation. Add as many H^+ ions to one side or the other as needed to make the charges on both sides the same.
   iv Add H_2O to the other side to balance the number of hydrogen atoms in the equation.

  b Construct the following half-equations using the same method as in part **a**:
   i $SO_2 \rightarrow SO_4^{2-}$ iii $BrO_3^- \rightarrow Br_2$
   ii $MnO_4^- \rightarrow Mn^{2+}$ iv $Cr^{3+} \rightarrow Cr_2O_7^{2-}$

The oxygen atoms should now balance too (for **2 a iv**).

3 Combine the following half-equations to determine the balanced overall equation:
  a $Zn(s) \rightarrow Zn^{2+}(aq) + 2e^-$ and $VO_2^+(aq) + 2H^+(aq) + e^- \rightarrow VO^{2+}(aq) + H_2O(l)$
  b $Cu^{2+}(aq) + e^- \rightarrow Cu^+(aq)$ and $2I^-(aq) \rightarrow I_2(aq) + 2e^-$
  c $IO_3^- + 6H^+ + 5e^- \rightarrow \frac{1}{2} I_2 + 3H_2O$ and $2I^- \rightarrow I_2 + 2e^-$
  d $H_2O_2 \rightarrow O_2 + 2H^+ + 2e^-$ and $MnO_4^- + 5e^- + 8H^+ \rightarrow Mn^{2+} + 4H_2O$

In parts **2 b iii** and **iv** you will firstly need to balance the number of bromine/chromium atoms.

Combining balanced half-equations can be accomplished by multiplying each half-equation by whatever factor is needed so that both half-equations have the same number of electrons. These will then cancel out when the two half-equations are combined.

4 Balance the following half-equations and then combine them to determine an overall
equation for each reaction.
 a $Fe^{3+} \rightarrow Fe^{2+}$ and $Zn \rightarrow Zn^{2+}$
 b $H^+ \rightarrow H_2$ and $Mg \rightarrow Mg^{2+}$
 c $MnO_4^- \rightarrow Mn^{2+}$ and $Fe^{2+} \rightarrow Fe^{3+}$
 d $S_2O_3^{2-} \rightarrow S_4O_6^{2-}$ and $I_2 \rightarrow I^-$
 e $C_2O_4^{2-} \rightarrow CO_2$ and $Cr_2O_7^{2-} \rightarrow Cr^{3+}$

5 Deduce the following redox equations:

> Remember charges as well as atoms must balance.
> Some of these equations can be easily balanced but others are more difficult. The best
> strategy if the balancing is not obvious is to use the change in the oxidation states; one
> substance's oxidation number increases by the same amount as another decreases.

 a $Cu + Ag^+ \rightarrow Cu^{2+} + Ag$
 b $Br_2 + SO_2 \rightarrow H_2SO_4 + HBr$
 c $H_2SO_4 + I^- \rightarrow I_2 + H_2S$

Exercise 9.4 – Using the reactivity series to predict the feasibility of a reaction

Table 25 of the data book lists the activity series of some common metals. This describes
the relative ease of oxidation. Metals near the top of the series lose electrons most easily to
form their positive ions.

1 Using the activity series, predict whether the following reactions will occur:
 a $Mg(s) + Zn^{2+}(aq) \rightarrow Mg^{2+}(aq) + Zn(s)$
 b $Bi(s) + 2H^+(aq) \rightarrow Bi^{2+}(aq) + H_2(g)$
 c $2Al(s) + Fe_2O_3(s) \rightarrow Al_2O_3(s) + 2Fe(s)$
 d $Sb_2S_3(s) + 2Sn(s) \rightarrow Sn_2S_3(s) + 2Sb(s)$

2 In an experiment to deduce the position of a metal in the activity series, the following
observations were made:
 1 When a small piece of the metal was placed into dilute acid, bubbles of hydrogen gas
 were produced.
 2 When a small piece of metal was placed into a solution of nickel nitrate solution, the
 surface of the metal became coated with a grey substance.
 3 When a small piece of metal was placed into a solution of chromium nitrate solution,
 there was no apparent reaction.
  a Use the activity series in the IB data book to suggest possible identities for the
  metal.
  b Design suitable simple displacement reactions that could be used to deduce the
  identity of the metal.

Exercise 9.5 – Redox titrations

Redox titrations often involve transition metal compounds and so often do not require an indicator as the transition metal compounds are often different colours in their different oxidation states. Many quantitative analysis procedures utilise redox reactions. Calculations are just the same as for those met in Topic 1 (stoichiometric relationships).

1 In an experiment to determine the oxalic acid ($H_2C_2O_4$) content of rhubarb leaves, a 100.0 g sample of leaves was processed resulting in 250.0 cm^3 of solution. When a 25.00 cm^3 portion of this solution was analysed by titration with $KMnO_4$ solution, it was found that 28.40 cm^3 of $KMnO_4$ of concentration 0.0100 mol dm^{-3} was required. The reaction between oxalic acid and potassium manganate(VII) can be represented by the equation:

$$2MnO_4^-(aq) + 5C_2O_4^{2-}(aq) + 16H^+(aq) \rightarrow 2Mn^{2+(aq)} + 10CO_2(g) + 8H_2O(l)$$

M_r(oxalic acid) = 90.04 g mol^{-1}

   a Calculate the number of moles of MnO_4^- used per titre.

   b Using the balanced equation, calculate the number of moles of oxalic acid present in each 25.00 cm^3 portion.

   c Calculate the number of moles of oxalic acid present in the full sample.

   d Calculate the mass of oxalic acid found in the leaves.

2 A 'copper' coin of mass 2.75 g was analysed to determine the copper content according to the following procedure.

   1 The coin was dissolved in an excess of concentrated nitric acid in a fume cupboard to form copper(II) ions and copious amounts of nitrogen(IV) oxide was produced. The solution formed was then quantitatively transferred into a volumetric flask and made up to 250 cm^3.

   2 A 25.00 cm^3 portion of the solution was transferred to a conical flask and an excess of potassium iodide solution was added, forming iodine and a white precipitate of copper(I) iodide. CuI I_2

   3 The quantity of iodine liberated was determined by titration with 0.100 mol dm^{-3} sodium thiosulfate solution. The average titre required was found to be 27.35 cm^3. The half-equation for the oxidation of sodium thiosulfate is:

   $$2S_2O_3^{2-}(aq) \rightarrow S_4O_6^{2-}(aq) + 2e^-$$

   a Deduce equations for the reactions in steps 1, 2 and 3.

   b Calculate the % of copper in the coin.

3 In order to accurately measure the amount of dissolved oxygen the following procedure can be used.

The Winkler method can be used to determine the amount of dissolved oxygen in water. The amount of dissolved oxygen required to support fish depends on the species and on the season. The biological oxygen demand (BOD) of the water can then be determined by comparing the amount of dissolved oxygen in the water before and after incubating a sample for 5 days at 20 °C.

It is anticipated that the BOD in a healthy stream is likely to be less than 1.00 mg dm^{-3}.

   Step 1 An excess of manganese(II) sulfate solution and sodium hydroxide solution is added to a sample of pond water forming a precipitate of manganese(II) hydroxide.

Step 2 The manganese(II) hydroxide formed is oxidised by the oxygen in the water to form manganese(IV) ions according to the following equation:
$$Mn(OH)_2(s) + O_2(g) \rightarrow 2MnO(OH)_2(s)$$

Step 3 The precipitate formed is then acidified with an excess of sulfuric acid:
$$MnO(OH)_2(s) + 4H^+(aq) \rightarrow Mn^{4+}(aq) + 3H_2O(l)$$

Step 4 An excess of potassium iodide is then added to the mixture to reduce the manganese ions to Mn^{2+}.

Step 5 The iodine liberated is then titrated with sodium thiosulfate. The equation for the reaction is as follows:
$$I_2(aq) + 2S_2O_3^{2-}(aq) \rightarrow 2I^-(aq) + S_4O_6^{2-}(aq)$$

Step 6 A second sample of water is incubated at 20 °C for 5 days in order for the microorganisms in it to use up some of the dissolved oxygen. This second sample is then analysed using the same procedure.

   a Give an equation for the reaction between manganese(II) ions and hydroxide ions in step 1 of the procedure.

   b Explain why the equation in step 3 is not a redox reaction.

   c Give an equation for the reaction in step 4.

   d Determine the ratio of the number of moles of dissolved oxygen to the number of moles of sodium thiosulfate.

   e Calculate what concentration of sodium thiosulfate would be suitable for use in this procedure for a sample of water of volume 100 cm³ if the expected dissolved oxygen level is 5 mg dm⁻³ and the anticipated average titre is 25.00 cm³.

Exercise 9.6 – Voltaic cells and their notation

In a voltaic cell a spontaneous chemical reaction is used to generate a voltage. During a redox reaction electrons are transferred directly from one species (the oxidised substance) to another (the reduced substance). In a voltaic cell, the oxidation half reaction and the reduction half reaction are physically separated and the electrons flow through an external circuit. Electrons are released to the external circuit by the half-cell which contains the species which is most easily oxidised (worse oxidising agent) towards the half-cell which includes the species which is most easily reduced (better oxidising agent). The species most easily reduced is conventionally written on the right. The greater the difference between the relative strengths as oxidising agents of the two species, the greater the voltage produced.

1 In Figure 9.1 Fe^{3+} ions are reduced to Fe^{2+} ions and zinc atoms are oxidised to Zn^{2+} ions.

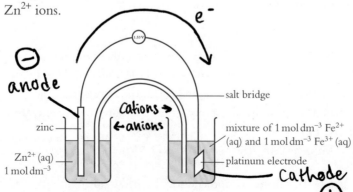

Figure 9.1 Voltaic cell; Zn(s) | Zn²⁺(aq) || Fe³⁺(aq), Fe²⁺(aq) | Pt.

a What is the purpose of the salt bridge?

b Why is a platinum electrode used in the Fe^{2+}/Fe^{3+} half-cell?

c Give equations for the reactions in each half-cell.

d What changes would be observed in each beaker?

e Copy and label Figure 9.1 to show the following:

   i the direction of electron flow through the external circuit

   ii the anode

   iii the cathode

   iv the positive electrode

   v the negative electrode

   vi the direction of ion flow in the salt bridge

> The electrodes are the parts of the cell where electrons move between the solutions and the wire in the external circuit; they are the rods that dip into the solutions.

2 Cell notation is used as shorthand to describe cells, for example:

$Cu(s) \mid Cu^{2+}(aq) \parallel H^+(aq), Cr_2O_7^{2-}(aq), Cr^{3+}(aq) \mid Pt(s)$

a What is the single vertical line used to represent?

b What is the double vertical line used to represent?

c What are the two electrodes made from in this cell?

d Give the half-equations occurring at each electrode.

e Why is platinum used in the right-hand half-cell?

f Give the overall equation for the cell.

> The convention is that the anode (oxidation) is shown on the left and the cathode (**R**eduction) on the **R**ight. Both half-equations can be read from left to right.

3 Determine the cell diagram for the cell that has the following overall equation in each part:

a $Ag^+(aq) + Cu(s) \rightarrow Ag(s) + Cu^{2+}(aq)$

b $Cu(s) + 2NO_3^-(aq) + 4H^+(aq) \rightarrow Cu^{2+}(aq) + 2NO_2(g) + 2H_2O(l)$

c $5IO_4^-(aq) + 2Mn^{2+}(aq) + 3H_2O(l) \rightarrow 5IO_3^-(aq) + 2MnO_4^{-(aq)} + 6H^+(aq)$

> Remember that **R**eduction is on the **R**ight and that the half-equations can be read from left to right. Start on the left with the oxidation process (in part **a** this is $Cu \rightarrow Cu^{2+}$) then $\parallel$ to represent the salt bridge followed by the reduction process ($Ag^+ \rightarrow Ag$). Include state symbols and a single vertical line to represent a phase boundary. In parts **b** and **c**, commas should be used to separate the species that are in the same solution and platinum will be required to provide a surface for the electron movement between the solutions and the wires.

HL Exercise 9.7 – Electrode potentials

The standard hydrogen electrode is defined as having a cell potential of 0.00 V and is used to determine the standard cell potential for all other half-cells. The standard electrode potential measures the tendency of a species to be reduced relative to that of hydrogen ions. A positive value means that reduction is more likely.

Remember that the data book gives a list of standard electrode potentials. Some of these reactions should be familiar. For example, the half-equation with the most positive value is $\frac{1}{2}F_2(g) + e^- \rightarrow F^-(aq)$; knowledge of the chemistry of group 17 tells you that fluorine is a very dangerous and reactive chemical because it is very easily reduced to fluoride ions.

Cell potentials can be calculated using the formula:
$E_{cell}^{\ominus} = E_{red}^{\ominus} - E_{ox}^{\ominus}$
When using this expression, the sign of the value must not be changed.

The difference in the strength as reducing agents between the zinc and the magnesium half-cells must be causing the difference in the voltages produced by the two cells.
Anode = Oxidation.
This is always true and applies to voltaic cells and in electrolysis (see Exercise 9.8).

1 The standard electrode potential for $Zn^{2+}(aq) + 2e^- \rightleftharpoons Zn(s)$ is -0.76 V.

   a What does this tell you about the tendency of Zn^{2+} ions to gain electrons compared to that of H^+ ions?

   b Using your answer to part **a**, determine the reactions that will occur in each half-cell when the following two half-cells are combined:
$Zn^{2+}(aq) + 2e^- \rightleftharpoons Zn(s)$ and $2H^+(aq) + 2e^- \rightleftharpoons H_2(g)$

2 An experiment was set up to compare the following two cells under standard conditions:

Cell 1: $Zn(s) \mid Zn^{2+}(aq) \parallel H^+(aq), Cr_2O_7^{2-}(aq), Cr^{3+}(aq) \mid Pt(s)$

Cell 2: $Mg(s) \mid Mg^{2+}(aq) \parallel H^+(aq), Cr_2O_7^{2-}(aq), Cr^{3+}(aq) \mid Pt(s)$

It was found that the voltage in cell 1 was $+2.09$ V and in cell 2 the voltage was $+3.69$ V.

   a Give the overall equations for these two cells and use the values of the cell potentials to deduce the relative strength of zinc and magnesium as reducing agents.

In simple terms, reading from left to right, the left-hand half-equation can be thought of as driving the right-hand half-equation forward. The oxidation of the zinc or magnesium (and therefore their 'power' as reducing agents) in this case is driving the reduction of the $Cr_2O_7^{2-}$ to Cr^{3+}. The more positive the overall voltage produced, then the more 'powerfully' the reaction is being driven.

   b Deduce the cell potential if a new cell was set up using the magnesium half-cell and the zinc half-cell. Which would be the anode in this new cell?

3 Conventionally in cell notation the oxidation half-equation is on the left and reduction on the right-hand side. The overall cell potential is the difference between these two and can be calculated using the equation: $E_{cell}^{\ominus} = E_{red}^{\ominus} - E_{ox}^{\ominus}$

   a In terms of the standard electrode potential for the left and right-hand-side half-cells ($E_{lhs}^{\ominus}$ and $E_{rhs}^{\ominus}$), deduce an expression for $E_{cell}^{\ominus}$.

   b As the anode is defined as the electrode at which oxidation occurs and the cathode is where reduction occurs, deduce an expression for $E_{cell}^{\ominus}$ in terms of $E_{anode}^{\ominus}$ and $E_{cathode}^{\ominus}$.

   c Using the standard electrode potentials given in the data book, write the overall reaction and calculate the electrode potential for the following reactions:

     i $Zn(s) \mid Zn^{2+}(aq) \parallel Cu^{2+}(aq) \mid Cu(s)$

     ii $Pt(s) \mid Fe^{2+}(aq), Fe^{3+}(aq) \parallel Cr_2O_7^{2-}(aq), H^+(aq), Cr^{3+}(aq) \mid Pt(s)$

     iii $Sn(s) \mid Sn^{2+}(aq) \parallel Cl_2(g) \mid Cl^-(aq) \mid Pt(s)$

Unlike enthalpy calculations, electrode potentials are not molar quantities and so are not multiplied to match the balancing of an equation; they represent the potential for a reaction to occur. It is true that standard conditions are for solutions with a concentration of $1\,mol\,dm^{-3}$ but this is the potential for the reaction at that concentration, not that a given number of moles have reacted. The units are volts, not volts per mole!

4 Using the electrode potentials in the data book, predict whether each of the following reactions will be spontaneous and explain your answer in each case. For those that are spontaneous, give the overall equation for the reaction.
   a $Fe(s)$ and $Sn^{2+}(aq)$
   b $H^+(aq)$ and $Mn^{2+}(aq)$
   c $I^-(aq)$ and $Fe^{3+}(aq)$

When there is a choice of half-equations, for example in part **b** there is a choice between Mn^{2+}/Mn and MnO_4^-/Mn^{2+}, it is important to remember that one equation must be reduction and the other oxidation. H^+ ions can only be reduced and so the Mn^{2+} must be oxidised.
For a spontaneous reaction $E_{cell}^{\ominus} > 0$, although the reaction would only be described as feasible; it may not actually occur.

5 For a spontaneous reaction $\Delta G^{\ominus} < 0$ and $\Delta G^{\ominus} = -nFE^{\ominus}$ where $F = 96\,500\,C\,mol^{-1}$. Calculate $\Delta G^{\ominus}$ for the following reactions met previously in Question 3.
   a $Zn(s) \mid Zn^{2+}(aq) \parallel Cu^{2+}(aq) \mid Cu(s)$
   b $Pt(s) \mid Fe^{2+}(aq), Fe^{3+}(aq) \parallel Cr_2O_7^{2-}(aq), H^+(aq), Cr^{3+}(aq) \mid Pt(s)$
   c $Sn(s) \mid Sn^{2+}(aq) \parallel Cl_2(g) \mid Cl^-(aq) \mid Pt(s)$

Exercise 9.8 – Electrolysis (SL)

Electrolysis occurs in electrolytic cells; it converts electrical energy into chemical energy by making non-spontaneous chemical reactions happen. Only ionic compounds undergo electrolysis, but this cannot occur in solid ionic compounds as the ions must be free to move under the influence of the applied voltage.

1 a Define the term 'electrolysis'.
   b What are the signs of the anode and cathode in an electrolytic cell?
   c At which electrode does oxidation occur in an electrolytic cell?
   d Why do the electrolytes need to be molten in order for electrolysis to occur?
   e Describe how current is carried both in the external circuit and in the electrolyte of an electrolytic cell.

2 Identify the products formed during the electrolysis of the following substances. In each case, identify which is produced at the anode and which at the cathode. Give the equation occurring at each electrode and the overall equation.
   a $CuCl_2(l)$
   b $ZnO(l)$
   c manganese(IV) oxide(l)
   d indium(III) bromide(l)

3 a Draw a diagram of the apparatus that could be used in a laboratory to electrolyse lead(II) bromide.
   b Give half-equations for the reaction at each electrode and the overall equation for the electrolysis.

When connected to an external power supply, it is always best to *PANIC*!
Positive Anode, Negative is Cathode

This is the same as for voltaic cells.

HL Exercise 9.9 – Electrolysis

The electrolysis of aqueous solutions is very similar to that of molten compounds but with the additional complication of there being a choice of ions which can undergo oxidation or reduction. The additional ions are H^+ and OH^- formed by the dissociation of water. The ions which are most easily oxidised will be discharged at the positive electrode (anode) and the ions which are most easily reduced (most positive electrode potential) will be discharged at the negative electrode (cathode).

1 Identify the ions present in the following solutions:
   a aqueous tin(II) chloride solution
   b aqueous magnesium sulfate solution
   c aqueous sodium nitrate solution
   d aqueous calcium bromide solution

2 A general principle is that during the electrolysis of aqueous solutions, oxygen or halogens are discharged at the anode and hydrogen or a metal is discharged at the cathode.
   a State three factors which affect the identity of the products formed during the electrolysis of an aqueous solution.
   b Identify the substance formed at the anode and cathode during the electrolysis of the aqueous solutions shown in Table 9.2, using inert electrodes under standard conditions and give the half-equations for the reaction at each electrode.

Anode = Oxidation

OIL RIG: Oxidation is Loss of electrons, Reduction is Gain of Electrons
The table of standard electrode potentials in the data book can be used to determine whether hydrogen or the metal is discharged at the cathode, although it is easier to refer to the activity series and note the position of hydrogen; metals below hydrogen are discharged in preference.

	Solution	Product at anode	Product at cathode
i	sodium chloride(aq)		
ii	magnesium bromide(aq)		
iii	copper(II) sulfate(aq)		
iv	acidified water		

Table 9.2

   c Why is it necessary to acidify the sample of water in part **iv** before electrolysis is possible?
   d Describe how the appearance and pH of the solution in part **iii** would change during the electrolysis.
3 a A solution contained a mixture of $1\,mol\,dm^{-3}$ of each of the following cations under standard conditions: Na^+, Mg^{2+}, Cu^{2+}, Mn^{2+} and Ag^+; during the electrolysis of this solution using inert electrodes, determine what substance will be produced at the cathode and justify your answer.

b A solution contained a mixture of $1\,mol\,dm^{-3}$ of each of the following anions under standard conditions: I^-, Br^-, Cl^-, SO_4^{2-} and NO_3^-; during the electrolysis of this solution using inert electrodes, determine what substance will be produced at the anode.

c In part **b** why is it not necessary to know the electrode potentials for the sulfate or nitrate ions?

4 An electrolytic cell was set up using an aqueous solution of copper(II) nitrate of concentration $1\,mol\,dm^{-3}$ using copper electrodes.

  a Give half-equations for the reactions at both electrodes.
  b How will the concentration of the copper(II) nitrate solution change over time?
  c Describe how the appearance of the electrodes will change over time.

> This is the basis of electroplating.

5 In the industrial manufacture of aluminium, a mixture of aluminium compounds is melted and electrolysed using carbon electrodes; however, the electrolyte can be considered to be aluminium oxide, Al_2O_3.

  a Write the overall equation for the electrolysis of molten aluminium oxide.
  b Write the half-equations for the reactions at the anode and the cathode.
  c Calculate the number of moles of electrons required to produce $500\,kg$ of aluminium.
  d If 1 mol of electrons has a charge of $96\,500\,C$ then calculate the charge required to produce $500\,kg$ of aluminium.
  e Using the expression $Q = It$, calculate the current required to produce $500\,kg$ of aluminium in one hour.
  f Calculate the number of moles of oxygen produced in one hour under the same conditions.
  g The anodes are normally made from carbon graphite. At the high temperatures at which electrolysis takes place the carbon reacts with the oxygen produced to form carbon dioxide. Calculate the mass of carbon reacting away per hour under these conditions.
  h Calculate the mass of carbon dioxide produced per hour under these conditions.

6 $200\,cm^3$ of a solution of $1.25\,mol\,dm^{-3}$ silver(I)nitrate was electrolysed using inert electrodes for $1\,h$ using a current of $0.5\,A$.

  a What mass of silver would be deposited during this process?
  b What will be the concentration of the $Ag^+(aq)$ ions remaining in the solution at the end of this time?

> In the expression $Q = It$, time is in seconds.

7 A series of electrolytic cells was set up as in Figure 9.2.

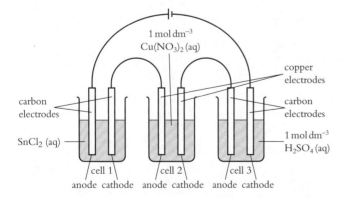

Figure 9.2 Electrolysis of a series of cells.

a Describe the observation in each cell.

b Give the equations for the reactions occurring at each electrode.

c If $0.54\,g$ of tin is produced in cell 1, what volume of oxygen gas will be produced in total by the complete series of cells? Assume $1\,mol$ of gas occupies $24\,000\,cm^3$ at the temperature and pressure of this experiment.

? Exam-style questions

1   Which is the correct name of $Co_2(SO_4)_3$?
   A cobalt sulfate
   B cobalt(II) sulfate
   C cobalt(III) sulfate(VI)
   D cobalt(II) sulfate(III)

2   In which compound does sulfur has the highest oxidation number?
   A SO_2Cl_2
   B H_2S
   C $Na_2S_2O_3$
   D SO_2

3   Determine the coefficient for the number of electrons in the following half-equation:
   ___ $Cr_2O_7^{2-}(aq) +$ ___ $H^+(aq) +$ ___ $e^- \rightarrow$ __ $Cr^{3+}(aq) +$ ___ $H_2O(l)$
   A 3
   B 4 $14H^+ + Cr_2O_7^{2-} \rightarrow 2Cr^{3+} + 7H_2O$
   C 5 $16e^-$ red.
   D 6

4   Consider the following reaction:
   $2MnO_4^-(aq) + 16H^+(aq) + 10Cl^-(aq) \rightarrow 2Mn^{2+}(aq) + 8H_2O(l) + 5Cl_2(g)$
   Which species have been correctly identified?

	Oxidising agent	Species oxidised
A	$MnO_4^-(aq)$	$Cl^-(aq)$
B	$MnO_4^-(aq)$	$Mn^{2+}(aq)$
C	$Cl^-(aq)$	$Cl_2(g)$
D	$Mn^{2+}(aq)$	$Cl^-(aq)$

Table 9.3

5   The results shown in Table 9.4 were obtained during a simple displacement
    experiment to deduce the reactivity of four metals, W, X, Y and Z.

	W(s)	X(s)	Y(s)	Z(s)
W nitrate(aq)		reaction	no reaction	reaction
X nitrate(aq)	no reaction		no reaction	no reaction
Y nitrate(aq)	reaction	reaction		reaction
Z nitrate(aq)	no reaction	reaction	no reaction	

Table 9.4

Deduce the order of reactivity of the metals from most reactive to least reactive.
A   X > Y > W > Z
B   Y > W > Z > X
C   Z > W > Y > X
D   X > Z > W > Y

6   For the voltaic cell shown in Figure 9.3, which statements are correct?

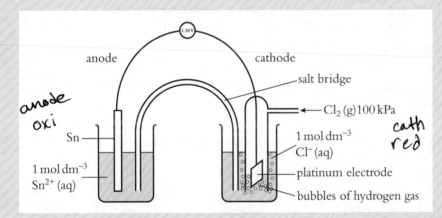

anode
oxi

cath
red

Figure 9.3 Sn/Sn^{2+} and Cl$_2$/Cl$^-$ voltaic cell.

I   Electrons move in the external circuit from the tin electrode to the chlorine electrode. ✓
II Positive ions in the salt bridge move towards the tin electrode. ✗
III The concentration of tin ions in solution increases during the process. ✓
A   I only
B   II only
C   I and III
D   II and III

7   In the following cell, which reactions occur at the anode and the cathode?

$Pb(s) \mid Pb^{2+}(aq) \parallel Cu^{2+}(aq) \mid Cu(s)$

	Anode	Cathode
A	$Pb^{2+}(aq) + 2e^- \rightarrow Pb(s)$	$Cu^{2+}(aq) + 2e^- \rightarrow Cu(s)$
B	$Pb(s) \rightarrow Pb^{2+}(aq) + 2e^-$	$Cu^{2+}(aq) + 2e^- \rightarrow Cu(s)$
C	$Cu^{2+}(aq) + 2e^- \rightarrow Cu(s)$	$Pb(s) \rightarrow Pb^{2+}(aq) + 2e^-$
D	$Cu^{2+}(aq) + 2e^- \rightarrow Cu(s)$	$Pb^{2+}(aq) + 2e^- \rightarrow Pb(s)$

Table 9.5

8   **HL** Consider the following reactions:

$SO_4^{2-}(aq) + 4H^+(aq) + 2e^- \rightleftharpoons H_2SO_3(aq) + H_2O(l)$ $\qquad E_{cell}^{\ominus} = +0.17\,V^{\ominus}$

$Ag^+(aq) + e^- \rightleftharpoons Ag(s)$ $\qquad E_{cell}^{\ominus} = +0.80\,V$

What is the cell potential, in V, for the spontaneous reaction that occurs when these two half-cells are connected?

A +0.97 V   C −0.63 V

B +0.43 V   D +0.63 V

9   **HL** Which statement is correct for the following spontaneous reaction?

$2Fe^{3+}(aq) + Sn^{2+}(aq) \rightarrow 2Fe^{2+}(aq) + Sn^{4+}(aq)$

A $E_{cell}^{\ominus} > 0$ and Fe^{3+} is a better reducing agent than Sn^{2+}.

B $E_{cell}^{\ominus} > 0$ and Fe^{3+} is a better oxidising agent than Sn^{4+}.

C $E_{cell}^{\ominus} < 0$ and Sn^{4+} is a better reducing agent than Fe^{3+}.

D $E_{cell}^{\ominus} < 0$ and Sn^{2+} is a better oxidising agent than Fe^{2+}.

10 **HL** Given the following electrode potentials, which statement is correct?

$Al^{3+}(aq) + 3e^- \rightleftharpoons Al(s)$ $\qquad E^{\ominus} = -1.66\,V$

$Zn^{2+}(aq) + 2e^- \rightleftharpoons Zn(s)$ $\qquad E^{\ominus} = -0.76\,V$

$\frac{1}{2}I_2(s) + e^- \rightleftharpoons I^-(aq)$ $\qquad E^{\ominus} = +0.54\,V$

$Fe^{3+}(aq) + e^- \rightleftharpoons Fe^{2+}(aq)$ $\qquad E^{\ominus} = +0.77\,V$

A For the reaction between iodine and aluminium, $E_{cell}^{\ominus} = 2.20\,V$ and the reaction will happen spontaneously.

B $\Delta G > 0$ for the reaction between Fe^{3+} and Al.

C If an Al^{3+}/Al half-cell is connected to a Zn^{2+}/Zn half-cell then under standard conditions the zinc half-cell will be the anode.

D If a current is passed through a mixture $1\,mol\,dm^{-3}$ of both Zn^{2+} and Al^{3+} ions then aluminium ions are more likely to be reduced than the zinc ions.

11 **HL** During the electrolysis of a solution of nickel(II) sulfate using platinum electrodes, 0.100 mol of nickel was deposited on one of the electrodes.

Given the half-equations below, which of the following statements is correct?

$$Ni^{2+}(aq) + 2e^- \rightleftharpoons Ni(s) \qquad\qquad E^\ominus = -0.26V$$
$$2H_2O(l) + 2e^- \rightleftharpoons H_2(g) + 2OH^-(aq) \qquad E^\ominus = -0.83V$$
$$O_2(g) + 4H^+(aq) + 4e^- \rightleftharpoons 2H_2O(l) \qquad E^\ominus = +1.23V$$

A 0.0500 mol of oxygen will be produced at the anode.

B 0.100 mol of oxygen will be produced at the anode.

C 0.200 mol of oxygen will be produced at the anode.

D 0.100 mol of hydrogen will be produced at the cathode.

12 **HL** During the electroplating of an object with chromium, a current of 0.75 A was passed through a solution of chromium(III) nitrate for a period of 2 minutes. What mass of chromium was deposited on the object?

($A_r(Cr) = 52.00\,g\,mol^{-1}$ and Faraday's constant (F) $= 96\,500\,C\,mol^{-1}$)

A $\dfrac{0.75 \times 2 \times 52.00}{96500 \times 3}$

B $\dfrac{0.75 \times 2 \times 60}{96500 \times 52.00}$

C $\dfrac{96500 \times 3 \times 2}{52.00 \times 0.75 \times 6}$

D $\dfrac{0.75 \times 2 \times 60 \times 52.00}{96500 \times 3}$

13 Vanadium is a typical transition metal in that it exhibits variable oxidation numbers.

   a Give the oxidation number of vanadium in the species shown in Table 9.6.

Species	Oxidation number
VCl_2	+ 2
VO_2^+	+ 5
NH_4VO_3	+ 5
VO^{2+}	+ 4
$V_2(SO_4)_3$	+ 3

[5]

Table 9.6

b The aqueous V^{3+} ion can be reduced to V^{2+} by reacting it with zinc. Give an equation for this reaction. [1]

c V^{2+} reacts with nitric acid according to the equation:

$$V^{2+}(aq) + 2NO_3^-(aq) + 2H^+(aq) \rightarrow VO^{2+}(aq) + 2NO_2(g) + H_2O(l)$$

Give the half-equations for this reaction, clearly stating which is reduction and which is oxidation. [3]

[Total 9]

14 A 0.50 g sample of hydrated ammonium iron(II) sulfate with formula $(NH_4)_2SO_4 \cdot FeSO_4 \cdot xH_2O$ was dissolved in dilute sulfuric acid and made up to a total volume of $250 \, cm^3$. A $25.00 \, cm^3$ portion of this was then analysed by titration with $0.00100 \, mol \, dm^3$ $KMnO_4$ solution; $25.50 \, cm^3$ of the $KMnO_4$ solution was required. In the reaction the iron(II) ions are oxidised to iron(III).

The half-equation for the reduction of the manganate(VII) ion is as follows:

$$MnO_4^-(aq) + 8H^+(aq) + 5e^- \rightarrow Mn^{2+}(aq) + 4H_2O(l)$$

a Deduce the balanced equation for the reaction between Fe^{2+} and MnO_4^- ions. [1]

b Calculate the number of moles of $KMnO_4$ used per titre. [1]

c Calculate the number of moles of Fe^{2+} ions that are oxidised during the reaction. [1]

d Calculate the number of moles of $(NH_4)_2SO_4 \cdot FeSO_4 \cdot xH_2O$ present in the original sample. [1]

e Deduce the relative formula mass of the $(NH_4)_2SO_4 \cdot FeSO_4 \cdot xH_2O$ and hence deduce the value of x. [3]

[Total 7]

15 In a voltaic cell chemical energy is converted into electrical energy. Figure 9.4 shows a voltaic cell made using iron and copper half-cells.

$$Cu^{2+}(aq) + 2e^- \rightleftharpoons Cu(s) \qquad E^\ominus = +0.34V \text{ cat red}$$
$$Fe^{2+}(aq) + 2e^- \rightleftharpoons Fe(s) \qquad E^\ominus = -0.45V \text{ ano oxi}$$

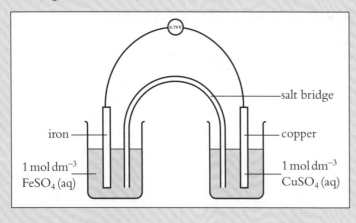

Figure 9.4 Iron copper cell.

a Give the half-equation for the reactions at each electrode. [3]

b Describe any changes that would be seen in each beaker. [4]

[Total 7]

Anode: $Fe_{(s)} \rightarrow Fe^{2+}_{(aq)} + 2e^-$

cathode: $Cu^{2+}_{(aq)} + 2e^- \rightarrow Cu_{(s)}$

cathode is fatter

anode is skinnier

solution will be less blue

16 Describe the similarities and differences between voltaic and electrolytic cells. [4]

[Total 4]

17 **HL** Describe additional similarities and differences between voltaic and electrolytic cells. [6]

[Total 6]

18 **HL** Describe a standard hydrogen electrode and explain how it can be used to find the standard electrode potential of a half-cell. [5]

[Total 5]

19 **HL** Electrolysis can yield different products under different conditions.
a Give the products obtained when sodium chloride is electrolysed under the following conditions. Include half-equations in your answer and indicate at which electrode each product is produced.
   i when molten
   ii in concentrated solution
   iii in dilute solutio. [6]
b Using electrode potential data from the data book, explain why different products are produced in parts **ii** and **iii**. [3]

[Total 9]

20 **HL**
a Explain the process of electroplating. [2]
b Draw a diagram of a simple cell that could be set up in a laboratory to coat a metal object with silver. [1]
c Name a suitable electrolyte and state from what substance each electrode should be made. [3]
d Give the half-equations for the reactions in your cell. [2]

[Total 8]

10 Organic chemistry

Chapter outline

- Recognise and identify the following families of organic molecules: alkanes, alkenes, alkynes, halogenoalkanes, alcohols, ethers, aldehydes, ketones, esters, carboxylic acids, amines, amides, nitriles, arenes and the functional groups that these molecules contain. Explain the trends in the boiling points of the members of a homologous series.
- Use different types of formulas for molecules including general formulas, molecular, empirical, skeletal, and full and condensed structural formulas.
- Draw and name non-cyclic alkanes and halogenoalkanes up to halohexanes, alkenes up to hexene and alkynes up to hexyne, compounds up to six carbon atoms (in the basic chain for nomenclature purposes) containing only one of the classes of functional groups: alcohols, ethers, aldehydes, halogenoalkanes, ketones, esters and carboxylic acids.
- Describe the characteristic reactions of alkanes, alkenes, alcohols, halogenoalkanes, polymers and benzene including the mechanism for the reaction of alkanes with halogens.
- Recall the following mechanisms: nucleophilic substitution including factors that affect the rate of S_N1 and S_N2 reactions, electrophilic addition including Markovnikov's rule and electrophilic substitution. **HL**
- Describe the reduction of carbonyl compounds and carboxylic acids and of nitrobenzene to phenylamine. **HL**
- Deduce a multi-step synthetic route given starting reagents and the desired product. **HL**
- Explain what is meant by stereoisomerism and describe *cis–trans*, *E/Z*, conformational and optical isomerism. **HL**
- Apply the Cahn–Ingold–Prelog system to the naming of *E/Z* isomers. **HL**
- Deduce whether a given molecule will exhibit optical isomerism and compare the physical and chemical properties of enantiomers including how optical isomers can be distinguished using a polarimeter. **HL**

KEY TERMS

Electrophile: A species that can accept a lone pair of electrons to form a coordinate bond; electrophiles are Lewis acids.

Heterolytic fission: The breaking of covalent bond where both electrons in the bond remain with one of the atoms in the bond.

Homologous series: A series of compounds of the same family, with the same general formula, which differ from each other by a common structural unit.

Homolytic fission: The breaking of a covalent bond where one electron in the bond remains with each of the atoms in the bond.

Isomerism: Where molecules have the same molecular formula but their atoms are arranged differently.

Nucleophile: A species that can donate a pair of electrons to form a coordinate bond; nucleophiles are Lewis bases.

Structural isomerism: Molecules with the same molecular formulas but with different structural formulas.

Chiral centre/chiral carbon: A carbon atom with four different atoms or groups attached to it (also known as an asymmetric carbon).

cis–trans **isomerism:** Two compounds that have the same structural formulas but the groups are arranged differently in space due to restricted rotation around a double bond or a ring.

Conformational isomerism: Forms of the same molecule that differ due to rotation about a σ bond.

Optical isomers: Molecules which are non-superimposable mirror images of each other.

Stereoisomerism: Molecules with the same molecular and structural formulas but with the atoms arranged differently in space.

Exercise 10.1 – Fundamentals of organic chemistry

Recognising different functional groups and naming compounds is a fundamental skill.

1 Copy and complete Table 10.1.

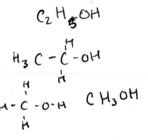

	Homologous series	Functional group	Name of functional group	General formula
a	alcohol	$-OH$	hydroxyl	$C_nH_{2n+1}OH$
b	aldehyde	$-C\!\!\begin{smallmatrix}O\\H\end{smallmatrix}$	~~aldehyde~~ carbonyl	$C_nH_{2n}O$
c	alkane		alkyl	C_nH_{2n+2}
d	alkene	$C=C$	alkenyl	C_nH_{2n}
e	alkyne	$C\equiv C$	alkynyl	C_nH_{2n-2}
f	amide	$O=C-NH_2$	amide	
g	amine	$-NH_2$ $-NHR$ $-NR_2$	amine	
h	arenes	$-C_6H_5$	phenyl	
i	carboxylic acid	$-COOH$	carboxyl	$C_nH_{2n+1}COOH$
j	ester	$R-C\!\!\begin{smallmatrix}O\end{smallmatrix}-O-R$	ester	
k	ether	$C-O-C$	ether	
l	halogenoalkane	$R-X$	alkyl	
m	ketone	$R-C\!\!\begin{smallmatrix}O\end{smallmatrix}-R$	~~ketone~~ carbonyl	$C_nH_{2n}O$
n	nitrile	$R-C\equiv N$	nitriles	

Table 10.1

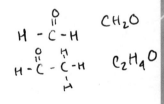

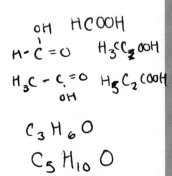

Take care to distinguish between the name of a homologous series and the name of the functional group; these are the same for some groups but not for all.

o The headings of the table include the terms 'homologous series' and 'functional group'. Define these terms.

2 As well as identifying functional groups, you will also need to be able to classify compounds as saturated, unsaturated, aliphatic, aromatic and be able to describe a functional group as primary, secondary or tertiary.
   a What is meant by the term 'saturated'? *every C single bonded to C*
   b What is meant by the term 'unsaturated'?
   c What is meant by the term 'aliphatic'? *straight chain*
   d What is meant by the term 'aromatic'? *rings w/ delocalized e⁻*
   e Name the following compounds and classify them as saturated, unsaturated, aliphatic, aromatic and primary, secondary or tertiary if applicable.

   i

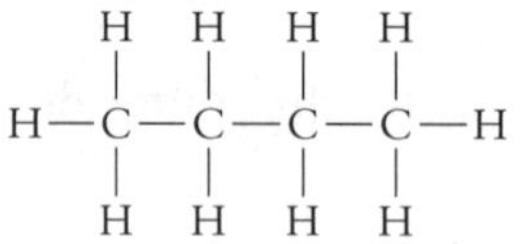

   butane, sat

   Figure 10.1

   ii

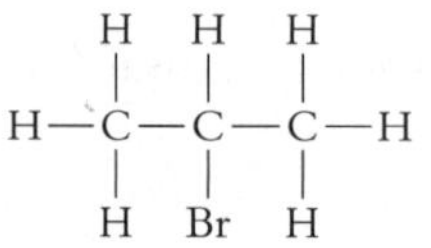

   2-bromopropane

   Figure 10.2

   iii

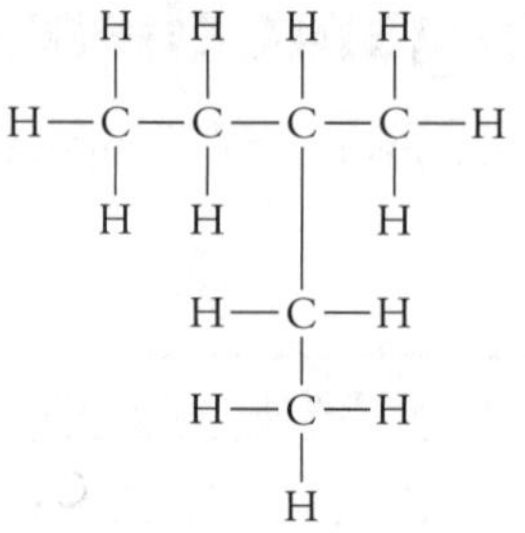

   3-methyl pentane
   sat

   Figure 10.3

   iv

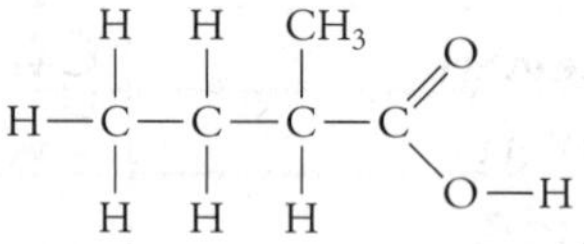

   2-methylbutanoic acid
   sat

   Figure 10.4

   v

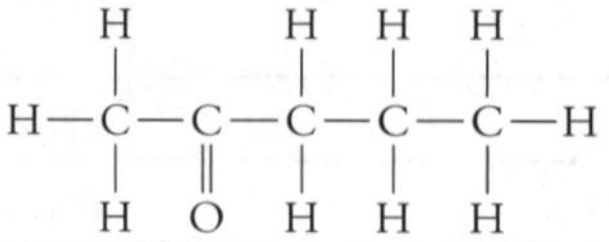

   sat
   pent-2-anone

   Figure 10.5

   vi

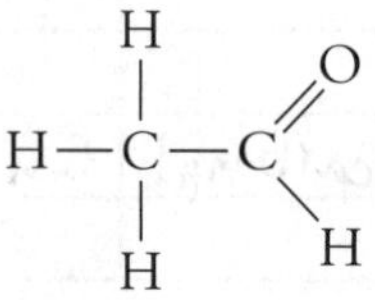

   ethanal

   Figure 10.6

vii

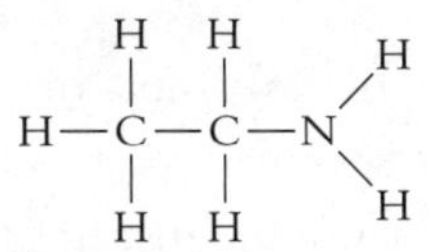

H—C—C—N (with H atoms) *amine*
methanamine

Figure 10.7

viii

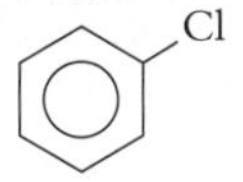

(benzene ring with Cl) *aromatic*
chlorobenzene

Figure 10.8

ix

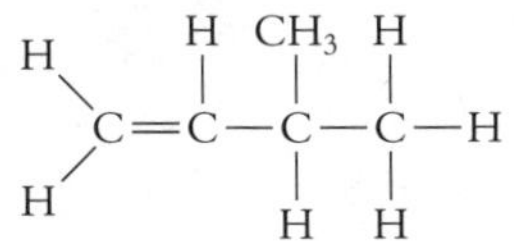

C=C—C—C—H (with H and CH₃) *3-methylbut-1-ene*

Figure 10.9

x

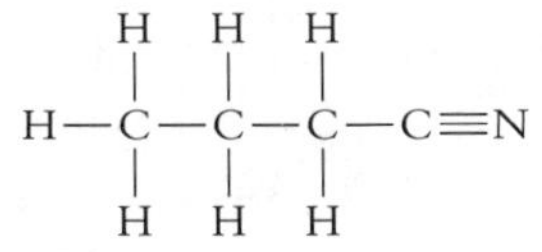

H—C—C—C—C≡N (with H atoms) *butanenitrile*

$-\overset{\text{O}}{\overset{\|}{C}}-O-CH_2CH_3$ (with H)

Figure 10.10

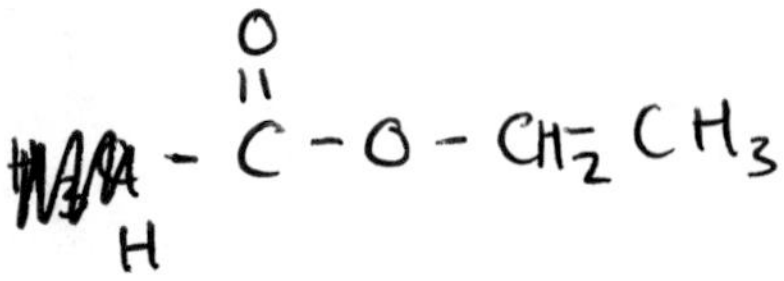

f Draw the following molecules:

  i hex-1-ene
  ii 3-methylbut-1-yne
  iii ethyl methanoate
  iv a tertiary bromoalkane with 5 carbon atoms
  v an ester containing 4 carbon atoms

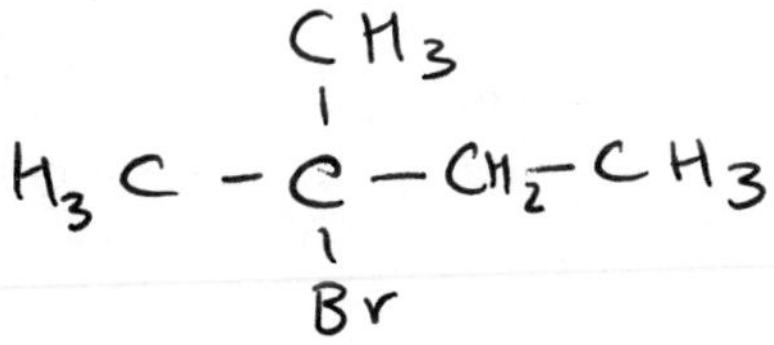

$H_3C-\overset{CH_3}{\underset{Br}{\overset{|}{\underset{|}{C}}}}-CH_2-CH_3$

Correct connectivity is important when drawing structural formulas. Bonds must be accurately placed to show which atom is joined to which. For example, the functional group of an alcohol must be written C–O–H and not C–H–O. The only exception is the case of alkyl groups which can always be written as CH_3-. They do not need to be written H_3C- when on the left-hand side of a structure.

3 Copy and complete Table 10.2 to show the different representations of organic molecules.

	Name	Molecular formula	Empirical formula	Full structural formula	Skeletal formula
a	butane				
b		C_6H_6			
c					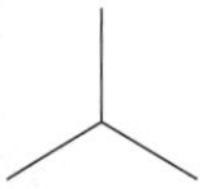 Figure 10.11
d				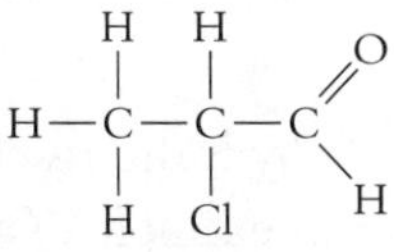 Figure 10.12	
e	ethyl ethanoate				

Table 10.2

c bonded to 2 C + 1H
delocalized electrons ring

Most of the time, it doesn't matter whether a skeletal, full structural formula or a mixture of the two is used as long as it is unambiguous. Occasionally a specific type of structure is called for in a question, in which case read the question and follow the instructions!

4 Benzene is an aromatic, unsaturated hydrocarbon with the molecular formula C_6H_6.
   a Describe the structure of benzene.

A labelled diagram would be useful here. At Higher Level, the answer could include reference to s and p bonding.

☆ b Describe the physical evidence which supports the delocalised structure of benzene rather than the Kekulé model.

same bond lengths / angles

Physical evidence includes bond lengths, bond strength and the number of di-substituted isomers.

c Describe the chemical evidence for the structure of benzene.

Chemical evidence includes enthalpy of hydrogenation and that benzene undergoes substitution reactions rather than addition reactions like alkenes.

C_2H_6

I
$Cl \rightarrow 2Cl\cdot$

P
$Cl\cdot + C_2H_6 \rightarrow C_2H_5\cdot + HCl$
$C_2H_5\cdot + Cl_2 \rightarrow C_2H_5Cl + Cl\cdot$

T
$C_2H_5\cdot + Cl\cdot \rightarrow C_2H_5Cl$

Exercise 10.2 – Functional group chemistry

1 Alkanes are generally unreactive but do react with halogens in the presence of UV light. Using the chlorination of methane as an example:
   a Give an equation for the initiation step.

The free radical must be represented by a single dot.
Initiation steps increase the number of free radicals.

b i Give equations to show the role of chlorine atoms in the propagation steps of the reaction.

Propagation steps maintain the number of free radicals; there are the same number on both the left- and right-hand sides of the equations.

ii Why is this reaction known as a chain reaction?
c Give an example of a termination step.

Termination steps involve a reduction in the number of free radicals.

d This reaction is known as a 'free radical substitution'. Explain what is meant by this term.

Both the term 'free radical' and the term 'substitution' need to be defined.

e This mechanism involves homolytic fission. Use one of the steps in the mechanism to explain this term showing the movement of electrons with curly arrows.

HL students should use 'fish hook' arrows here.

f Explain why this reaction often produces a mixture of halogenated products.

2 The reactions of alkenes are characterised by addition reactions.
  a Complete the following equations:
     i $C_3H_6 + Br_2 \rightarrow$ **ii** $CH_3CH = CHCH_3 + HBr \rightarrow$
     iii $C_2H_4 + H_2O \rightarrow$ **iv** $CH_3CH_2CH = CH_2 + H_2 \rightarrow$
  b Alkenes also undergo addition polymerisation.
  Copy and complete Table 10.3 to show the monomer or repeating unit for the following polymers:

Monomer	Repeating unit
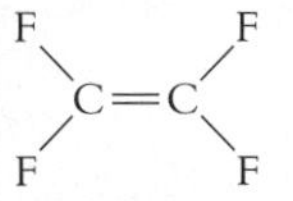 Figure 10.13	
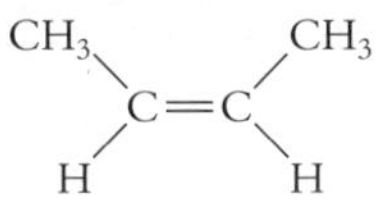 Figure 10.14	
	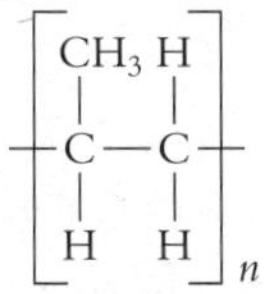 Figure 10.15
	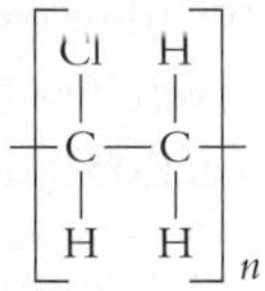 Figure 10.16

Table 10.3

Repeating units must have bonds extending out at both sides to show how the units are connected to one another. Square brackets and the subscript 'n' are also recommended but are not essential.

3 All alcohols undergo combustion as well as condensation reactions to produce esters. Some alcohols can also undergo oxidation reactions.

   a Give an equation for the complete combustion of propan-2-ol.

   b The formation of an ester can also be described as nucleophilic substitution. What is meant by the term 'nucleophilic substitution'?

   c Ethanol reacts with propanoic acid to form an ester.

      i   Give the equation of the reaction and the name of the ester formed.

      ii   State the reagents and conditions required for the reaction.

   d Ethyl ethanoate is an ester which has a number of structural isomers.

      i   Draw all of these which are esters.

      ii   These esters are isomers of carboxylic acids. Draw and name these.

4 a Not all alcohols undergo oxidation. Which type of alcohols are resistant to oxidation?

   b Name two suitable reagents that can be used for the oxidation of an alcohol and the colour changes that would be observed when each of these is used.

   c A mixture of ethanol and a suitable oxidising agent can produce two different products depending on the apparatus used as shown in Figure 10.17a and b.

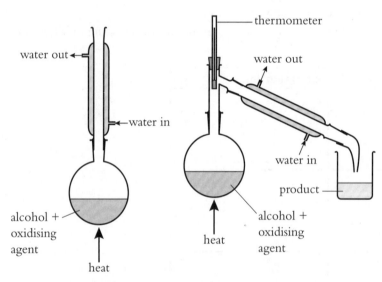

Figure 10.17 a and b: Oxidation of ethanol.

      i   Give equations for the reactions that occur in these two experiments and suggest why the two different methods are required.

      ii   What name is given to the two practical techniques shown in Figure 10.17?

      iii What would be produced if propan-2-ol were used in these experiments rather than ethanol? Give an equation for any reactions showing the structural formulas of the reactants and products.

5 Halogenoalkanes undergo substitution reactions with aqueous sodium hydroxide.

   a Give an equation for the reaction between 1-bromobutane and aqueous sodium hydroxide.

   b The hydroxide ion donates a pair of electrons to form a covalent bond with the carbon atom of the halogenoalkane. What name is given to this type of reagent?

HL Exercise 10.3 – Types of organic reactions

1 Nucleophilic substitution is explored in more depth in this part of the syllabus. In primary halogenoalkanes the reaction occurs via an S_N2 mechanism whereas S_N1 is more common in tertiary halogenoalkanes.

  a What do the numbers 1 and 2 represent in the names of these two mechanisms?

  b Describe the mechanism for the reaction of 1-bromoethane with aqueous sodium hydroxide.

'Describe' does not mean that the answer must be given in words – use a diagram/equation including curly arrows.

These mechanisms should include lone pairs of electrons on the nucleophile and the dipole on the carbon–halogen bond as well as the curly arrows. Curly arrows must start at a pair of electrons or a bond and end where the electrons move to: a new bond or on an atom as a lone pair.

  c Describe the mechanism for the reaction of 2-bromo-2-methylpropane with aqueous sodium hydroxide.

  d The rate of hydrolysis depends on a number of different factors. One of these is the identity of the halogen.

  i Describe the trend in the rate of hydrolysis of 1-iodoethane, 1-bromoethane and 1-chloroethane.

  ii Explain the trend in the rate of hydrolysis of 1-iodoethane, 1-bromoethane and 1-chloroethane.

  e Another factor in the rate of hydrolysis is the identity of the nucleophile.

  i Explain why a hydroxide ion is a stronger nucleophile than water.

  ii The identity of the nucleophile does not affect the rate of an S_N1 reaction but it does affect the rate of an S_N2 reaction. With reference to these mechanisms, explain this difference.

  f A third factor that affects the rate of hydrolysis is the identity of the solvent. Protic polar solvents favour the S_N1 mechanism whereas aprotic polar solvents favour S_N2 mechanisms.

  i What is meant by a 'protic polar solvent'? Give an example of a protic polar solvent.

  ii What is meant by an 'aprotic polar solvent'?

> Did you explain this in your answer to part **i**? Read the question carefully and take note of the command term. 'Describe' and 'explain' have different meanings.

2 Alkenes generally react via an electrophilic addition reaction.

  a Describe this mechanism using the reaction of ethene with hydrogen bromide to illustrate your answer.

  b Unsymmetrical alkenes such as propene undergo addition reactions to produce a mixture of products.

  i Draw the structures of the two possible products formed when propene reacts with hydrogen bromide.

  ii Suggest which will be the major product.

  iii Explain your answer to part **ii**.

> Markovnikov's rule allows the major product to be identified; it does not explain why. The reason is linked to the stability of the carbocation intermediate.

3 Benzene undergoes substitution reactions which occur via an electrophilic mechanism.

  a Complete the equation for the nitration of benzene.

   $C_6H_6 + HNO_3 \rightarrow$

  b This reaction is catalysed by concentrated sulfuric acid. Show how the sulfuric acid and nitric acid react with each other to produce the electrophile.

  c Give the mechanism for the reaction between the electrophile and benzene.

  d Give an equation to show how the sulfuric acid catalyst is regenerated.

4 Carboxylic acids, aldehydes and ketones can undergo reduction reactions.

  a Complete and balance the following equations:

   i $CH_3CH_2CHO + [H] \rightarrow$

   ii $CH_3CH_2COCH_3 + [H] \rightarrow$

   iii $CH_3CH_2COOH + [H] \rightarrow$

  b Suggest a suitable reagent for all three reactions in part **a**.

  c Suggest a reagent that is suitable for the reactions in parts **a i** and **ii** but that would be unsuitable for **a iii**.

  d Another reduction reaction is the reduction of nitrobenzene.

   i Write the equation for this reaction and give the name of the organic product.

   ii State the reagents required to bring about this reaction.

> This is a two-stage reaction.

HL Exercise 10.4 – Synthetic routes

It is essential to know the reactions of the different functional groups individually and to recognise the role of a particular reagent in order to devise a synthetic route. One way to learn these is to use reaction schemes which link the different functional groups to each other. Practise drawing these out until you can draw it all from a blank piece of paper.

These next few questions give you a skeleton broken down into smaller parts to make this easier.

1 Copy and complete the gaps in the following reaction schemes to give either the formulas of the products or the reagents and conditions as indicated in the questions.

  a Give the displayed formulas for the products in Figure 10.18.

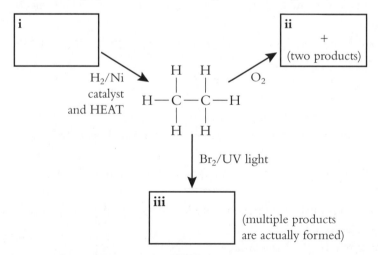

Figure 10.18 Reaction scheme for alkanes.

b Give the displayed formulas for the products in Figure 10.19.

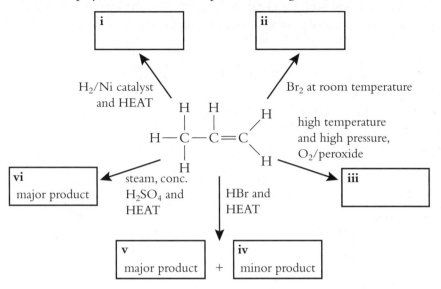

Figure 10.19 Reaction scheme for alkenes.

c Give the reagents and conditions for the reactions shown in Figure 10.20.

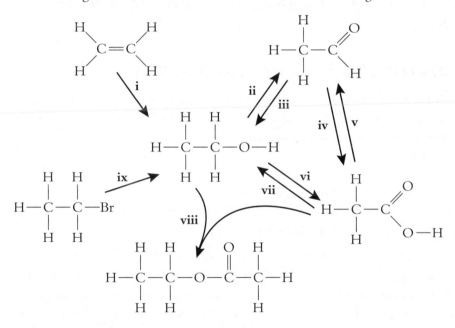

Figure 10.20 Reaction scheme for alcohols.

d Suggest a suitable reaction pathway for the following conversions and give the equations for each step:

i from but–2-ene to butanone

ii from propane to propanal

iii from 3-phenylpropene to 2-phenylpropan-1,2-diol (see Figure 10.21)

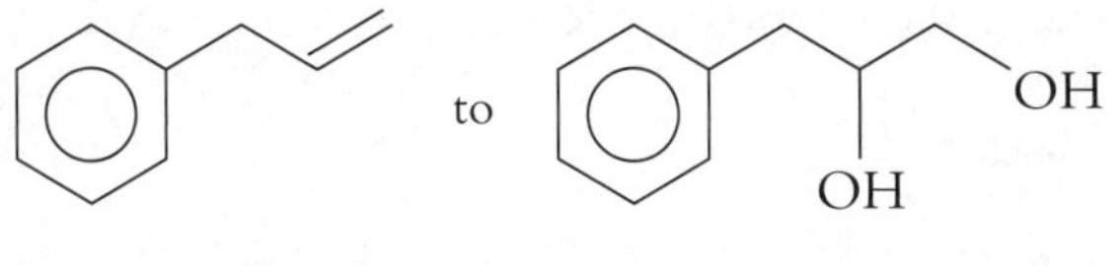

to

Figure 10.21 From 3-phenyl propene to 3-phenylpropan-1-2-diol.

As long as the functional group is not directly attached to the benzene ring, the reactions will be the same as those of aliphatic compounds.

e Chemists often design synthetic pathways like those in part **d** using retrosynthesis. What does this term mean?

2 A similar synthetic pathway can be developed for aromatic compounds.

a Copy Figure 10.22 and complete the spaces to show the missing products and reagents and conditions.

Figure 10.22 Aromatic reaction scheme.

b What is the name of the final product in the reaction scheme shown in Figure 10.22?

c For each step in the reaction scheme, name the type of reaction.

HL Exercise 10.5 – Stereoisomerism

Isomerism can be subdivided into different types in a number of different ways. Structural isomerism occurs when molecules have the same molecular formula but different structural formulas (their atoms are joined together in a different order). This section looks at stereoisomerism.

1 a Define the term 'stereoisomerism'.

b Stereoisomerism can be further subdivided into 'configurational isomerism' and 'conformational isomerism'. Define these two terms.

Conformational isomers constantly interconvert and cannot be isolated. Covalent bonds do not need to be broken in this process. One isomer may be slightly more stable (and therefore more common) than another, but the energy barrier to rotation is often very low. Configurational isomers can only interconvert by the breaking and re-forming of a covalent bond.

c Configurational isomerism can be divided into '*cis–trans* isomerism' and 'optical isomerism'. Define these terms.

You have probably come to realise the importance of learning definitions by this point in the course!

d Identify the type of isomerism shown by the following pairs of molecules:

i

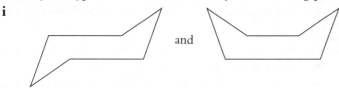

Figure 10.23 Aromatic reaction scheme.

ii

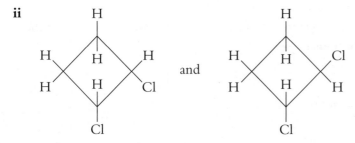

Figure 10.24 1,2-dichlorocyclobutane.

iii

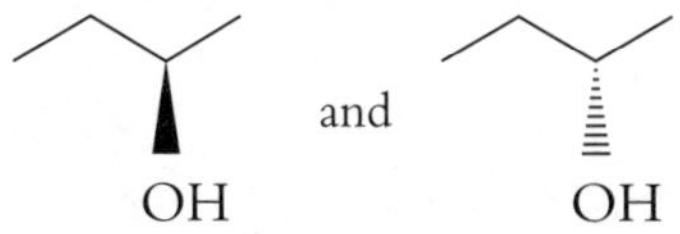

and

OH   OH

Figure 10.25 Butan-2-ol.

e With reference to the bonding in the molecules, explain why alkenes exhibit *cis–trans* isomerism.

2 a Draw the *cis–trans* isomers of the following compounds, clearly identifying which is *cis* and which is *trans*.
 i pent-2-ene
 ii 1,2–dichlorobut-1-ene

b Naming *cis–trans* isomers cannot be used when there are four different groups attached to the double bond. When four different groups are present, the *E/Z* naming system is used which is based on the Cahn–Ingold–Prelog priority rules. Identify the following isomers as *E* or *Z*.

i

CH₂OH   Cl   Br   Cl
  C=C   and   C=C
Br   H   CH₂OH   H
 isomer A   isomer B

ii

CH₃   CH₂CH₃   CH₃   C—OH
  C=C   and   C=C   ‖ O
HO   C=O   HO   CH₂CH₃
 isomer A | isomer B
          OH

iii

CH₃   CH₂OH   CH₃   CH₂CH₂OH
  C=C   and   C=C
Br   CH₂CH₂OH   Br   CH₂OH
 isomer A   isomer B

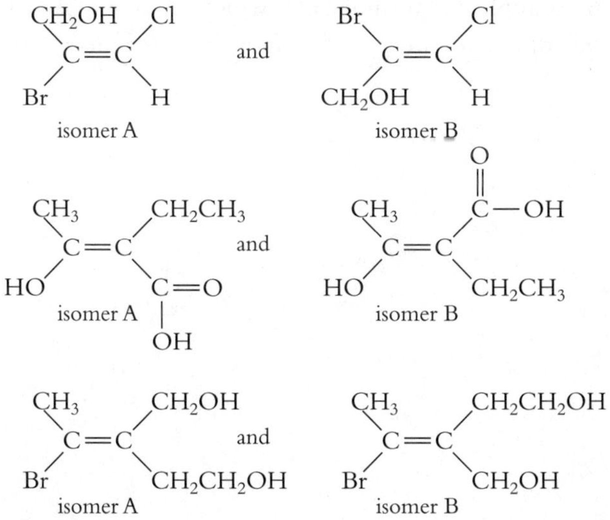

Figure 10.26 *E/Z* isomers.

Priority is assigned by looking at the atomic number of the atom attached to the carbon of the double bond. If this is the same in two cases, then the atomic number of the next atom along the chain is considered. This process continues until a difference is found. Double-bonded atoms such as the oxygen in –CHO count as two groups and so have higher priority than single bonded groups like – CH₂OH.

3 It is possible to draw a mirror image of anything: a person, a tree, a house or a molecule. Optical isomerism occurs when two molecules are mirror images of each other but these mirror images are non-superimposable.

  a Optical isomerism occurs when a molecule possesses a chiral or asymmetric centre. Explain what is meant by a chiral or asymmetric centre.

  b What is the effect on plane-polarised light when it is passed through an optically active compound?

  c What name is given to optical isomers?

  d Determine which of the following compounds are optically active and, for those which are, draw both isomers.

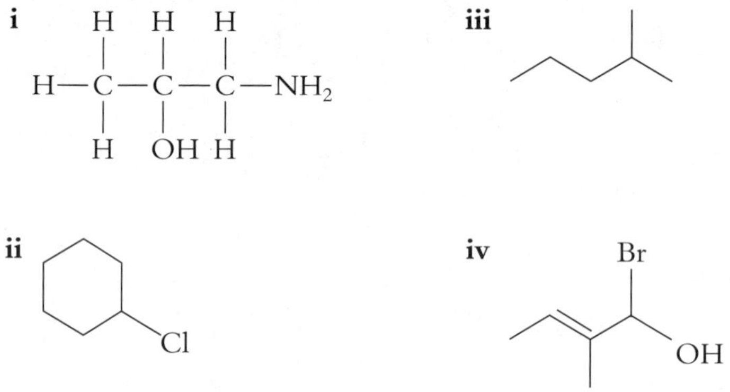

Figure 10.27 Optical isomers.

When drawing optical isomers, 3D notation must be used, but this is only needed around the chiral centre. Draw a basic 3D tetrahedral shape with the chiral carbon at the centre and then place the four groups around it. Take care to show correct connectivity: HO–C and not OH–C, for example.

4 a What name is given to an equimolar mixture of two optical isomers?

  b What effect would this have on the rotation of plane of plane-polarised light?

  c Figure 10.28 shows an example of two molecules which are stereoisomers because their atoms are arranged differently in space but are not mirror images of one another.

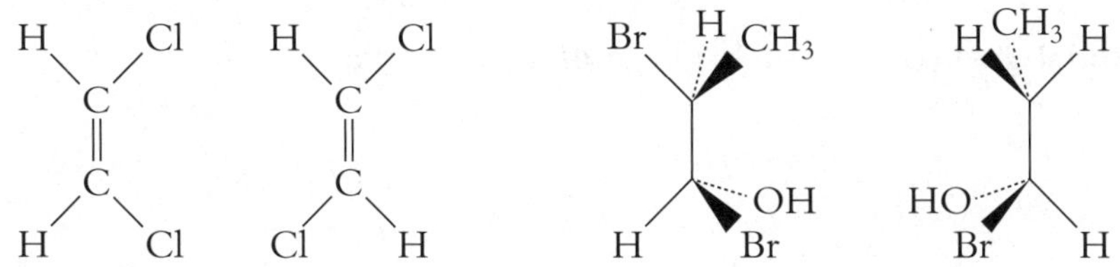

cis– and trans–1,
2–dichloroethene

1,2–dibromopropan–1–ol

Figure 10.28 Stereoisomers which are not mirror images.

What name is given to these types of molecules?

d Describe the differences in the chemical and physical properties of optically active compounds.

e Optical isomerism in cyclic compounds can be determined by considering whether or not the molecule has a plane of symmetry. If there is a plane of symmetry, then the molecule will not be optically active.

Identify whether the following molecules have a plane of symmetry and therefore whether or not they are optically active:

i   *cis*–1,2–dibromocyclopropane
ii *trans*–1,2–dimethylcyclopropane
iii *cis*–1,2–diiodocyclobutane
iv *trans*–cyclobutan–1,2–diol

? Exam-style questions

1   **Which is the correct name for this molecule?**

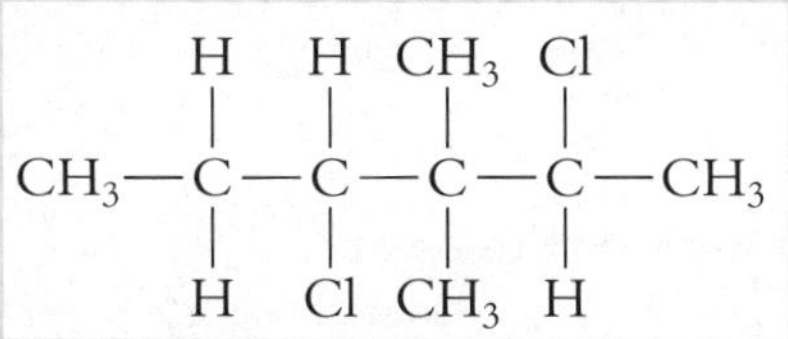

Figure 10.29

 A 1,3–dichloro 1,2,2,4–tetramethylbutane
 B 2,4–dichloro–3–dimethylhexane
 C 2,4–dichloro–3,3–dimethylhexane
 D 3,5–dichloro–4,4–dimethylhexane

2   **Which of the following molecules is a tertiary alcohol?**
 A 2,4–dimethylpentan–2–ol
 B 2–methylpentan–3–ol
 C 2,2–dimethylpentan–1–ol
 D 2,2–dimethylpentan–3–ol

3   Identify the names of the functional groups present in the molecule shown in Figure 10.30.

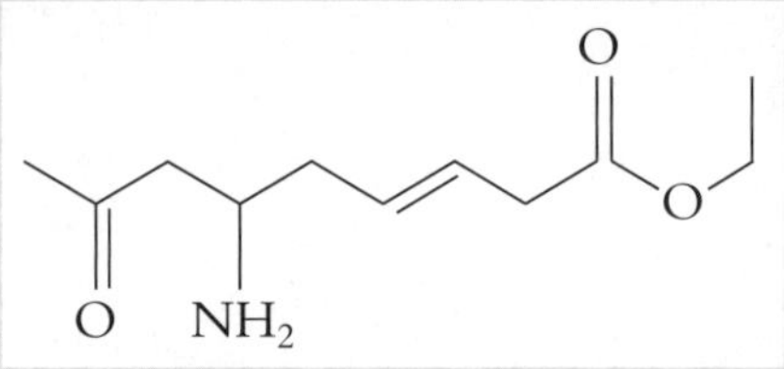

Figure 10.30

A ketone, amine, alkene, ester
B carbonyl, amine, alkenyl, ester
C amide, alkenyl, carbonyl, ether
D carboxamide, alkenyl, ester

4   **Which statements are true about the reaction of methane with bromine?**
I   The reaction occurs in the dark.
II The reaction involves homolytic fission.
III A mixture of products is formed.
A I only
B I and II only
C II and III only
D I, II and III

5   **Which of the following reagents can be used to convert a halogenoalkane into an alcohol?**
A acidified potassium manganate(VII) solution
B concentrated sulfuric acid
C lithium aluminium hydride
D aqueous sodium hydroxide

6   **Ethanoic acid and propan-2-ol acid react together to form which of the esters shown in Figure 10.31?**

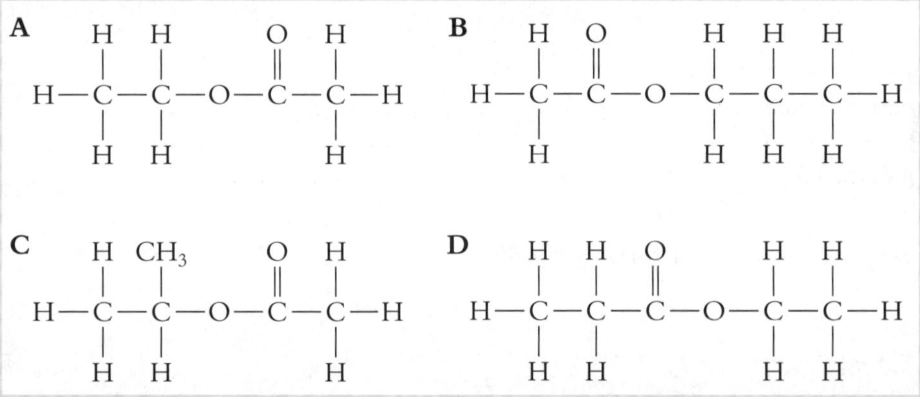

Figure 10.31

7 **HL** Which of these mechanisms includes homolytic fission?

A electrophilic addition

B nucleophilic addition

C electrophilic substitution

D free radical substitution

8 **HL** Which of the following reactions occurs via a nucleophilic mechanism?

A $CH_3CH_2OH + 2[O] \rightarrow CH_3COOH + H_2O$

B $C_2H_4 + HBr \rightarrow CH_3CH_2Br$

C $C_6H_6 + HNO_3 \rightarrow C_6H_5NO_2 + H_2O$

D $CH_3CH_2CH_2Br + OH^- \rightarrow CH_3CH_2CH_2OH + Br^-$

9 **HL** Which of the following molecules exhibits optical isomerism?

A butane

B 1-chlorobutane

C 2-chlorobutane

D 2-chloro-2-methylbutane

10 **HL** Which of the following molecules would be produced by the reaction of propanone with lithium aluminium hydride?

A propan-1-ol

B propan-2-ol

C propanal

D propanoic acid

11 Benzene is an unsaturated hydrocarbon. Its skeletal formula can be represented by either of the diagrams in Figure 10.32.

Figure 10.32 Skeletal formula of benzene.

a Define the terms 'unsaturated' and 'hydrocarbon'. [2]

b Give the molecular formula of benzene. [1]

c Give the empirical formula of benzene. [1]

d The hydrogenation of cyclohexene and of benzene can be represented by the equations shown in Figure 10.33.

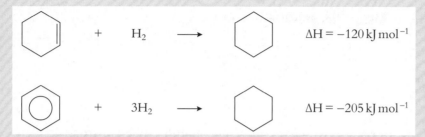

Figure 10.33 Hydrogenation of cyclohexene.

Using this information, draw an energy level diagram to explain which of the representations of benzene in Figure 10.32 is believed to be more accurate. [4]

e Benzene does not decolourise bromine water and only reacts with halogens in the presence of a catalyst. Under these conditions an electrophilic substitution reaction occurs.

   i   What can be deduced about the structure of benzene from the fact that it undergoes electrophilic reactions. [1]

   ii What can be deduced from the fact that benzene undergoes substitution rather than addition reactions. [2]

   iii Explain how the answers to parts **i** and **ii** support ideas about both models for the structure of benzene. [2]

[Total 13]

12 **Figure 10.34 shows the trend in the boiling points of three different homologous series, straight-chain alkanes, straight-chain primary chloroalkanes and straight-chain primary alcohols.**

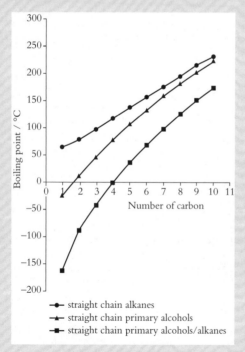

Figure 10.34 Boiling points in three homologous series.

a Explain the general trend in the boiling points of the alkanes. [2]

b Explain why the relationship between boiling point and the number of carbon atoms is not linear. [1]

c Explain why it would not be fair to compare the boiling points of molecules from each series with the same number of carbon atoms such as comparing the boiling points of ethane, chloroethane and ethanol. [1]

d Choose one molecule from each homologous series to illustrate the effect of the nature of the functional group on boiling point. [3]

[Total 7]

13 **Alkanes have relatively low reactivity but undergo both combustion and halogenation.**

a Alkanes can produce carbon dioxide, carbon monoxide and carbon as combustion products depending on the conditions.

Give separate equations for the formation of these three products from the combustion of propane and state the different conditions that lead to their formation. [5]

b Propane reacts with bromine according to the equation given in Figure 10.35, in the presence of UV light.

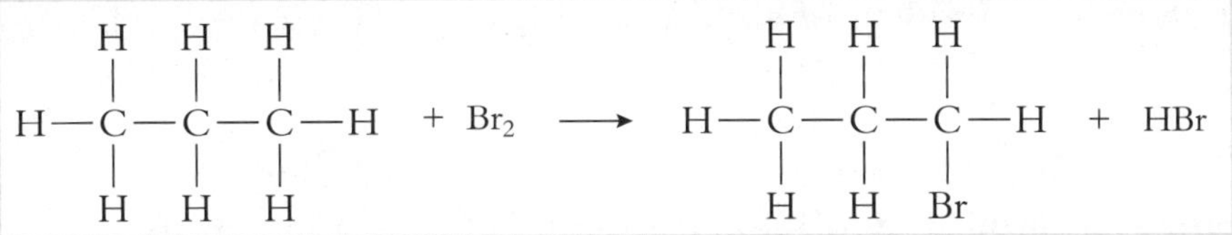

Figure 10.35 Bromination of propane.

i Describe the mechanism for this reaction including the role of UV light. [5]

ii State the name given to this mechanism. [1]

iii Small amounts of hexane are often formed during this reaction as well as traces of other bromoalkanes such as 2-bromopropane and multi-substituted alkanes. Explain how these substances are formed. [3]

[Total 14]

14 **Describe what would be observed in the following laboratory experiments and give an equation for any reactions that occur:**

a Shaking hexane with a few drops of bromine. [1]

b Shaking hexene with a few drops of bromine. [2]

c Refluxing a mixture of acidified potassium dichromate solution and propan-1-ol. [2]

d Refluxing a mixture of acidified potassium manganate(VII) solution and ethanol. [2]

e Refluxing a mixture of ethanol, ethanoic acid and sulfuric acid. [2]

[Total 9]

15 **HL** **Alcohols can be prepared both from alkenes and from halogenoalkanes.**

a i Give an equation for the reaction of propene with H_2O to form propanol. The formula of the product can be represented as C_3H_7OH. [1]

ii This is an electrophilic addition reaction and the mechanism is the same as that for the reaction of ethene with a hydrogen halide. Describe the mechanism for the electrophilic addition of H_2O to propene. [3]

iii The reaction of propene with H_2O gives a mixture of two organic products. Give the structural formulas of these two compounds and explain which will be the major product. [2]

b i Give an equation for the hydrolysis of 2-iodobutane with aqueous hydroxide ions to form an alcohol. [1]

ii This reaction occurs via a mixture of both S_N1 and S_N2 mechanisms.
The S_N1 mechanism is not stereospecific whereas the S_N2 mechanism is stereospecific. Explain this difference in the products, giving equations to illustrate your answer. [4]

[Total 11]

16 **HL** **Starting from 1-chlorobutane as the only organic reagent, outline the preparation of butyl butanoate. Include all relevant reagents and conditions but you do not need to describe how the product of each step is separated or purified. [6]**

[Total 6]

17 **HL** **It is possible to distinguish between optical isomers of a particular compound by comparing their effect on plane-polarised light using a polarimeter.**

a Describe the effect of optical isomers on plane-polarised light and how a polarimeter can be used to distinguish them. [4]

b Apart from their effect on plane-polarised light, describe the other features of optical isomers. [1]

c i The first member of the homologous series of alkanes which is optically active has the molecular formula C_7H_{16}. Draw both enantiomers of this molecule. [2]

ii Cyclic compounds can also exhibit optical isomerism. The first cyclic alkane to do so has the molecular formula C_5H_{10}. Draw the enantiomers and name this molecule. [2]

[Total 9]

Measurement, data processing 11 and analysis

Chapter outline

- Distinguish between qualitative and quantitative data and recall that quantitative data obtained from measurements are always associated with random errors/uncertainties due to the limitations of the apparatus and by human limitations including the calculation of the random error in a final result.
- Explain the difference between random and systematic errors, discuss their impact on processed data and suggest how these might be reduced.
- Recall the difference between accuracy and precision when evaluating results.
- Use decimal places and significant figures appropriately in calculations.
- Draw and interpret graphs including drawing lines of best fit and the calculation of a gradient at a given point.
- Calculate the index of hydrogen deficiency (IHD) of an organic compound.
- Deduce information about the structural features of a compound from percentage composition data, MS, ^{1}H NMR or IR.
- Interpret ^{1}H NMR spectra using chemical shift data, the number of peaks, the area under each peak and splitting patterns and the use of TMS as a reference standard in ^{1}H NMR. **HL**
- Recall that X-ray crystallography can be used to identify the bond lengths and bond angles of crystalline compounds. **HL**
- Identify a compound using a combination of IR, ^{1}H NMR and MS data. **HL**

KEY TERMS AND FORMULAS

Absolute uncertainty: The uncertainty in a value quoted in the same units as the value itself.

Accuracy: How close a measurement is to the true value.

Index of hydrogen deficiency: The number of double-bond equivalents or the degree of unsaturation. (A ring is equivalent to a double bond,)

Infrared spectroscopy: An analytical technique used to identify the functional groups in an organic molecule due to their absorption of radiation in the infrared region of the electromagnetic spectrum.

Mass spectrometry: An analytical technique which is used for structural determination. The sample is bombarded with high-energy electrons and forms positively charged ions. The mass-to-charge ratio of the ions is then measured, giving rise to the different peaks on the spectrum.

NMR (nuclear magnetic resonance) spectroscopy: An analytical technique used for structural determination. It is used to identify the hydrogen atoms (protons) in a molecule.

Precision: The reproducibility of results. Precise values are ones that lie close together and are close to the mean value.

Random uncertainty: Uncertainties in a measurement due to the limitations of the measuring equipment and other uncontrollable variables. Random uncertainties result in values that are distributed on both sides of the mean.

Significant figures: The number of digits that have meaning. All non-zero digits are significant. Zeros between non-zero digits are significant. Leading zeros are never significant.

Systematic error: An error due to the apparatus or procedure used. Systematic errors result in a value being further away from the true value. Systematic errors are always in the same direction: making a value always too big or always too small. They are not reduced by repeating the results.

Spin–spin coupling: The splitting of a signal in NMR spectroscopy due to the presence of protons adjacent to those giving rise to the signal.

X-ray crystallography: An analytical technique used to produce a three-dimensional picture of the structure of a crystal. It can be used to measure bond lengths and bond angles.

$$\text{Percentage error} = \frac{(\text{experimental value} - \text{accepted value}) \times 100}{\text{accepted value}}$$

$$\text{Percentage uncertainty} = \frac{\text{uncertainty} \times 100}{\text{measured value}}$$

Index of hydrogen deficiency (IHD)

For a molecule with the formula $C_cH_hN_nO_oX_x$, where X is a halogen:

$$\text{IHD} = \frac{1}{2}(2c + 2 - h - x + n)$$

Exercise 11.1 – Uncertainties and errors in measurements and results

1 This question is about decimal places and significant figures.

   a Write the following numbers to the specified number of decimal places:

   i   69.49   2 d.p.

   ii 0.4993   3 d.p.

   iii 345.670   1 d.p.

   iv 0.0042097   4 d.p.

   b To how many significant figures have the following values been quoted?

   i   7895.40

   ii 0.00304

   iii 0.023050

   iv 3390

All non-zero digits are significant. Zeros between non-zero digits are significant. Leading zeros are never significant. In a number with a decimal point, trailing zeros (those to the right of the last non-zero digit) are significant. In a number without a decimal point, trailing zeros may or may not be significant.

c Write the following numbers to the specified number of significant figures:

i   346720   4 s.f.
ii 345.732   3 s.f.
iii 0.00595   2 s.f.
iv 4.66666×10^4 4 s.f.

d Write the following numbers in standard form to the specified number of significant figures:

i   8489.33   3 s.f.
ii 0.00045560   3 s.f.
iii 4500498   4 s.f.
iv 34.04992   3 s.f.

e Complete the following, giving the answer to the appropriate number of significant figures or decimal places.

i $345.3 + 0.034$

ii $56300 - 432$

iii $\dfrac{252}{6}$

iv $1.452 \times 10^{-3} \times 2.0$

v $456.2 - 1.45$

vi $\dfrac{3.564 \times 10^3}{0.22}$

vii $0.05 + 0.05$

viii 0.05×2

> For addition and subtraction, the final answer should be to the same number of decimal places as the original data with the fewest number of decimal places. For multiplication and division, the final answer should be quoted to the number of significant figures of the piece of data with the fewest significant figures.

$$\text{Percentage uncertainty} = \frac{\text{uncertainty} \times 100}{\text{measured value}}$$

2 This question is about random uncertainties in measurements.

a What is meant by the term 'random uncertainty'?

b Random uncertainties can be quoted as an absolute random uncertainty or as a percentage random uncertainty. Explain the difference between these two terms.

c Other than by repeating a measurement, how can absolute random uncertainties be reduced?

d Other than by repeating a measurement, how can percentage random uncertainties be reduced?

e What is the value of the following measurements? Give the uncertainty in each case.

> Think about the instrument or measuring equipment.

As a general rule the uncertainty in an analogue instrument is half the smallest division. The uncertainty in a digital instrument is one unit in the last decimal place.

i   **Figure 11.1** pH meter.

ii **Figure 11.2** A measuring cylinder.

iii **Figure 11.3** A burette.

iv **Figure 11.4** A stop-clock.

f During an experiment to measure the time taken for a reaction to happen using the stop-clock shown in part **e iv**, the experimenter guessed that the uncertainty in their reaction time was ±2 s. If the reading on the stop-clock was as shown in the figure, what value should be recorded in the results table?

g The data in Table 11.1 were obtained by repeated measurements of the mass of a piece of corn.

Reading	Mass/g ±0.001 g
1	0.133
2	0.135
3	0.132
4	0.136
5	0.136
6	0.135

Table 11.1

    i Calculate the mean mass of a piece of corn.

    ii The uncertainty in each value is 0.001 g. What is the uncertainty in the mean value?

The uncertainty in a mean value can be found in a number of ways.
1 Half the difference between the maximum and minimum values (the range) after anomalous results have been ignored.
   This gives a pessimistic value for the uncertainty.
2 Half of the deviation of the maximum and minimum values from the mean. This also gives a pessimistic value and the mean does not always lie in the middle of the range.
3 Two thirds of the deviation from the mean. This gives a better but still rough estimate.
4 The overall uncertainty can be quoted as the largest of the percentage uncertainties in the original data. For example
ΔH mean = [+100 kJ mol^{-1} (±10%) + 110 kJ mol^{-1} (±1%) + 108 kJ mol^{-1} (±3%)]/3
ΔH mean = +106 kJ mol^{-1} (±10%)
Statistical analysis of data would give a much better indication of the uncertainties but this is not a requirement of the IB Chemistry syllabus. It is a good idea to make a simple note of how an uncertainty has been calculated: e.g. mean mass = 123.4 g ± 0.1 g (half the range)

h In a series of experiments to measure the value of the volume occupied by 1 mole of an ideal gas at STP, the results shown in Table 11.2 were obtained. Each value was obtained using a different method. The accepted value is 22.7 dm^3 mol^{-1}.

Method	Value / dm^3 mol^{-1}
1	23 ± 1
2	21.0422 ± 0.0001
3	21.5 ± 0.1
4	21.97 ± 0.01

Table 11.2

Evaluate the data by finding:

   i the method which gave the most accurate result.

   ii the method which gave the least accurate result.

   iii the percentage error in the value obtained by method 3.

3 In an experiment to find the enthalpy change of neutralisation when hydrochloric acid and sodium hydroxide are reacted together, the following data were obtained.

Volume of hydrochloric acid of concentration $1.00\,mol\,dm^3 = 25.0\,cm^3 \pm 0.1\,cm^3$

Volume of sodium hydroxide of concentration $1.00\,mol\,dm^3 = 25.0\,cm^3 \pm 0.1\,cm^3$

Initial temperature = $22.5\,°C \pm 0.5\,°C$

Final temperature = $29.0\,°C \pm 0.5\,°C$

a Assuming that the specific heat capacity of the solution is $4.18\,J\,K^{-1}\,mol^{-1}$ and the density of the solution is $1.00\,g\,cm^{-3}$, calculate the value of the enthalpy change of neutralisation in $kJ\,mol^{-1}$.

b Calculate the percentage and absolute uncertainty in the final calculated value for ΔH.

c The following suggestions were made to improve the accuracy and precision of the experiment:

  1 Insulate the beaker.

  2 Measure the mass of the solutions using a 2 decimal place balance rather than measuring their volumes.

  3 Stir the reaction mixture.

  4 Use a digital thermometer that reads to 1 decimal place.

  5 Repeat the experiment a number of times.

  6 Use a burette rather than a measuring cylinder to measure the volumes of the solutions.

Which of the suggestions 1–6 above would have the following effects? Each suggestion can be used once, more than once or not at all.

   i   reduce the random uncertainties

   ii reduce the systematic errors

   iii make the results more precise

   iv make the result more accurate

> Use the formula $\Delta H = -mc\Delta T$ to find the enthalpy change for the number of moles used in the reaction. Enthalpy change of neutralisation is for one mole of water.

> When quantities with uncertainties are added or subtracted, the absolute uncertainties are added. When quantities with uncertainties are multiplied or divided, the percentage uncertainties are added. In essence, you cannot add uncertainties if they have different units so percentage uncertainties must be used.

Exercise 11.2 – Graphical techniques

1 Describe the relationships shown in Figures 11.5–11.9.

a

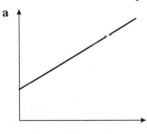

Figure 11.5

b

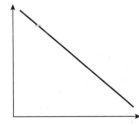

Figure 11.6

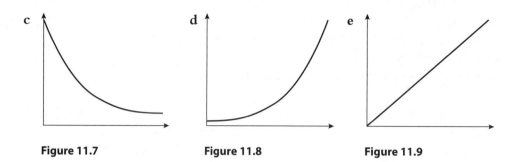

Figure 11.7   **Figure 11.8**   **Figure 11.9**

f Conventionally, is the independent variable or the dependent variable plotted along the *x*-axis of a graph?

The independent variable is the variable for which the experimenter chooses the values.

The dependent variable is what is measured; its value depends on the value of the independent variable chosen.

For example, in an experiment to measure the volume of gas given off against time, the experimenter chooses the time intervals, say every 30 s, and measures the volume of gas. Time is the independent variable; the volume of gas given off depends on the time so volume of gas is the dependent variable. Time should be plotted on the *x*-axis.

2 Sketch a line of best fit for Figures 11.10–11.14.

Proportional and directly proportional both mean the same thing.
You are not expected to deduce the equation for a non-linear relationship but could comment on whether the gradient increases or decreases.
HL: you may be asked to deduce the half-life from a concentration vs time graph in Topic 15.

Lines of best fit should be smooth, ignore obviously anomalous points and there should be an approximately equal number of points on both sides of the line.
A line of best fit does not need to go through any of the points.
Sometimes, there is no obvious relationship between two variables.

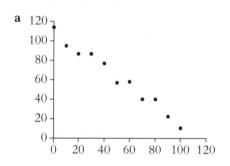

Figure 11.10

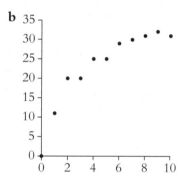

Figure 11.11

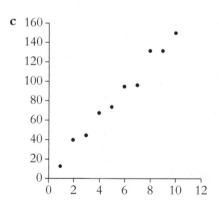

Figure 11.12

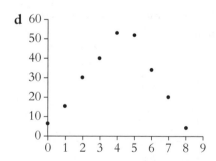

Figure 11.13

e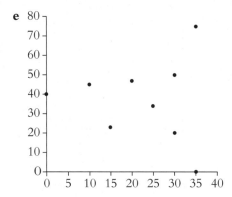

Figure 11.14

f Complete Table 11.3 identifying whether the following data are continuous/discrete and, for line graphs, whether a line of best fit should be drawn or the points joined dot to dot.

y-axis	x-axis	Continuous or discrete?	Bar chart or line graph?	Line of best fit or points joined dot to dot?
temperature	time			
concentration	time			
boiling point	number of carbon atoms in a homologous series			
rate	concentration			
ionisation energy	atomic number			
$\log_{10}$(ionisation energy)	number of ionisation energy (1st, 2nd, 3rd and so on)			
melting point of the group 16 hydrides	period in the periodic table			
boiling point of alkanes	relative molar mass			

Table 11.3

3 Draw a line of best fit and then determine the gradients of the graphs shown in Figures 11.15–11.18, including units.

Continuous or discrete data refers to the data on the *x*-axis.

a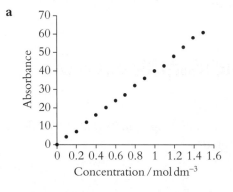

Figure 11.15

b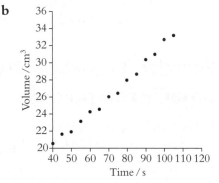

Figure 11.16

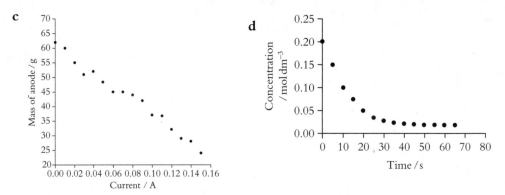

Figure 11.17

Figure 11.18

  i Look at Figure 11.18. Determine the gradient at $x = 0$.

  ii Look at Figure 11.18. Determine the gradient at $x = 30$.

4 Identify which of the following statements correctly describes the graphs in Figure 11.19.

> Always draw construction lines on the graph to show how the gradient has been calculated.

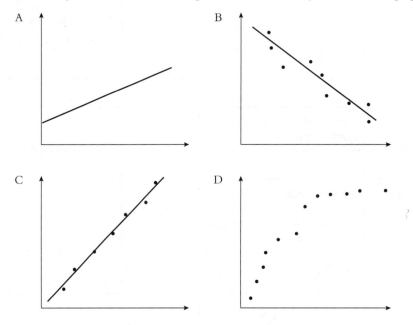

Figure 11.19 Identifying errors from graphs.

1 The experiment has a high degree of precision.

2 The experiment was not very precise.

3 As the relationship is meant to be proportional, there is evidence of a systematic error.

4 The experiment has produced an anomalous result.

Exercise 11.3 – Spectroscopic identification of organic compounds

1 The number of multiple bonds and rings in an organic compound is called its index of hydrogen deficiency (IHD) or degree of unsaturation.

a Determine the IHD of the following compounds:

i

H—C—C=C—C—H with H atoms on top (H H H H) and bottom H's

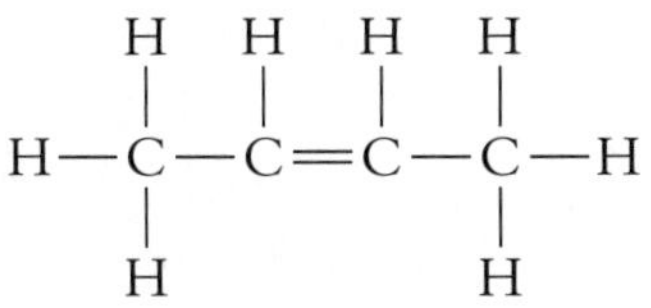

Figure 11.20

ii

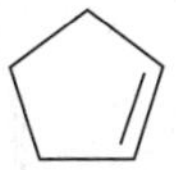

Figure 11.21

iii

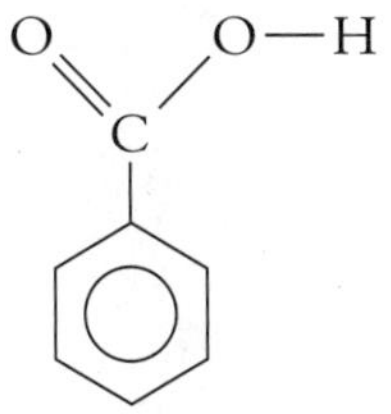

Figure 11.22

iv

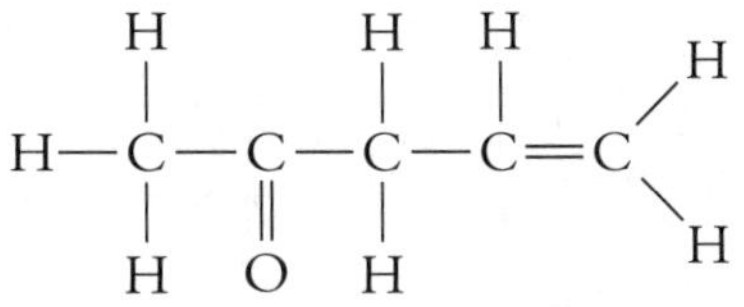

H—C—C—C—C=C

Figure 11.23

b Determine the IHD of the following compounds:
  i C_3H_6
  ii $C_5H_8Cl_2$
  iii $C_8H_{10}O$
  iv C_4H_5N
  v C_8H_9NO

2 Infrared spectroscopy can be used to identify the functional groups present in a compound. The characteristic ranges for infrared absorption due to stretching vibrations in organic molecules are given in the data book.

  a The segment of an infrared spectrum with wavenumbers below around $1500\,\text{cm}^{-1}$ can be used to positively identify a molecule by comparing it to a database of spectra. What name is given to this region?

  b Describe the regions in which you would expect to see key absorptions for the following molecules:
  i pentan-1-ol
  ii cyclohexene
  iii ethanoic acid
  iv ethyl propanoate

  c Identify the functional groups present in the IR spectra shown in Figures 11.24–11.27.:

i

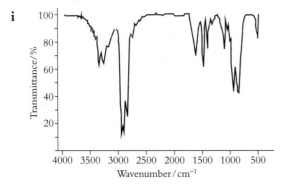

Figure 11.24

ii

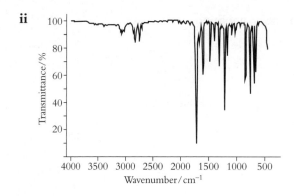

Figure 11.25

iii

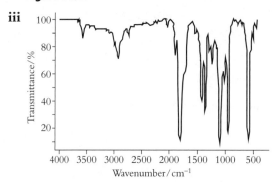

Figure 11.26

iv

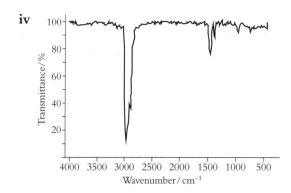

Figure 11.27

3 Mass spectrometry can be used to find the relative molecular mass of a compound and identify some of its structural components by analysing the fragmentation pattern.

   a State what is meant by 'fragmentation pattern'.

   b In the mass spectrum of a hydrocarbon a number of peaks were observed.
   Suggest the formulas of the species that could be responsible for the following peaks:

   i 15

   ii 27

   iii 29

   iv 57

c Figure 11.28 shows the mass spectrum of propan-1-ol. Suggest the identity of the species giving rise to the peaks at *m/z* values of 29, 31, 59 and 60.

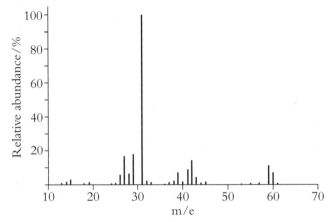

Figure 11.28 Mass spectrum of propan-1-ol.

4 NMR is another technique that is used to identify the structure of a compound.
  a What does NMR stand for?
  b The signals in an NMR spectrum are due to the presence of atoms of which element?
  c Energy in which region of the electromagnetic spectrum is used to produce the signals in an NMR spectrum?
  d What information can be deduced from the following aspects of an NMR spectrum?
    i the number of signals
    ii the integration trace of the signals
  e Suggest the number of signals and the ratio of the integration trace in an NMR spectrum for the following molecules:
    i propanone
    ii 1-chlorobutane
    iii 2-chlorobutane
    iv methyl ethanoate

HL Exercise 11.4 – Spectroscopic identification of organic compounds

Additional information from NMR spectroscopy is considered at HL in addition to X-ray crystallography and combined techniques.

1 Two additional pieces of information about NMR are considered at HL: the chemical shift of each signal and any splitting pattern.
  a What information does the chemical shift give?
  b What information does the splitting pattern give?
  c Chemical shift values are given relative to the signal produced by tetramethylsilane, TMS. The structure of TMS is given in Figure 11.29.

The energy causes the nuclei of the atoms to change their orientation in an external magnetic field. The amount of energy required is different depending on the position of the atom in the molecule which is why atoms in different positions give different signals.

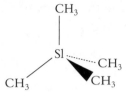

Figure 11.29 TMS.

Why is TMS used as the standard for chemical shift values?

d Using the values in the data book, suggest the number of peaks that would be found in the NMR spectrum of the following molecules and the range of the chemical shift values for each one:

i ethanoic acid

ii pentan-2-one

iii 2-chloroethanal

e Figure 11.30 shows the NMR spectrum of a hydrocarbon with the formula C_7H_8. Suggest the identity of this compound.

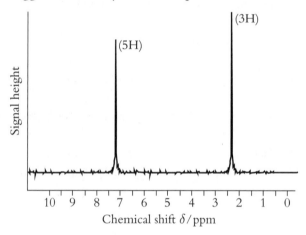

Figure 11.30 NMR of C_7H_8.

2 High-resolution NMR reveals additional detail and the splitting pattern of the signals can be seen. Splitting occurs when protons on adjacent carbon atoms cause a signal to be split. An adjacent proton is one that is three bonds away. The number of peaks in the signal is one more than the number of adjacent protons.

a Suggest the number of signals and splitting pattern that would be seen in the following molecules:

i

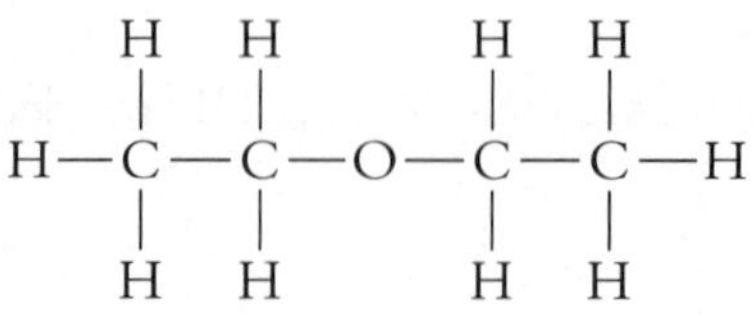

$$H-\underset{\underset{H}{|}}{\overset{\overset{H}{|}}{C}}-\underset{\underset{H}{|}}{\overset{\overset{H}{|}}{C}}-O-\underset{\underset{H}{|}}{\overset{\overset{H}{|}}{C}}-\underset{\underset{H}{|}}{\overset{\overset{H}{|}}{C}}-H$$

Figure 11.31 Ethoxyethane.

ii

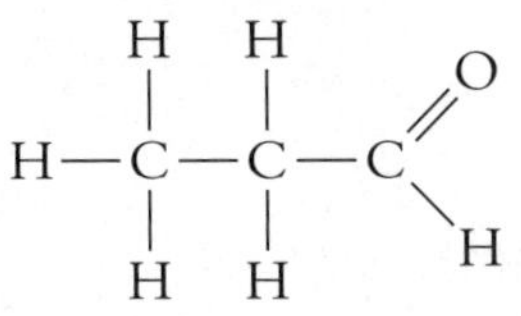

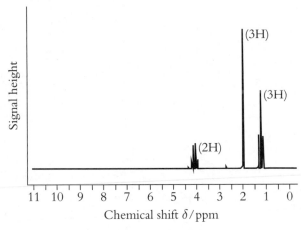

Figure 11.32 Propanal.

iii

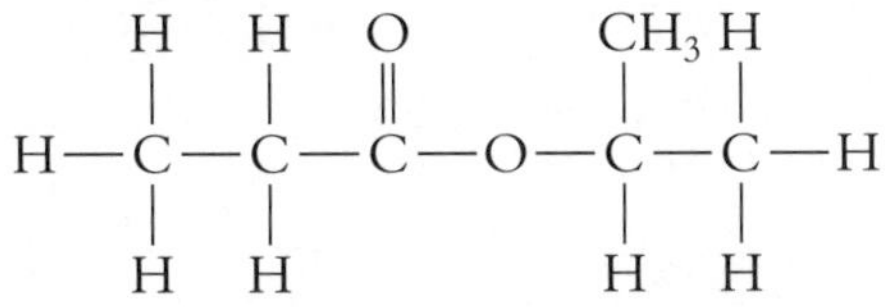

Figure 11.33 1–methylethyl ethanoate.

b Figure 11.34 shows the NMR spectrum of an organic compound containing carbon, hydrogen and oxygen with a molar mass of 88 g mol^{-1}. Suggest an identity for this compound.

(3H)

(3H)

(2H)

Signal height

11 10 9 8 7 6 5 4 3 2 1 0

Chemical shift δ/ppm

Figure 11.34 NMR of an unknown compound].

3 Single-crystal X-ray crystallography produces a three-dimensional picture of a molecule. State what other information can be deduced from this type of image.

1 How many significant figures and decimal places are there in 2.020×10^2?

	Significant figures	Decimal places
A	3	3
B	4	1
C	4	3
D	6	4

Table 11.4

2 Calculate the volume used from the burette readings shown in Table 11.5.

	Value	Uncertainty
Final reading / cm³	25.50	±0.05
Initial reading / cm3	1.30	±0.05

Table 11.5

A $24.2 \pm 0.1 \, \text{cm}^3$
B $24.20 \pm 0.1 \, \text{cm}^3$
C $24.20 \pm 0.05 \, \text{cm}^3$
D $24.2 \pm 0.10 \, \text{cm}^3$

3 What is the total uncertainty in the following calculation?

$$\Delta H = \frac{-mc\Delta T}{n} = \frac{-2.35\,(\pm 2\%) \times 4.18 \times 12.2\,(\pm 8\%)}{0.023\,(\pm 5\%)}$$

A $\dfrac{16}{5}\%$

B 8%

C 2%

D 15%

4 Which statements are correct about the data in Table 11.6, collected from a series of experiments to measure the molar gas volume at STP? (actual value = $22.7 \, \text{dm}^3 \, \text{mol}^{-1}$)

	Experiment 1	Experiment 2	Experiment 3
Result 1	23.4	22.23	23.4
Result 2	23.5	23.43	23.5
Result 3	21.2	24.78	24.5
Result 4	23.3	24.34	23.0
Result 5	22.4	21.99	23.1
Mean value	22.8	23.35	23.5

Table 11.6

I   The results of experiment 1 were the most accurate.

II   The results of experiment 2 were the most precise.

III Experiment 3 probably contains a systematic error.

A I only

B I and III only

C II and III only

D II and III

5   **Which of the following molecules has an index of hydrogen deficiency of 3?**

A

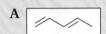

Figure 11.35 Molecule A.

B

Figure 11.36 Molecule B.

C

Figure 11.37 Molecule C.

D

Figure 11.38 Molecule D.

6   **Which technique can be used to determine the functional groups in a compound?**

A infrared spectroscopy

B NMR spectroscopy

C mass spectroscopy

D colorimetery

7   **HL** **The high-resolution NMR spectrum of ethanol is made up of three signals. The ratio of the areas under each peak is 3 : 2 : 1. Which of the following correctly describes the splitting pattern?**

A triplet : doublet : singlet

B doublet : triplet : doublet

C triplet : quartet : singlet

D triplet : quartet : triplet

8 **HL** How many proton environments are there in the following molecule?

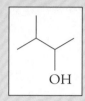

Figure 11.39 3-methylbutan-2-ol.

A 3
B 4
C 5
D 6

9 **HL** Which analytical method can be used to determine bond angles in solid compounds?

A X-ray crystallography
B infrared spectroscopy
C mass spectrometry
D NMR spectroscopy

10 **HL** Use the following information to deduce the identity of the unknown compound.

The infrared spectrum has a strong broad peak at $3300\,cm^{-1}$ and a sharp peak at $1750\,cm^{-1}$.

The molecular ion peak in the mass spectrum occurs at $m/z = 60$.

The NMR spectrum has two peaks with a peak area ratio of 3 : 1.

It has a IHD of 1.

A

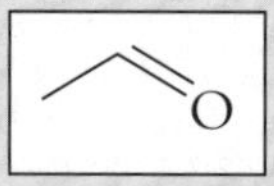

Figure 11.40

B

Figure 11.41

C

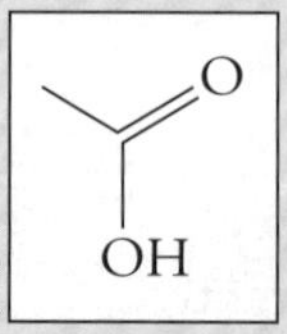

Figure 11.42

D

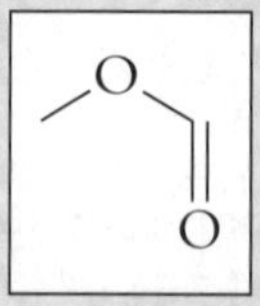

Figure 11.43

11 In an experiment to find the density of a solution, the mass and volume of samples of the solution were measured using a measuring cylinder marked in $1\,cm^3$ divisions and a 2 decimal place balance. The experiment was repeated three times as shown in Table 11.7.

Experiment	Volume of solution / cm³	Mass of solution / g
1	25.5	25.03
2	13.0	13.10
3	24.0	23.96

Table 11.7

a State the uncertainty in the readings on the measuring cylinder. [1]

b If the measuring cylinder only has $1\,cm^3$ divisions on it, explain why it is appropriate to give values as 0.0 or $0.5\,cm^3$ as in Table 11.7 [1]

c Calculate the percentage uncertainty in the volume measurements for all three experiments given in the table. [2]

d State the uncertainty in the balance readings. [1]

e Calculate the percentage uncertainty in the mass measurements for all three experiments given in Table 11.7 [2]

f Using the formula density $= \dfrac{mass}{volume}$, calculate the density of the solution for all three sets of data, including its absolute uncertainty. [2]

g Calculate the mean value for the density and its uncertainty. Give your answer to an appropriate number of significant figures. [3]

h Suggest two ways that the percentage uncertainty in the final value for the density of the solution could be reduced. [3]

[Total 15]

12 The data shown in Table 11.8 were obtained in a series of experiments to find number of moles of an ideal gas at a constant pressure of 101021 Pa.
As $PV = nRT$ then a graph of V against T should have a gradient $= \dfrac{nR}{P}$ where R is the gas constant.
Plot the data and use the graph to deduce the number of moles of gas used in the experiment, showing your working. [8]

Temperature / K	Volume / dm³
250	21.0
275	22.7
300	25.5
325	27.0
350	29.7
375	31.0
400	32.7
425	35.0

Table 11.8

[Total 8]

13 **Limonene is a hydrocarbon with the molecular formula $C_{10}H_{16}$. Its structure is shown in Figure 11.44.**

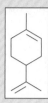

Figure 11.44 Structure of limonene.

a Give the empirical formula of limonene. [1]
b Deduce its index of hydrogen deficiency. [1]
c Figure 11.45 shows the infrared spectrum of limonene.

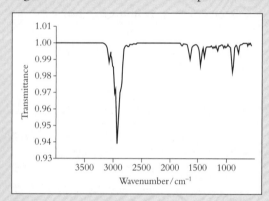

Figure 11.45 Infrared spectrum of limonene.

Identify the peaks at 1630 and 2900 cm^{-1}. [2]
d Suggest identities and m/z values of likely fragments in the mass spectrum of limonene. [2]
e Suggest how many signals might be seen in the proton NMR spectrum of limonene. [1]

[Total 7]

14 **HL** **Figures 11.46, 11.47 and 11.48 show the infrared, mass and NMR spectra of compound A, respectively.**

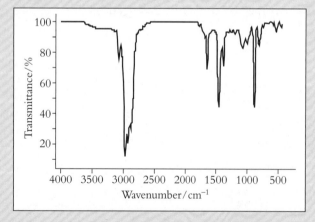

Figure 11.46 Infrared spectrum of compound A.

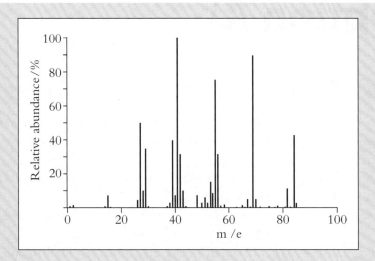

Figure 11.47 Mass spectrum of compound A.

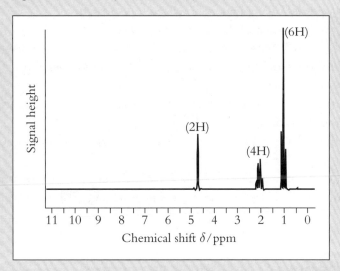

Figure 11.48 NMR spectrum of compound A.

Compound A was found to have a composition of 85.7% carbon and 14.3% hydrogen.

a Deduce the empirical and molecular formulas of compound A. [2]

b Determine the index of hydrogen deficiency of compound A. [1]

c Use the spectra given in Figures 11.46, 11.47 and 11.48 to suggest a possible structure for compound A. [6]

[Total 9]

12 Materials (Option A)

Chapter outline

- Recall that materials are classified based on their uses, properties, or bonding and structure and use a bonding triangle diagram to classify a binary compound.
- Recall that metals are obtained from their ores by reduction with carbon or by electrolysis, that most metals are used as alloys and that trace amounts of metals can be detected using ICP-MS or ICP-OES techniques.
- Recall how catalysts work and explain the factors involved in choosing a catalyst for a process.
- Explain how different types of liquid crystal behave on a molecular level and the properties needed for a substance to be used in a liquid crystal display.
- Describe how the properties of a polymer are related to its structure.
- Explain the environmental impact of the use and disposal of plastics.
- Recall that nanotechnology is the production and application of structures, devices and systems on a nanometre scale and describe the structure, properties and production of carbon nanotubes.
- Recall the properties of superconducting materials and the use of X-ray diffraction to analyse metallic and ionic compounds. **HL**
- Describe the formation of condensation polymers and compare these to addition polymers. **HL**
- Explain the environmental impact of heavy metals and how chelating substances can be used to remove these, including calculations involving K_{sp}. **HL**

KEY TERMS AND FORMULAS

Composite material: A mixture containing two or more different materials present as distinct, separate phases. Synthetic composite materials consist of a reinforcing phase embedded in a matrix.

Diamagnetism: A very weak magnetic effect caused by paired electrons. Diamagnetic materials are repelled by a magnetic field.

Heterogeneous catalyst: A catalyst that is in a different phase (state) from the reactants.

Homogeneous catalyst: A catalyst that is in the same phase (state) as the reactants.

Liquid crystal: A phase of matter in which the properties of a compound may exhibit the characteristics of both a solid and a liquid.

Lyotropic liquid crystal: A substance in which, when in solution, the molecules form into clusters with a regular orientation but these clusters are randomly arranged.

Nematic liquid crystal: A liquid crystal in which the molecules are aligned, on average, in the same direction but are positioned randomly relative to each other (no positional order).

Paramagnetism: A weak magnetic effect caused by unpaired electrons. Paramagnetic materials are attracted towards a magnetic field.

Plasma: A fully or partially ionised gas consisting of positive ions and electrons.

Thermotropic liquid crystal: A substance for which the liquid-crystal phase is only stable over a small temperature range.

Unit cell: The simplest repeating unit from which a whole crystal can be built up.

Superconductor: A material that has zero electrical resistance below a critical temperature.

$$Q = It$$

where
Q = amount of charge/C
I = current/A
t = time/s

Solubility product constant:

For a solid MX dissolving to form M^{n+} and X^{n-} ions

$$K_{sp} = [M^{n+}][X^{n-}]$$

Exercise 12.1 – Materials science introduction

1 Materials can be classed as distinct types in a number of ways, for example as metals, ceramics or polymers. Most materials are mixtures known as composites. Mixing different materials enables the properties to be tailored to suit a particular use.
  a State whether the following materials are metals, polymers, ceramics or composites:
    i silicon dioxide
    ii tungsten
    iii PVC
    iv fibre glass
  b Materials can also be classified according to their properties.
    Give the meaning of the following properties:
    i electrical conductivity
    ii permeability
    iii elasticity
    iv brittleness
    v malleability/ductility

c The properties of a material can be matched to its structure and bonding. The statements below describe the structure and bonding found in different materials. From the list below, state which property (or properties) is a result of each statement.

high melting point   good electrical conductors   permeable   malleable   brittle

i   strong forces between the particles
ii   contain mobile electrons
iii particles can slide over one another
iv   contains gaps within the structure
v   contains mobile ions when liquid or aqueous
vi   lattice of oppositely charged ions which repel each other when a force is applied
vii giant covalent lattice composed of localised shared pairs of electrons.

> The properties of polymers have not been included here as these are met later in Exercise 12.5.

2 Ionic and covalent bonding were examined in Topic 4 as being at either end of a linear scale. In this topic, metallic bonding is also considered alongside ionic and covalent bonding giving rise to a 2-dimensional scale known as a bonding triangle. This bonding triangle is given in section 29 of the data book. It is used for elements and for binary substances.

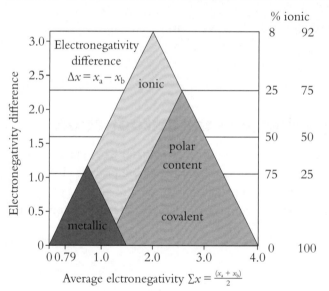

Figure 12.1 Triangular bonding diagram.

> For compounds, determine the difference between the electronegativity values and the average electronegativity value and plot these on the graph.
> For elements the difference in the electronegativity value is zero.

Use Figure 12.1 to classify the following substances. The electronegativity values can be found in the data book.

a TiO_2

b Cu

c Al_2O_3

d Ge

e H_2O

f $AlCl_3$

g $MgBr_2$

Exercise 12.2 – Metals and inductively coupled plasma spectroscopy

1 The method used for extracting a metal from its ore depends on its position in the activity series.

a What type of chemical reaction do most of these metal extractions involve?

b Describe the relationship between the position of a metal in the activity series and the ease with which it is extracted from its ore.

c Tin can be extracted from its ore, SnO_2, by heating the ore with carbon. Give an equation for this process.

d A metal can also be produced from the reaction of its ore with a more reactive metal.
For example, aluminium can be used to extract chromium from its ore, Cr_2O_3. Give an equation for this reaction.

> The activity series is given in section 25 of the data book.

2 Aluminium is commonly produced by the electrolysis of bauxite. There are three main steps to this process: purification of the ore, solvation in molten cryolite, and electrolysis.

a Purification involves dissolving the ore, which is a mostly mixture of aluminium hydroxide and various impurities, in hot sodium hydroxide to form $NaAl(OH)_4$. This is then cooled and the $Al(OH)_3$ precipitates out, leaving the impurities dissolved. The purified aluminium hydroxide is removed and then heated to produce alumina, Al_2O_3.

   i   Give an equation for the reaction of aluminium hydroxide with sodium hydroxide. (The impurities can be ignored.)

   ii   Metal hydroxides are normally basic. What name is given to substances that react with both acids and bases?

   iii Give an equation for the reaction that occurs when the purified aluminium hydroxide is heated to form alumina.

   iv   What name is given to the process in part **iii**?

> Cryolite does not lower the melting point of the aluminium oxide.

b Why is the purified Al_2O_3 dissolved in molten cryolite before electrolysis rather than simply melted?

c Both electrodes in the electrolysis cell are made from graphite.

   i   Give the half-equation that occurs at the cathode.

   ii   Give the half-equation that occurs at the anode.

   iii Give the overall equation for the electrolysis process.

   iv   Why do the anodes of the cell need to be periodically replaced? Include an equation in your answer.

> The cathode is the negative electrode and the anode is the positive electrode. This is met in Topic 9.

d The amount of a substance formed at an electrode can be calculated from the amount of charge that passes through the electrode in a given time period using the equation $Q = It$, where Q = amount of charge (C), I = current (A) and t = time (s).

Calculate the mass of aluminium produced when a current of 3000A is passed through molten aluminium oxide for 1 hour by following the steps below.

i   Using $Q = It$, calculate the amount of charge.

ii   One mole of electrons carries a charge of $96\,500\,C\,mol^{-1}$ (Faraday's constant). Calculate the number of moles of electrons flowing through the circuit.

iii Write the half-equation for the reaction at the electrode at which aluminium is produced.

iv   Using the answers to parts **ii** and **iii**, calculate the number of moles of aluminium produced.

v   Calculate the mass of aluminium produced.

HL Electrolysis calculations are part of Topic 19 The value of Faraday's constant is given in the data book.

3 Most metals are used in the form of alloys rather than as pure elements.

a What is meant by the term 'alloy'?

b Why are pure metals rarely used?

c Explain why most alloys are stronger than the metals from which they are made. Use a diagram in your answer.

4 Most people are familiar with magnetic materials like iron. Iron exhibits ferromagnetism; however, there are other types of magnetism which are much weaker: paramagnetism and diamagnetism.

a Describe paramagnetism.

b Describe diamagnetism.

c Identify whether the following compounds are diamagnetic or paramagnetic:

   i O_2

   ii $FeCl_3$

   iii ZnO

d Place the following metals in order of increasing paramagnetism: Na, As, Cr, Sc and Ti

Firstly, deduce the electron configuration for each substance.
HL Diamagnetism and paramagnetism are met in Topic 13.

5 The presence and amount of small traces of metals (and some non-metals) can be determined using inductively coupled plasma (ICP) techniques. The two main variations of this technique are ICP-MS and ICP-OES.

a What do the initials OES and MS mean?

b In both techniques the sample is injected into a high-temperature argon plasma. What is an argon plasma?

c How is the argon plasma produced?

d What effects does the argon plasma have on the atoms in the sample material?

e The methods of analysis used in the two techniques differ and both are described in the Table 12.1.

Technique 1	Technique 2
Electrons fall back down to a lower energy level producing an emission spectrum.	The ions are introduced into the instrument at low pressure.
The different spectral lines are separated using a prism.	The ions are accelerated using a magnetic field.
The wavelengths are converted into an electrical signal.	The ions are deflected by a magnetic field.
The magnitude of each signal is used to determine the identity and amount of the element present.	The detector converts the ions that reach it into an electrical signal which is in proportion to the number of ions reaching it.

Table 12.1

   i   Which column describes ICP-MS and which ICP-OES?
   ii   What is required in both of these techniques to accurately determine the concentration of a particular element?
f Give an example of an industrial application of ICP.

Exercise 12.3 – Catalysts

1 a Catalysts can be classed as homogeneous or heterogeneous. What is the difference between these two types of catalyst?
  b Describe how a heterogeneous catalyst works.
  c Carbon nanocatalysts and zeolites are often used as heterogeneous catalysts. Explain what properties of these substances make them particularly useful.
  d Describe how a homogeneous catalyst works. Include a sketch of an energy profile diagram in your answer.

Exercise 12.4 – Liquid crystals

A liquid crystal is a phase of matter in which the properties of a compound may exhibit the characteristics of both a solid and a liquid.
When most substances melt, the neat order of the molecules is broken down. In some substances, the liquid state retains some of this order; this is the liquid-crystal state.
Liquid crystals can be classified into a number of different types such as thermotropic and lyotropic.

1 a Some liquid crystals are described as nematic. This relates to their shape. What shape are the molecules in this type of liquid crystal and how are they arranged in the liquid crystal state?
  b Describe one major difference in the composition of thermotropic and lyotropic liquid crystals.

How are these techniques used to measure the amount of an element present? What sort of graph is required?

Key ideas: adsorption, desorption, weakening of bonds, molecular orientation, activation energy.

c Figures 12.2 and 12.3 describe thermotropic and lyotropic liquid crystals.

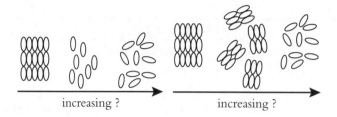

increasing ? increasing ?

Figure 12.2 and 12.3 Transitions in liquid crystals.

    i Which diagram shows a thermotropic and which a lyotropic liquid crystal?

    ii What factor brings about the change in the order of the molecules in each case?

d Place each statement under the correct heading.

Thermotropic	Lyotropic

Table 12.2

- An example of this type of liquid crystal is soap and water.
- Examples of this type of liquid crystal include biphenyl nitriles.
- These liquid crystals are pure substances.
- These liquid crystals are solutions.
- This liquid-crystal phase depends on concentration.
- This liquid-crystal phase is dependent on temperature.

e The properties of liquid crystals can depend on the orientation of their molecules. List three properties of liquid crystals that can be affected by their molecular orientation.

2 One of the most widespread uses of liquid crystals is in LCD displays. The molecules are sandwiched between polarising filters. The transmission of plane-polarised light matches the orientation of the molecules which can be changed by an external stimulus.

a What stimulus is used to switch the orientation of the molecules?

b Why must the molecules used in LCDs be polar?

c What other properties make a compound suitable for use in LCDs?

Exercise 12.5 – Polymers

There are numerous naturally occurring polymers such as proteins, silk and cellulose but this section of the syllabus focuses on synthetic polymers which are commonly called plastics.

1 a Define the term 'polymer'.

   b One type of polymer is a thermoplastic.

    i Describe the effect of heat on a thermoplastic.

    ii What type of forces hold the chains of a thermoplastic together and how does this give rise to their thermoplastic properties?

c Another type of polymer is a thermosetting polymer.

   i What is meant by a thermosetting polymer?

   ii Describe the bonding in thermosetting polymers.

d A third type of polymer is an elastomer.

   i Describe the properties of a typical elastomer.

   ii Describe the structure of an elastomer.

2 The properties of a polymer can be manipulated by altering their structural features.

a Explain why polymers with longer chain lengths tend to be stronger and have higher melting points than those with shorter polymer chains.

b Low-density polyethene (LDPE) is composed of branched chains whereas high-density polyethene (HDPE) has very little branching.

Explain the effect of these differences on the strength and melting points of these polymers.

c The position of the side chains on a polymer chain can also affect the intermolecular forces between the chains. For example, the polymerisation of propene can result in isotactic or atactic polypropene.

   i Draw diagrams to show the difference between isotactic and atactic polypropene.

   ii State whether atactic or isotactic polypropene will have a more crystalline and therefore rigid structure.

   iii Why does poly(2-methylpropene) not have atactic or isotactic forms?

d Plasticisers can also be added to a polymer to increase its flexibility.

   i Describe how a plasticiser works.

   ii Give examples of the use of plasticised and unplasticised polyvinylchloride.

e The properties of polystyrene can be altered by the addition of a volatile hydrocarbon during its manufacture and then heat-treating the polymer.

   i What is the purpose of the hydrocarbon?

   ii What effect does this process have on the properties of the polystyrene?

3 Atom economy can be used as a measure of the efficiency of a reaction. The formula for atom economy is given in the data book.

Calculate the atom economy of the following processes:

a the manufacture of cyclohexene from cyclohexanol:

$$C_6H_{11}OH \rightarrow C_6H_{10} + H_2O$$

b the production of iron from iron(III) oxide:

$$Fe_2O_3 + 3CO \rightarrow 2Fe + 3CO_2$$

c the preparation of ethyne from calcium carbide:

$$CaC_2 + 2H_2O \rightarrow C_2H_2 + Ca(OH)_2$$

Exercise 12.6 – Nanotechnology

Many substances exhibit novel properties when their size falls below around 100 nm. This section looks at nanotechnology.

1 a It is possible to produce nanoparticles by breaking down a bulk material into ever smaller pieces (top-down approach). Other approaches are called bottom-up or molecular self-assembly.

What is meant by 'bottom-up' and 'molecular self-assembly'?

b Give an example of molecular self-assembly.

c A scanning tunnelling microscope can be used to position atoms on a surface; this is referred to as a physical technique. Chemical techniques can also be used. Describe the difference between chemical and physical techniques.

2 Harry Kroto, Robert Curl and Richard Smalley were awarded the Nobel Prize for Chemistry in 1996 for deducing the structure of C_{60}. The molecule was named Buckminsterfullerene and given the nickname 'the buckyball'. Their discovery, it could be argued, has spawned a new branch of chemistry, that of carbon nanotechnology: carbon nanotubes and graphene.

a Describe the arrangement of the carbon atoms in carbon nanotubes and in graphene.

b Carbon nanotubes have been created with a diameter of around 1–2 nm and can have open or capped ends.

Explain the following properties of carbon nanotubes and graphene with reference to their bonding and structure.

i electrical conductivity

ii strength

c Carbon nanotubes can be produced in a number of ways, some of which are described in Table 12.3.

Arc discharge	Two metal rods are placed close together in a hydrocarbon solvent. A high current causes an arc between the electrodes causing the hydrocarbon to be decomposed. Rod-like deposits are formed on the anode.
CVD	A hydrocarbon gas such as ethyne or methane is passed over a metal catalyst on a silica or zeolite support at a high temperature in an inert atmosphere. Nanotubes are formed on the catalyst surface.
HIPCO	Carbon monoxide and an iron complex containing carbon monoxide, $Fe(CO)_5$, are subjected to high temperatures and pressures. Iron nanoparticles are produced which catalyse the disproportion of carbon monoxide, producing carbon nanotubes on their surface.

Table 12.3

i What do the initials CVD stand for?

ii What do the initials HIPCO stand for?

d Using methylbenzene ($C_6H_5CH_3$) as an example of a suitable hydrocarbon solvent in the arc-discharge method described in the table, explain why the production of carbon nanotubes is an oxidation reaction.

e Describe an alternative arc-discharge method which is different from that described in the table.

f Why is an inert atmosphere needed in the CVD process?

g Give an equation for the disproportionation reaction described in the HIPCO process.

Exercise 12.7 – Environmental impact: plastics

There are a number of environmental concerns about the use and disposal of plastics. Most plastics are made from non-renewable crude oil and do not biodegrade. When disposed of via landfill, they persist for hundreds of years.

1 This question is about the disposal of plastic waste by incineration.
  a State three factors on which the substances produced when a plastic is combusted depend.
  b Suggest the likely products formed when the following polymers are combusted:
    i   polypropene in a plentiful supply of oxygen
    ii   polyethene in a limited supply of oxygen
    iii PVC in a plentiful supply of oxygen at high temperatures
  c Construct simple equations for the reactions in part **b**.
  d When PVC undergoes incomplete combustion or the temperature at which it is incinerated is too low then PCDDs and a compound which is an unsaturated heterocyclic ring with two oxygen atoms at the 1 and 4 positions can be produced.
    i   What do the initials PCDD stand for?
    ii   What is the name of the compound which is an unsaturated heterocyclic ring with two oxygen atoms at the 1 and 4 positions?
    iii Why are these combustion products of environmental concern?

> The structure of this molecule is given in the data book. Can you identify it from its description?

2 PCBs or polychlorinated biphenyls were used in the manufacture of electronic components such as transformers and capacitors. They are thought to be carcinogenic.
  a Why are PCBs suited to these uses?
  b Draw the structure of a typical PCB.
  c Suggest whether PCBs are likely to accumulate in aqueous or fatty tissues.
  d Why are PCBs non-biodegradable?

> Are the molecules able to form hydrogen bonds with water?

3 Another group of compounds that are thought to be carcinogenic are phthalate esters.
  a These compounds are often added to plastics to increase their flexibility. What name is given to substances that have this role?
  b What feature of the bonding between the phthalate molecules and the polymer to which they are added is the reason why these molecules are released into the environment?
  c Why is the use of these plastics containing these compounds to wrap fatty foods of concern?

4 An alternative to landfill or incineration as a way of disposing of plastics is to recycle them.
  a Outline the advantages and disadvantages of recycling.
  b Most objects made from plastics contain a resin identification code. What is the purpose of these codes?
  c One of the major costs in the recycling of plastics is the sorting of the waste into its different types. IR spectroscopy can be used to identify and assess the purity of plastic waste.
    Figures 12.4a and b show the IR spectra of two different compounds found in plastic waste. The structures of these compounds are given in Figure 12.5.

> These are given in the data book.

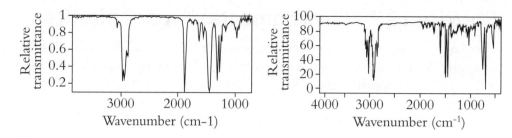

Figure 12.4a and 12.4b IR of compounds found in plastic waste.

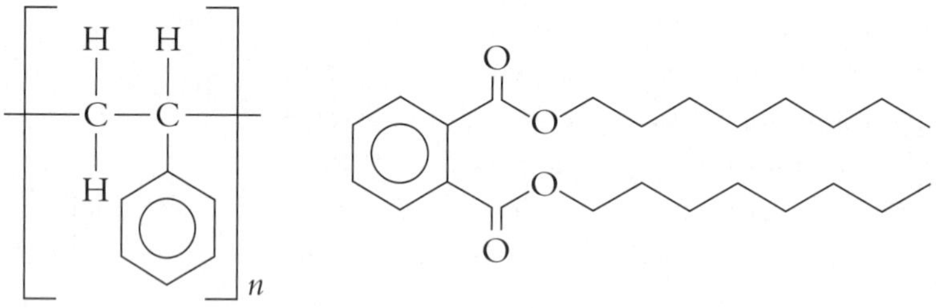

polystyrene   di–n–octylphthalate

Figure 12.5 Structure of polystyrene and di n-octyl phthalate.

Using the information in section 26 of the data book, identify which is which and justify your answer.

HL Exercise 12.8 – Superconducting metals and X-ray crystallography

The bonding and structure of metals was met in Topic 4. Metals are described as having a lattice of positive ions surrounded by a sea of delocalised electrons. The electrostatic forces of attraction between these particles holds the structure together.

1 All metals conduct electricity because the delocalised electrons can move through their structure. Some metals are better conductors than others.
   a Describe what causes resistance in metals.
   b Explain why resistance increases with temperature?
   c Some materials exhibit superconductivity. What is meant by this term?
   d The Bardeen–Cooper–Schrieffer (BCS) theory suggests that superconduction occurs via a Cooper pair of electrons.
      Describe the origin of a Cooper pair.

2 Superconductors can be divided into two types depending on their behaviour in a magnetic field.
   a All superconductors expel an external magnetic field below their critical temperature.
      i   What name is given to this effect?
      ii   What causes this effect?

b Figure 12.6 shows the resistance of a metal and a type 1 superconductor at different temperatures.

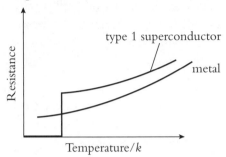

Figure 12.6 Variation in resistance with temperature.

Sketch the graph and add a line to show the resistance of a typical type 2 superconductor.

There are two key differences: the critical temperature and the sharpness of the change in the resistance.

3 In Topic 4 the lattice structures of sodium chloride, and diamond were introduced. There are lots of other lattice structures which give rise to the shapes of different crystals. In this section, the crystal structures of metals are examined by considering the arrangement of the particles in their unit cell.

a What is meant by the term 'unit cell'?

b Figure 12.7 shows the unit cells of some different materials.

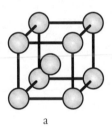 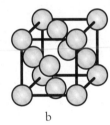 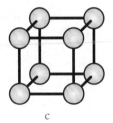

      a   b   c

Figure 12.7 Lattice structures.

   i   Name each type of lattice.

   ii   Deduce the coordination number for each lattice.

To find the coordination number, consider the adjacent unit cells too. An atom at a corner position is shared between eight unit cells. An atom on a face is shared by two unit cells. Being able to imagine these in three dimensions is a difficult but useful skill. The most difficult coordination to 'see' is often the fcc structure. Consider the atom in the centre of the top face and count the number of atoms in the same layer, the layer above and the layer below.

   iii Calculate the number of atoms (or ions) in each unit cell.

To deduce the number of atoms in a unit cell, you need to consider the fraction of each atom that is inside the cubic structure. Atoms in the corner of a cell are shared between 8 cells so only $\frac{1}{8}$ of an atom is inside the unit cell. Atoms on a face are shared between 2 cells so are $\frac{1}{2}$ in the cell. Atoms at the centre of a cell are wholly within it. Calculate this for each atom and add them up to find the total.

The Bragg equation is given in the data book.

c What is the name of the analytical technique often used to determine the structure of an ionic or metallic lattice?

d The size of a unit cell can be determined using the Bragg equation.

$n\lambda = 2d\sin\theta$

Use this expression to calculate the interatomic distance and the atomic radius of the metal if the crystal has a simple cubic structure and X-rays of wavelength 5.53×10^{-10} m produce a first order reflection at an angle of 14.3°.

The interatomic distance equals the length of the unit cell for a simple cubic structure. For a simple cubic structure, the length of the unit cell equals twice the atomic radius as can be seen in Figure 12.8.

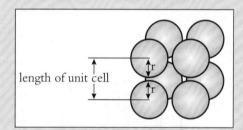

length of unit cell

Figure 12.8 A simple cubic structure.

e Copper was analysed by X-ray crystallography and its unit cell was found to have a face-centred cubic structure with a dimension of 361 pm (3.61×10^{-10} m). Follow the steps below to calculate the density of copper.

  i Calculate the mass of one atom of copper using its relative atomic mass and the Avogadro constant.

  ii Deduce the number of atoms in a unit cell from the cell's structure.

  iii Calculate the mass of one unit cell by multiplying the mass of one atom (see part **i**) by the number of atoms in unit cell (see part **ii**).

  iv Work out the volume of the unit cell using the cell dimensions given in the question.

  v Calculate the density using:

$$\text{density} = \frac{\text{mass of unit cell}}{\text{volume of unit cell}} = \frac{\text{part } \textbf{iii}}{\text{part } \textbf{iv}}$$

HL Exercise 12.9 – Condensation polymers

Many naturally occurring substances like proteins and starch are condensation polymers. Condensation polymers can also be synthesised. This section of the syllabus is about synthetic condensation polymers.

1 a What is meant by the term 'condensation polymer'?
   b Two types of condensation polymers are polyesters and polyamides. Draw the linkages in these molecules.
   c Describe the monomers required to make a typical polyester.
   d Describe the monomers required to make a typical polyamide.
   e Compare addition and condensation polymerisation.

Bullet points can be used in Question 1e so that the key points are not lost.

2 Kevlar® is a polyamide that is used in bullet-proof vests and protective clothing. Its monomers are shown below.

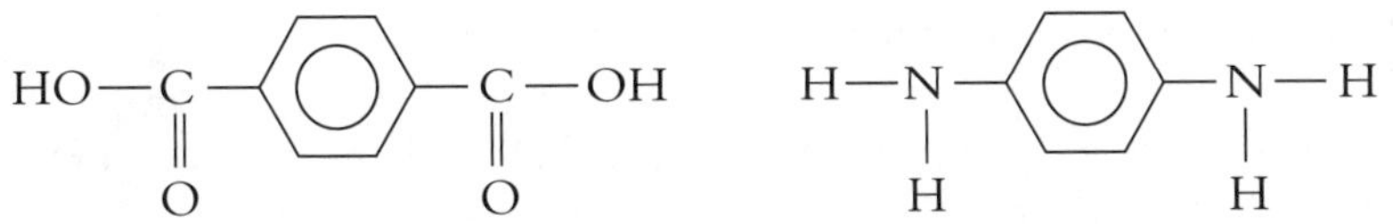

Figure 12.9 The monomers of Kevlar®.

a Give a balanced equation to show the formation of Kevlar®.
b Explain why Kevlar® is strong enough for use in bullet-proof materials.
c Kevlar® is only soluble in concentrated sulfuric acid. Explain how the sulfuric acid breaks up the structure of the polymer.

This is a Chemistry question – refer to the specific type of bonding and state which atoms these bonds are between; use a diagram.

Again diagrams would be useful in this answer.

3 Most addition polymers are not biodegradable due to the strong covalent bonds in the polymer chain. This leads to disposal problems as discussed in Exercise 12.7. One solution is to use polymers made from natural materials; these are referred to as bioplastics.
   a Explain why most biodegradable polymers are condensation polymers.
   b One example of a bioplastic is PLA which can be made from corn starch. A section of polymer chain is shown in Figure 12.10. It is formed from a single monomer. Deduce the monomer from which PLA is made.

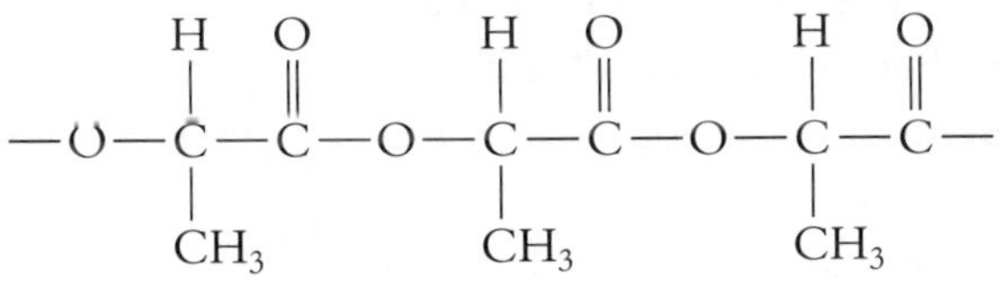

Figure 12.10 PLA.

   c Other than biodegradability, give one advantage of plastics derived from plant materials.
   d Outline two concerns about the use and manufacture of bioplastics.

Find the ester linkage; add H to the –O– to make a hydroxyl group and add OH to the C=O group to make a carboxyl group.

(HL) Exercise 12.10 – Environmental impact: heavy metals

Heavy metals such as copper, chromium, lead, nickel and cadmium are classed as pollutants. They can get into the environment through a wide range of industrial processes.

1 Many biological processes are redox processes.
Many heavy metals are transition metals.

   a In what way does the second statement explain why heavy metals are considered toxic in high concentrations?

   b Hydroxyl radicals, •OH, are a highly reactive species; they interact with many biological molecules, for example DNA and proteins, and damage them.
Hydroxyl radicals are produced by the Haber–Weiss reaction according to the equation:
$$•O_2^- + H_2O_2 \rightarrow •OH + OH^- + O_2$$
This reaction is catalysed by Fe^{3+} which reacts with the $•O_2^-$ ion.

      i Deduce the two-step mechanism for the catalysed reaction.

> The reactants of the first step are given in the question: 'Fe^{3+} which reacts with the $•O_2^-$ ion'.
>
> As this is a redox reaction, Fe^{3+} must be reduced and the $•O_2^-$ ion oxidised. It is unlikely that atomic iron is formed and so the product is probably Fe^{2+}. The other product is O_2 as the oxidation state of the oxygen must be increasing from $-\frac{1}{2}$ to 0. In the second step, the Fe^{2+} must be reacting with the other reactant (H_2O_2); the Fe^{3+} must be regenerated (it is acting as a catalyst) and the other products ($•OH + OH^-$) must be formed.

      ii What name is given to the second step in the mechanism?

2 Heavy metals can be removed from aqueous solution such as water supplies in a number of ways including precipitation, adsorption and chelation.

   a i Name a solution that could be used to remove chromium(III) ions from water by precipitation.

     ii Give an equation for your answer to part **i**.

   b i Some metal ions such as Pb^{2+} are removed as their sulfide precipitate. What gas is passed through the water to produce an insoluble sulfide?

     ii Give an equation for the precipitation of lead(II) sulfide.

   c What does the term adsorption mean in the context of removing heavy metal ions form water?

   d Outline how chelation is used to remove heavy metal poisoning.

3 This question explores complex ions in more detail. These were first met in Topic 13 (see Chapter 3).
Complex ions are composed of a central metal atom or ion surrounded by a number of ligands.

   a What feature must all ligands have?

   b Describe the bonding between the central atom/ion and the ligands.

   c Ethane-1,2-diamine is a bidentate ligand; its structure is shown in Figure 12.11 below.

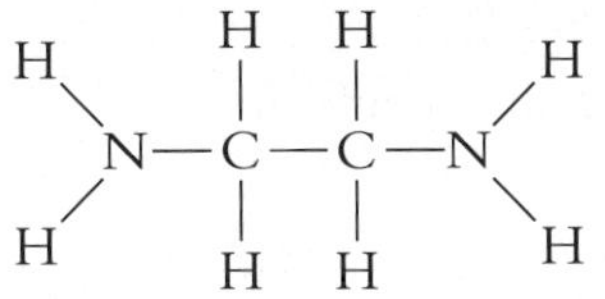

Figure 12.11 Ethane-1,2-diamine.

What is meant by the term bidentate?

d EDTA is a hexadentate ligand shown in Figure 12.12:

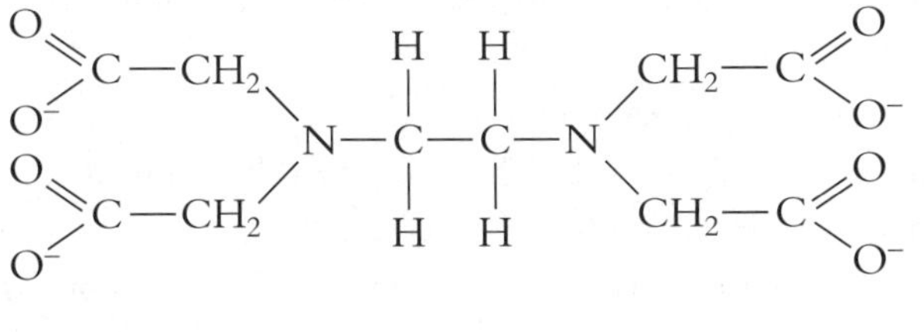

Figure 12.12 EDTA.

Copy and indicate on the diagram the six atoms which can attach to a central metal atom/ion.

e Polydentate ligands like EDTA can be used to remove heavy metal ions as they form stable complexes. An example is the removal of nickel in a case of nickel poisoning, for example if a child swallowed a battery. The nickel/EDTA complex is held in solution to be excreted and so prevents the Ni^{2+} ions from binding to other biologically significant molecules.

  i Give an equation to show the reaction of aqueous nickel ions, $[Ni(H_2O)_6]^{2+}$, with EDTA.

  ii Explain why this reaction is energetically favourable even though the enthalpy change is approximately zero.

> EDTA has a charge of −4.

4 When ideas about solubility are discussed, substances are often described as being soluble or insoluble but this is a simplification.
Consider the equation for the solvation of a simple salt, MX:
$$MX(s) \rightleftharpoons M^{n+}(aq) + X^{n-}(aq)$$
For an insoluble salt, the equilibrium lies to the left and its equilibrium constant, K_{sp}, will be very small. For a soluble salt, the value of the equilibrium constant will be large.

a What name is given to these equilibrium constants?

b Deduce an expression for the K_{sp} of the salt MX for the equation given above.

c Deduce the K_{sp} expressions, and the units of K_{sp}, for the following salts:

  i AgBr

  ii $Mg(OH)_2$

  iii $Fe_2(CO_3)_3$

> A common confusion is solubility and K_{sp}. Solubility describes the number of moles of a compound that is dissolved in a given volume of solution, its units are $mol\,dm^{-3}$. K_{sp} is an equilibrium constant.

5 This question is designed to provide practice in carrying out solubility calculations.

a The solubility of $PbCO_3$ is $2.60 \times 10^{-7}\,mol\,dm^{-3}$ at 298 K. Following the steps outlined, calculate the solubility product constant.

  i Write an equation for the solvation of $PbCO_3$.

  ii Deduce an expression for K_{sp}.

  iii Calculate K_{sp}.

> There is a hint on how to answer this question on the next page.

If the number of moles of $PbCO_3$ dissolving in 1 dm^3 is 2.72×10^{-7} then the concentrations of both Pb^{2+} and CO_3^{2-} will be 2.72×10^{-7} mol dm^{-3}, therefore these values can be substituted into the expression derived in part **ii**.

b The solubility of $Zn(OH)_2$ is 1.96×10^{-6} mol dm^{-3} at 298 K. Following the steps outlined, calculate the solubility product constant.

   i   Write an equation for the solvation of $Zn(OH)_2$.

   ii Deduce an expression for K_{sp}.

   iii Calculate K_{sp}.

c The solubility product of Ag_2SO_4 is 1.2×10^{-5} at 298 K. Following the steps outlined below, calculate its solubility at this temperature.

   i   Write an equation for the solvation of Ag_2SO_4.

   ii Calculate the solubility of Ag_2SO_4 at 298 K.

d The solubility product of Hg_2CO_3 is 3.6×10^{-17} at 298 K. Hg_2CO_3 contains the cation Hg_2^{2+}.

   i   Calculate its solubility in water at this temperature.

   ii Calculate its solubility if carbon dioxide is bubbled through the solution and the concentration of carbonate ions increases to 0.10 mol dm^{-3}.

   iii Explain the effect of carbon dioxide ions in terms of the equilibrium for the reaction.

The concentration of carbonate ions can be assumed to be equal to 0.10 mol dm^{-3} as the amount of carbonate ions present due to Hg_2CO_3 dissolving is very small and can be ignored.

❓ Exam-style questions

1   **a** Copy and complete the gaps in Table 12.4 showing the properties of metals, ceramics and polymers.

	Metals	Ceramics	Polymers
Melting points: high or low?	high	high	low, although thermosets burn rather than melt
Electrical conductivity: good or poor?		poor	
Permeability: high or low?	low		
Elasticity: high or low?			generally low, apart from elastomers
Brittleness: high or low?	low		
Malleability/ductility: high or low?			variable

Table 12.4

[5]

  b In terms of their structure, explain why most ceramics are poor electrical conductors. [2]

  c Comparing the structure of metals, ceramics and polymers, explain the difference in their melting points. [3]

d Figure 12.13 shows a triangular bonding diagram.

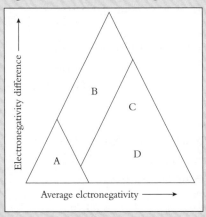

Figure 12.13 Triangular bonding diagram.

In which region or regions of the triangle would ceramic materials be found? [1]

[Total 11]

2 **The thermite reaction is used to make small quantities of molten iron. This process is sometimes used in remote areas to produce sufficient iron for repairing railway lines. A mixture of iron(III) oxide and aluminium powder is ignited and a redox reaction occurs forming iron and aluminium oxide.**

a Construct an equation for the reaction. [1]

b Identify which species is oxidised and which is reduced. [1]

c Iron is a ferromagnetic material in that it forms permanent magnets. Aluminium oxide and aluminium exhibit different types of magnetism.

What name is given to these types of magnetism? Explain their cause using the electron configurations of these substances in your answer. [2]

d Most iron is formed into alloys as these are stronger than the pure element.

Explain how alloying increases the strength of a metal. [1]

e i The amount of a trace element in an alloy can be determined using inductively coupled plasma detection techniques.

Figure 12.14 shows the calibration curve for manganese obtained from an ICP-OES instrument.

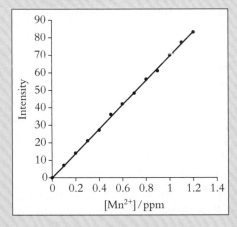

Figure 12.14 Calibration curve for ICP-OES instrument.

A 0.10 g sample of an alloy was dissolved in acid to produce a solution with a volume of 100 cm^3. The Mn^{2+} ion concentration of the solution was then measured. It was found to have an intensity of 64.

Outline how the metal ions are separated and quantified using ICP-OES. [4]

ii Calculate the percentage of manganese in the 0.1 g sample. (1 ppm = 1 mg dm^{-3}) [2]

[Total 11]

3 **Many transition metals and their compounds can be used as catalysts. Heterogeneous catalysts work by providing a surface onto which the reactants can be adsorbed. Current research into zeolites and into carbon nanotubes includes research into their use as supports for catalysts or as catalysts themselves.**

a What is meant by a zeolite. [1]

b Why are carbon nanotubes and zeolites likely to be useful as catalyst supports or as catalysts? [1]

c Describe a concern that people may have about the use of nano-sized particles. [1]

d One advantage of zeolites as catalysts or catalyst supports is the idea that they can be shape-selective.

What is meant by this and what structural feature do zeolites have that might enable them to act this way. [2]

e Some reactions can be catalysed by a number of different catalysts.

Outline the factors that may be relevant to the choice of catalyst used. [3]

f How does a catalyst affect the atom economy of a process. [1]

[Total 9]

4 **The properties of a plastic can be modified in a number of ways.**

Explain the effect of the different modifications described below, using examples where possible:

a the degree of branching in the polymer chain. [4]

b the addition of a phthalate este. [4]

c the position of the side group. [4]

d the addition of a volatile hydrocarbon and heating during manufacturing [3]

[Total 15]

5 a What feature of the molecule shown in Figure 12.15 makes it likely to be useful for a liquid crystal display. [1]

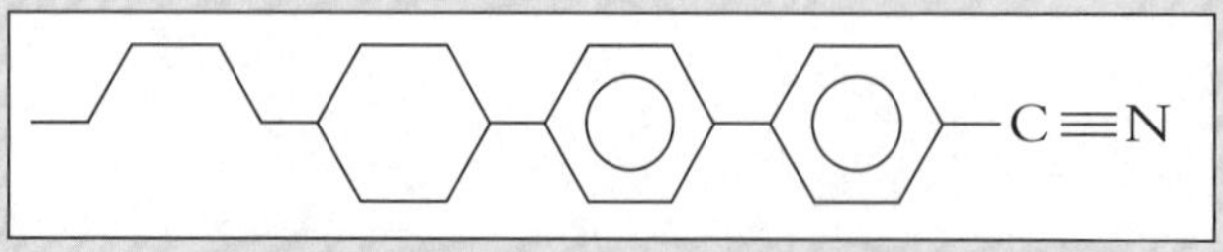

Figure 12.15 Compound for use in LCDs.

b What effect does an electric field have on these types of molecules. [1]

c Soap molecules can behave as liquid crystals in solution as the molecules can arrange themselves into spheres and layers.

i Of what type of liquid crystal is soap solution an example. [1]

ii What factor affects the liquid-crystal behaviour of the soap molecules. [1]

d In the solid state, molecules of the compound in Figure 12.15 are arranged in a neat regular arrangement. When heated it goes through a liquid-crystal state and then eventually melts to form a liquid with randomly arranged and orientated molecules. Describe the arrangement of the molecules in the liquid-crystal state. [1]

[Total 5]

6   **HL** **Nylon-6,10 is a polyamide made from the monomers shown in Figure 12.16.**

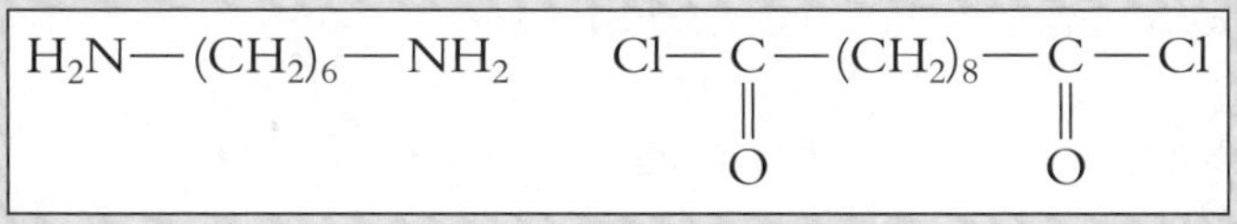

$$H_2N-(CH_2)_6-NH_2 \qquad Cl-\underset{\underset{O}{\|}}{C}-(CH_2)_8-\underset{\underset{O}{\|}}{C}-Cl$$

Figure 12.16 Monomers of nylon 6,10.

a Draw a section of the polymer chain and identify the other product formed in the reaction. [3]
b Nylon forms long chains with intermolecular forces between different polymer chains. What type of intermolecular forces are formed between the amide linkages. [1]
c Figure 12.17 shows the structure of Bakelite. Bakelite is a thermosetting plastic made from phenol and methanal.

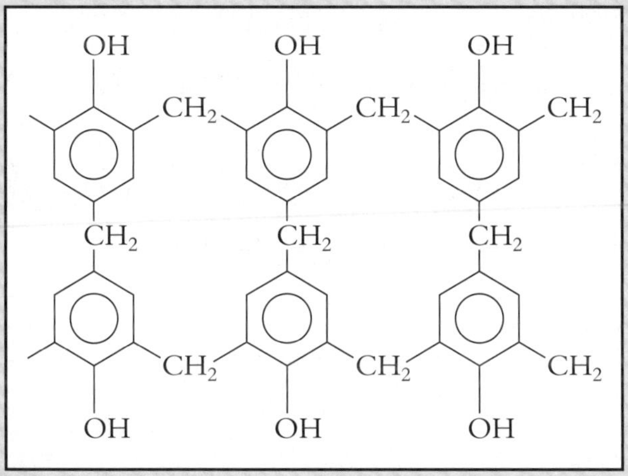

Figure 12.17 Bakelite.

i Describe what is meant by the term 'thermosetting'. [1]
ii State what type of bonding links the chains in a thermosetting polymer. [1]
iii Suggest the likely properties of Bakelite. [1]
d Waste plastics can be disposed of through landfill or by incineration.
i Identify a different environmental concern linked to both of these disposal methods. [2]
ii The combustion of nylon produces CO, H_2O and HCN. Construct an equation for this reaction. Use $(C_{16}H_{30}N_2O_2)_n$ as the formula for nylon. [2]
iii Outline why the recycling of plastics is an energy-intensive process. [2]
e One solution to the problem of plastic waste is the use of biodegradable plastics.
i Name a substance that is commonly used to make biodegradable plastics. [1]
ii Explain why most synthetic polymers are not biodegradable. [1]

f PVC is a widely used polymer but its use in some situations has been under scrutiny.

   i State why its use in food packaging is of concern. [2]

   ii Suggest why it is being replaced by low-smoke, zero-halogen cabling in some circumstances. [1]

[Total 18]

7 **HL** Perovskite is a naturally occurring mineral with the formula CaTiO$_3$ but the term is now used to describe any ceramic material with the same crystal structure.

  a State the name of the analytical method that can be used to determine crystal structure. [1]

  b Figure 12.18 shows the structure of CaTiO$_3$.

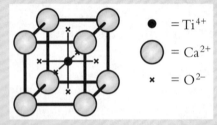

    ● = Ti^{4+}

    ◯ = Ca^{2+}

    × = O^{2-}

Figure 12.18 CaTiO$_3$.

It can be thought of as a cube with Ca^{2+} ions at the corners of the cube, a Ti^{4+} ion in the centre and 6 O^{2-} ions on the six faces of the cube.

   i Considering the position of the Ca^{2+} and Ti^{4+} ions only, give the name for this arrangement. [1]

   ii Considering the position of the Ca^{2+} and O^{2-} ions only, what give the name for this arrangement? [1]

   iii Deduce the number of ions in one unit cell of CaTiO$_3$. [1]

  c Metallic calcium has a face-centred cubic structure with a unit cell length of 5.56×10^{-10} m. Calculate:

   i the atomic radius of calcium [3]

   ii the density of calcium [5]

[Total 12]

8 **HL** Heavy metals can be removed from water supplies by precipitation using hydroxide ions or by bubbling hydrogen sulfide gas through the water.

  a Give equations for the reaction of Pb^{2+} ions with these reagents. [2]

  b The concentration of sodium hydroxide needed to precipitate the Pb^{2+} ions from a contaminated water supply is 0.001 mol dm^{-3} at 298 K. Given that the solubility product constant of lead(II) hydroxide is 1.43×10^{-20}, calculate the concentration of Pb^{2+} in the water at this temperature. [2]

  c The solubility product constant of PbI$_2$ is approximately 8.5×10^{-9} at 298 K.

   i Calculate its solubility at this temperature. [2]

   ii The value of the solubility product constant increases as the temperature increases. Predict the effect of increasing the temperature on the solubility of PbI$_2$. [1]

[Total 7]

Biochemistry (Option B) 13

Chapter outline

- Recall that the diverse functions of biological molecules depend on their structures and shapes and that metabolic processes involve both catabolic and anabolic processes.
- Describe the structure of proteins and explain the role of enzymes in catalysing biological reactions.
- Explain the role of inhibitors in regulating the activity of enzymes and interpret data on enzyme kinetics and protein assays. **HL**
- Explain how amino acids and proteins can act as buffer solutions and calculate the pH of a buffer solution from given data. **HL**
- Describe the structure and functions of lipids including triglycerides, phospholipids and steroids.
- Describe the structure and functions of mono-, di- and polysaccharides.
- Recall that vitamins are micronutrients that are essential to health and relate their structure to their solubility in water or fat.
- Explain the potential impact of plastics, antibiotics, enzymes, pesticides and other xenobiotic compounds on the environment.
- Describe the structure of DNA and RNA and discuss the benefits and concerns of using genetically modified foods. **HL**
- Explain the origin of colour, stability and function in biological pigments, and the role of hemoglobin in oxygen transport. **HL**
- Recognise that most biochemical processes are stereospecific and recall examples of stereoisomerism including glucose, amino acids, *cis*/*trans*-fats and the role of vitamin A in vision.

KEY TERMS AND FORMULAS

Anabolism: The process of synthesising molecules needed by cells; this requires energy.

Biomagnification: The increase in concentration of a substance as it passes up a food chain.

Catabolism: The process of breaking down larger molecules into smaller ones with the release of energy.

Isoelectric point: The pH at which an amino acid has no overall charge.

Metabolism: The chemical reactions that occur within cells. It involves both the breakdown of molecules with the release of energy and the synthesis of molecules that are required by cells.

Xenobiotics: Compounds found in a living organism that should not normally be found there.

Zwitterion: The form of an amino acid that has no overall charge.

Allosteric effect: The binding of a ligand to one site on a protein molecule in such a way that the properties of another site on the same protein are affected.

Conjugated system: A system of connected p-orbitals with delocalized electrons in molecules with alternating single and multiple bonds.

Genetic code: The sequence of bases in DNA that determines the sequence of amino acids in a protein.

Genetically modified organism (GMO): Organisms in which the genetic code has been changed in some way by genetic engineering.

Michaelis constant, K_m: The concentration of substrate when the rate of an enzyme catalysed reaction is half the maximum rate.

$$\text{Atom economy} = \frac{\text{molar mass of desired products}}{\text{molar mass of all reactants}} \times 100$$

$$R_f = \frac{\text{distance travelled by the spot}}{\text{distance travelled by the solvent front}}$$

$$\text{Iodine number} = \frac{M_r(I_2) \times \text{number of C} = \text{C double bonds} \times 100}{\text{relative molecular mass of the molecule}}$$

(Relative molecular mass of $I_2 = 253.80$)

Exercise 13.1 – Introduction to biochemistry

1 Biological molecules have many roles in living organisms. Many of these functions depend on the structure and shape of the molecules. The chemical reactions that occur within cells occur in a highly controlled aqueous environment and involve both the breakdown and synthesis of molecules.

   a What general name is given to the processes that occur in cells?

   b What name is given specifically to the breakdown of larger molecules in cells into smaller ones with the release of energy?

   c What name is given to the process of synthesising the molecules needed by cells?

   d Photosynthesis is a reaction that occurs in cells. It uses light energy to produce glucose from carbon dioxide and water.

      i Give a simple equation to represent photosynthesis.

      ii The breakdown of glucose occurs via a series of complex steps eventually producing carbon dioxide and water. What name is given to this process?

   e What is the significance of photosynthesis and the process described in part **d ii** to the composition of the atmosphere?

Learning definitions is important in chemistry but so too is recognising a definition.

2 Condensation reactions and hydrolysis reactions are both important in biological systems.

  a What is meant by the term 'condensation reaction'?
  b What is meant by the term 'hydrolysis'?
  c Name a biologically important molecule that is formed by a condensation reaction.
  d Give an example of a biological process that involves hydrolysis.

You may not be able to answer parts **c** and **d** until you have covered more of this topic. Just leave these parts for now and come back to them later.

Exercise 13.2 – Proteins and enzymes

1 This question is about amino acids; the structures of the 20 naturally occurring 2-amino acids can be found in the data book.

  a Give the general formula of a 2-amino acid.
  b Amino acids are amphoteric. Explain what this term means and explain why amino acids exhibit this property. Give equations to illustrate your answer.
  c 'The charge on an amino acid depends on the pH of the solution.'
     Using equations as appropriate, explain this statement.
  d What name is given to the form of an amino acid that has no overall charge?
  e What name is given to the pH at which an amino acid has no overall charge?
  f Describe two physical properties of amino acids and account for these properties in terms of their structure.

Suitable physical properties include melting points and solubility.

2 This question is about the structure of proteins.

  a What is meant by the 'primary structure' of a protein?
  b What is meant by the 'secondary structure' of a protein?
  c What is meant by the 'tertiary structure' of a protein?
  d What is meant by the 'quaternary structure' of a protein?
  e Give equations for the formation of the two different dipeptides that can be formed from the two amino acids shown in Figure 13.1

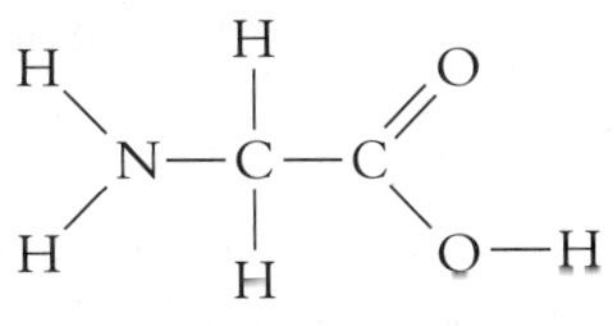

glycine 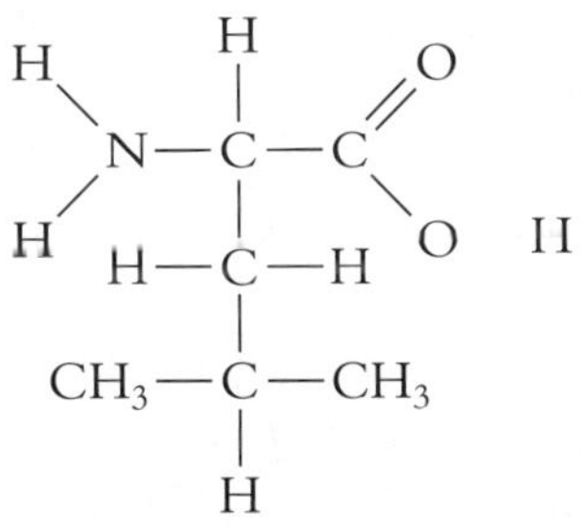   leucine

Figure 13.1 Glycine and leucine.

As no pH is stated, these can be drawn without charges, i.e. $-NH_2$ and –COOH

f The tripeptide shown in Figure 13.2 was heated with concentrated sodium hydroxide solution in order to hydrolyse it into separate amino acids.
Give the structure of the three amino acids formed under these conditions.

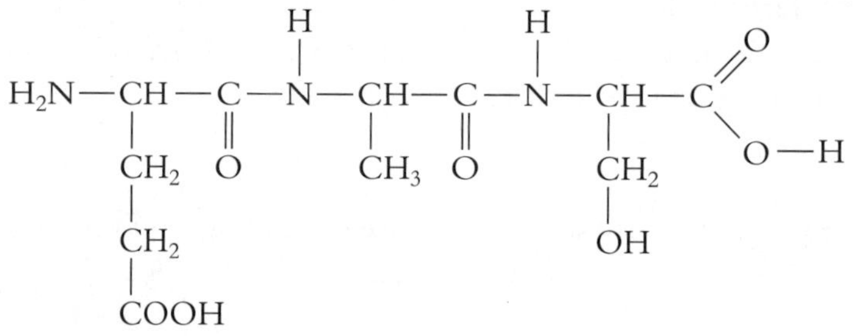

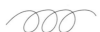

Figure 13.2 Glu-Ala-Ser.

This time you do need to think about any charges on $-NH_2$ and –COOH groups.

g Give three examples of the functions of proteins in humans.

Specific examples are not required in the syllabus but it is useful to know a few examples.
Give a variety of examples – try to use examples from different categories such as a structural protein, a catalyst, a hormone, a transport protein, an immunological protein or as an energy source.

3 The diagrams and statements below describe the structure of proteins. Identify which Figures and statements refer to either the primary, secondary, tertiary or quaternary structure.

Figure 13.3

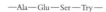

—Ala—Glu—Ser—Try—

Figure 13.4

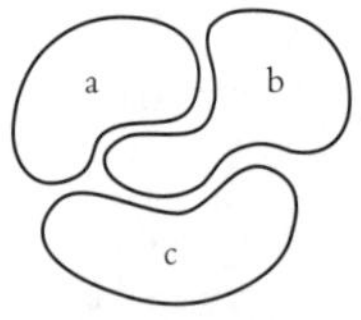

Figure 13.5

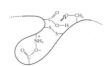

Figure 13.6

a Covalent bond in an amide link.

b Interactions between groups in different protein chains.

c Hydrogen bonds between the C=O of one peptide bond and the N-H of another.

d Interactions between the R groups of different amino acids.

4 This question is about the analysis of proteins.

 a The statements below describe the analysis of a protein by paper chromatography or by TLC.

   List the statements in the correct order.
   1 Spray the plate with a locating agent.
   2 Calculate the R_f value.
   3 Mark the position of the solvent front.
   4 Place a small sample of the unknown and any reference samples on the bottom of a TLC plate or piece of chromatography paper.
   5 Compare with the values for known amino acids.
   6 Heat with concentrated hydrochloric acid.
   7 Place the paper or TLC plate into a tank containing a suitable solvent.
   8 Allow the solvent to rise up the paper or TLC plate.

 b What is the purpose of step 6 in part **a**?
 c Define R_f as mentioned in step 2.
 d Outline the analysis of a protein by gel electrophoresis.

5 Enzymes are proteins made by living organisms that catalyse a biological reaction. They differ from inorganic catalysts in a number of ways.
 a Outline the similarities and differences between inorganic catalysts and enzymes.
 b The action of an enzyme can be described by the equation:

   $E + S \rightleftharpoons ES \rightarrow E + P$

   where E is the enzyme, S is the substrate, P is the product and ES is an enzyme–substrate complex.
   i Why is the way that enzymes act sometimes described as the 'lock and key' hypothesis?
   ii The 'lock and key' hypothesis has been replaced by the induced-fit hypothesis. What is the difference between these two ideas?
 c Figure 13.7 shows how the rate of an enzyme-catalysed reaction varies with substrate concentration using a constant amount of enzyme.

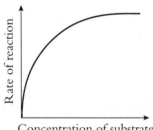

Figure 13.17 The kinetics of an enzyme catalysed reaction.

   Why does the rate of the reaction become constant at high substrate concentrations?

> It is very easy to only focus on the differences – include some similarities too.

d Figure 13.8 shows how the rate of an enzyme-catalysed reaction varies with
temperature and pH. Explain the shapes of these graphs.

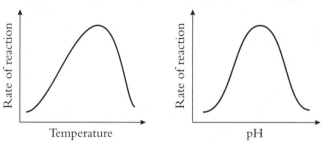

Figure 13.8 The effect of temperature and pH on enzyme kinetics.

Exercise 13.3 – Lipids

1 a Name three types of lipids found in the human body.
b State four uses of lipids in the human body.
c By reference to the formula of a typical carbohydrate as $C_6H_{12}O_6$ and a typical
fat as $C_{51}H_{98}O_6$, explain why lipid molecules contain more energy per gram than
carbohydrates.

2 Triglycerides are tri-esters of glycerol and three fatty acid molecules.
a Draw the structure of a typical triglyceride, use R to represent a fatty acid molecule
but include the ester linkage in your answer.
b What type of reaction occurs when these molecules are formed?
c The following terms can all be used to describe fatty acids, saturated, unsaturated and
polyunsaturated.
Draw the following molecules
i a saturated fatty acid with the formula $C_{17}H_{36}O_2$
ii an unsaturated fatty acid with the formula $C_{17}H_{34}O_2$
iii a polyunsaturated fatty acid with the formula $C_{17}H_{30}O_2$

Skeletal formulas can be used.

Don't forget to count the C of COOH.

Double bonds can be positioned anywhere in the hydrocarbon chain.

If you have already completed Exercise 11.3 then you could calculate the index of
hydrogen deficiency for the polyunsaturated molecule in part **iii** to find the number of
double bonds.

d Explain why triglycerides containing a high proportion of saturated fatty acids tend
to have higher melting points than unsaturated fats of similar molecular mass.

You must first deduce the number of C=C bonds in the molecule. If you have already completed Exercise 11.3 then you could calculate the index of hydrogen deficiency to do this. If not, then consider the formula as $C_{17}H_{29}COOH$ rather than $C_{18}H_{30}O_2$ and deduce how many double bonds there are compared to a saturated molecule with the formula $C_nH_{2n+1}COOH$.

The second step is to calculate the relative molecular mass of the molecule and then apply the formula:

$$\text{iodine number} = \frac{M_r(I_2) \times \text{number of C=C double bonds} \times 100}{\text{relative molecular mass of the molecule}}$$

3 Fats and oils can be compared using their iodine number.
  a Define the term iodine number and state what it measures.
  b Calculate the iodine number of a fatty acid with the formula $C_{18}H_{30}O_2$.
  c A sample of a lipid with an average relative molecular mass of 786.78 has an iodine number of 43. Calculate the average number of C=C double bonds in the lipid.
  d Explain why the answer to part c is not a whole number.

4 Figure 13.9 shows the structure of a typical phospholipid.

H—C—O—P—O—H with H and O⁻ above, and O double bonded below phosphorus; H—C—O—C chain with a C=C double bond; H—C—O—C chain; structural diagram of phospholipid.

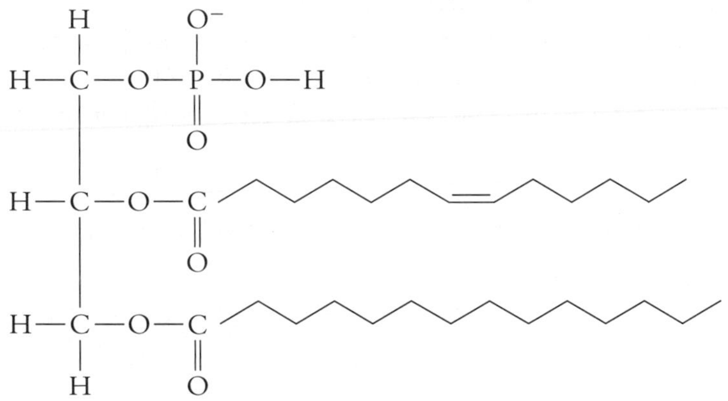

Figure 13.9 A typical phospholipid.

'Linkage' implies not just a single bond but a group of atoms.

  a Indicate on the diagram the phosphate–ester linkage.
  b The phosphate group can form a second ester linkage to other molecules which are often polar in nature. Explain how the presence of polar and non-polar parts of the molecule enables them to form bilayers as shown in Figure 13.10.

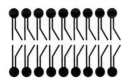

Figure 13.10 Phospholipid bilayer.

5 a Give an equation for the reaction that occurs when the triglyceride in Figure 13.11 is heated under reflux in the presence of aqueous acid.

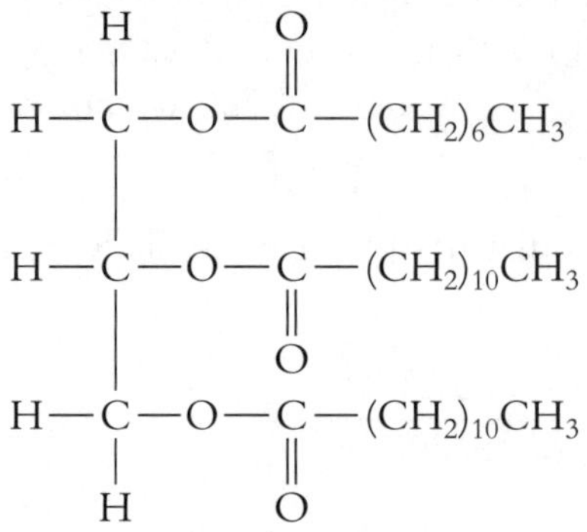

$$H-\underset{\underset{H}{|}}{\overset{\overset{H}{|}}{C}}-O-\overset{\overset{O}{\|}}{C}-(CH_2)_6CH_3$$

$$H-\underset{|}{\overset{|}{C}}-O-\overset{\underset{O}{\|}}{C}-(CH_2)_{10}CH_3$$

$$H-\underset{\underset{H}{|}}{\overset{|}{C}}-O-\overset{\underset{O}{\|}}{C}-(CH_2)_{10}CH_3$$

Figure 13.11 A triglyceride.

b What name is given to this type of reaction?
c What would be the difference in the products if an alkali was used rather than an acid?

> Think about the reaction between the fatty acid molecules and an alkali.

6 When fats go off they develop an unpleasant smell and are described as rancid. There are two main types of reaction that cause rancidity.
  a Name the two main types of reaction that cause rancidity.
  b Which of these most commonly causes rancidity in saturated fats?
  c Which of these most commonly causes rancidity in unsaturated fats?
  d The rate of rancidity is affected by a number of factors including temperature and the presence of enzymes. Give one other major factor for each type of rancidity.
  e At which part of the molecules do these processes occur in saturated and unsaturated fats?

7 A steroid is a type of lipid that has the common structure shown in Figure 13.12.

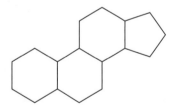

Figure 13.12 Steroid backbone.

  a Suggest whether steroids are likely to be water- or fat-soluble.
  b Two examples of steroids found in the body are testosterone and cholesterol. Cholesterol has an important function in the body as a precursor for other steroids as well as in cell membranes. Cholesterol is transported around the body in the form of low-density lipoproteins (LDLs) and high-density lipoproteins (HDLs).
  i State the role of LDLs and their impact on health.
  ii State the role of HDLs and their impact on health.

   iii Different types of fat are thought to be either beneficial or harmful in a balanced
     diet.
   Suggest whether a healthy diet should contain high or low levels of saturated,
   unsaturated and *trans*-fats.
c Testosterone is a naturally occurring anabolic steroid hormone.
   Give a medical use of this hormone and suggest why it can sometimes be misused.

Exercise 13.4 – Carbohydrates

1 Carbohydrates range from simple sugars to complex polymers known as
polysaccharides.
  a Give the two major functions of carbohydrates in the human body.
  b What is the general formula of carbohydrates?
  c The simplest sugars are monosaccharides.
    Monosaccharides include hexose and pentose sugars; both of these can be aldoses or
    ketoses. Monosaccharides can join together to form disaccharides.
    i Describe what is meant by the term 'disaccharide'.
    ii What is meant by the terms 'hexose', 'pentose', 'aldose' and 'ketose'?
    iii Other than a carbonyl group, what other functional group do all
      monosaccharides include?
  d Glucose exists in solution in both its straight-chain and ring forms as shown in
    Figure 13.13.

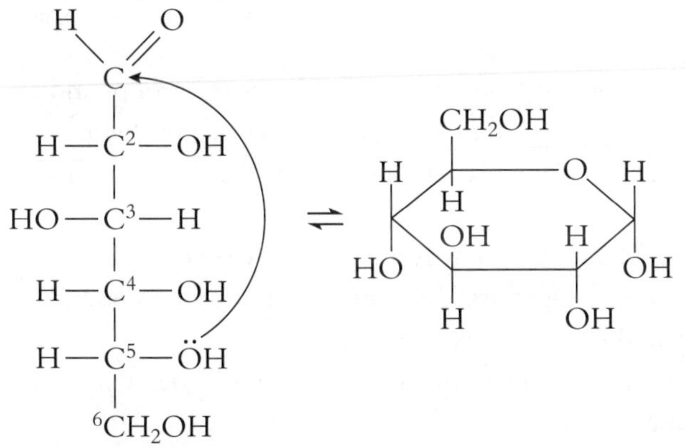

Figure 13.13 Chain and ring forms of glucose.

    i What name is given to the C–O–C linkage in the ring form of glucose?
    ii Figure 13.13 shows the ring form using a Haworth projection. Number the
      carbon atoms in this projection to match those in the chain form.

2 Monosaccharides join to form disaccharides.
  a What type of reaction is this?
  b During the reaction between two monosaccharides to form a disaccharide, what
    other small molecule is formed?

The syllabus states that you should understand the relationship of the properties and functions of monosaccharides and polysaccharides to their chemical structures. It is important to bear in mind that this is a chemistry syllabus and so answers should be based on specific types of intermolecular forces, hydrogen bonding in this case.

Specific polysaccharides are not required but the principles about properties and structure from Topic 4 can be applied in a biochemical context.

The structures of some monosaccharides are given in the data book. Note that C^1 is drawn on the right of these molecules.

For this question, rotate monosaccharide 2 around by 180° so that C^2 is adjacent to the C^1 of the first molecule.

c Draw the disaccharide formed when the two monosaccharides shown in Figure 13.14 form a disaccharide with a 1,2-linkage.

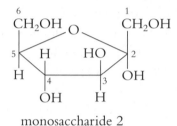

Figure 13.14 Two monosaccharides.

3 Examples of polysaccharides include starch, glycogen and cellulose. These are sometimes called complex carbohydrates.

Monosaccharides such as glucose contain large numbers of hydroxyl groups and are water-soluble. Glucose is stored in plants as starch and in animals, as glycogen.

a Why is glucose stored in the form of complex carbohydrates rather than as a simple sugar?

b Cellulose is found in the cell walls of plants. It is made up of closely packed long chains of glucose molecules joined together. Describe how the properties and functions of cellulose are related to its molecular structure.

c What type of reaction occurs when storage molecules such as glycogen and starch are broken down to produce glucose?

Exercise 13.5 – Vitamins

1 Vitamins are micronutrients; most are not synthesised in the body but are derived from food. Their solubility in fat or in water can be deduced from their structure.

a Define the term 'micronutrient'.

b The structures of some common vitamins are given in Figure 13.15. Predict their solubility in fat and water.

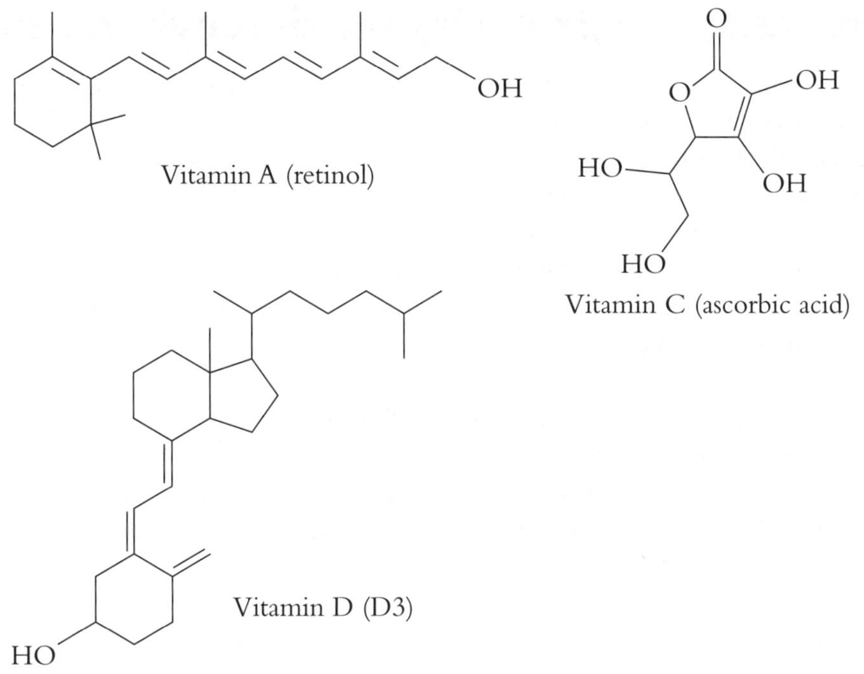

Vitamin A (retinol)

Vitamin C (ascorbic acid)

Vitamin D (D3)

Figure 13.15 Structure of common vitamins.

Consider whether the molecule contains polar groups such as OH and so can form hydrogen bonds with water.

c Give two reasons why the vitamin C content of vegetables is reduced when they are boiled.

d Table 13.1 gives examples of the sources of some common vitamins and problems associated with their deficiency in the diet.

Vitamin	Source	Deficiency
vitamin A	animal products such as liver, dairy products, egg yolk, carrots and other orange/yellow fruits and vegetables	Poor vision in low light intensity/ night blindness, poor growth and development, weakened immune system
vitamin B	whole grains	beriberi, anaemia, muscle weakness
vitamin C	fresh fruit and vegetables, particularly citrus fruits	scurvy, swollen bleeding gums, muscle and joint pain
vitamin D	butter, cheese, milk, fish oils Can also be synthesised by the action of sunlight	rickets – softening and deformity of the bones

Table 13.1

i Suggest why vitamin D deficiencies are increasing in more economically developed countries.

ii Vitamin A deficiency is more common in less economically developed countries. One controversial solution to this is the development of genetically modified crops such as 'golden rice' which is rich in molecules that can be converted into vitamin A in the body.

Suggest an alternative, less controversial solution.

Exercise 13.6 – Biochemistry and the environment

Choose three different types of examples; don't choose three different drugs for example.

1 Antibiotics are examples of xenobiotics and are molecules that are found in a living organism but should not be present.

   a Give three other examples of xenobiotic substances.

   b Many xenobiotics enter the environment via the water supply. Give three possible ways that these molecules get into the water supply.

   c Why is the presence of antibiotics in the environment of particular concern?

   d The concentration of some substances can increase as it passes up the food chain. What name is given to this process?

2 One of the solutions to plastic waste is the use of biodegradable plastics.

   a What is meant by the term 'biodegradable'?

   b What feature in the structure of polyalkenes means that they are non-biodegradable?

   c Poly(lactic acid) (PLA) is a biodegradable polymer made from corn starch. A section of its polymer chain is shown in Figure 13.16.

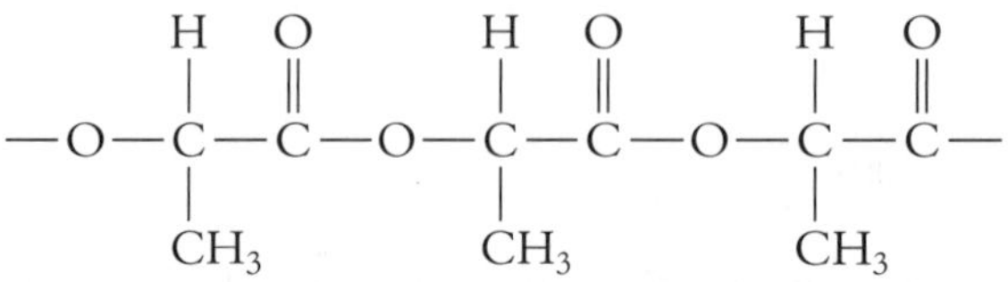

Figure 13.16 PLA.

     i What is the name of the functional group linking the lactic acid monomers together in PLA?

     ii What type of reaction occurs when PLA is broken down into lactic acid?

     iii Deduce the structure of lactic acid.

3 Host–guest chemistry is a technique used to remove toxic chemicals from the environment.

   a Describe what is meant by 'host–guest chemistry'.

   b What type of interactions hold the 'guest' and 'host' complex together?

   c Apart from the nature of the interactions between the host and the guest, describe one other similarity and one difference between host–guest chemistry and enzyme–substrate complexes.

   d Give an example of a pollutant that can be removed from the environment using host–guest chemistry.

4 a Microorganisms such as bacteria can be used to clean up the environment, for example in the treatment of oil spills.
     Outline how bacteria are able to do this.

   b Biological detergents are designed to clean effectively at lower temperatures than non-biological detergents and so save energy.

     i What ingredient do biological detergents contain that enables them to work more effectively at lower temperatures?

     ii Explain why biological detergents are less effective than non-biological detergents at higher temperatures.

5 Some of the principles of green chemistry are outlined below.
   1. prevention of waste
   2. high atom economy
   3. reduced toxicity of reactants, solvents and products
   4. energy efficiency
   5. renewable feedstocks
   6. biodegradable products
      a What is meant by 'green chemistry'?
      b Ethanol can be produced by fermentation of sugars using yeast or by the reaction of ethene with steam according to the following equations:
      fermentation: $C_6H_{12}O_6 \rightarrow 2C_2H_5OH + 2CO_2$
      reaction of ethene with steam: $C_2H_4 + H_2O \rightarrow C_2H_5OH$
         i Calculate the atom economy of both processes.
         ii In terms of green chemistry, discuss the advantages and disadvantages of both methods.

HL Exercise 13.7 – Proteins and enzymes

1 This question is about enzyme kinetics.
Figure 13.17 shows the relationship between the rate of an enzyme-catalysed reaction and the substrate concentration.

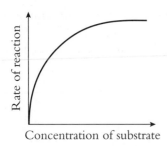

Figure 13.17 The kinetics of an enzyme catalysed reaction.

   a Explain why the relationship is directly proportional at low substrate concentrations.
   b Explain why the rate of reaction becomes constant at high substrate concentrations.
   c The affinity of an enzyme for a substrate can be described by the Michaelis constant.
      i Use Figure 13.17 to explain how this value is obtained.
      ii What does a large Michaelis constant imply about the stability of the enzyme–substrate complex?

2 The action of an enzyme can be reduced by the presence of an inhibitor.
The two main types of enzyme inhibitors are competitive and non-competitive inhibitors.
   a Outline the features of a competitive inhibitor.
   b i Outline the features of a non-competitive inhibitor.
      ii What name is given to the site where a non-competitive inhibitor binds?

c **i** Sketch a graph of the rate of an enzyme-catalysed reaction to show the effect of a competitive inhibitor and a non-competitive inhibitor.

ii What is the effect of these inhibitors on the maximum rate of reaction and on the value of the Michaelis constant?

d Explain why inhibitors are important in biological systems.

3 Amino acids and proteins can both act as buffers in solution.

a Explain why amino-acid solutions can act as buffers. Give an equation to explain your answer.

b The isoelectric point of valine is 6.0. Suggest the range of pH inside which valine could act as a buffer.

c Proteins can also act as buffers. What type of amino acids must a protein contain in order to do this?

d A buffer solution consisted of glycine, H_2NCH_2COOH, in both its zwitterion and protonated forms.

The concentration of the protonated form was found to be $0.125\,mol\,dm^{-3}$ and the concentration of the zwitterion form was $0.100\,mol\,dm^{-3}$.

i Give an equation for the reaction to show the equilibrium between the two forms of glycine.

ii Given that the pK_a for glycine is 2.35, calculate the pH of the solution.

4 The concentration of a protein can be found using UV-Vis spectroscopy by reference to a calibration curve obtained using solutions of known concentration.

a Outline the procedure to obtain the concentration of a protein in solution. You do not need to describe how the standard solutions are made.

b Figure 13.18 shows the calibration curve obtained during an experiment to find the concentration of a protein.

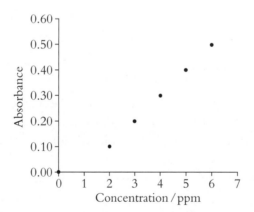

Figure 13.18 Calibration curve for a protein assay.

The absorbance of the unknown protein solution was found to be 0.45. Calculate the concentration of the protein solution.

c In a separate experiment using a different protein solution, the molar absorptivity of the protein at a given wavelength was found to be $732\,cm^{-1}\,mol^{-1}\,dm^3$. The absorbance of a solution of unknown concentration of this protein was measured as 0.38 with a path length of $1.0\,cm$. Calculate the concentration of the protein.

The Beer–Lambert law is given in the data book. It describes the relationship between the amount of light absorbed by a solution and its concentration. It can be simplified to:

absorbance = ecl

HL Exercise 13.8 – Nucleic acids

1 Nucleic acids are condensation polymers made up of nucleotides. Nucleotides consist of a five-carbon sugar, an organic nitrogen-containing base and a phosphate group. Figure 13.19 gives the general structure of a nucleotide.

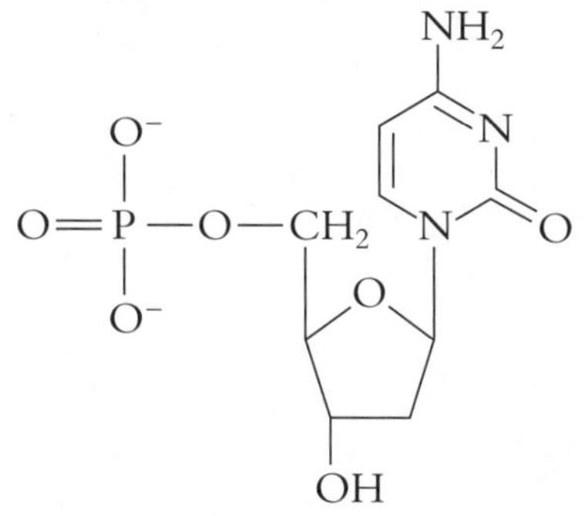

Figure 13.19 General structure of a nucleotide.

a Indicate on the diagram the two positions where the nucleotides join together to make a polynucleotide.

b Figure 13.19 shows a nucleotide from deoxyribonucleic acid. Indicate on the diagram the position on the ribose sugar which differs in ribonucleic acid.

c Another difference between DNA and RNA is the identity of the bases. The structures of the bases are give in the data book.

   i   Name the bases found in DNA.

   ii   Name the bases found in RNA.

   iii The structure of DNA involves complementary base pairs. Identify which bases pair together.

   iv Describe the bonding between the base pairs.

d Apart from the identity of the bases and the sugar, describe another difference between the structure of DNA and RNA.

2 The genetic information of a cell is found in the nucleus of a cell. Long strands of DNA are coiled into chromosomes which are wrapped around proteins called histones.

a Describe the interactions that hold the chromosomes and proteins together, identifying the parts of each molecule involved.

b How does DNA hold the genetic information required to code for the primary sequence of a protein?

c What aspect of the structure of DNA enables it to accurately undergo replication?

d A single strand of DNA was found to have the following sequence of bases:

   –T–A–G–G–C–A–T–C–G–T–A–G–G–T–A–A–

   i   Deduce the sequence of bases in its complementary strand.

   ii   Deduce the sequence of bases in a strand of RNA that is complementary to the sequence given in the question.

Details of protein formation (transcription and translation) are not required.

This is a chemistry syllabus so ensure that answers refer to the chemistry. Many students who also study biology fall into the trap of giving a biology answer which does not include enough reference to the bonding in these molecules.

3 Genetically modified organisms are a controversial issue in different parts of the world. The most common type of genetically modified organisms are GM foods.
   a What is meant by a genetically modified organism?
   b Describe three possible advantages of genetically modified foods.
   c Describe three possible concerns about the use of GM foods.

HL Exercise 13.9 – Biological pigments

1 This question is about biological pigments.
   a What is meant by the term 'biological pigment'?
   b Biological pigments absorb light in which region of the electromagnetic spectrum?
   c The absorption of light by biological pigments is linked to the presence of chromophores within the molecules.
      What is meant by the term 'chromophore'?
   d Figure 13.20 gives the structure of a biological pigment. Indicate on the diagram the part of the molecule that is responsible for its colour.

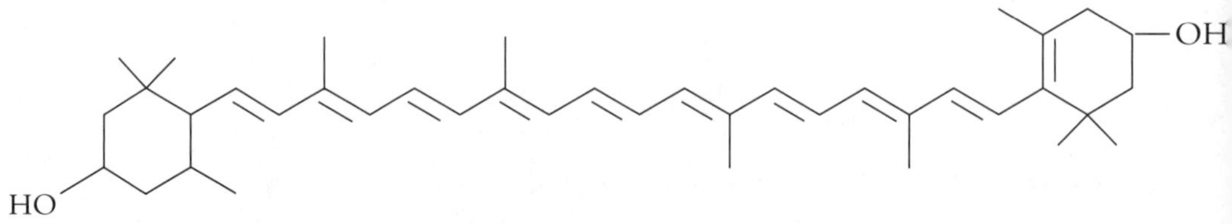

Figure 13.20 A biological pigment

2 The data book gives the structure of some biological pigments. These molecules all have extensive delocalised systems which are chromophores.
   a Anthocyanins are aromatic water-soluble pigments found in plants such as blackcurrants, blueberries and other red, blue and purple fruits, flowers and vegetables.
      Figure 13.21 shows the structure of an anthocyanin found in blue flowers.

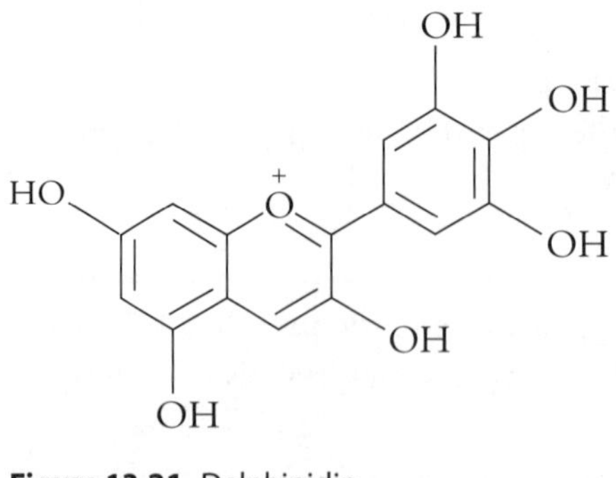

Figure 13.21 Delphinidin.

   i   What features of this molecule make it water-soluble?
   ii What factors affect the colour of anthocyanin pigments?
   b Carotenoids are a widespread type of pigment which absorb light in the blue–violet region of the electromagnetic spectrum.
      i   What colour do fruits and vegetables that contain high levels of carotenoids most commonly appear?

Consider the colour of carotenoids. How does this affect the range of wavelengths of light that can be absorbed?

ii Two examples of carotenoids given in the data book are α- and β-carotene. Predict whether these molecules are likely to be water- or fat-soluble, justifying your answer.

iii Carotenoids are susceptible to oxidation catalysed by light. What structural feature of the molecules is responsible for this?

iv Carotenoids are also found in leaves but their colour is often masked by the presence of chlorophyll. They absorb light causing the promotion of electrons which are passed on via a series of redox reactions.

Explain how the presence of carotenoids increases the amount of energy that leaves can obtain from light.

3 Hemoglobin, myoglobin, chlorophyll and cytochromes contain groups which contain a porphyrin ring and a central metal ion.

a Describe the bonding between the metal ion and the porphyrin ring.

b Porphyrin rings can be described as macrocyclic ligands. What does this term mean?

c Hemoglobin and myoglobin both consist of a heme unit and a globin molecule. What type of molecule is globin?

d Identify the charges on the ions which are associated with heme and with chlorophyll.

e Outline the role of hemoglobin in the transport of oxygen.

f The ability of hemoglobin to bind oxygen can be represented by the equation:

$$HbO_2 + H^+ \rightleftharpoons HbH^+ + O_2$$

where HbO_2 represents the oxygenated form of hemoglobin.

i Carbon dioxide dissolves in blood plasma to form an acidic solution. Give an equation for the process.

ii Using the equilibrium given in the question, describe the effect of a change in the pH of the blood on the ability of hemoglobin to bind oxygen.

iii Describe the effect of temperature on the ability of hemoglobin to bind oxygen.

g Carbon monoxide binds to the iron ions more strongly than oxygen and so acts as an inhibitor.

What name is given to this type of inhibitor?

h Cytochromes are proteins that contain heme groups. They are involved in key redox reactions in cells. Give equations to show the role that the central metal ion of the heme group plays in these processes.

4 Outline the use of chromatography to separate and identify pigments.

HL Exercise 13.10 – Stereochemistry in biomolecules

Topic 20.3 of the IB syllabus introduces the idea of stereochemistry. Stereochemistry is divided into conformational and configurational isomerism. Configurational isomerism is divided into *cis–trans*/*E–Z* isomerism and optical isomerism. This section of the biochemistry option is concerned with *cis–trans* and optical isomerism in biological molecules.

The structures of heme and chlorophyll are given in the data book although these do not show the charges on the ions.

Include ideas about the structure of hemoglobin, how it binds to oxygen reversibly, how the affinity for oxygen changes as the partial pressure of oxygen changes. These ideas do not need to be discussed in depth as the command term 'outline' is used here.

At a very simple level, the binding of oxygen can be thought of as a 'bond-forming' process.
$$Hb + O_2 \rightleftharpoons HbO_2$$

Outline means 'give a brief account or summary'. Key terms here include adsorption, stationary phase, mobile phase and solvent.

1 This question is about optical isomerism in amino acids and in sugars.

a Apart from glycine, all naturally occurring amino acids are optically active. Using the structures of the amino acids given in the data book, explain why glycine is not optically active.

b The optical isomers of amino acids are named using a d– and l– convention. However. only one form is found in natural proteins – which one?

c Are d– or l– forms of sugars more common in nature?

d The naming of d– and l–sugars is based on the configuration of only one of the chiral carbon atoms as drawn in a Fischer projection – which one and what is the convention?

e Sugar molecules exist in both chain and ring forms when in solution as shown in Figure 13.22.

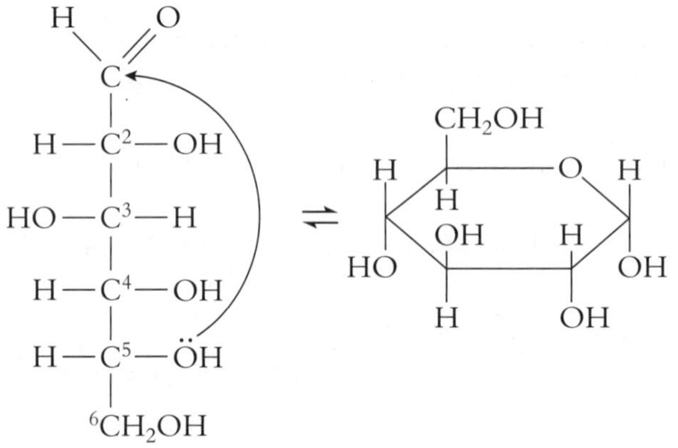

Figure 13.22 Chain and ring forms of glucose.

Carbon number 1, which is not chiral in the chain form, is a chiral centre in the ring form. This results in two possible ring forms which are designated α and β. Figure 13.23 shows the ring forms of fructose. Identify which is the α form and which is the β form.

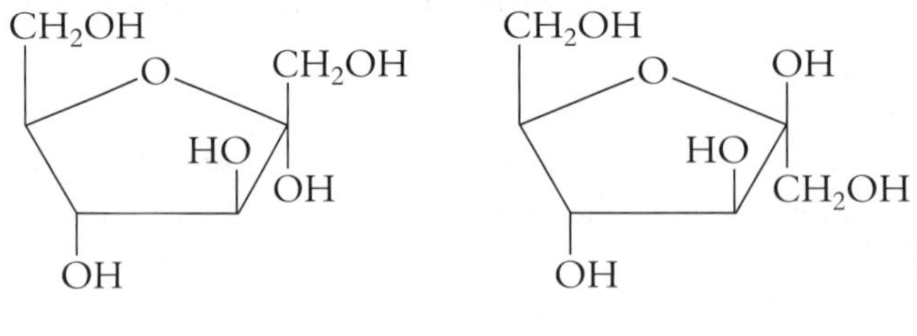

Figure 13.23 α and β forms of fructose

The α and β naming depends on the orientation of the OH group on the carbon which was part of the carbonyl group (carbon number 2 in fructose, carbon number 1 in glucose). The α molecule has this OH group below the plane of the ring.

2 Section 4 of the biochemistry topic introduces polysaccharides. This question examines the structure of two polysaccharides of glucose: starch and cellulose.

Compare and contrast the structure and properties of starch and cellulose and relate this to the bonding in these substances.

3 Unsaturated fats commonly contain *cis* C=C bonds rather than *trans*.

  a Describe the effect of the presence of *cis* C=C bonds on the melting and boiling points of fats compared to saturated fats and those with *trans* C=C bonds.

  b Describe the process of hydrogenation and partial hydrogenation of fats, and the effect on melting points.

  c Describe the advantages and disadvantages of hydrogenation.

This is linked to the packing of the fatty acid chains and the strength of the intermolecular forces.

4 Figure 13.24 shows the structure of *cis*-retinal which is also given in the data book. Cells in the retina of the eye contain *cis*-retinal bonded to the protein opsin.

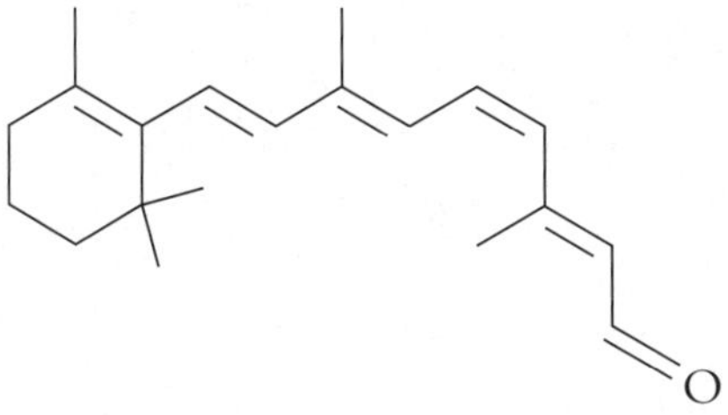

Figure 13.24 11 *cis*-retinal.

  a What name is given to the protein made of opsin in combination with retinal?

  b Copy the structure of *cis*-retinal and mark the *cis* group.

  c What is the effect on the structure of *cis*-retinal when a photon of light is absorbed by the molecule?

  d How does this lead to a signal being sent to the brain?

  e What happens to the retinal after the signal has been sent?

  f Figure 13.25 shows the structure of Vitamin A, retinol.

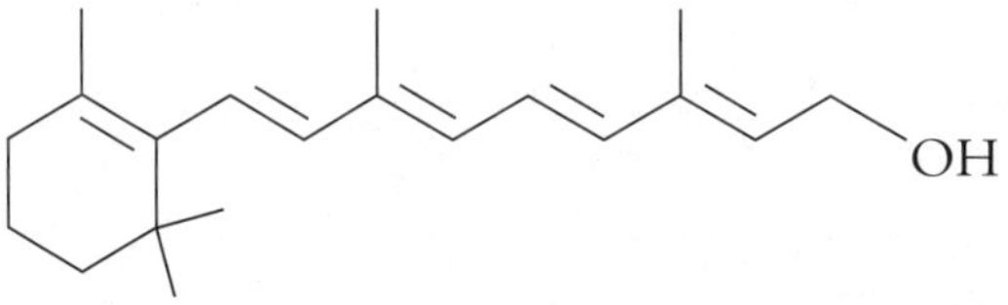

Figure 13.25 Vitamin A, retinol

This is also given in the data book.

Looking at the functional groups in retinol (Figure 13.23) and retinal (Figure 13.22), what type of reaction occurs when retinol is converted into retinal?

1   **a** **The general formula of an amino acid can be written as $H_2NCH(R)COOH$.**
   i Name the two functional groups in these molecules. [2]
   ii Naturally occurring amino acids are called 2-amino acids. To what does the '2' refer? [1]
  b The data book gives the structures and isoelectric points of 20 amino acids.
    Draw the structures of the following amino acids at the pH stated:
   i alanine at pH 6 [1]
   ii isoleucine at pH 9 [1]
   iii phenylalanine at pH 5.5 [1]
   iv aspartic acid at pH 7 [1]
   v lysine at pH 9.7 [1]
  c The structure of the dipeptide Val–Tyr is shown in Figure 13.26.

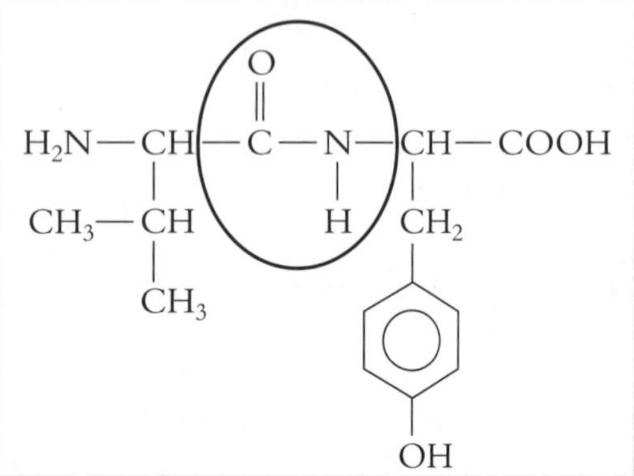

Figure 13.26 Val–Tyr.

   i Draw the structure of a different dipeptide that contains the same two amino acids. [1]
   ii Give the name of the section circled in Figure 13.26. [1]
   iii The dipeptide shown in Figure 13.26 forms two different molecules on heating with sodium hydroxide. Give the structures of these molecules. [2]

                                       [Total 12]

2   **Examples of biological molecules include proteins, lipids, carbohydrates and vitamins.**
  a From the list above give the name of the type or types of biological molecules that:
   i contain ether linkages. [1]
   ii contain ester linkages. [1]
   iii contain amide linkages. [1]
   iv are classed as micronutrients. [1]

b Lipids and carbohydrates are both used for energy storage.
Compare the roles of these two classes of compounds with reference to their solubility and how easily the energy they contain is released. **[5]**

c In order to release the stored energy both lipids and carbohydrates undergo oxidation reactions. Explain why lipids release more energy per gram than carbohydrates. **[2]**

[Total 11]

3 **Lipids used for energy storage are commonly triglycerides.**

a Describe the structure of a typical triglyceride. **[1]**

b Triglycerides can be described as saturated or unsaturated.
Describe how this affects the melting points of triglycerides. **[1]**

c The degree of unsaturation of a lipid is indicated by its iodine number.
   i Define the term 'iodine number'. **[1]**
   ii A lipid X contains an average of 3.75 C=C bonds and has an iodine number of 157.
   Calculate its relative molecular mass. (M_r of I_2 = 253.80) **[2]**

d Lipids can undergo both hydrolytic and oxidative rancidity.
   i Describe these two processes and the parts of a lipid molecule where each reaction occurs. **[4]**
   ii Give an equation for the process that occurs when the triglyceride shown in Figure 13.27 undergoes hydrolytic rancidity. **[2]**

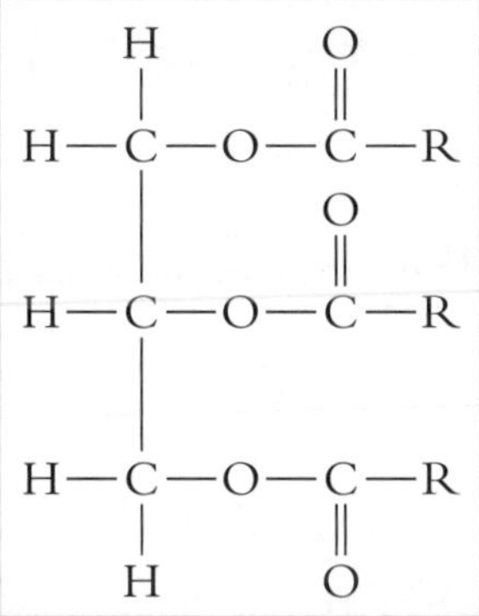

Figure 13.27 A triglyceride.

e Outline how the water content of food, pH, temperature and the availability of oxygen and light affects the storage of fatty food in terms of the ease of hydrolytic and oxidative rancidity. **[4]**

[Total 15]

4 **The impact of different biological molecules on health is a topic of much research.**

a Triglycerides and cholesterol are transported around the body as part of lipoproteins. These are described as LDL or HDL.
   i State what the letters LDL and HDL stand for. **[1]**
   ii Outline the role of LDL and HDL and their impact on health. **[4]**

b Cholesterol is essential to the human body as it serves an important role in the synthesis of other molecules including steroid hormones.
   i Name a biological molecule that is formed from cholesterol. **[1]**
   ii Steroids can be useful medicinally but can also be abused. Name the effect these compounds have that makes them suitable for both use and abuse. **[1]**

[Total 7]

5 **This question is about green chemistry.**

The presence of biological molecules in the environment can lead to a number of undesirable effects.

a What name is given to molecules found in the environment that ought not to be present? [1]

b One of the issues with these molecules is that they can lead to biomagnification.

  i Define the term 'biomagnification'. [1]

  ii List the properties that lead to a molecule being more likely to cause biomagnification. [3]

  iii Give a specific example of biomagnification, its use, and consequent negative impact. [4]

  [Total 9]

6 **HL**

a Explain the different modes of action of competitive and non-competitive inhibitors in enzyme-catalysed reactions. [3]

b The action of an inhibitor was investigated by following the kinetics of the reaction.
It was found that for the uninhibited enzyme the Michaelis constant, $K_m = 2.233$, whereas in the presence of an inhibitor, its value was 4.322.

  i Explain the term 'Michaelis constant'. [2]

  ii Deduce whether the inhibitor is acting competitively or non-competitively. Justify your answer. [2]

  iii Sketch a graph to show the kinetics of the reaction both with and without the inhibitor. [4]

  [Total 11]

7 **HL**

a Describe the structure of DNA including the types of bonding and the nature of the linkages between its different components. [4]

b Explain the stability of DNA in terms of the hydrophilic and hydrophobic interactions between its different parts. [3]

c Explain the origin of the negative charge on DNA and the role of this charge in the structure of chromosomes. [2]

d Figure 13.28 shows cytosine–guanine and adenine–thymine base pairs.
Show the position of the hydrogen bonds that hold these bases together. [2]

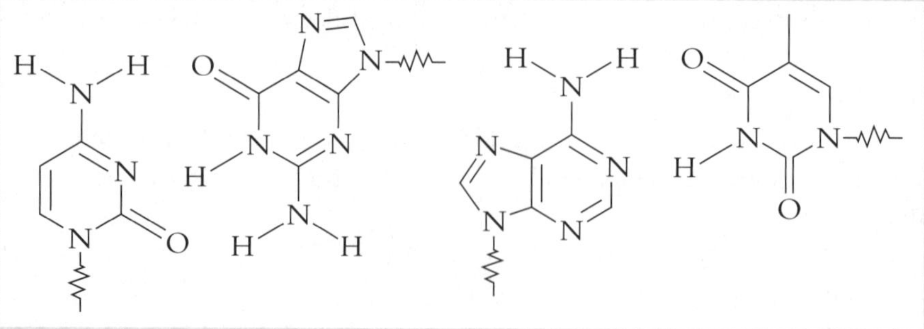

Figure 13.28 C–G and A–T base pairs.

[Total 11]

8   **HL** **Biological pigments include anthocyanins, carotenoids and chlorophyll. These molecules absorb light in the visible part of the electromagnetic spectrum.**
   a Name the feature of these molecules that enables them to appear coloured. [1]
   b Outline the factors that affect the stabilities of anthocyanins, carotenoids and chlorophyll in relation to their structures. [4]
   c Anthocyanins can act as indicators because of their sensitivity to pH.
      Figure 13.29 shows the structure of a typical anthocyanin found in a variety of red cabbage.

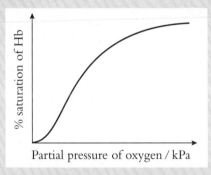

violet   blue

Figure 13.29 Anthocyanin from cabbage.

Give the colour of this substance at high pH. [1]

[Total 6]

9   **HL** **Figure 13.30 shows the oxygen binding curve for hemoglobin.**

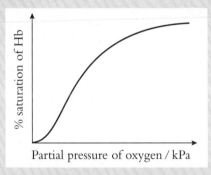

Figure 13.30 Oxygen binding curve for hemoglobin.

   a Sketch a line on the graph to show the curve for foetal hemoglobin. [1]
   b State the importance of this difference. [2]
   c Carbon monoxide is toxic. Compare the bonding of oxygen and carbon monoxide to hemoglobin and explain how carbon monoxide prevents oxygen transport. [4]

[Total 7]

10　**HL**　Figure 13.31 shows the Fischer projection for a molecule of D-mannose.

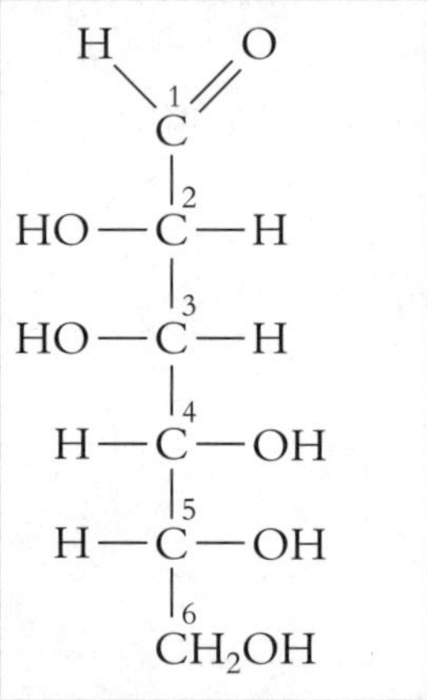

Figure 13.31 D mannose.

D mannose can be described as both an aldose and as a hexose.

a　Explain why it can correctly be described as an aldose. [1]

b　Explain why it can correctly be described as a hexose. [1]

c　Indicate which part of the molecule identifies it as the d-isomer. [1]

d　d-mannose has a number of stereoisomers.

　　i　Draw the structure of its enantiomer. [1]

　　ii　Draw the structure of a diastereoisomer of d-mannose. [1]

e　D-mannose has two different cyclic forms known as α- and β-D-mannose.

　　Draw these two cyclic forms, clearly indicating which is the α form and which is the β form.

　　You do not need to show the position of all of the OH groups, only those relevant to the α and β nomenclature. [2]

[Total 7]

Energy (Option C) 14

Chapter outline

- Discuss the use of different sources of renewable and non–renewable energy and calculate the energy density and specific energy of different fuels.
- Recall the origin and processing of fossil fuels and the environmental impact of their use.
- Explain the processes of nuclear fusion, nuclear fission and radioactive decay, including half–life calculations involving integer numbers of half–lives. (**HL** includes calculations involving non–integer numbers of half–lives.)
- Discuss problems associated with nuclear waste.
- Identify the features of molecules that allow them to absorb visible light and their role in photosynthesis.
- Describe how plant material can be used to make bioethanol and biodiesel.
- Explain how greenhouse gases absorb infrared radiation and discuss their role in the greenhouse effect and other factors which lead to global warming.
- Describe different types of electrochemical cell along with the associated calculations. **HL**
- Calculate the energy produced by nuclear fission reactions and describe how the fuel for nuclear reactors is enriched. **HL**
- Recall that solar energy can be converted to electrical energy in a photovoltaic cell and explain how photovoltaic cells and dye–sensitised solar cells operate. **HL**

KEY TERMS AND FORMULAS

Breeder reactor: A nuclear reactor that produces more fissionable material than it consumes.

Half–life: The time taken for the number of radioactive nuclei in a sample to fall to half its value.

Nuclear fission: The breakdown of a larger nucleus into smaller fragments.

Nuclear fusion: The joining together of smaller nuclei to make a larger one.

Anode: The electrode at which oxidation occurs.

Cathode: The electrode at which reduction occurs.

Effusion: The process by which a gas escapes through a very small hole in a container.

Electrochemical cell: A device capable of either generating electrical energy from chemical reactions or facilitating chemical reactions through the introduction of electrical energy.

Fuel cell: A type of electrochemical cell that uses the reaction of a fuel and an oxidising agent to produce electrical energy directly; it uses a continuous supply of reactants from an external source.

Nuclear binding energy: The energy required to completely separate the nucleons in a nucleus.

Photovoltaic cell: A device that converts solar energy into electrical energy.

Voltaic cell: An electrochemical cell that converts chemical energy into electrical energy.

$$\text{thermodynamic efficiency} = \frac{\Delta G}{\Delta H}$$

Equations for use when calculating binding energies:

$E = mc^2$

where

E = energy, J

m = mass, kg

c = speed of light = $3.00 \times 10^8 \, \text{m s}^{-1}$ – this value is given in the data book.

Exercise 14.1 – Energy sources

Energy is the ability to do work. It can neither be created nor destroyed but can be transformed from one type to another. In doing so, work is done and some energy is 'lost' as heat to the surroundings. The quality of the energy is said to have been degraded.

1 When energy is transferred from one type to another, it goes from a more concentrated to a less concentrated (dispersed) form.

    a Calculate the efficiency of the following energy transformations:

        i An electric fire consumes 1000 J of energy and produces 700 J as heat and 300 J as light.

        ii A candle made of wax was calculated to contain 25 J of energy. When burnt, the amount of light produced was calculated as 1 J and heat as 24 J. Calculate the efficiency of the candle.

> Use the expression: $\text{efficiency} = \dfrac{\text{useful energy out}}{\text{total energy in}} \times 100$
>
> You will need to decide which of the types of energy output is 'useful'.

    b The amount of energy contained in a fuel can be described by its energy density and its specific energy.

        i Define these two terms.

ii Calculate the specific energy and the energy density of methane at standard temperature and pressure given that its standard enthalpy of combustion is $-891 \, \text{kJ mol}^{-1}$.

The enthalpy change of combustion is in kJ mol^{-1} so the first step is to convert this to kJ g^{-1} by dividing by the molar mass of methane. This is the specific energy.

To find the energy density, the volume occupied by one mole is required.

Use $PV = nRT$ to find the volume at 298 K and 100 kPa.

The energy density can be calculated by dividing the enthalpy (kJ mol^{-1}) by this volume. The units of volume will be m^3. It is more usual to convert this into kJ dm^{-3}.

It is important to take particular care when converting units and always state the units of a value.

c The specific energy of a fuel is determined by its chemical composition and does not depend on the conditions whereas the energy density depends on both temperature and pressure.

How could the conditions be changed to increase the energy density of methane as calculated in part **b ii**?

2 Energy sources can be broadly divided into renewable and non-renewable.
   a Give three examples of non-renewable energy sources.
   b Give five examples of renewable energy sources.
   c For an energy source to be described as 'useful' it should release energy at a reasonable rate. What other qualities are desirable in a useful fuel?

Exercise 14.2 – Fossil fuels

The main fossil fuels are coal, oil and gas. They were formed from things that lived millions of years ago.

1 Coal was mostly formed from trees and plants whereas oil and gas were formed from aquatic organisms.
   a Coal is mostly composed of carbon. What other elements are most likely to be present?
   b Describe the chemical composition of crude oil.
   c What type of chemical reaction best describes the formation of coal, oil and gas from biological molecules?
   d State one advantage of oil as a fuel compared to coal.
   e State one advantage of gas as a fuel compared to oil.
   f Give a major disadvantage associated with all fossil fuels.
   g Rank coal, oil and gas in order of:
      i cost of production.
      ii likely world reserves/availability.

2 Crude oil has very little use in its raw form and must be processed by fractional distillation.
   a What physical property of the different substances in crude oil allows them to be separated by fractional distillation?
   b Outline the process of fractional distillation.
   c The main fractions obtained by the fractional distillation of crude oil are listed in Table 14.1.

Name of fraction	Approximate chain length
refinery gases	1–4
gasoline	5–9
naphtha	6–12
kerosene	10–16
gasoil	13–20
fuel/lubricating oils	20–25
bitumen	>25

Table 14.1

   i Give a use for each fraction.
   ii Describe the trends in boiling points and volatility of the fractions with chain length.

3 The proportion of each fraction in crude oil will depend on its source. The demand for the different fractions also varies but inevitably does not match the supply. Further processing enables 'less useful' fractions to be converted into 'more useful' fractions. This question explores these.

One of the fractions most in demand is gasoline. One problem associated with some of the molecules in the gasoline fraction is that they auto-ignite; this is often called 'knocking'.

Fuels are often assigned octane ratings to compare their tendency to cause knocking. Most modern cars require a fuel with an octane rating of around 95.

   a Describe the effect of chain length and the amount of branching on the octane number of a compound.
   b The yield of gasoline can be increased by a number of processes including catalytic reforming and cracking.
      i Describe cracking.
      ii Describe reforming.
   c Identify whether each of the following equations represents cracking or reforming:
      i $C_{20}H_{42} \rightarrow C_8H_{18} + C_{12}H_{24}$
      ii $C_6H_{14} \rightarrow C_6H_{12} + H_2$

   iii

Figure 14.1

      iv $C_6H_{14} \rightarrow C_6H_6 + 4H_2$
      v $C_{12}H_{26} \rightarrow C_{10}H_{22} + C_2H_4$

The general formula for an alkane is C_nH_{2n+2} and for an alkene is C_nH_{2n}. These formulas can help in the identification of the products. Cracking always produces a mixture of alkanes and alkenes.

4 Coal gasification and liquefaction are methods of converting coal in to other fuels.

   a **i**   State what is meant by coal gasification.

      ii   Give an equation to represent this process.

   b **i**   State what is meant by coal liquefaction.

      ii   Give an equation to represent this process.

5 All fossil fuels contain carbon and so release carbon dioxide when they are burnt.

   a What is the main environmental concern about the release of carbon dioxide into the environment?

   b The 'carbon footprint' is often used as a measure of the total amount of carbon dioxide emitted as a result of a given activity. In what units is this usually expressed?

   c Calculate the mass of carbon dioxide produced per gram of fuel burnt and per J of energy released for the following fuels given the data provided:

     i   methane $\Delta H_c = -891 \, \text{kJ} \, \text{mol}^{-1}$

     ii   octane $\Delta H_c = -5470 \, \text{kJ} \, \text{mol}^{-1}$

     iii methanol $\Delta H_c = -726 \, \text{kJ} \, \text{mol}^{-1}$

Step 1: Write the equations for the complete combustion of these fuels.

Step 2: Calculate the mass of CO_2 produced per mole of fuel.

Step 3: Use the molar mass of each fuel to find the mass of CO_2 per gram of fuel or use the enthalpy of combustion to find the mass of CO_2 per kJ of energy produced.

Exercise 14.3 – Nuclear fusion and fission

Chemical reactions involve electrons whereas nuclear fission and fusion involve the nuclei of atoms. During nuclear reactions, the identity of an atom may change.

1 **a** Describe what is meant by:

     i   nuclear fission.

     ii   nuclear fusion.

   b The force holding the protons and neutrons together in a nucleus is termed the nuclear binding energy. Figure 14.2 shows the average binding energy per nucleon of different isotopes.

Understanding the difference between these two is an essential starting point.

This is also in section 36 of the data book.

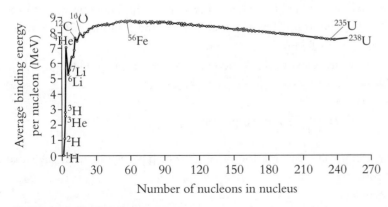

Figure 14.2 Binding energy curve.

> **i** What does this graph show about the stability of different nuclei?
> **ii** Which isotopes are the most stable?
> **iii** Indicate on the graph the region where isotopes that are likely to undergo nuclear fusion are found.
> **iv** Indicate on the graph the region where isotopes that are likely to undergo nuclear fission are found.

The easiest approach to these questions is to calculate the mass number and atomic number of the unknown species. These numbers must balance. Once the atomic number is known then the identity of the species can be deduced.

2 a Consider the nuclear fusion reaction between two deuterium nuclei:

$$^2_1H + ^2_1H \rightarrow ^4_2He$$

Using the binding energy curve given in Figure 14.2, explain why this reaction leads to the release of energy.

b Deuterium nuclei can also undergo different fusion reactions. Complete the equations to indicate the products of the equations below.

i $^2_1H + ^2_1H \rightarrow ^3_2He + ?$

ii $^2_1H + ^2_1H \rightarrow ^3_1H + ?$

c What are the advantages of using nuclear reactions for energy generation rather than fossil fuels?

d Nuclear fusion occurs in stars and is the origin of some elements. How can the elements present in a star be identified?

3 a Although nuclear fission is the opposite of nuclear fusion in that fission involves the breakdown of a large nucleus and fission is the joining of nuclei, both processes release energy.

Explain this statement.

b The main fuel used in nuclear fission reactors is $^{235}_{92}U$. Its fission is initiated by absorbing a neutron. A number of different products are possible.

Complete the equation for the products of the following series:

$$^{235}_{92}U + ^1_0n \rightarrow ? \rightarrow ^{108}_{43}Tc + ? + 3\,^1_0n$$

c Why are nuclear reactions like the one above referred to as chain reactions?

d Chain reactions have potentially catastrophic consequences in a nuclear reactor. Control rods are used to prevent these from occurring. They can also be controlled by using a critical mass of uranium fuel.

i Explain what is meant by the term 'critical mass'.

ii What would be the result of using a sub-critical mass?

iii What would be the result if the reaction is not controlled sufficiently?

e An alternative nuclear reactor is known as a breeder reactor. These produce more nuclear fuel than they consume. The reaction involves the collision of $^{238}_{92}U$ with fast-moving neutrons, eventually producing $^{239}_{94}Pu$.

Complete the equations below to show the steps involved in the production of $^{239}_{94}Pu$.

i $^{238}_{92}U + ^1_0n \rightarrow ^{239}_{92}? \rightarrow ^{239}_{?}Np + ^0_{-1}e \rightarrow ^{239}_{94}Pu + 2\,^0_{-1}e$

ii $^{239}_{?}Np \rightarrow ^{239}_{94}Pu + ^0_{-1}e$

f List four major concerns about nuclear power.

4 Radioactive decay can involve the emission of either α or β particles as well as γ radiation.

a What is an α particle?

b What is a β particle?

c What is γ radiation?

d Although radioactive decay is a random process, it is a first-order process and the half-life for a given isotope can be measured.
Define the term 'half-life'.

e Figure 14.3 shows the radioactive decay of an isotope. Determine its half-life.

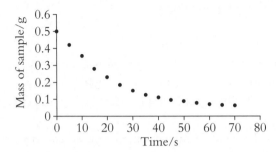

Figure 14.3 Decay of a radioactive isotope.

f The half-life of a radioactive isotope is 25 days.
Calculate:
i the amount of a 0.025 g sample that will remain after 75 days.
ii the amount remaining after 150 days.

g Calculate the half-life of a radioactive substance if it takes 30 s for a 2.40 mg sample to decay to 0.075 mg.

h Calculate how long it will take for a 500.0 mg sample of a radioactive substance with a half-life of 150 years to decay to 62.5 g.

Exercise 14.4 – Solar energy

The Sun's energy comes from nuclear fusion reactions in which small nuclei join together. Plants have evolved to harness that energy through photosynthesis and we too harness that energy indirectly by using plants for food and as fuels. (**HL** Exercise 14.8 looks at harnessing the Sun's energy in photovoltaic cells.)

1 Plants contain coloured compounds known as chromophores; some of these are used in photosynthesis, such as chlorophyll and carotenes, while others are used to produce the colour in their flowers to attract pollinating insects.

a In order to absorb energy in the UV-visible region of the electromagnetic spectrum, what molecular features/bonds are required and how must these be arranged?

b The molecules in Figure 14.4 all contain conjugated double bonds.

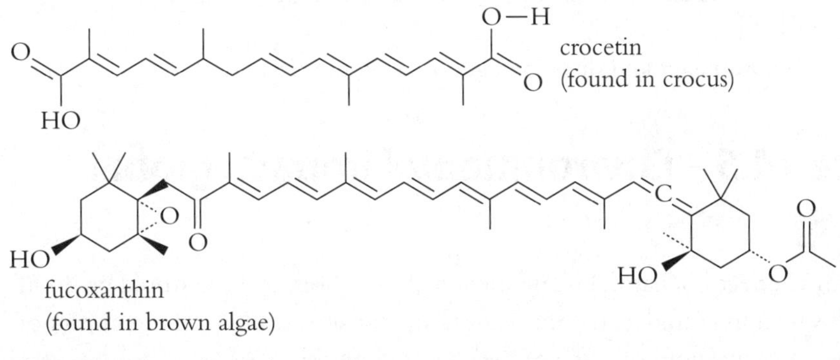

crocetin
(found in crocus)

fucoxanthin
(found in brown algae)

Figure 14.4 Examples of chromophores.

It is not clear that this knowledge is required as part of the syllabus but it's useful to know.

Draw construction lines on the graph to find this.

As this is clearly three half-lives then the amount of sample should be halved three times or multiplied by $(\frac{1}{2})^3$. The formulas,

$t_{\frac{1}{2}} = \dfrac{\ln 2}{\lambda}$ and $N = N_0 e^{-\lambda t}$ are given in the data book and can be used but at SL you will only encounter integer numbers of half-lives so these formulas are not needed.

    i   What does the term 'conjugated' mean?

    ii   How many conjugated double bonds are there in each molecule?

  c Photosynthesis is used by plants to produce glucose, $C_6H_{12}O_6$. The substances needed for photosynthesis are carbon dioxide, water, sunlight and plant pigments like chlorophyll. Give a simple equation for photosynthesis.

2 This question is about the production and use of biofuels.

A biofuel is a fuel produced from organic matter obtained from plants, waste material and so on. The biggest demand for biofuels is as liquid fuels for vehicles. The most common are bioethanol and biodiesel. The 'bio' prefix simply refers to how the ethanol and diesel have been produced.

Be precise about the catalyst. Yeast is not the catalyst; there is something in the yeast that is – but what?

  a **i**   Outline the production of bioethanol by fermentation; include an equation for its formation in your answer.

       ii   Explain why it is only possible to produce a solution of ethanol with a concentration of around 8–12% by fermentation.

      iii How is the ethanol separated from the fermentation mixture?

  b Biodiesel is made from vegetable oils by transesterification.

      i   Explain the term 'transesterification'.

      ii   Copy and complete the equation in Figure 14.5 which shows the transesterification of a typical vegetable oil with methanol.

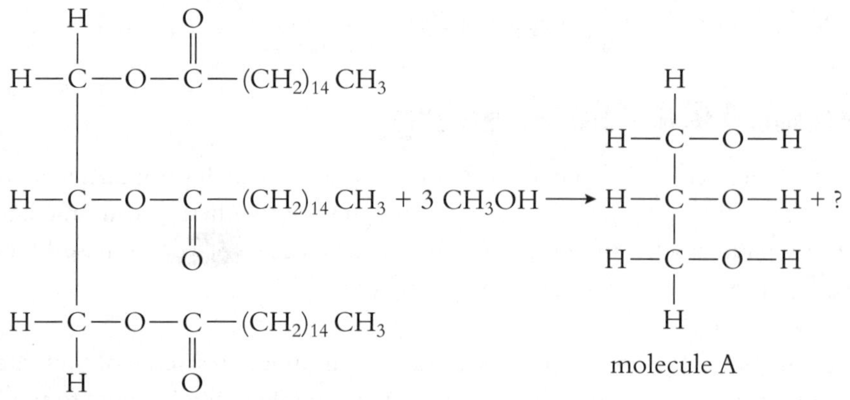

Figure 14.5 A transesterification reaction.

     iii What is the name of molecule A?

     iv Name a suitable catalyst that can be used during transesterification.

     v   Why can vegetable oils not be used in a diesel engine without first being processed into biodiesel?

  c Discuss the advantages and disadvantages of using biofuels.

Exercise 14.5 – Environmental impact: global warming

The greenhouse effect is a natural phenomenon and without it there would be no life on Earth. This section considers the mechanism of global warming and the impact of changing the concentrations of some of the gases responsible.

1 The temperature of the Earth is maintained by the balance between the absorption by the Earth of incoming solar radiation and energy being reflected back into space from the Earth's surface. This is often shown in diagrammatic form as in Figure 14.6.

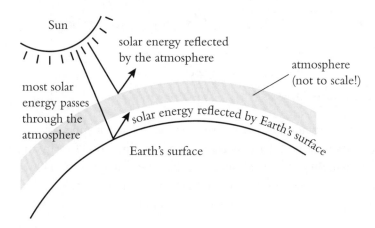

Figure 14.6 The greenhouse effect.

a Describe the change in the wavelength of the solar energy when it is reflected by the Earth's surface.

b The reflected energy is absorbed by molecules in the atmosphere. Why do these molecules absorb the radiation?

c **i** Name three gases chiefly responsible for natural global warming.

 ii What structural feature must a molecule have to be able to act as a greenhouse gas?

2 **a** Table 14.2 lists a number of greenhouse gases, their relative abundance in the atmosphere and their relative effectiveness at absorbing infrared radiation.

Gas	Relative abundance / %	Relative effectiveness
H_2O	0.10	0.1
CO_2	0.036	1
CH_4	0.0017	26

Table 14.2

 i Describe the main sources of these greenhouse gases.

 ii Why is carbon dioxide of more concern than water vapour despite its lower relative abundance?

b Figure 14.7 shows the variation in global temperatures and in carbon dioxide levels over the last 800 000 years.

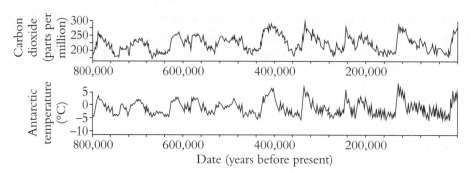

Figure 14.7 Global temperatures and CO_2 levels.

    i Outline how these data provide evidence in support of global warming.
    ii Atmospheric carbon dioxide levels have increased rapidly in the last 100 years and are currently higher than they have ever thought to have been in over 500 000 years. Suggest why carbon dioxide levels have increased so rapidly in recent times.
  c State five consequences which have been predicted as a result of climate change.

3 There is a large amount of research into a wide range of strategies to control carbon dioxide emissions and combat global warming: (i) reduce its production, (ii) reduce its release into the atmosphere and (iii) increase natural processes which remove it from the atmosphere.
  a Methods of reducing the release of carbon dioxide into the atmosphere include carbon capture and storage techniques. Outline what is meant by this.
  b Other than carbon capture and storage, describe three ways in which the amount of carbon dioxide produced can be reduced.
  c Photosynthesis is one major natural process that removes carbon dioxide from the atmosphere. Discuss the impact of deforestation.

HL Exercise 14.6 – Electrochemistry, rechargeable batteries and fuel cells

Electrochemical cells were first met in Topic 9. This section of Option C explores these in more detail.

1 Electrochemical cells can refer to both voltaic cells and electrolytic cells.
  a Describe the fundamental difference between electrolytic and voltaic cells.
  b Figure 14.8 shows a diagram of a typical voltaic cell of the type met in Topic 9.

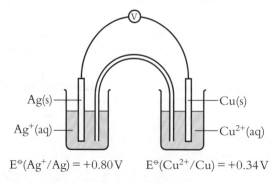

$E^{\ominus}(Ag^+/Ag) = +0.80\,V$ $E^{\ominus}(Cu^{2+}/Cu) = +0.34\,V$

Figure 14.8 A typical voltaic cell.

Label the following parts of the cell:

i anode

ii cathode

iii positive electrode

iv negative electrode

v salt bridge

vi direction of flow of the electrons in the external circuit

c Describe the factors that affect the voltage of a typical electrochemical cell as shown in Figure 14.8.

d All voltaic cells have an internal resistance which limits the maximum current that can be obtained from the cell. What causes this internal resistance?

2 There are several different types of cells.
Briefly describe the following:

a a primary cell

b a rechargeable cell

c a fuel cell

d a concentration cell

3 A fuel cell is a type of electrochemical cell that uses the reaction of a fuel and an oxidising agent to produce electrical energy directly; it uses a continuous supply of reactants from an external source.
This question focuses on several different types of fuels cells.

a Figure 14.9 represents a hydrogen–oxygen fuel cell with an acidic electrolyte.

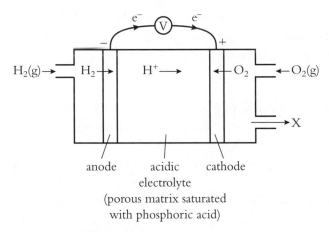

Figure 14.9 Hydrogen oxygen fuel cell with an acidic electrode.

Use $\Delta G^{\ominus} = -nFE^{\ominus}$ to find $\Delta G^{\ominus}$. The number of electrons must match the definitions.

The definition of $\Delta H^{\ominus}$ is the enthalpy of combustion when 1 mole of hydrogen… and so on.

i What is produced at the point marked X on the diagram?

ii Give an equation for the reaction occurring at the anode.

iii Give an equation for the reaction occurring at the cathode.

iv Give the overall equation for the cell.

v Given that $E^{\ominus}(H^+/H_2) = 0.00V$ and $E^{\ominus}(O_2/H_2O) = 1.23V$, calculate the standard cell potential for the cell.

b The thermodynamic efficiency of fuel cells can be calculated using the expression:

thermodynamic efficiency $= \dfrac{\Delta G}{\Delta H}$ where $\Delta G^{\ominus} = -nFE^{\ominus}$

Given that the standard enthalpy of combustion of hydrogen is $-286\,kJ\,mol^{-1}$, calculate the thermodynamic efficiency of a hydrogen fuel cell.

c An alternative design to the one in Figure 14.9 is known as a PEM fuel cell. What do the letters PEM stand for?

d Another alternative to the fuel cell in Figure 14.9 uses an alkaline electrolyte.

i Give the equation for the reaction occurring at the anode in this cell.

ii Give an equation for the reaction occurring at the cathode.

iii Give the overall equation for the cell.

e An alternative to hydrogen as a fuel in fuel cells is to use methanol.

i Why is methanol more practical than hydrogen as a fuel in fuel cell vehicles?

ii Give one disadvantage of methanol in these vehicles.

iii The overall equation for a methanol fuel cell is:

$$CH_3OH + \frac{3}{2}O_2 \rightarrow CO_2 + 2H_2O$$

Construct the half-cell equations for a methanol fuel cell using a PEM between the electrodes. Identify which reaction is occurring at which anode.

The oxidation of methanol is best deduced using oxidation numbers adopting the strategy met in Topic 9.

Step 1: Deduce the change in oxidation state of carbon and add this number of electrons to the right-hand side of the equation (on the right because oxidation is loss of electrons).

Step 2: Add sufficient H^+ ions on the right to make the charges on both sides of the equation balance.

Step 3: Add H_2O to the left of the equation to make the number of hydrogen and oxygen atoms on both sides balance.
Follow the same process for the oxygen half-equation.

f Microbial fuel cells utilise the oxidation of waste materials by bacteria as a source of energy. *Geobacter* produce a much higher current density than any other organism. They are able to oxidise ethanoate ions under acid conditions.

i Construct the half-cell equation for the oxidation of ethanoate ions to carbon dioxide and water.

ii Do the bacteria in a microbial fuel cell colonise the anode or the cathode of the cell?

4 Rechargeable batteries are a portable type of electrochemical cell that generates current via electrically reversible reactions.

a When the engine of a vehicle containing a lead–acid battery is running then the lead–acid battery is charged up by the following reactions:

anode: $PbSO_4(s) + 2H_2O(l) \rightarrow PbO_2(s) + 2e^- + 4H^+(aq) + SO_4^{2-}(aq)$

cathode: $PbSO_4(s) + 2e^- \rightarrow Pb(s) + SO_4^{2-}(aq)$

The lead(II) sulfate occurs as an insoluble coating on the surface of both metal electrodes.

  i Give the equations when the lead–acid battery is being used without the engine running.

  ii What is the electrolyte in a lead–acid battery?

  iii What is the major disadvantage of lead–acid batteries?

b Some of the first readily available rechargeable batteries for use in household gadgets like toys and clocks were nickel–cadmium batteries. These use a metallic cadmium electrode and a nickel oxide hydroxide NiO(OH) electrode separated by a potassium hydroxide electrolyte.

The equations for the reactions at the electrodes are as follows:

negative electrode: $Cd(s) + 2OH^-(aq) \rightarrow Cd(OH)_2(s) + 2e^-$

positive electrode: $2NiO(OH)(s) + 2H_2O(l) + 2e^- \rightarrow 2Ni(OH)_2(s) + 2OH^-(aq)$

  i Deduce the overall reaction equation.

  ii Do the equations above represent the reactions during the use of a nickel–cadmium battery or during the recharging process?

c Most laptops and mobile phones use lithium-ion batteries. These can generate higher voltages than nickel–cadmium batteries. Figure 14.10 shows a lithium-ion battery.

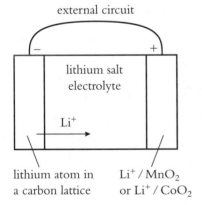

Figure 14.10 Lithium-ion battery.

  i What happens to the lithium atoms at the anode while the battery is being used?

  ii At the cathode lithium ions become inserted into the lattice of the manganese(IV) oxide or cobalt(IV) oxide (electrode material) causing the transition metal ion to be reduced to an oxidation state of +3.

    Give an equation for the reduction of Co^{4+} to Co^{3+}.

  iii Apart from the voltages that they produce, what is the major advantage of lithium-ion batteries compared to nickel–cadmium batteries?

The difference between discharging (using) and recharging is the poles of the electrodes. During use, the cell is acting as a voltaic cell and oxidation (always at the anode), releases electrons and is the negative electrode. During recharging, the external power supply effectively makes the cell an electrolytic cell; the anode is positive as this is where electrons are removed from the cell by the power supply.

Write the overall cell equation and use this to determine the reaction quotient.

5 Standard cell potentials are measured under standard conditions.

a Describe standard conditions.

b The Nernst equation is given in the data book and can be used to calculate the voltage under non-standard conditions.

Calculate the electrode potential for the following half-cells at 300 K:

i Ag^+/Ag half-cell with a concentration of $0.01 \, mol \, dm^{-3}$ ($E^{\ominus}(Ag^+/Ag) = 0.80V$)

ii Fe^{2+}/Fe^{3+} half-cell in which $[Fe^{2+}] = 0.10 \, mol \, dm^{-3}$ and $[Fe^{3+}] = 0.20 \, mol \, dm^{-3}$ ($E^{\ominus}(Fe^{3+}/Fe^{2+}) = 0.77V$)

The reaction quotient can be found by considering the half-equation. The concentration of a solid can be considered to be 1.

c Calculate the electrode potential of a $Pb \, | \, Pb^{2+} \, || \, Cu^{2+} \, | \, Cu$ cell at 298 K if $[Pb^{2+}] = 0.010 \, mol \, dm^{-3}$ and $[Cu^{2+}] = 0.20 \, mol \, dm^{-3}$.

$E^{\ominus}(Pb^{2+}/Pb) = -0.13V$

$E^{\ominus}(Cu^{2+}/Cu) = +0.34V$

d As the electrode potential of a half-cell depends on the concentration of the electrolyte, it is possible to generate a voltage from two half-cells using the same chemicals but in different concentrations.

What name is given to this type of cell?

HL Exercise 14.7 – Nuclear fusion and nuclear fission

This section examines some of the ideas met in Exercise 14.3 in more detail.

1 The total mass of a nucleus is less than the mass calculated by adding the mass of all the protons and neutrons it contains. The difference is called the mass defect, Δm.

a Calculate the mass defect in kg of the following nuclei given the data in Table 14.3.

These values are given in the data book.

Particle	Mass / kg
proton	1.672622×10^{-27}
neutron	1.674927×10^{-27}
electron	9.109383×10^{-31}

Table 14.3

$1 \, u = 1.66 \times 10^{-27} \, kg$

i ^{12}C (mass of atom, 12.000 000 u)

ii ^{56}Fe (mass of atom, 55.934 942 u)

iii ^{238}U (mass of atom, 238.050 783 u)

Step 1: Calculate the mass (in kg) of all of the electrons by multiplying the mass of one electron by the number of electrons in the atom.

Step 2: Convert this value into atomic mass units using the conversion factor given in the question.

Step 3: Find the mass of the nucleus by subtracting the mass of all of the electrons from the value of the mass of the atom in u.

Step 4: Calculate the mass of all of the nucleons (in u) using the values for the mass of a proton and neutron and the conversion factor.

Step 4: Subtract the mass of the nucleus calculated in step 3 from its theoretical mass in step 4. This is the mass defect in amu.

Step 5: Multiply the mass defect in amu by 1.66×10^{-27} to find its value in kg.

N.B. The value used to convert amu to kg and vice versa is only given to 3 significant figures.

b Calculate the binding energy of the nuclei of the isotopes in part **a** in $J\,mol^{-1}$.
c Calculate the binding energy per nucleon for the isotopes in part **a** in J.
d What can be deduced about the relative stability of these nuclei from the relative magnitudes of their binding energies?
e Given the data below, calculate the change in mass and the energy released in $J\,mol^{-1}$ for the following reactions:
  i $^{2}_{1}H + {}^{2}_{1}H \rightarrow {}^{4}_{2}He$
    mass of $^{2}_{1}H = 2.014\,102\,u$
    mass of $^{4}_{2}He = 4.002\,60\,u$
  ii $^{226}_{88}Ra \rightarrow {}^{222}_{86}Rn + {}^{4}_{2}He$
    mass of $^{226}_{88}Ra = 226.025\,403\,u$
    mass of $^{222}_{86}Rn = 222.017\,570\,u$
    mass of $^{4}_{2}He = 4.002\,60\,u$

2 This question extends ideas about half-life met in Exercise 14.3. At HL you are expected to perform calculations using non-integer numbers of half-lives. These are done using the decay constant for an isotope, λ.
  a The half-life of ^{253}No is 97 s. Calculate the decay constant and the amount of a $1.00 \times 10^{-2}\,g$ sample of nobelium that would remain after 1 hour.
  b A 0.250 g sample of a radioactive isotope was found to weigh 0.212 g after a period of 25 days. Calculate its half-life.

3 The abundance of ^{235}U in naturally occurring uranium ores is less than 1%. In order to sustain the chain reaction in nuclear power plants the percentage of ^{235}U needs to be increased.
  a What name is given to this process?
  b The main ore of uranium contains uranium(IV) oxide, UO_2. The processing of uranium involves converting the ore into uranium(VI) fluoride, UF_6.
    UO_2 is a high melting point solid whereas UF_6 is a low melting point solid.
    i Describe the differences in the bonding in these two compounds.
    ii Why does the UO_2 need to be converted into UF_6 before the ore is processed?
  c There are two main techniques for increasing the proportion of ^{235}U in the fuel used in nuclear reactors: gaseous diffusion and gas centrifugation.
    Diffusion is based on Graham's law of effusion which is given in the data book as:
    $$\frac{\text{rate}_1}{\text{rate}_2} = \sqrt{\frac{M_1}{M_2}}$$
    i What is meant by the term 'effusion'?
    ii The rate of effusion depends on the kinetic energy of the gas. State the relationship between kinetic energy, mass and particle velocity.

This can be calculated using:
$E = mc^2$

The value of c is $3.00 \times 10^8\,m\,s^{-1}$ and is given in the data book.

The energy produced in a fusion reaction can be calculated by finding the change in mass of the products and the reactants. This can be converted into kg by multiplying by 1.66×10^{-27} and then converted into energy using $E = mc^2$.

The formula $l = \dfrac{\ln 2}{t_{\frac{1}{2}}}$ should be used, where $t_{\frac{1}{2}}$ is the half-life and λ is the decay constant. Once the decay constant has been calculated then the formula $N = N_0 e^{-\lambda t}$ can be used.

The formula $N = N_0 e^{-\lambda t}$ is used first to find λ and then $t_{\frac{1}{2}} = \dfrac{\ln 2}{\lambda}$ is used to find the half-life.

    iii Outline how gaseous diffusion works.

    iv Outline how gas centrifugation works.

4 There are many concerns about the use of nuclear technology. Nuclear energy produces ionising radiation which can damage living cells by the production of free radicals, for example, when ionising radiation interacts with water and with oxygen.

  a State the formulas of two free radicals that can be formed in these reactions.

  b Other than health risks associated with ionising radiation, state two other common concerns about nuclear reactions.

HL Exercise 14.8 – Photovoltaic and dye-sensitised solar cells

This section of Option C revisits and extends ideas met earlier in the topic: ideas about chromophores, conductivity and nanoparticles, for example.

1 Exercise 14.4 introduced chromophores as compounds with conjugated double bonds. These molecules are used along with semiconductors in photovoltaic cells.

  a How does the size of the conjugated system affect the wavelength of light that a molecule absorbs?

  b Describe how electrical conductivity varies with temperature:

    i in metals.

    ii in semiconductors.

  c In terms of their ionisation energies, explain the following statements:

    i Metals such as copper are good electrical conductors.

    ii Non-metals such as sulfur are poor electrical conductors.

    iii Elements such as silicon are semiconductors.

  d Doping can increase the conductivity of a semiconductor. Name two elements that could be used to dope silicon.

  e Semiconductors that have been doped are called p-type and n-type. Describe the difference between these two types of semiconductor.

2 This question looks at how photovoltaic cells work.

  a Silicon semiconductors are made of both n-type and p-type materials. At the junction between the two materials a voltage is produced that prevents further movement between the two materials; this is shown in Figure 14.11.

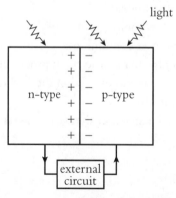

Figure 14.11 Silicon photovoltaic cell.

What effect does light have on the semiconductor materials?

The more conjugated the delocalised system, the smaller the difference in the energy levels between which the excited electron moves.

Doping works by either providing extra electrons or providing spaces that electrons can move in and out of.

b DSSCs are an alternative to silicon-based photovoltaic cells.
   i What do the initials DSSC stand for?
   ii A DSSC is shown in Figure 14.12.

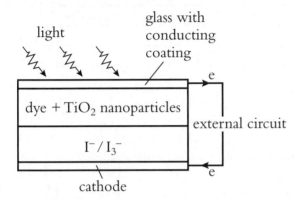

Figure 14.12 A typical DSSC

The anode of a DSSC is made up of a dye and TiO_2 nanoparticles. Light excites electrons in the dye which 'injects' them into the TiO_2 semiconductor. The loss of electrons by the dye is effectively an oxidation reaction. Electrons flow from the TiO_2 semiconductor through the external circuit to the cathode.

Give a half-equation for the reaction of substances in the cathode of the cell shown in Figure 14.12 and an equation for how the dye is reduced back to its original state. Use "Dye$^+$" to represent its oxidised state in your equations.

   iii Why is TiO_2 used in the form of nanoparticles?

c State two advantages of DSSCs compared to silicon-based solar cells.

The mechanism by which DSSCs work is similar to that of natural chromophores used in photosynthesis: the absorbed light does not cause the movement of electrons directly but triggers the movement of electrons in other reactions.

? Exam-style questions

1 **The increase in global temperatures has been linked to the global increase in the levels of carbon dioxide in the atmosphere.**
   a Explain why, despite being non-polar, carbon dioxide acts as a greenhouse gas. [2]
   b Calculate the carbon footprint of a gas-powered heating system and an oil-powered heating system. The amount of heat energy needed in an average UK home in December is 1.5×10^6 kJ. [5]

Use the data provided in Table 14.4 in your calculations.

Fuel	Empirical formula	Specific energy/kJ g^{-1}	Efficiency of heating /%
gas	CH_4	55.5	45
oil	CH_2	48.0	40

Table 14.4

c The specific energies of gas and oil are given in Table 14.4.
Explain what is meant by the term 'specific energy'. [1]

d Using the data calculated in the question, compare the advantages and disadvantages of gas and oil for heating homes. [1]

e As well as the specific energies, the energy densities of different fuels can also be compared.
i State what is meant by 'energy density'. [1]
ii Explain why the energy density of a fuel is also important when considering the suitability of a fuel for use in a vehicle. [1]

f The incomplete combustion of fossil fuels produces soot and other particulates. These can lead to global dimming.
Explain what is meant by global dimming and state its effect on global temperatures. [2]

[Total 13]

2 **Figure 14.13 gives some equations for reactions that occur during the processing of oil to make gasoline for cars.**

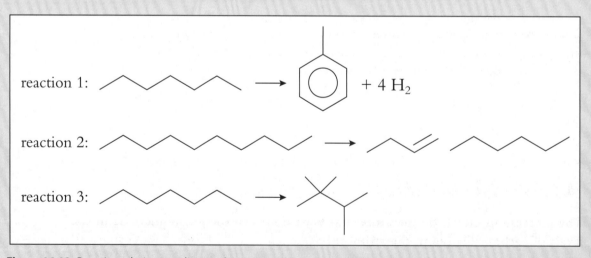

Figure 14.13 Reactions during gasoline production.

a Reaction 2 in Figure 14.13 produces a mixture of an alkane and an alkene.
i Name this process. [1]
ii Give an alternative equation for this process using the same reactant but producing different products. [1]

b Reactions 1 and 3 in Figure 14.13 do not result in molecules with different numbers of carbon atoms. Name this type of process. [1]

c The production of shorter molecules is a method of making less useful fractions obtained from the fractional distillation of crude oil into more useful ones.
State the purpose of Reactions 1 and 3. [1]

d The octane number is a measure of the tendency of a fuel not to undergo auto-ignition in an engine. Rank the molecules shown in Figure 14.14 in order of increasing octane number. [1]

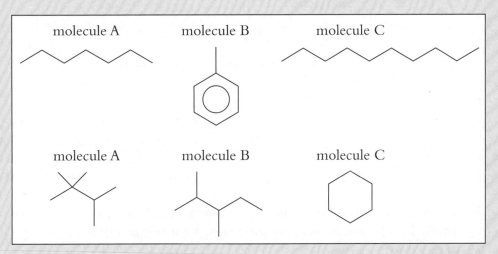

Figure 14.14 Octane rating of different molecules.

e Liquid hydrocarbons can also be produced from coal.
  i Name this process. [1]
  ii In one such process coal is mixed with a solvent and hydrogen and subjected to high temperatures and pressures in the presence of a catalyst.
  Give an equation for the production of C_8H_{18} by this method. [1]

f Diesel for cars can be obtained from vegetable oils. Vegetable oils have a higher energy density than the biodiesel that they are used to produce. Vegetable oils cannot be used directly in vehicle engines because they are too viscous.
  i Explain why vegetable oils are more viscous than biodiesel. [3]
  ii Outline how biodiesel is made from vegetable oils. [3]

[Total 13]

3 One type of nuclear power generation uses a breeder reactor. Breeder reactors use ^{239}Pu as a fuel. This fuel is produced from ^{238}U in three steps: neutron capture and two further steps, both of which involve the loss of an electron which can be represented by $_{-1}^{0}e$.

a Deduce equations for these three steps. [3]

b In some nuclear reactions small nuclei join together to make a larger one.

   i Name this type of nuclear reaction. [1]

   ii Deduce the equation for the reaction when a $_1^2$H nucleus combines with a $_1^3$H nucleus to form a $_2^4$He nucleus and another particle. [1]

c One of the problems associated with nuclear power is the generation and therefore disposal of nuclear waste. Nuclear waste can be divided into two types: low-level waste and high-level waste.

   i Describe the difference in the half-lives of the radioisotopes in these two types of waste. [1]

   ii One solution for the disposal of nuclear waste is to store it underground. Suggest the possible problems associated with this solution. [1]

   iii One of the isotopes present in the waste from nuclear fuel rods is ^{239}Pu. Calculate how long it would take for a sample to fall to 12.5% of its original activity level if ^{239}Pu has a half-life of 24 110 years. [2]

[Total 9]

4 **HL** Cars can be powered by a number of different methods, including the combustion of a fuel such as petrol, diesel or hydrogen or by using an electric motor.

Electric motors can be powered using fuel cells or using rechargeable batteries.

a Outline the difference between a fuel cell and a rechargeable battery. [2]

b One type of fuel cell uses methanol and an alkaline electrolyte.
The overall equation for the reaction is:

$$CH_3OH + \frac{3}{2}O_2 \rightarrow CO_2 + 2H_2O$$

   i Deduce the anode half-equation for the oxidation of methanol under alkaline conditions. [1]

   ii Deduce the half-equation for the reaction at the cathode. [1]

c The enthalpy of combustion of methanol is $-726\,kJ\,mol^{-1}$ and the maximum voltage produced by a methanol fuel cell under the same conditions is 1.21 V.
Calculate the thermodynamic efficiency of the cell and compare this to the thermodynamic efficiency of a hydrogen cell which is 82.9%. [4]

d State one other advantage of a methanol fuel cell over a hydrogen fuel cell. [1]

e One disadvantage of methanol fuel cells compared to hydrogen-powered fuel cells is that methanol fuel cells release carbon dioxide. One effect of the increasing atmospheric carbon dioxide level is the acidification of the oceans.

   i Explain why increasing CO_2 levels in the atmosphere are lowering the pH of the oceans. Give appropriate equations in your answer. [2]

   ii Describe the effect of a lowering of oceanic pH on marine species. [1]

[Total 12]

5 **HL** The Solar Impulse is a solar-powered aircraft that completed the first solar-powered circumnavigation of the globe in July 2016. The 17-stage journey covered some 42 000 km and was powered by 17 000 solar cells on the wings and upper surfaces of the aircraft.

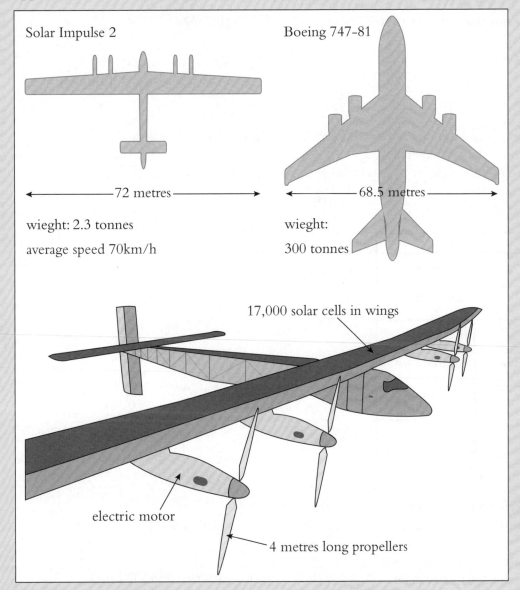

Solar Impulse 2

72 metres

wieght: 2.3 tonnes

average speed 70 km/h

Boeing 747-81

68.5 metres

wieght:

300 tonnes

17,000 solar cells in wings

electric motor

4 metres long propellers

Figure 14.15 The Solar Impulse

a The solar cells in the Solar Impulse are made from semiconductor materials. Outline how sunlight interacts with a semiconductor to produce electrical energy. [1]

b Solar energy is absorbed by plants by compounds such as chlorophyll. Describe the features of chlorophyll molecules that enable them to absorb energy from sunlight. [1]

c Synthetic dyes can also be used in solar cells in association with a semiconductor material. These are known as dye-sensitised solar cells (DSSCs). Their action is similar to that of plant pigments. Outline how these solar cells work. [3]

d Electrical energy can also be generated using electrochemical cells.

Calculate the cell potential for the following concentration cell at 298 K: [4]

$Pt(s)|Fe^{2+}(aq)[1.0\,mol\,dm^{-3}],Fe^{3+}(aq)[0.10\,mol\,dm^{-3}]||Fe^{3+}(aq)[1.5\,mol\,dm^{-3}],Fe^{2+}(aq)$
$[0.010\,mol\,dm^{-3}]|Pt(s)$
$E^{\ominus}(Fe^{3+}/Fe^{2+}) = +0.77V$

[Total 9]

6 HL

a The energy released during a nuclear fission reaction can be calculated by deducing the change in mass during the reaction.

Using the data given in Table 14.5, calculate the energy released per mole of ^{235}U during the following reaction: [6]

$$^{235}_{92}U + ^1_0n \rightarrow ^{130}_{52}I + ^{96}_{38}Sr + ^4_2He + 5^1_0n$$

Atom	Mass/u
$^{235}_{92}U$	235.043 923
$^{130}_{52}I$	129.854 731
$^{96}_{38}Sr$	95.347 821
^4_2He	4.002 60
^1_0n	1.008 665
^1_1p	1.007 276

Table 14.5

b The proportion of ^{235}U in nuclear fuel is increased by enriching.

  i Explain why the proportion of ^{235}U in the ore needs to be increased. [1]

  ii Name two methods used to enrich uranium ores. [2]

  iii Calculate the relative rates of effusion of $^{235}UF_6$ and $^{238}UF_6$. [1]

c One of the isotopes present in the waste from nuclear fuel rods is ^{239}Pu. Calculate how long it would take for a 1.0 g sample to fall to 10% of its original activity level if ^{239}Pu has a half-life of 24 110 years. [3]

Medicinal chemistry (Option D) 15

Chapter outline

- Describe the main steps in drug development, the nature of drug–receptor interactions, assessment of dosage, drug administration and the effect of this on bioavailability.
- Describe the use of aspirin and penicillin and how the structures of these molecules can be modified to facilitate bioavailability and overcome resistance.
- Explain the use and abuse of opiates and relate their structure to their potency.
- Describe how the pH of the stomach is regulated including calculations using the Henderson–Hasselbalch equation.
- Explain how antiviral medications work and discuss the difficulties of solving the AIDS problem.
- Explain the environmental problems associated with some medications such as the disposal of radioactive waste, the use of solvents and the dangers of antibiotic waste.
- Describe the use of chiral auxiliaries in drug manufacture and the use of taxol as a chemotherapeutic agent. **HL**
- Describe the use of nuclear radiation in the detection and treatment of disease. **HL**
- Solve calculations involving half-lives. **HL**
- Describe the process of extraction and purification of organic products including the use of fractional distillation and describe how organic structures can be analysed through the use of IR, MS and ^{1}H NMR spectroscopy. **HL**

KEY TERMS AND FORMULAS

Active metabolites: Active forms of a drug after they have been processed in the body.

Analgesic: Drug that reduces pain.

Antibiotic: Drug that kills bacteria.

Bioavailability: The proportion of the administered dosage of a drug that is transferred into the blood stream.

Drug: A substance that, when applied to or introduced to a living organism, brings about a change in the biological function through chemical action.

Opiates: Natural narcotic (sleep-inducing) analgesics derived from the opium poppy.

Prophylactic: A drug given for prevention rather than as a treatment.

Side-effect: An unintended secondary effect of a drug on the body; it is usually an undesirable effect.

Synergism: The effect when two or more drugs, given at the same time, have a greater effect than the sum of the individual drugs.

Therapeutic effect: A desirable and beneficial effect of a drug; one that alleviates symptoms or treats a particular disease.

Tolerance: When an organism becomes less responsive to the effects of a drug – larger and larger doses need to be used to produce the same effect which means that there is a greater risk of toxic side-effects.

Chiral auxiliary: An optically active substance that is temporarily incorporated into an organic synthesis so that the synthesis can be carried out asymmetrically with the selective formation of a single enantiomer.

$$\text{atom economy} = \frac{\text{molar mass of desired products}}{\text{total molar mass of all reactants}} \times 100$$

therapeutic index (TI)

$$TI = \frac{LD_{50}}{ED_{50}} \text{ or } \frac{TD_{50}}{ED_{50}}$$

where
LD_{50} is the dose required to kill 50% of the test population
ED_{50} is the dose that has a therapeutic effect in 50% of the test population
TD_{50} is the dose that produces a toxic effect in 50% of the test population

Raoult's law:

$$A = \frac{\text{number of moles of A}}{\text{total number of moles}} = \frac{n(A)}{n(A) + n(B)} \text{ and similarly,}$$

$$B = \frac{\text{number of moles of B}}{\text{total number of moles}} = \frac{n(B)}{n(A) + n(B)}$$

where
χ_A and χ_B are the mole fractions of A and B in an ideal solution of A and B
$n(A)$ and $n(B)$ are the number of moles of A and B in the mixture

Partial pressure, P_x:

$$P_A = P_A^O \times \chi_A \text{ and } P_B^O \times \chi_B \text{ and } P_T = P_A + P_B$$

where

P_A and P_B are the partial pressures of substance A and B
P_T is the total vapour pressure
P_A^O and P_B^O are the vapour pressures of pure A and B, respectively

Exercise 15.1 – Pharmaceutical products and drug action

Drugs and medicines can be naturally occurring, synthetic or semi-synthetic substances but must go through a variety of tests to determine their effectiveness and safety before they are made commercially available.

1 Drug development is a long and expensive process. This question explores the different stages of that process.

  a The first stage in drug development is often the identification of lead chemicals which are then modified.

    i What is meant by a lead chemical?

    ii How can a knowledge of the structure of the target molecule help with the identification of suitable lead chemicals?

  b Many hundreds of chemicals which are similar in structure to the lead chemical are then tested for their toxicity and biological effectiveness on biological tissues and eventually on animals. Data collected includes LD_{50}, TD_{50} and ED_{50}.
Explain these three terms.

  c Following the successful identification and testing of a potential new drug, human clinical trials can be conducted. This stage is normally broken into three phases. Outline these three phases.

  d What is the final phase that the pharmaceutical company must follow if the drug passes all three phases of its clinical trials?

  e What factors must be considered when choosing the method by which the new drug is synthesised on a large scale?

2 There are a number of different considerations that must be taken into account when developing a new drug. This question looks at a number of these.

  a What is meant by the therapeutic index of a drug?

  b What is meant by the therapeutic window of a drug?

  c i What is meant by the bioavailability of a drug?

    ii What factors affect a drug's bioavailability?

  d What other factors also need to be considered when developing a new drug?

  e List at least six different ways that a drug can be administered.

Exercise 15.2 – Aspirin and penicillin

1 This question is about aspirin.

  a Aspirin is an example of a mild analgesic and anti-inflammatory agent. What is meant by the term 'analgesic'?

  b Outline how mild analgesics like aspirin work.

  c As well as its use as an analgesic and an anti-inflammatory, aspirin can also be used as a prophylactic. Give an example of its use as a prophylactic.

  d One of the side-effects of aspirin is that it irritates the lining of the stomach and can lead to stomach ulcers and bleeding. The risk is increased if aspirin is taken with alcohol. What name is given to the effect when one drug increases the effectiveness of another?

> Prophylactics are substances that prevent disease.

2 Aspirin is made from salicylic acid by warming it with an excess of $(CH_3CO)_2O$.

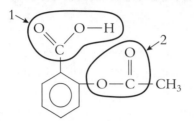

Figure 15.1 shows the structure of aspirin.

a Name the functional groups labelled 1 and 2 in Figure 15.1.

b Figure 15.2 shows part of the equation for the synthesis of aspirin from salicylic acid.

Figure 15.2 The synthesis of aspirin.

This reaction is an esterification reaction and so the catalyst met in Topic 10 is suitable here.

   i   Name substance A.

   ii   Draw the structure of salicylic acid.

   iii Name substance B.

   iv Name a suitable catalyst for the reaction.

c Aspirin is not very soluble and, when the reaction mixture is cooled, it forms as a white precipitate. The impurities are then removed.

   i   What name is given to the process used to purify an impure solid?

   ii   Outline the steps in this process.

d The bioavailability of aspirin can be increased by chemically modifying it.

   i   Describe the modification made.

   ii   Why does this increase its bioavailability?

e The purity of aspirin can be determined using IR spectroscopy.

   i   Apart from differences in the fingerprint region of the spectrum, suggest two other differences in the spectra of salicylic acid and aspirin.

   ii   Suggest a non-spectroscopic method of determining the purity of aspirin.

3 This question is about penicillin.

Penicillins were first discovered in 1928 by a Scottish doctor, Alexander Fleming. They are a group of compounds which are produced by fungi.

a What type of drugs are penicillins?

b All penicillins have the same core structure, a β-lactam ring.

Circle this part of the molecule in Figure 15.3.

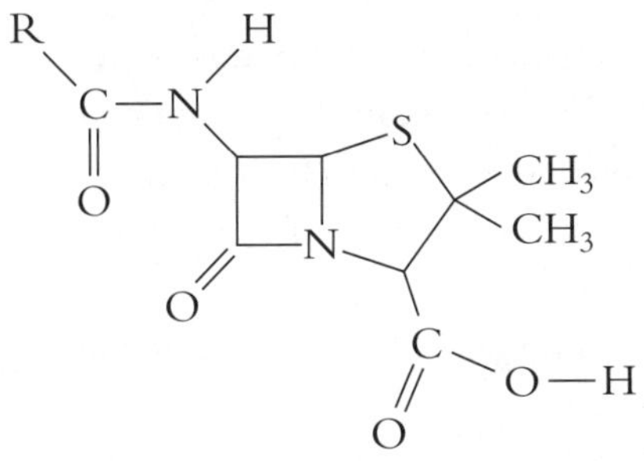

Figure 15.3 General structure of penicillin.

Only a brief description is needed.

c Outline how penicillins work, including the role of the β-lactam ring.
d Over time the effectiveness of penicillins has decreased due to resistance.
  i   Explain why this has arisen in the target organisms.
  ii Suggest how human behaviour has led to this resistance.
  iii In what way have scientists sought to tackle this problem?

Exercise 15.3 – Opiates

1 Opiates are natural narcotic analgesics derived from the opium poppy.
  a What does the term 'narcotic' mean?
  b Opiates are strong analgesics whereas aspirin is a mild analgesic.
    What is the difference between the actions of these two groups of compounds?
  c In what circumstances are strong analgesics used in medicine?
  d Opiates all have similar chemical structures which include a tertiary amine group and a benzene ring.
    Describe what is meant by a tertiary amine group.
  e Diamorphine (heroin) and codeine are synthetic morphine derivatives. Diamorphine contains two ester groups.
    i   Name the reagent used to convert morphine into diamorphine.
    ii Codeine can be synthesised from morphine either using iodomethane in the presence of a strong base or using a quaternary ammonium salt. These reagents convert the phenol group of morphine into a different functional group.
        What is the name of the functional group produced?
  f The analgesic potency of codeine, morphine and diamorphine is linked to their structures and solubility in lipids. Why is this key to their effectiveness?

2 One of the problems with opiates is that they cause dependency and tolerance.
  a What is meant by the term 'dependency'?
  b What does the term 'tolerance' mean?
  c Apart from tolerance and dependency, what are some of the known side-effects of opiates?
  d Opiate dependence is a worldwide issue. State some examples of other social issues that can be linked to drug dependency.

The structures of morphine, codeine and diamorphine are given in section 37 of the IB data book.

Diamorphine is the fastest acting as it is the most lipid-soluble of the three: it has two ester groups rather than the two phenol groups in morphine. Codeine's lipid solubility is between that of morphine and diamorphine. Diamorphine is hydrolysed into morphine once it has crossed the lipid barrier. This also happens to codeine but to a lesser extent.

The structure of ranitidine is given in the data book but, considering how most biological molecules work, its mode of action can be easily guessed at.

Cell membranes are composed of phospholipids.

Other examples are codeine which is converted to morphine in the body and aspirin which is converted to salicylic acid in the body.

Sodium bicarbonate is sodium hydrogen-carbonate.

HL Buffer solutions are part of Topic 18.

Exercise 15.4 – pH regulation of the stomach

The stomach contains hydrochloric acid at a pH of between 1 and 2 as this is the optimum pH for digestive enzymes such as pepsin. The very acidic environment also kills bacteria which are ingested with food. The acid is produced by cells known as parietal cells. The acid is then pumped into the stomach by a mechanism known as a proton pump.

1 The production of stomach acid is triggered by a number of mechanisms including the release of histamine (Figure 15.4).

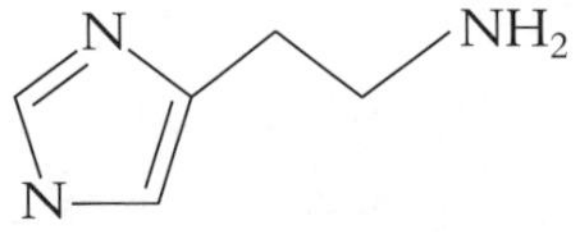

Figure 15.4 Histamine.

a Ranitidine is a drug that inhibits the production of stomach acid by binding to the same receptors as histamine and blocking them.
What feature of the structure of ranitidine enables it to block the same sites as histamine?

b Omeprazole (Prilosec) and Esomeprazole (Nexium) are drugs that act by preventing the acid produced in the parietal cells from being released into the stomach.

- **i** What feature of these molecules allows them to pass through cell membranes?
- **ii** The environment inside the parietal cells is acidic. This protonates the drug molecule which changes into its active form. What name is given to the products of a drug which are formed in the body and have the desired therapeutic effect?
- **iii** What are the advantages of using drugs that are not active until they reach their target site?

2 Irritation of the stomach lining following the production of excess stomach acid can be caused by alcohol, over eating, smoking and stress. Medications like aspirin also lower the production of the stomach's protective mucous lining. A simple treatment is to neutralise the excess acid using an antacid.
A number of difference weak bases can be used as antacids. Construct equations for the reactions of the following substances with hydrochloric acid:

a magnesium hydroxide
b aluminium hydroxide
c sodium carbonate
d sodium bicarbonate

3 The structure of many biological molecules depends on pH. The pH of blood is tightly regulated by the body's own systems to a pH of between 7.35 and 7.45. This is achieved through the use of natural buffer solutions.

a Define the term 'buffer'.
b Describe the composition of a typical acidic buffer solution.
c Describe the composition of a typical basic buffer solution.
d Explain how an acidic buffer works.

e The pH of a buffer can be calculated using the Henderson–Hasselbalch equation which is given in the data book.

Calculate the pH of the following solutions:

  i a buffer made from a mixture containing $0.125\,mol\,dm^{-3}$ of CH_3COO^- and $0.252\,mol\,dm^{-3}$ CH_3COOH ($pK_a = 4.76$)

  ii a buffer made when $0.35\,g$ of sodium ethanoate, $CH_3COO^-Na^+$ is dissolved in $100\,cm^3$ of $0.100\,mol\,dm^{-3}$ CH_3COOH ($pK_a = 4.76$)

  iii a buffer made by mixing $100\,cm^3$ of $0.200\,mol\,dm^{-3}$ CH_3COOH ($pK_a = 4.76$) with $30\,cm^3$ of $0.400\,mol\,dm^{-3}$ NaOH

Any explanation about how a buffer works must have an equation in it showing the equilibrium between the acid–base conjugate pair.

Ethanoic acid and sodium hydroxide do react with each other. You will need to:

1 Find the number of moles of each being used and so which is in excess.
2 Find the number of moles of excess in the mixture.
3 Find the number of moles of salt formed.
4 Use the results of steps 2 and 3 to find the concentration of both the acid and the salt.
5 Use the Henderson–Hasselbalch equation to find the pH.

Sodium ethanoate and ethanoic acid do not react with each other; this is a mixture.
You will first need to calculate the concentration of the ethanoate ions.

f Determine the composition of the following buffer:

A buffer has a pH of 4.20 and was made by mixing $50\,cm^3$ of a weak acid of concentration $0.200\,mol\,dm^{-3}$ with $50\,cm^3$ of its salt.

What concentration of salt solution is needed?

The pK_a of the acid is 3.98.

1 Use the Henderson–Hasselbalch equation to find [salt].
N.B. [acid] = $0.100\,mol\,dm^{-3}$ in the mixture as it has been diluted to twice its original volume when it is mixed with the salt.
2 Find the concentration of the salt before it is diluted by adding it to the acid solution.

Exercise 15.5 – Antiviral medications

Viruses are parasites. A large number of diseases ranging from the common cold to polio and HIV are caused by viruses.

1 a Describe the differences between viruses and bacteria.
  b Why is it difficult to design drugs to target viruses?
  c Viruses work by attaching themselves to the surface of a host cell and releasing their genetic material into the cytoplasm of the host. The viral genetic information then becomes incorporated into the DNA of the host cell and the host cell then acts as a factory for new viral material. The new viral material is assembled into new virus particles which then break free of the cell and go on to infect new host cells. Antiviral drugs can tackle this mechanism in a number of ways.
    Briefly outline how antiviral drugs work.
  d Oseltamivir (Tamiflu) and zanamivir (Relenza) are antiviral drugs that target a protein found on the surfaces of a specific type of virus.
    i What disease do these antivirals tackle?

ii Outline how these antivirals work.

iii Both oseltamivir (Tamiflu) and zanamivir (Relenza) are given as prophylactics. What does this term mean?

iv Figure 15.5 shows the structures of oseltamivir and zanamivir. Name the functional groups A–G and suggest why zanamivir cannot pass through cell membranes as easily as oseltamivir.

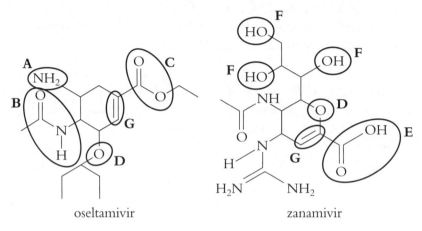

oseltamivir   zanamivir

Figure 15.5 Oseltamivir and zanamivir.

2 HIV is a virus that infects the white blood cells and leads to AIDS.

a Why are people with AIDS susceptible to infections with the result that simple infections can become life-threatening?

b Suggest why the development of antiviral drugs to combat HIV is especially difficult.

c HIV was first diagnosed in humans in 1981 and since then has spread rapidly around the globe.

i Outline how the virus is spread.

ii Outline possible prevention measures against HIV infection.

Exercise 15.6 – Environmental impact of some medications

1 Some medical treatments use radioactive materials. For example, ^{131}I is used to treat thyroid cancer. Radioactive waste is categorised into high-level waste and low-level waste.

a Describe the differences between high-level and low-level waste.

b Into which category does most radioactive medical waste fall?

c Outline the disposal of radioactive waste.

2 The release of antibiotics into the environment is a cause of concern.

a Describe a potential impact of the release of antibiotics into the environment.

b Suggest two ways in which antibiotics may enter the water supply.

3 The basic principles of green chemistry are to minimise the production of hazardous substances and their release into the environment.

a One way of minimising waste is to choose a manufacturing method that has a high atom economy.

i What is meant by the term 'atom economy'?

ii How is the atom economy of a reaction different from its yield?

iii Calculate the atom economy of the preparation of aspirin, $C_9H_8O_4$, from salicylic acid according to the equation:

$$C_4H_6O_3 + C_7H_6O_3 \rightarrow C_9H_8O_4 + C_2H_4O_2$$

b Many of the solvents used in drug manufacture are organic.
   i   How does this affect the 'greenness' of the process?
   ii Suggest some possible solutions to decrease the impact of organic solvents.
c Oseltamivir is used as a treatment for influenza. It can be made from compounds that are obtained from the fruits of chinese star anise plants. The demand for oseltamivir during times of high need led to worldwide efforts to find an alternative source for the precursor molecules. One solution is to use the fermentation of sugar using genetically modified bacteria.
   Which principle of green chemistry does this alternative method exemplify?

> Consider the solvent and conditions required for fermentation.

HL Exercise 15.7 – Taxol: a chiral auxiliary case study

Stereoisomerism was met in Chapter 10 as part of IB Topic 20.

1 a What effect do optical isomers have on plane-polarised light?
  b What feature of a molecule gives rise to optical isomerism?
  c What is the definition of optical isomerism?
  d Why do optical isomers often have different biological effects?
  e What name is given to the apparatus that is used to distinguish optical isomers?
  f Why is it necessary to test both enantiomers of a compound for their therapeutic effect?

2 Taxol occurs naturally in yew trees but can also be synthesised.
  a For what is taxol used as a treatment?
  b Taxol has 11 chiral centres and so there are a large number of different optical isomers only one of which has the desired biological activity.
    The structure of taxol is shown in Figure 15.6. Place an asterisk next to all the chiral carbons in the section of the molecule within the box indicated.

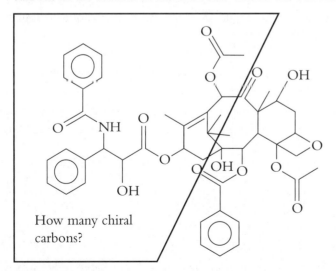

How many chiral carbons?

Figure 15.6 Taxol.

c Taxol is synthesised using a chiral auxiliary. Explain what this means.

HL Exercise 15.8 – Nuclear medicine

Radioactive isotopes can be used in medicine in a number of ways, including for both diagnosis and treatment.

1 This question explores radioactive decay.

a Radioactive decay includes the formation of α particles, β particles, positrons and γ-radiation.

  i What is an α particle?
  ii What is a β particle?
  iii What is a positron?
  iv What is γ-radiation?

b In equations for radioactive decay the following symbols are sometimes used:
  $_{-1}^{0}e$, $_{2}^{4}He$ and $_{0}^{1}n$
  Which type of radiative decay do these symbols represent?

c Copy and complete or construct the following equations:

  i $_{90}^{234}Th \rightarrow \ _{-1}^{0}e + ?$

  ii $_{86}^{219}Th \rightarrow \ _{84}^{215}Po + ?$

  iii $? \rightarrow \ _{2}^{4}He + \ _{66}^{167}Dy$

  iv $_{83}^{214}Bi \rightarrow \ _{0}^{1}n + ?$

  v ^{214}Pb decays by emitting a β particle

  vi ^{214}Pb is formed by the emission of an α particle

> Equations for radioactive decay must balance but, whereas in ordinary equations the **elements** must balance, it is the **total of the mass numbers and atomic numbers** that must balance for radioactive decay equations because the identity of an element can change.

2 The rate of radioactive decay varies from fractions of a second to thousands of years. The rate of decay is indicated by the half-life of an isotope.

a Define the term 'half-life'.

b Calculate the following:

  i the mass of ^{214}Bi remaining from a sample containing 0.0100 g of ^{214}Bi after 1 hour (half-life of ^{214}Bi = 20 minutes).

  ii the half-life of a radioactive isotope if after 15 minutes only 25% of a sample remained.

  iii the time taken for the mass of a sample of ^{89}Sr to fall to 6.25% of its original level (half-life of ^{89}Sr is 50.5 days).

c Calculate the following:

  i the mass of ^{214}Bi remaining from a sample containing 0.0100 g of ^{214}Bi after 30 minutes. (half-life of ^{214}Bi = 20 minutes).

  ii the half-life of a radioactive isotope if after 15 minutes, only 35% of a sample remained.

  iii the time taken for the mass of a sample of ^{89}Sr to fall to 5% of its original level (half-life of ^{89}Sr is 50.5 days).

> These questions involve whole numbers of half-lives and so can be performed using relatively simple sequences. For example, in part **i**: 1 hour is three half-lives, so mass will fall from 0.0100 → 0.00500 → 0.00250 → ?

> Use the expressions: $N_t = N_0 \left(\dfrac{1}{2}\right)^{\frac{t}{t_{\frac{1}{2}}}}$ in part **i** and $\lambda = \dfrac{\ln 2}{t_{\frac{1}{2}}}$ and $\left(\text{or } t_{\frac{1}{2}} = \dfrac{\ln 2}{\lambda}\right)$ and
>
> $N_t = N_0\,e^{-\lambda t}$ in parts **ii** and **iii**.
> All these formulas are given in the data book.
> Very similar questions have been chosen here so that you will be able to judge if your answer is approximately correct by comparing your answer to those in part **b**.

3 Radiotherapy can be used in medicine both internally or externally. ^{99}Tc is often used in imaging. It is incorporated into a drug, given orally or by injection and its progress (and therefore that of the drug) can be detected.

Consider its half-life, emission type and chemistry.

  a Outline why ^{99}Tc is suitable for use in this way.

  b ^{90}Y, ^{131}I and ^{177}Lu are β-emitters commonly used in radiotherapy for the treatment of cancer.

    Describe the effect that β-emitters used in this way have on cells.

  c Suggest some of the more common side-effects caused by radiotherapy.

  d Targeted alpha therapy (TAT) uses α-emitting radioisotopes such as ^{212}Pb.

    i Outline how this is used.

    ii Why does this have the potential to be used for the treatment of cancers that have spread from their primary site?

  e Another potential new radiotherapy is BNCT.

    i What do the letters BNCT stand for?

    ii Outline the principle of BNCT.

    iii During this process ^{10}B atoms are converted into ^{7}Li atoms. Give an equation for this process.

4 MRI scanning is an extremely useful diagnostic tool.

  a What do the letters MRI stand for?

  b MRI uses nuclear magnetic resonance to produce three-dimensional images. What changes in the nucleus of an atom does this technique rely on?

  c Which analytical technique is based on the same principle as MRI scanning?

  d Which element in the body does MRI scanning interact with?

  e MRI scanning involves the use of which part of the electromagnetic spectrum?

HL Exercise 15.9 – Drug detection and analysis

The separation and identification of compounds are important tools in chemistry and different techniques are used in different circumstances.

1 During development and manufacturing, a target compound needs to be separated from a reaction mixture. This can be achieved because the substance has a different solubility at different temperatures in different solvents, or because it has a different boiling point from the other components in a mixture.

  a What is the name of the technique used to separate a substance that has different solubilities in a solvent at different temperatures?

b The molecules shown in Figure 15.7 have very different solubilities in water and in non-polar solvents. Suggest which will be soluble in water and which will be soluble in non-polar solvents.

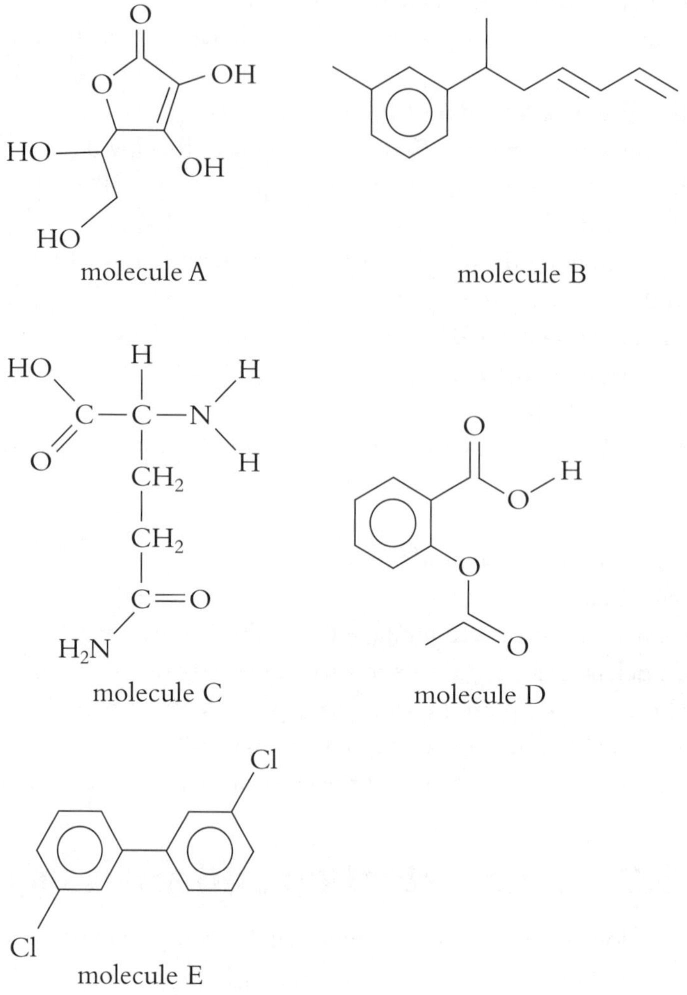

molecule A

molecule B

molecule C

molecule D

molecule E

Figure 15.7 A range of organic molecules.

c Given the data in Table 15.1, describe how substance X could be separated from an aqueous mixture of X and Y.

Substance	Solubility in water	Solubility in hexane
X	medium	very high
Y	high	low

Table 15.1

The syllabus does not state that this needs to be known but it is useful as an aid to understanding the way that fraction distillation works.

d A mixture of liquids with very different boiling points can be separated by simple distillation. What technique would be used for a mixture of liquids with very similar boiling points?

2 This question explores fractional distillation and Raoult's law.

a State Raoult's law.

b Raoult's law refers to partial pressure, mole fractions and ideal solutions.

  i What is meant by the term 'partial pressure'?

  ii What is meant by the term 'mole fraction'?

  iii What is meant by the term 'an ideal solution'?

c A mixture containing 100 g of ethanol and 500 g of water was placed in a sealed flask at 298 K and allowed to reach equilibrium. The vapour pressures of water and ethanol at this temperature are 3.17 kPa and 7.80 kPa, respectively.

  i Calculate the mole fraction of ethanol and water in the mixture.

  ii Calculate the vapour pressure in the flask.

  iii Calculate the mole fraction of each of the two gases in the vapour.

d A liquid boils when its vapour pressure equals the external pressure. The vapour pressure of a mixture depends on its composition and so the boiling point of a mixture also depends on its composition. This is the basis of how fractional distillation works and can be explained using Raoult's law.

    If one of the components of a mixture is more volatile than the other, then the vapour produced by the mixture will contain a higher proportion of the more volatile component than the liquid mixture. This can be seen in the graph in Figure 15.8. A horizontal line drawn at any point gives the composition of the mixture in the liquid phase and the composition of the mixture in the vapour phase. Using the graph in Figure 15.8, follow the steps below and the lines drawn on the graph to follow this logic as a mixture of 10% X and 90% Y are separated by fractional distillation. The percentages represent the mole fractions.

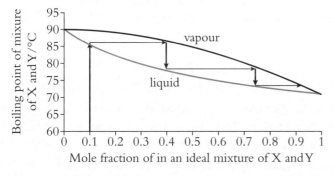

Figure 15.8 Boiling point composition diagram for an ideal solution of X and Y.

  i What is the boiling point of the liquid mixture containing 10% X and 90% Y?

  ii What will the composition of the vapour be at this temperature?

  iii This vapour moves up the column where the temperature is cooler. At this cooler temperature the vapour condenses to form a liquid with the same composition as the vapour. What is the boiling point of this liquid?

  iv When the liquid trickles down to the point in the column at which the temperature is above its boiling point, it will turn to vapour.

    What is the composition of the vapour at this temperature?

  v Follow the line for one more cycle of vapour rising, condensing and re-boiling. What is the composition of the vapour?

This is the same reaction as you met in Chapter 10.

3 The detection of alcohol is an important tool in road safety. It can be detected in a number of ways.

  a **i**   Describe how the amount of ethanol can be measured using a chemical oxidising agent.

      ii   Give an equation for the oxidation of ethanol into ethanoic acid using [O] to represent the oxidising agent.

  b A more accurate type of breathalyser uses a fuel cell. These use the ethanol in the breath to produce an electrical current; the more ethanol, the higher current produced. The half-equations for the reactions at the anode and cathode are given below:

anode: $C_2H_5OH + H_2O \rightarrow CH_3COOH + 4H^+ + 4e^-$

cathode: $O_2 + 4H^+ + 4e^{-+} \rightarrow 2H_2O$

Give the overall reaction for the fuel cell.

  c Name a spectroscopic method that can be used to detect ethanol in breath.

4 Spectroscopic techniques were met in Chapter 11 as they are part of Topics 11 and 21. These are re-visited as part of this Option D.

  a Figure 15.9 shows the structure of paracetamol.

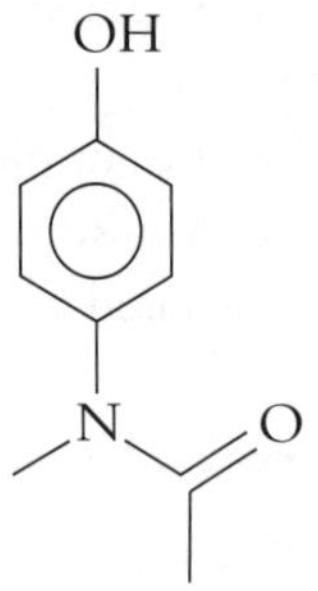

$C_8H_9NO_2$

Figure 15.9 Paracetamol.

Paracetamol contains an amide group but in this question we can consider the C=O and N–H parts separately.

    i   Using the data tables in section 26 of the IB data book, suggest the wavenumber of some significant peaks that might be expected to be seen in the IR spectrum.

    ii   The mass spectrum of paracetamol includes peaks at $m/z = 58, 93, 108$ and 151. Suggest the identity of these peaks.

    iii   Ignoring any coupling, suggest how many peaks might be expected in the NMR spectrum of paracetamol.

  b Mass spectrometry is often used forensically: for example, when detecting the presence of banned substances in blood and urine samples from athletes. These samples contain hundreds of different compounds, most of which are not suspicious but are the normal substances found in healthy humans. The first stage in analysis is to separate the components in the mixture from one another.

    i   What is the name of the analytical technique used to separate the components in a complex mixture?

    ii   In one type of instrument, the vaporised mixture is carried through a heated column by a carrier gas such as nitrogen or helium. The column is packed with beads coated in a non-volatile liquid. Separation depends on the extent to which each component in the mixture dissolves in the non-volatile liquid. The more soluble, the longer the time taken for that component to pass through the column.

What name is given to the time taken for a component to pass through the column?

iii Once the components are separated, how are they identified?

iv One class of compounds that can be detected using this method is the anabolic steroids.

What effect do anabolic steroids have on the body?

? Exam-style questions

1 **Analgesics can be classed as strong or mild.**
   a Give examples of a mild analgesic and of a strong analgesic. [2]
   b Compare the different ways in which these two type of painkiller work. [3]
   c Aspirin is hydrolysed in the body to salicylic acid which is the active form of the drug. State the name given to the active form of a drug that is produced in the body. [1]
   d In an experiment to prepare a sample of solid analgesic with the formula $C_9H_8O_4$, 1.0 g of $C_4H_6O_3$ was reacted with 1.0 g of $C_7H_6O_3$. A mass of 0.97 g of the product was obtained.

   The equation for the reaction is:

   $$C_4H_6O_3 + C_7H_6O_3 \rightarrow C_9H_8O_4 + C_2H_4O_2$$

   i Calculate the percentage yield. [4]
   ii State one method that could be used to assess the purity of the product. [1]
   e A newly developed analgesic was found to contain an amine group but was not very soluble.
   i State how its solubility could be increased. [1]
   ii Other than by increasing its solubility, describe how the bioavailability of the drug could be increased. [1]
   iii The new drug was found to have a large therapeutic window and a low value therapeutic index. Explain these terms and comment on whether these values are desirable in a medicine. [4]

   [Total 17]

2 a **The action of most drugs depends on the interaction of a drug with receptors on target molecules.**
   Explain how this principle applies to the action of the antibiotic penicillin. [3]
   b Bacterial resistance is an increasing problem.
   i Suggest how not finishing a course of antibiotics can lead to increased bacterial resistance. [1]
   ii It has been found that resistant bacteria produce an enzyme that renders the penicillin inactive. New forms of penicillin have been developed which are able to withstand the action of this enzyme. Describe the modifications made to penicillin that have been developed. [1]

c Morphine, diamorphine and codeine are classed as opiates. Their structures are given in the data book. These drugs act on the brain. The brain is surrounded by a lipid membrane.

i Name the features of these molecules that enable then to cross this blood–brain barrier. [1]

ii Of these three opiates, state which molecule can cross the blood–brain barrier least easily. [1]

iii In the brain, the ester linkages in diamorphine are hydrolysed. Give an equation for this hydrolysis, using $R(OCOCH_3)_2$ to represent the formula of diamorphine. [2]

[Total 9]

3 **a** An excess of stomach acid can be treated with a simple antacid preparation obtainable from pharmacists and a wide range of other shops.

The contents of one such antacid were analysed in a laboratory by reacting it with dilute hydrochloric acid. It was found that a 500 mg tablet was neutralised by 35.2 cm³ of 0.100 mol dm⁻³ HCl. If the active ingredient in the tablet was $Mg(OH)_2$ then calculate what percentage of active ingredient the tablet contains. [4]

b An alternative treatment for chronic excess acid is to use drugs like ranitidine. Outline how drugs like ranitidine control excess acid. [1]

[Total 5]

4 **a** Describe one difference between bacteria and viruses. [1]

b Developing drugs to tackle diseases caused by viruses and by bacteria can be difficult. Outline two of these difficulties. [2]

c Explain two ways in which antiviral medications work. [2]

d Oseltamivir (Tamiflu) and zanamivir (Relenza) are both antiviral medicines that can be used preventatively. Suggest what they can be used to prevent. [1]

[Total 6]

5 **HL** **Figure 15.10 shows a simple polarimeter.**

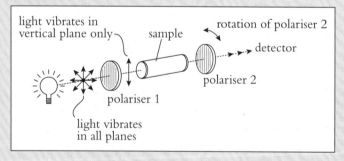

Figure 15.10 A simple polarimeter.

a State why the second polarising filter (polariser 2) would need to be rotated to allow light to pass through to the detector when a solution of an optically active compound is placed in the sample tube. [1]

b Give two reasons why optical isomerism is important in medicinal chemistry. [2]

c Explain how chiral auxiliary substances are used in drug synthesis. [3]

d Taxol is a drug that is synthesised using a chiral auxiliary.

    i Name the disease for which taxol is used as a treatment. [1]

    ii Name the plant which produces the precursor for the synthesis of taxol. [1]

    iii Describe one way that the synthesis of taxol is an example of green chemistry. [1]

[Total 9]

6 **HL**

a Hair loss is a common side-effect of some forms of cancer treatment such as radiotherapy. Suggest why hair follicles are prone to damage by radioactive isotopes. [1]

b ^{131}I is used treat some forms of cancer as it emits both β particles and γ-radiation.

    i Give an equation for the loss of a β particle from ^{131}I. [1]

    ii The half-life of ^{131}I is 8 days. Calculate the percentage of the isotope remaining after 30 days. [3]

c State why α- and β-emitters are particularly useful in cancer treatments which are delivered directly to the site of a cancer. [1]

d A new approach to cancer treatment is targeted alpha therapy (TAT).

    i State how the cancer cells are targeted. [1]

    ii Name the type of cancers for which it is hoped that this treatment will be particularly useful. [1]

[Total 8]

7 **HL** Figure 15.11 shows the structure of warfarin and Figure 15.12 shows its IR spectrum. Warfarin is used to stop the blood from clotting and so prevent heart attacks and strokes.

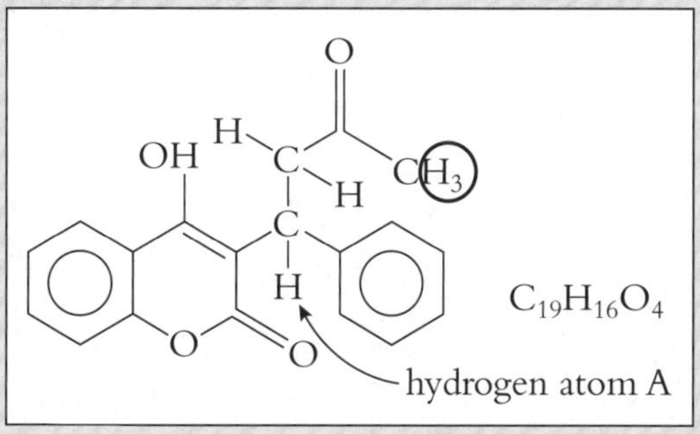

Figure 15.11 Warfarin.

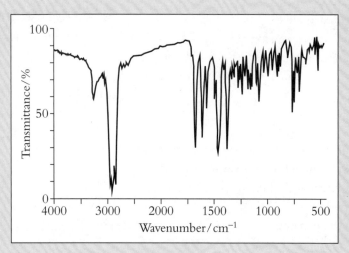

Figure 15.12 IR spectrum of warfarin.

a Suggest the identity of the functional groups responsible for the following peaks:

  i 1750 cm^{-1} [1]

  ii 3200 cm^{-1} [1]

  iii 2800–2900 cm^{-1} [1]

b Warfarin is optically active. Draw an asterisk ($\star$) next to the chiral centre. [1]

c The mass spectrum of warfarin is shown in Figure 15.13.

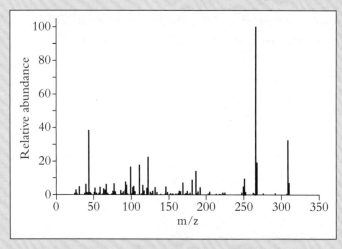

Figure 15.13 Mass spectrum of warfarin.

Suggest the moleculas formulas of the fragments that are responsible for the following fragments. The molar mass of warfarin is 308 g mol^{-1}.

  i m/z = 265 [1]

  ii m/z = 43 [1]

  iii Suggest an identity for the fragment at m/z = 43. [1]

d i State how many signals there would be in the NMR spectrum of warfarin, ignoring any coupling. [1]

  ii State the range of the chemical shift of the hydrogen atoms circled in Figure 15.11. [1]

  iii State the multiplicity of the signal produced by the hydrogen atom labelled 'A' in Figure 15.11. [1]

[Total 10]

Glossary

Absolute scale of temperature   Absolute scale of temperature, which starts at zero; an interval of 1 °C is the same as an interval of 1 K and so 0 °C is equivalent to 273 K.

Absolute uncertainty   The uncertainty in a value quoted in the same units as the value itself.

Absolute zero   The temperature at which everything would be in its lowest energy state; 0 K or −273 °C.

Accuracy   How close a measurement is to the true value.

Acid–base indicator   A weak acid or base for which the ionised and unionised forms are different colours.

Acid deposition   A more general term than acid rain; it refers to any process in which acidic substances leave the atmosphere and are deposited on the Earth's surface.

Acid dissociation constant, K_a   The equilibrium constant for the dissociation of a weak acid. For an acid HA, then its dissociation can be represented by the equation $HA(aq) \rightleftharpoons H^+(aq) + A^-(aq)$ and:

$$K_a = \frac{[H^+][A^-]}{[HA]}$$

Activation energy   The minimum amount of energy that colliding species must have before a collision results in a chemical reaction.

Active metabolites   Active forms of a drug after they have been processed in the body.

Actual yield   The actual amount of product formed in a reaction.

Addition reaction   A reaction in which one molecule is added to a compound containing a multiple bond without the loss of another group.

Adsorption   The attachment of one substance onto the surface of another.

Aldose   a monosaccharide that contains only one aldehyde (−CH=O) group per molecule.

Aliphatic   An organic compound whose carbon atoms are linked in open chains (branched or straight).

Alkali   A soluble base.

Allosteric effect   The binding of a ligand to one site on a protein molecule in such a way that the properties of another site on the same protein are affected.

Allotrope   Different forms of the same element; e.g. diamond, graphite and fullerene are allotropes of carbon.

Alloy   A homogeneous mixture of a metal with other metals or non-metals.

Amphiprotic   A substance that can both donate a proton (act as a Brønsted–Lowry acid) and accept a proton (act as a Brønsted–Lowry base).

Amphoteric   A substance that can act as both an acid and a base.

Anabolism   The process of synthesising molecules needed by cells; this requires energy.

Analgesic   Drug that reduces pain.

Analogue instrument   An instrument that is not digital, one which has a scale. As a general rule the uncertainty in an analogue instrument is half the smallest division.

Anhydrous   Without water of crystallisation.

Anode   The electrode at which oxidation occurs.

Anthropogenic   Something that is the result of human activity.

Anthropomorphic   Something that is as a result of human action.

Antibiotic   Drug that kills bacteria.

Aprotic   a solvent that does not contain a hydrogen ion (a proton).

Aromatic   An organic compound containing planar rings with a delocalised π electron cloud.

Atactic polymer   A polymer that has side groups orientated randomly on both sides of the main chain.

Atom   The smallest part of an element that can still be recognised as the element. In the simplest picture of the atom, the electrons orbit around the central nucleus; the nucleus is made up of protons and neutrons (except for a hydrogen atom, which has no neutrons).

Atom economy   A measure of the efficiency of a process often used in green chemistry; a measure of the proportion of the reactant atoms that are found in the desired product.

$$\text{atom economy} = \frac{\text{molar mass of desired products}}{\text{molar mass of all reactants}} \times 100$$

Atomic number, Z   The number of protons in the nucleus of an atom.

Atomic radius   Half the inter-nuclear distance between two atoms of the same element covalently bonded together.

Aufbau principle   The idea that electrons always fill the sub-levels of the lowest energy first.

Average bond enthalpy   The average amount of energy required to break one mole of covalent bonds in a gaseous molecule under standard conditions. Average refers to the fact that the actual bond enthalpy will vary in different molecules. Bond enthalpies are always endothermic ($\Delta H^{\ominus} = +ve$).

Avogadro's constant, L 6.02×10^{23} mol^{-1}

Avogadro's law   Equal volumes of ideal gases measured at the same temperature and pressure contain the same number of molecules.

Base   A substance that reacts with an acid in a neutralisation reaction.

Base ionisation (dissociation) constant, K_b   The equilibrium constant for the dissociation of a weak base. For a base B, then its dissociation can be represented by the equation $B(aq) + H_2O(l) \rightleftharpoons BH^+(aq) + OH^-(aq)$ and

$$K_b = \frac{[BH^+][OH^-]}{[B]}$$

Bidentate   a ligand having two atoms from which electrons can be donated to the central coordinated atom.

Binary substance   A compound made of just two elements.

Bioavailability   The proportion of the administered dosage of a drug that is transferred into the blood stream.

Biofuel   A fuel produced from organic matter obtained from plants, waste materials and so on.

Biomagnification   The increase in concentration of a substance as it passes up a food chain.

Boiling   Change of state from liquid to gas at a temperature at or above the boiling point of the substance. It differs from evaporation in that boiling occurs throughout a liquid and not just at the surface.

Boiling point   The temperature at which the vapour pressure of a liquid equals the atmospheric pressure. This definition strays into Physics and is not part of the Chemistry course; however, in simple terms the boiling point can be thought of as the temperature above which a substance will be in its gaseous state.

Bottom-up   a technique used in nanotechnology to build or grow larger structures atom by atom or molecule by molecule.

Born–Haber cycle   An enthalpy level diagram showing the formation of an ionic compound in a number of simpler steps.

Breeder reactor   A nuclear reactor that produces more fissionable material than it consumes.

Brittle   A material that breaks when it is stretched.

Brønsted–Lowry acid   A proton (H^+) donor.

Brønsted–Lowry base   A proton (H^+) acceptor.

Buffer solution   A solution that resists changes in pH when a small amount of acid or alkali is added to it.

Calorimetry   A practical technique where the heat change brought about by a chemical reaction is used to produce a temperature change in a substance of known specific heat capacity.

Carbocation   An ion with a positively charged carbon atom.

Carbon footprint   A measure of the total amount of greenhouse gases emitted as a result of human activity.

Catabolism   The process of breaking down larger molecules into smaller ones with the release of energy.

Catalyst   A substance that increases the rate of a chemical reaction by providing an alternative pathway of lower activation energy and is not consumed by the reaction.

Cathode   The electrode at which reduction occurs.

Chelation   The formation of a complex which includes a ring containing the central atom/ion. These are formed by bidentate and multidentate ligands.

Chemical properties   How a substance behaves in chemical reactions.

Chemical shift, δ/ppm   The scale used in NMR spectroscopy. The distance (shift) along the horizontal axis that the signal appears relative to TMS (which is given an arbitrary value of 0 ppm).

Chiral auxiliary   An optically active substance that is temporarily incorporated into an organic synthesis so that the synthesis can be carried out asymmetrically with the selective formation of a single enantiomer.

Chiral centre/chiral carbon   A carbon atom with four different atoms or groups attached to it (also known as an asymmetric carbon).

Chromophore   The part of a molecule which gives rise to its colour.

***cis–trans* isomerism**   Two compounds that have the same structural formulas but the groups are arranged differently in space due to restricted rotation around a double bond or a ring.

Closed system   A system where there is no exchange of matter with the surroundings.

Coefficient   The number placed in front of the formula of the substances in a balanced equation to represent the relative amounts of each substance. The number 1 is not normally used.

Collision theory   A reaction can only occur when the particles collide in the correct orientation and with energy greater than or equal to the activation energy.

Complex   A species consisting of a central atom or ion surrounded by a number of ligands to which it is bonded by dative covalent bonds.

Composite material   A mixture containing two or more different materials present as distinct, separate phases. Synthetic composite materials consist of a reinforcing phase embedded in a matrix.

Compound   A substance composed of two or more different elements chemically bonded together in a fixed ratio.

Concentration   Amount of solute dissolved in a unit volume of solution; the volume that is usually taken is 1 dm^3 (one litre); the amount of solute may be expressed in g or mol, so the units of concentration are g dm^{-3} or mol dm^{-3}

Condensation   The change of state from gas to liquid.

Condensation polymer   a small molecule formed as a by-product each time a bond is formed between two monomers.

Condensation reaction   A type of chemical reaction involving the joining together of two or more molecules with the formation of a covalent bond and the elimination of a small molecule such as water.

Configurational isomers   stereoisomers that can cannot be converted into one another by rotation around a single bond. The two main types of configurational isomers are geometric isomers and optical isomers.

Conformational isomerism   Forms of the same molecule that differ due to rotation about a σ bond.

Conjugate acid–base pair   Two species that differ from each other by one proton (H^+). When an acid donates a proton it forms its conjugate base and vice versa.

Conjugated system   A system of connected p-orbitals with delocalised electrons in molecules with alternating single and multiple bonds.

Continuous spectrum   A spectrum in which all frequencies/wavelengths are present.

Convergence limit   The lines in a line spectrum fall into several series or groups. Within each series the lines get closer together at higher frequency, eventually converging. The convergence limit is the frequency at which this convergence occurs.

Cooper pair   a pair of weakly bound electrons responsible for the transfer of charge in a superconducting material.

Coordinate bond   A covalent bond in which both electrons in the shared pair come from the same atom – also known as a dative covalent bond.

Coordination number   The number of nearest neighbours for an atom or ion in a crystal.

Covalent bond   The electrostatic force of attraction between the shared pair of electrons and the nuclei of the atoms making up the bond.

Cracking   The process of converting a long-chain alkane into shorter-chain alkanes and alkenes.

Critical mass   the smallest mass of fissionable material that can sustain fission reactions.

Decimal places   The total number of digits after the decimal point in a value.

Degenerate   The term used to describe orbitals of equal energy.

Delocalisation   The sharing of a pair of electrons between three or more atoms.

Deposition   The change of state from gas to solid without going through a liquid phase; the reverse of sublimation.

Diamagnetism   A weak magnetic force cause by the presence of paired electrons. Diamagnetic materials are repelled by a magnetic field.

Diastereoisomers   Stereoisomers that are not mirror images of each other.

Digital instrument   An instrument with an electronic display that gives a numerical value with no scale. The uncertainty in a digital instrument is one unit in the last decimal place.

Dipole   The separation of charge due to its uneven distribution.

Distillation   A practical technique which is used to separate compounds with different boiling points.

Drug   A substance that, when applied to or introduced to a living organism, brings about a change in the biological function through chemical action.

Ductile   Able to be drawn into wires.

Dynamic equilibrium   A system is said to be in a state of dynamic equilibrium when there appears to be no change in the macroscopic properties (e.g. all concentrations are constant); however, both forward and backward reactions are still continuing but at equal rates.

ED$_{50}$ The dose of a drug required to produce a therapeutic effect in 50% of the test population (ED = effective dose).

Effective nuclear charge   The attractive force experienced by an electron taking into account the shielding effect of inner electron shells.

Efficiency   A measure of the amount of useful energy compared to the energy input.

Effusion   The process by which a gas escapes through a very small hole in a container.

Elasticity   The ability of a material to return to its original shape once a stretching force has been removed.

Elastomer   Polymers that display rubber-like elasticity. They are flexible and can be stretched many times by the application of a force; they return to their original size and shape once the force is removed.

Electrical conductivity   The degree to which a substance conducts electricity.

Electrochemical cell   A device capable of either generating electrical energy from chemical reactions or facilitating chemical reactions through the introduction of electrical energy.

Electrolysis   The breaking down of a substance (in the molten state or in solution) by the passage of electricity through it.

Electrolyte   A solution or a molten compound that is broken down when electricity is passed through it.

Electron affinity   The energy change when one electron is added to each atom in a mole of gaseous atoms to form a mole of gaseous ions each with a 1− charge under standard conditions.

Electron domain   An area in which electrons are found around an atom or in a molecule. The number of electron domains refers to the number of lone pairs or bond locations; bond location is independent of whether the bond is a single, double or triple bond.

Electronegativity   A measure of the the tendency of a covalently bonded atom to attract the shared pair of electrons towards itself.

Electrophile   A species that can accept a lone pair of electrons to form a coordinate bond; electrophiles are Lewis acids.

Element   A substance containing only one type of atom (although these may be isotopes of each other).

Emission spectrum   The line spectrum produced when light is emitted by a gas due to the fall of electrons from higher to lower energy levels. That only certain lines are present is evidence that only certain energy levels are possible and supports the idea of electron shells.

Empirical formula   The simplest whole-number ratio of the elements present in a compound.

Enantiomers   Optical isomers (see below).

End point of titration   The point at which an indicator changes colour in a titration.

Endothermic   A chemical reaction in which heat is taken in from the surroundings, ΔH is positive for endothermic reactions.

Energy density   A measure of the amount of energy per unit volume of a fuel.

Energy level This describes the 'energetic distance' of an electron from the nucleus. Only certain discrete energy levels exist in a given atom and so these energy levels are also referred to as 'shells'.

Enrichment an isotopic separation process that increases the proportion of the uranium-235 isotope in relation to uranium-238 in natural uranium.

Enthalpy change, ΔH The heat exchanged with the surroundings at constant pressure.

Entropy, $S^{\ominus}$ A measure of the available energy is distributed among the particles. The standard entropy is the entropy of a substance at 100 kPa and 298 K. It can also be thought of as the amount of disorder of a substance, solids have a lower entropy than liquids as solids are more ordered. Entropy is measured in $J\,K^{-1}\,mol^{-1}$.

Entropy change, $\Delta S^{\ominus}$ The change in entropy under standard conditions. An increase in the entropy ($\Delta S^{\ominus} > 0$) represents an increase in the disorder; the energy is more spread out, for example, changing from liquid to gas.

Equilibrium law This states that the ratio of the products of the concentrations of the products (raised to the power of their coefficients in the balanced equation) to the product of the concentrations of the reactants (raised to the power of their coefficients in the balanced equation) is constant at a given temperature.

Equivalence point The point at which exact stoichiometric amounts of the reacting species have been mixed in a titration.

Evaporation The change of state from liquid to gas that occurs at the surface of a liquid. Evaporation occurs at all temperatures.

Exothermic A chemical reaction in which heat is released to the surroundings, ΔH is negative for exothermic reactions.

Fatty acid A long-chain carboxylic acid found in triglycerides and phospholipids.

Fenton reaction the use of hydrogen peroxide and ferrous salts (Fenton reagent) to oxidize α-hydroxy acids to α-keto acids or to convert 1,2-glycols to α-hydroxy aldehydes.

Fingerprint region the region to the right-hand side of an infrared spectrum that is almost unique for any given compound.

First electron affinity The enthalpy change when one electron is added to each atom in one mole of gaseous atoms under standard conditions of 298 K and 100 kPa; $X(g) + e^- \rightarrow X^-(g)$.

First ionisation energy The minimum amount of energy required to remove to infinity the outermost electron from each atom in one mole of gaseous atoms to form a mole of gaseous ions each with a 1+ charge under standard conditions of 298 K and 100 kPa; $X(g) \rightarrow X^+(g) + e^-$

Formal charge A concept used to identify the most likely Lewis structure for a molecule or ion. It is the charge that an atom would have if all the atoms had equal electronegativity.

Fossil fuel Fuels formed from the geological remains of organisms that lived millions of years ago.

Fragmentation pattern The pattern of peaks in mass spectrometry due to the breaking of a molecule into smaller parts (fragments).

Free energy change/Gibbs free energy, $\Delta G^{\ominus}$ This is related to the entropy of the universe. It can be used to predict whether a reaction will occur spontaneously at a given temperature; for spontaneous reactions $\Delta G < 0$ where $\Delta G = \Delta H - T\Delta S$

Free radical A species (atom or group of atoms) with an unpaired electron. Free radicals are generally very reactive.

Free radical substitution a substitution reaction involving free radicals as a reactive intermediate.

Freezing The change of state from liquid to solid.

Fuel cell A type of electrochemical cell that uses the reaction of a fuel and an oxidising agent to produce electrical energy directly; it uses a continuous supply of reactants from an external source.

Functional group An atom or group of atoms that gives an organic molecule its characteristic properties.

Functional group isomerism Isomers with different functional groups.

General formula The formula of a family of molecules which can be used to determine the molecular formula of any member of the series.

Genetic code The sequence of bases in DNA that determines the sequence of amino acids in a protein.

Genetically modified organism (GMO) Organisms in which the genetic code has been changed in some way by genetic engineering.

Giant structure A structure which is not composed of individual molecules.

Green chemistry the design of chemical products and processes that reduce or eliminate the use and generation of hazardous substances.

Group A vertical column of the periodic table.

Half-life The time taken for the concentration of a reactant or number of radioactive nuclei in a sample to fall to half of its original value.

Hess's law This states that the enthalpy change for a reaction is independent of the route taken provided that the conditions remain constant.

Heterogeneous catalyst A catalyst that is in a different phase (state) from the reactants.

Heterogeneous mixture A mixture that does not have a uniform composition and consists of separate phases; it can be separated by mechanical means.

Heterolytic fission The breaking of covalent bond where both electrons in the bond remain with one of the atoms in the bond.

Hexose a monosaccharide with six carbon atoms, having the chemical formula $C_6H_{12}O_6$.

Homogeneous catalyst A catalyst that is in the same phase (state) as the reactants.

Homogeneous mixture A mixture that has a uniform composition throughout the mixture and consists of only one phase.

Homologous series   A series of compounds of the same family, with the same general formula, which differ from each other by a common structural unit.

Homolytic fission   The breaking of a covalent bond where one electron in the bond remains with each of the atoms in the bond.

Hund's rule   The idea that electrons fill degenerate orbitals so as to give the maximum number of electrons with the same spin. This leads to all the degenerate orbitals being half-filled rather than some being occupied by a pair of electrons and some empty.

Hybridisation   The mixing of atomic orbitals when a compound is formed to produce a new set of orbitals. The total energy and the total number of orbitals is conserved but their shape and orientation differ from the atomic orbitals from which they have been formed.

Hydrated   The term used to describe crystals that contain water of crystallisation bound within their structure.

Hydration   A reaction in which water combines with an unsaturated molecule.

Hydrocarbon   An organic molecule composed of only hydrogen atoms and carbon atoms.

Hydrogen bonding   Intermolecular force between a lone pair of electrons on the nitrogen, oxygen or fluorine atom of one molecule and a hydrogen atom attached to a nitrogen, fluorine or oxygen atom of another molecule. These forces can also form intramolecularly.

Hydrogenation   A reaction in which hydrogen is added to an unsaturated compound.

Hydrolysis   A reaction in which a covalent bond is broken by the reaction with water.

Ideal gas   A theoretical model that approximates the behaviour of real gases. It can be defined in terms of macroscopic properties (a gas that obeys the equation $PV = nRT$) or in terms of microscopic properties (the main assumptions that define an ideal gas on a microscopic scale are that the molecules are point masses – their volume is negligible compared with the volume of the container – and that there are no intermolecular forces except during a collision).

Index of hydrogen deficiency   The number of double-bond equivalents or the degree of unsaturation. (A ring is equivalent to a double bond.)

Infrared spectroscopy   An analytical technique used to identify the functional groups in an organic molecule due to their absorption of radiation in the infrared region of the electromagnetic spectrum.

Inhibitor   a substance which slows down or prevents a particular chemical reaction.

Integration trace   The stepped line on an NMR spectrum which measures the area under each peak. The ratio of the heights of the steps is equal to the ratio of the number of hydrogen atoms giving rise to each peak.

Intermolecular forces   Forces between different molecules.

Intramolecular forces   Forces within a molecule.

Iodine number   A measure of the degree of unsaturation in a fat or oil. It is the number of grams of iodine that reacts with 100 g of fat or oil.

Ion   An atom or group of atoms that have lost or gained one or more electrons and so is electrically charged. N.B. It is not correct to define an ion as a charged particle because protons and neutrons are charged particles but they are not ions.

Ionic bond   The electrostatic force of attraction between oppositely charged ions.

Ionic product constant for water, K_w   The equilibrium constant representing the dissociation of water. $K_w = [H^+(aq)][OH^-(aq)]$. The value of K_w at 298 K is given in the data book (1.00×10^{-14}).

Ionic radius   The distance between the nucleus and the electron in the outermost shell of an ion.

Ionisation energy   This can be thought of as the minimum amount of energy required to remove the outermost electron from a gaseous atom.

Isoelectric point   The pH at which an amino acid has no overall charge.

Isomerism   Where molecules have the same molecular formula but their atoms are arranged differently.

Isotactic polymer   A polymer that has side groups all arranged on the same side of the main chain.

Isotope   Different atoms of an element; they have the same number of protons but different numbers of neutrons.

Ketose   a monosaccharide containing one ketone group per molecule.

LD$_{50}$ The dose of a drug required to kill 50% of the test population, normally expressed in mass per kg bodyweight (LD = lethal dose). LD$_{50}$ is not determined in humans!

Le Chatelier's principle   This states that if a system in a state of dynamic equilibrium is subject to some change then the position of the equilibrium will shift in order to minimise the effect of that change.

Lewis acid   An electron (lone) pair acceptor.

Lewis base   An electron (lone) pair donor.

Lewis structure   A diagram showing the arrangement of electrons in a molecule (or ion). Normally only the outer-shell electrons are shown.

Ligand   A species (neutral molecule or negative ion) which can donate a pair of electrons to form a dative covalent bond with an atom or ion to form a complex.

Limiting reactant   The reactant that is used up first in a chemical reaction. When the number of moles of each species is divided by its coefficient in the stoichiometric equation, the limiting reactant is the one with the lowest number; all other reactants are in excess.

Line spectrum   An emission spectrum of an atom composed of lines because only certain frequencies/wavelengths of light are present. The frequency of each line represents a particular transition between different energy levels when an electron falls from a higher to a lower energy level.

Lipid A group of biological molecules including steroids, triglycerides and phospholipids.

Liquid crystal A phase of matter in which the properties of a compound may exhibit the characteristics of both a solid and a liquid.

London forces Intermolecular forces arising from temporary dipole–induced dipole interactions.

Lyotropic liquid crystal A substance in which, when in solution, the molecules form into clusters with a regular orientation but these clusters are randomly arranged.

Macrocyclic ligand a macrocycle with three or more donor sites. Macrocyclic ligands exhibit particularly high affinity for metal ions.

Malleable Able to be hammered into sheets.

Mass defect The difference between the mass of a nucleus and the sum of the masses of the individual nucleons.

Mass number, A The sum of the number of protons and neutrons in the nucleus of an atom.

Mass spectrometry An analytical technique which is used for structural determination. The sample is bombarded with high-energy electrons and forms positively charged ions. The mass-to-charge ratio of the ions is then measured, giving rise to the different peaks on the spectrum.

Markovnikov's rule When HX adds across a double bond of an alkene, the H atom attaches to the carbon atom which has the greater number of hydrogen atoms on it already.

Mean value The sum of all the values divided by the number of values.

Mechanism A series of steps that make up a more complex reaction. Each step involves the collision of two particles.

Medicine Something that treats, prevents or alleviates the symptoms of disease.

Meissner effect the effect in which a superconductor negates all magnetic fields inside of the superconducting material.

Melting The change of state from solid to liquid.

Melting point The temperature at which a substance changes state from solid to liquid. Above this temperature the substance will all be in the liquid state.

Metabolism The chemical reactions that occur within cells. It involves both the breakdown of molecules with the release of energy and the synthesis of molecules that are required by cells.

Metallic bonding The electrostatic force of attraction between the lattice of positive ions in a metal and the sea of delocalised electrons.

Michaelis constant, K_m The concentration of substrate when the rate of an enzyme catalysed reaction is half the maximum rate.

Micronutrient A substance required by an organism but in relatively small amounts. Vitamins and minerals are classed as micronutrients.

Mixture A mixture contains two or more substances mixed together and not chemically joined. The exact composition of a mixture is not fixed. It is worth remembering that all solutions are mixtures.

Molar mass, M This is the relative atomic mass, relative formula mass or relative molecular mass of a substance in grams. Its units are $g\,mol^{-1}$.

Mole The amount of substance that contains the same number of particles (atoms, ions, molecules, and so on) as there are carbon atoms in 12 g of carbon-12 (6.02×10^{23}).

Molecular formula The total number of atoms of each element present in a molecule of the compound; the molecular formula is a multiple of the empirical formula.

Molecular ion, M^+ The ion produced in mass spectrometry when just one electron is removed from a molecule and the molecule does not fragment.

Molecular self-assembly A bottom-up approach to the production of nanoparticles, where molecules come together reversibly and spontaneously to create a larger structure.

Molecularity The number of 'molecules' that react in a particular step (usually the rate-determining step) in a chemical reaction.

Molecule An electrically neutral particle consisting of two or more atoms chemically bonded together.

Monoprotic acid/diprotic acid etc. An acid that dissociates to form one proton/two protons etc. per molecule.

Monosaccharide A simple sugar with the general formula $C_x(H_2O)_y$ which includes a carbonyl group and at least two hydroxyl groups.

Nanotechnology The production and application of structures, devices and systems at the nanometre scale. These are general man-made structures with one dimension smaller than 100 nm.

Nematic liquid crystal A liquid crystal in which the molecules are aligned, on average, in the same direction but are positioned randomly relative to each other (no positional order).

Neutralisation reaction The reaction between an acid and a base which produces a salt and water only.

NMR (nuclear magnetic resonance) spectroscopy An analytical technique used for structural determination. It is used to identify the hydrogen atoms (protons) in a molecule.

Nuclear binding energy The energy required to completely separate the nucleons in a nucleus.

Nuclear fission The breakdown of a larger nucleus into smaller fragments.

Nuclear fusion The joining together of smaller nuclei to make a larger one.

Nucleon A sub-atomic particle found in the nucleus of an atom. (The IB Chemistry syllabus only considers protons and neutrons as nucleons.)

Nucleophile A species that can donate a pair of electrons to form a coordinate bond; nucleophiles are Lewis bases.

Octane number A measure of the tendency of a compound not to cause knocking or auto-ignition in an engine.

OES Optical Emissions Spectrometer, an instrument for testing chemical composition of metals.

Opiates Natural narcotic (sleep-inducing) analgesics derived from the opium poppy.

Optical isomers Molecules which are non-superimposable mirror images of each other.

Orbital The region or **volume** (not area as orbitals are 3-dimensional) of space in which there is a high probability of finding a maximum of two electrons.

Order of reaction The power to which the concentration of a substance is raised in the experimentally determined rate expression.

Overall order of reaction The sum of the powers of the concentration terms in the experimentally determined rate equation.

Oxidation The addition of oxygen or removal of hydrogen, loss of electrons or an increase in oxidation number.

Oxidation number The imagined charge on an atom if it were considered to be purely ionic.

Oxidising agent The species in a reaction that oxidises another substance.

Paramagnetism A weak magnetic force caused by the presence of unpaired electrons. Paramagnetic substances are attracted to a magnetic field.

Pauli exclusion principle The idea that two electrons within the same orbital must have opposite spins.

Pentose a monosaccharide with five carbon atoms, having the chemical formula $C_5H_{10}O_5$.

Period A horizontal row of the periodic table.

Permeability The degree to which a material allows liquids or gases to pass through it.

pH A measure of the concentration of hydrogen ions in an aqueous solution. $pH = -\log_{10}[H^+]$

Photovoltaic cell A device that converts solar energy into electrical energy.

Physical properties Properties such as melting point, solubility and electrical conductivity, relating to the physical state of a substance and the physical changes it can undergo.

Pi bond A bond formed from the sideways overlap of parallel p orbitals. The electron density lies in two regions above and below the inter-nuclear axis.

Plane-polarised light Light that vibrates in only one plane.

Plasma A fully or partially ionised gas consisting of positive ions and electrons.

Plasticiser Small molecules that are added to a polymer to increase its flexibility.

Point of inflexion The point where the gradient of a curve stops increasing and starts decreasing or vice versa.

Polar A bond or molecule in which there is an uneven distribution of charge.

Polarimeter An instrument that is used to measure the extent to which plane-polarised light is rotated by an optically active compound.

Polychlorinated dibenzodioxins (PCDDs) also known simply as dioxins, are a group of polyhalogenated organic compounds that are significant environmental pollutants.

Polymer A long-chain molecule formed when large numbers of small molecules (monomers) are joined together.

Polymerisation The process by which polymers are formed.

Precipitation A reaction in which a solid is formed when two solutions are mixed.

Precision The reproducibility of results. Precise values are ones that lie close together and are close to the mean value.

Primary cell A cell that cannot be recharged – its reaction is non-reversible.

Primary structure of a protein The linear sequence of amino acids in a polypeptide chain.

Principal quantum number The number used to describe the main energy level or shell. The first shell has the principal quantum number 1, the second, 2 and so on. The symbol n is sometimes used. The maximum number of electrons in a given shell can be calculated using the formula $2n^2$.

Prophylactic A drug given for prevention rather than as a treatment.

Protic a solvent or acid that contains and can donate a hydrogen ion (a proton).

Qualitative data Data that is not numerical.

Quantitative data Numerical data.

Quaternary structure of a protein The structure due to the combination of two or more polypeptide chains and any prosthetic groups.

Racemic mixture An equimolar mixture of two enantiomers of a chiral compound; it has no effect on plane-polarised light.

Rancidity an unpleasant taste or smell through the decomposition of fats or oils.

Random uncertainty Uncertainties in a measurement due to the limitations of the measuring equipment and other uncontrollable variables. Random uncertainties result in values that are distributed on both sides of the mean. Random uncertainties can be reduced by repeating measurements; they can not be eliminated. Random uncertainties are usually quoted to only one significant figure.

Raoult's Law The partial vapour pressure of a component in an ideal solution is equal to the vapour pressure of the pure component at that temperature multiplied by its mole fraction in the mixture.

Rate constant, k The proportionality constant in the experimentally determined rate equation.

Rate equation/rate expression An experimentally determined equation that relates the rate of a reaction to the concentrations of the substances in the reaction mixture.

Rate of reaction The change in the concentration of reactants or products per unit time.

Rate-determining step The slowest step in a reaction mechanism.

Reaction quotient The ratio of the products of the concentrations of the products (raised to the power of their coefficients in the balanced equation) to the product of the concentrations of the reactants (raised to the power of their coefficients in the balanced equation) at any given point in time (i.e. not just at equilibrium). At equilibrium the reaction quotient is equal to the equilibrium constant.

Redox reaction A reaction which involves both oxidation and reduction.

Reducing agent The species in a reaction that reduces another species.

Reduction The removal of oxygen or addition of hydrogen, gain of electrons or decrease in oxidation number.

Reflux A practical technique in which a mixture is heated without the loss of any vapours as these are condensed and returned to the flask.

Reforming The process of converting a hydrocarbon molecule into a more branched, cyclic or aromatic structure.

Relative atomic mass, A_r The weighted mean mass of an atom of an element taking into account all of its isotopes and their relative abundances, relative to $\frac{1}{12}$th the mass of an atom of carbon-12.

Relative formula mass If a compound contains ions, the relative formula mass is the mass of the formula unit relative to the mass of $\frac{1}{12}$ of an atom of carbon-12.

Relative molecular mass, M_r The mass of a molecule of a compound relative to the mass of $\frac{1}{12}$ of an atom of carbon-12; the M_r is the sum of the relative atomic masses of the individual atoms making up the molecule.

Resonance structure One of several Lewis structures for a substance. The actual structure of the substance is a hybrid of its resonance structures.

Retrosynthesis The process of devising a synthetic route to a compound by starting with the target molecule and working backwards.

Reversible reaction A reaction that can occur in either direction.

Salt A compound formed when the hydrogen ions in an acid are replaced by a metal ion or the ammonium ion.

Salt hydrolysis The reaction of the conjugate base of a weak acid or the conjugate acid of a weak base with water. This is why solutions of the salt of a weak acid or weak base are not neutral.

SATP (standard ambient temperature and pressure) 298 K and 100 kPa.

Saturated A molecule that contains only single bonds.

Second electron affinity The enthalpy change when one electron is added to each 1− charged ion in one mole of gaseous ions under standard conditions of 298 K and 100 kPa; $X^-(g) + e^- \rightarrow X^{2-}(g)$

Second ionisation energy The minimum amount of energy required to remove one electron from each 1+ charged ion in one mole of gaseous ions under standard conditions of 298 K and 100 kPa; $X^+(g) \rightarrow X^{2+}(g) + e^-$

Secondary structure of a protein The regular folding of a protein chain held by hydrogen bonds between peptide links in different parts of the chain.

Shielding The idea that complete inner shells of electrons shield or screen outer electrons from the full attractive force of the nucleus.

Side-effect An unintended secondary effect of a drug on the body; it is usually an undesirable effect.

Sigma bond A bond formed by the axial overlap of atomic orbitals. The electron density lies along the axis joining the two nuclei.

Significant figures The number of digits that have meaning. All non-zero digits are significant. Zeros between non-zero digits are significant. Leading zeros are never significant. In a number with a decimal point, trailing zeros (those to the right of the last non-zero digit) are significant. In a number without a decimal point, trailing zeros may or may not be significant.

Skeletal formula A representation of the structure of a molecule which only shows the essential structure of the compound with the hydrogen atoms removed and using straight lines to represent carbon–carbon bonds.

Solubility A measure of the maximum amount of a solute that can dissolve in a given volume of solvent.

Solubility product constant The equilibrium constant for the dissolving of a sparingly soluble substance.

Solute A substance that is dissolved in another (the solvent).

Solution That which is formed when a solute dissolves in a solvent.

Solvent A substance that dissolves another substance (the solute); the solvent should be present in excess of the solute.

Specific energy A measure of the energy released by a fuel per unit mass.

Specific heat capacity, c The amount of energy needed to raise the temperature of one gramme of a substance by 1 K, units are $J\,g^{-1}\,K^{-1}$

Spin–spin coupling The splitting of a signal in NMR spectroscopy due to the presence of protons adjacent to those giving rise to the signal.

Spontaneous reaction A reaction that occurs without any outside influence at a given temperature.

Standard cell potential The voltage produced when two half-cells are combined under standard conditions.

Standard conditions A common set of agreed conditions used to compare data. Most commonly a temperature of 298 K, a pressure of 100 kPa and with all solutions of concentration $1\,mol\,dm^{-3}$.

Standard electrode potential The voltage of a half-cell connected to a standard hydrogen electrode measured under standard conditions. It shows the tendency of a species to be reduced compared to that of hydrogen ions.

Standard enthalpy change of atomisation, $\Delta H_{at}^{\ominus}$ The enthalpy change to form one mole of gaseous atoms from an element under standard conditions of 298 K and 100 kPa.

Standard enthalpy change of combustion, $\Delta H_{c}^{\ominus}$ The enthalpy change when one mole of a substance in completely burnt in oxygen under standard conditions of 298 K and 100 kPa.

Standard enthalpy change of formation, $\Delta H_{f}^{\ominus}$ The enthalpy change when one mole of a substance is formed from its elements in their standard states under standard conditions of 298 K and 100 kPa.

Standard enthalpy change of hydration, $\Delta H_{hyd}^{\ominus}$ The enthalpy change when one mole of gaseous ions are surrounded by water to form an infinitely dilute solution under standard conditions of 298 K and 100 kPa.

Standard enthalpy change of neutralisation, $\Delta H_{n}^{\ominus}$ The enthalpy change when one mole of water is formed by the reaction of an acid with an alkali under standard conditions of 298 K and 100 kPa.

Standard enthalpy change of reaction, $\Delta H_{r}^{\ominus}$ The enthalpy change when the molar amounts in a given a balanced equation react together under standard conditions of 298 K and 100 kPa.

Standard enthalpy change of solution, $\Delta H_{sol}^{\ominus}$ The enthalpy change when one mole of a substance is dissolved in excess solvent to form a solution of infinite dilution under standard conditions of 298 K and 100 kPa.

Standard hydrogen electrode The standard half-cell relative to which standard electrode potentials are measured. It is defined as having a value of 0.00 V.

Standard lattice (dissociation) enthalpy, $\Delta H_{latt}^{\ominus}$ The enthalpy change when one mole of an ionic substance dissociates into its gaseous ions under standard conditions of 298 K and 100 kPa. $\Delta H_{latt}^{\ominus} > 0$.

Standard state The state (solid, liquid or gas) of a pure substance at a pressure of 100 kPa, at a specified temperature, most commonly 298 K.

State symbols Used to indicate the physical state of an element or compound; these may be written as subscripts after the chemical formula or in normal type: (aq) = aqueous (dissolved in water), (g) = gas, (l) = liquid, (s) = solid. Note that lower-case letters are used.

Stereoisomerism Molecules with the same molecular and structural formulas but with the atoms arranged differently in space.

Stoichiometry This describes the relationship between amounts of substance; the ratio in which one substance reacts with another given by the coefficients in a balanced equation.

STP (standard temperature and pressure) 273 K and 100 kPa.

Strong acid/base An acid/base that is completely dissociated into its ions in aqueous solution.

Structural formula A representation of a molecule which shows the arrangement of the atoms.

Structural isomerism Molecules with the same molecular formulas but with different structural formulas.

Sub-energy level A group of degenerate orbitals in an atom.

Sublimation/subliming The change of state from solid to gas without going through the liquid phase.

Substitution reaction A reaction in which one atom or group of atoms is replaced by another atom or group of atoms.

Superconductor A material that has zero electrical resistance below a critical temperature.

Synergism The effect when two or more drugs, given at the same time, have a greater effect than the sum of the individual drugs.

System/surroundings System refers to the chemicals themselves whereas the surrounding refers to the solvent, the air, the apparatus – all that surrounds the chemicals.

Systematic error An error due to the apparatus or procedure used. Systematic errors result in a value being further away from the true value. Systematic errors are always in the same direction: making a value always too big or always too small. They are not reduced by repeating the results.

TD$_{50}$ The dose of a drug required to produce a toxic effect in 50% of the test population (TD = toxic dose).

Tertiary structure of a protein The folding of sections of protein which gives the three-dimensional shape of the protein. This is formed by the interactions between the R groups of the different amino-acid residues.

Theoretical yield The maximum possible amount of product that could be formed if all of the limiting reactant is converted to the required product.

Therapeutic effect A desirable and beneficial effect of a drug; one that alleviates symptoms or treats a particular disease.

Therapeutic index The ratio of the toxic dose to the therapeutic dose of a drug.

Therapeutic window The range of dosage between the minimum required to cause a therapeutic effect and the level which produces unacceptable side-effects.

Thermodynamic efficiency A measure of the ratio of the change in free energy to the enthalpy change for a reaction.

Thermoplastic A type of polymer that softens when heated and hardens when cooled. These polymers can be repeatedly heated and cooled and remoulded into different shapes.

Thermoset A pre-polymer in a soft solid or viscous state that changes irreversibly into a polymer network by curing.

Thermotropic liquid crystal A substance for which the liquid-crystal phase is only stable over a small temperature range.

Titration An analytical technique used where one solution is reacted with the exact stoichiometric amount of another solution. It is often used to find the concentration of one of the solutions.

Tolerance When an organism becomes less responsive to the effects of a drug – larger and larger doses need to be used to produce the same effect which means that there is a greater risk of toxic side-effects.

Transesterification A process in which an ester is hydrolysed in the presence of another alcohol which substitutes for the original alcohol to form a different ester.

Transition element An element that forms at least one stable ion with a partially filled d sub-shell.

Triglyceride A type of lipid molecule; a tri-ester of glycerol and three fatty acid molecules.

Unit cell The simplest repeating unit from which a whole crystal can be built up.

Unsaturated Organic compounds which contain multiple bonds.

Valence shell/electrons The outermost electrons.

van de Waals' forces The collective name for weak intermolecular forces. It includes London forces, dipole–induced dipole forces and permanent dipole–dipole forces but not hydrogen bonding or ion–dipole forces.

Vaporisation The change of state from liquid to gas including both evaporation and boiling.

Viscosity A measure of the resistance of a liquid to flow.

Volatility A measure of how easily a substance evaporates.

Voltaic cell An electrochemical cell that converts chemical energy into electrical energy.

VSEPR Valence-Shell Electron-Pair Repulsion. This is the theory by which the shapes of molecules and ions can be deduced.

Water of crystallisation Water that is present in definite proportions in the crystals of hydrated salts (e.g. $CuSO_4 \cdot 5H_2O$). The water may not be directly bonded to the metal (e.g. in hydrated copper sulfate, four water molecules are bonded to the copper ion and one is not).

Wavenumber/cm^{-1} $\dfrac{1}{\text{wavelength/cm}}$ The units used along the axis in infrared spectroscopy.

Weak acid/base An acid/base that is only partially dissociated into its ions in aqueous solution.

Xenobiotics Compounds found in a living organism that should not normally be found there.

X-ray crystallography An analytical technique used to produce a three-dimensional picture of the structure of a crystal. It can be used to measure bond lengths and bond angles.

Yield The amount of product obtained from a chemical reaction.

Zeolites Porous crystalline materials, often aluminosilicate minerals.

Zwitterion The form of an amino acid that has no overall charge.

CD-ROM terms and conditions of use

CD-ROM Terms and conditions of use This is a legal agreement between 'You' (which for individual purchasers means the individual customer and, for network purchasers, means the Educational Institution and its authorised users) and Cambridge University Press ('the Licensor') for *Chemistry for the IB Diploma Workbook*. By placing this CD in the CD-ROM drive of your computer You agree to the terms of this licence.

1 Limited licence

a You are purchasing only the right to use the CDROM and are acquiring no rights, express or implied to it or to the software ('Software' being the CD-ROM software, as installed on your computer terminals or server), other than those rights granted in this limited licence for not-for-profit educational use only.

b Cambridge University Press grants the customer the licence to use one copy of this CD-ROM either (i) on a single computer for use by one or more people at different times, or (ii) by a single person on one or more computers (provided the CD-ROM is only used on one computer at any one time and is only used by the customer), but not both.

c You shall not: (i) copy or authorise copying of the CD-ROM, (ii) translate the CD-ROM, (iii) reverse engineer, alter, adapt, disassemble or decompile the CD-ROM, (iv) transfer, sell, lease, lend, profit from, assign or otherwise convey all or any portion of the CD-ROM or (v) operate the CD-ROM from a mainframe system, except as provided in these terms and conditions.

2 Copyright

a All original content is provided as part of the CD-ROM (including text, images and ancillary material) and is the copyright of, or licensed by a third party to, the Licensor, protected by copyright and all other applicable intellectual property laws and international treaties.

b You may not copy the CD-ROM except for making one copy of the CD-ROM solely for backup or archival purposes. You may not alter, remove or destroy any copyright notice or other material placed on or with this CD-ROM.

c The CD-ROM contains Adobe® Flash® Player. Adobe® Flash® Player Copyright © 1996−2010 Adobe Systems Incorporated. All Rights Reserved. Protected by U.S. Patent 6,879,327; Patents Pending in the United States and other countries. Adobe and Flash are either trademarks or registered trademarks in the United States and/or other countries.

3 Liability and Indemnification

a The CD-ROM is supplied 'as-is' with no express guarantee as to its suitability. To the extent permitted by applicable law, the Licensor is not liable for costs of procurement of substitute products, damages or losses of any kind whatsoever resulting from the use of this product, or errors or faults in the CD-ROM, and in every case the Licensor's liability shall be limited to the suggested list price or the amount actually paid by You for the product, whichever is lower.

b You accept that the Licensor is not responsible for the persistency, accuracy or availability of any urls of external or third party internet websites referred to on the CD-ROM and does not guarantee that any content on such websites is, or will remain, accurate, appropriate or available. The Licensor shall not be liable for any content made available from any websites and urls outside the Software.

c Where, through use of the CD-ROM and content you infringe the copyright of the Licensor you undertake to indemnify and keep indemnified the Licensor from and against any loss, cost, damage or expense (including without limitation damages paid to a third party and any reasonable legal costs) incurred by the Licensor as a result of such infringement.

4 Termination

Without prejudice to any other rights, the Licensor may terminate this licence if You fail to comply with the terms and conditions of the licence. In such event, You must destroy all copies of the CD-ROM.

5 Governing law

This agreement is governed by the laws of England, without regard to its conflict of laws provision, and each party irrevocably submits to the exclusive jurisdiction of the English courts.